LANDSCAPES OF FREEDOM

LATIN AMERICAN LANDSCAPES

CLAUDIA LEAL

LANDSCAPES OF FREEDOM

Building a Postemancipation Society in the Rainforests of Western Colombia

THE UNIVERSITY OF ARIZONA PRESS
TUCSON

The University of Arizona Press
www.uapress.arizona.edu

First paperback edition 2020

ISBN-13: 978-0-8165-3674-0 (cloth)
ISBN-13: 978-0-8165-4149-2 (paper)

Cover design by Leigh McDonald
Cover photo: Most likely lower Atrato River. 1954. Photograph by Robert C. West (R35 N24) Archivo Fotográfico Robert West, Las Tierras Bajas del Pacífico Colombiano. Biblioteca Luis Angel Arango and Biblioteca Universidad de los Andes. https://robertwest.uniandes.edu.co.

Publication of this book is made possible in part by the proceeds of a permanent endowment created with the assistance of a Challenge Grant from the National Endowment for the Humanities, a federal agency.

Library of Congress Cataloging-in-Publication Data
Names: Leal, Claudia, 1970– author.
Title: Landscapes of freedom : building a postemancipation society in the rainforests of western Colombia / Claudia Leal.
Other titles: Latin American landscapes.
Description: Tucson : The University of Arizona Press, 2018. | Series: Latin American landscapes | Includes bibliographical references and index.
Identifiers: LCCN 2017047630 | ISBN 9780816536740 (cloth : alk. paper)
Subjects: LCSH: Blacks—Colombia—History. | Colombia—Race relations. | Mineral industries—Colombia—History. | Forest products industry—Colombia—History.
Classification: LCC F2299.B55 L43 2018 | DDC 305.8009861—dc23 LC record available at https://lccn.loc.gov/2017047630

Printed in the United States of America
∞ This paper meets the requirements of ANSI/NISO Z39.48–1992 (Permanence of Paper).

Para Pacho y Magdalena,
que me hablaron del Pacífico y me llevaron a conocerlo,
y que me contagiaron su pasión por investigar y escribir.

CONTENTS

ILLUSTRATIONS

FIGURES

MAPS

GRAPHS

TABLES

ACKNOWLEDGMENTS

CURIOSITY AND FASCINATION with the Pacific coast led me to delve into its past and try to make sense of it. In this very long journey many generous people contributed to conceive and shape the words that follow. That the coast had a place in my mind from early on, and that I ended up working there, I owe to my parents, Pacho and Magdalena, who besides telling me stories and taking me and my sister to Utría, made sure—against my wishes—that I missed the Mother's Day celebration in the Amazonian boarding school where I taught in 1993 to attend a job interview. I spent the years that followed working for Proyecto Biopacífico, a very rewarding time when two people greatly influenced my view of the lowlands. Enrique Sánchez, who knew the place well through many years of experience, guided me gently and with good humor as I came to make sense of it, while Eduardo Restrepo—through long talks in Bogotá, Buenaventura, and elsewhere—shared with me his understanding of the latest turns in the region's cultural politics. I thank them both deeply for their insights and our long-lasting friendships. Those were times of constant learning, in which I travelled, talked, and shared beers with many fascinating people, more than I acknowledge here. Among the closest were my colleagues and friends from Biopacífico: Fernando Gast, Juan Manuel Navarrete, Mary Lucía Hurtado, Robin Hissong, Luz Marina Rincón, Mirta Bosoni, Jairo Miguel Guerra, Antonio María Cardona, Elías Córdoba, Libia Grueso, Alfredo Vanín, and Oscar Alzate. From those days I have admired William Villa and have had the good fortune to personally share some of his wise and informed views of the lowlands. My penchant for history drew me close to Orián Jiménez, Oscar Almario, Sergio Mosquera, and Luis Fernando González, all of whom were very kind in sharing their knowledge and camaraderie with me. To all of them my love and gratitude.

This book is based on the dissertation with which I graduated from the Department of Geography at the University of California, Berkeley. I did research in many places, including Bogotá, Quibdó, Cali, Popayán, Guapi, and Washington, D.C., where I received help from archivists and librarians, from people who opened their homes to me, and from others who shared their knowledge and even their research notes with me. I would particularly like to thank here Mauricio Tovar from the Archivo General de la Nación, Adriana Rodríguez Castañeda, Mario Diego Romero, Guido Barona, and Ann Farnsworth-Alvear. In Berkeley I was lucky enough to work with Michael Johns, who had the ability of pointing out my weaknesses while always making me feel good and enthusiastic about my research. He was a very generous adviser, whose uneasiness with academia forced me—I believe—to become a better scholar. I also learned a great deal from other wonderful Berkeley professors, especially Margaret Chowning, Roger Byrne, Michael Watts, and Nancy Peluso. While doing my PhD I also had the good luck of having my then-boyfriend Shawn's company and being welcome into his family. His grandmother, Hilda White, gave me the best tips I ever received for improving my writing in English, while Laurie and Jerry, his parents, and the entire crew made my life in Berkeley warmer and less transient.

Back in Bogotá I found the best possible home at the Department of History at Universidad de los Andes. For many years I taught a course on race and nation in Latin America that greatly contributed to the process of making a book out of the dissertation. Through this course I continued the inquiries I started at Berkeley with Nancy Appelbaum and Luz Mena. Nancy and Eduardo Restrepo read the dissertation and gave me detailed and very useful feedback, for which I am very grateful. That their suggestions ever made it into this book is something that I owe to the Rachel Carson Center for Environment and Society (RCC) in Munich, where I had time to organize my thoughts and write after several years largely devoted to becoming a professor and starting a family. I especially thank Christof Mauch, the center's director, for his support and for creating, along with Helmut Trischler, the inspiring community that the RCC has come to be. From my days in Munich I also thank warmly Katie Ritson, Tim LeCain, Eagle Glassheim, and Marlene Dado, plus the colleagues who the day after we enjoyed Oktoberfest attended the Works in Progress session in which I presented part of my work.

I am grateful to many other people, including Bernardo Leal, who kindly responded to several queries; Juan Sebastián Moreno, who assisted me in many ways; and Paola Luna, the best cartographer I know. American scholars James Sanders, Jason McGraw, and George Reid Andrews, who work on similar issues, have been a source of inspiration and support. Similarly encouraging has been the community of friends and colleagues that has grown around the Latin American and Caribbean Society for Environmental History. Among them, Stefania Gallini has been a particularly enthusiastic and supportive voyage partner. I have learned much from her and the group and consider this book a product of our collaboration.

To Shawn, I owe having written this book at all—and so much more. He has been part of it from the first words to the last. In the process he made sure we would not be lonely, and now our children, Siena and Niko, and also our dog, Rosita, have us constantly busy and often smiling. I hope Niko and Siena will someday read this book and share part of my passion for this singular history. But to love and understand the lowlands you have to go there, so I promise to take them to Utría, as my parents did with me. I am sure Shawn will love the ocean and might even remember that the very first words he ever said to me referred precisely to that enchanting coast. That trip will be just one way of thanking him for his endless support.

I cannot end without thanking Chris Boyer's and Kris Lane's generous and thorough comments of previous versions of this book, which without doubt contributed to making it much better. I hope that they, and everyone else who helped me throughout these long years, will enjoy this final version and forgive me for its shortcomings.

LANDSCAPES OF FREEDOM

VOYAGES INTO THE RAINFOREST

An Introduction in Three Acts

MY OWN JOURNEYS

For three years of my life, I cherished those brief moments, after the plane dived into the thick cloud cover and before it landed, when I could look at the seemingly endless jungle. Once I stepped off the plane, it was like walking into a sauna: my skin felt moist, my hair curled up, and my whole body relaxed. I had landed in Quibdó, the capital city of the department of Chocó, built at the edge of the majestic Atrato River (map 1). Arriving further south in the Pacific port of Tumaco, or even in Buenaventura, the region's largest port, which was reached by minibus for it had no airport, gave me a similar comforting feeling. Soon it would rain—perhaps just a quick shower or maybe an endless drizzle. With an umbrella in hand and plastic shoes, I would continue about my business like everyone else. Yet I stood out among the black people populating the streets. More than once, to my dismay, I was referred to as *blanca* (white), despite not being pale and having dark-brown hair and eyes. In Bogotá, where I grew up, I learned to think of myself as *mestiza* (mixed-blood). But that Andean world felt quite distant from these lowlands I was getting to know. Navigating in a motorboat or a canoe along one of many rivers with banks covered by intermixed crops, wooden houses, and lush vegetation was a pleasant and unusual experience to me. These scenes repeated themselves throughout a large territory that spans 1,300 kilometers from Panama to Ecuador along

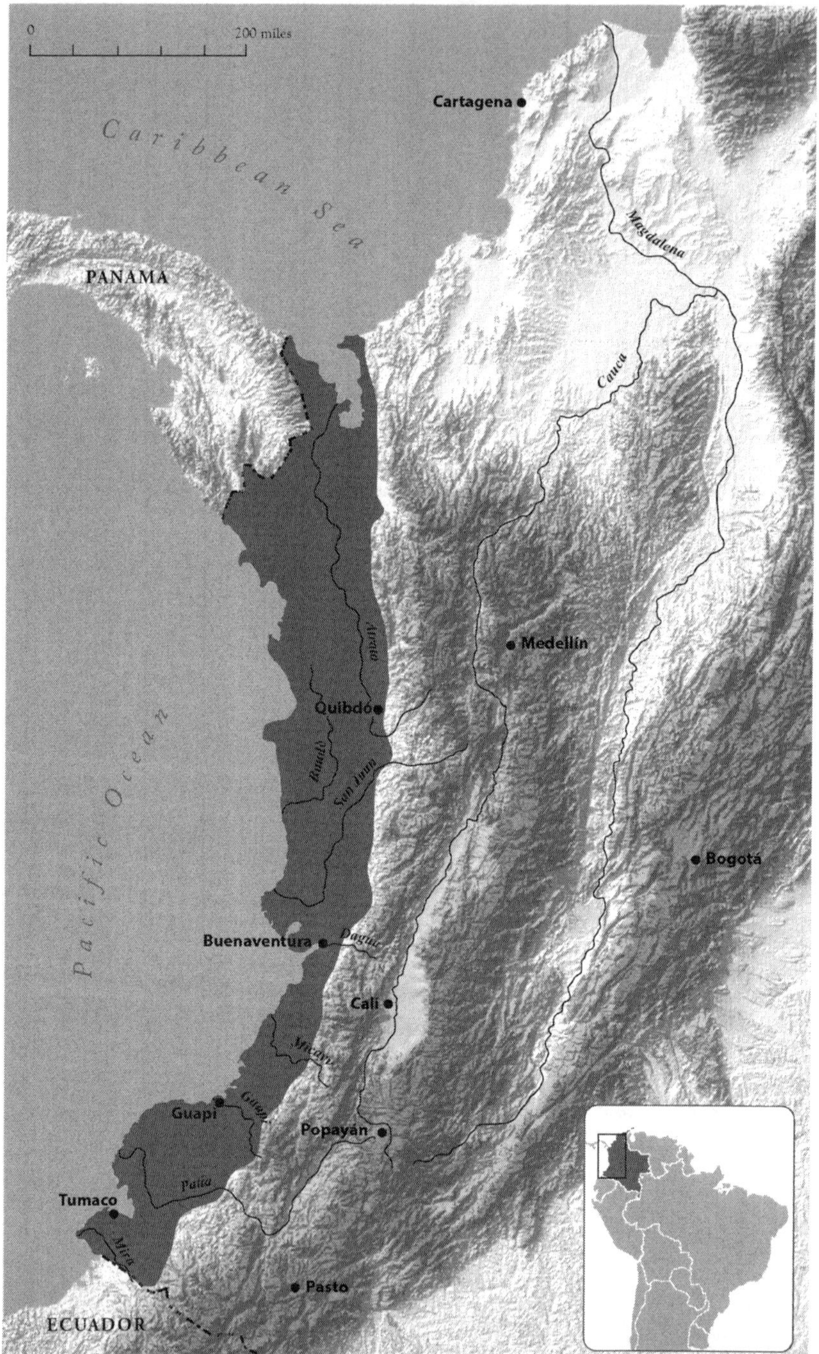

MAP 1 The Pacific lowlands of Colombia. Map by Paola Luna, Cartography Lab, Universidad de los Andes, Bogotá.

Colombia's Pacific coast—the largest area in the Americas inhabited primarily by black people.[1]

It was the mid-1990s, a time when this region came into the spotlight, conceived in a novel manner through the double lens of biodiversity conservation and black ethnicity. The ethos that enveloped us, which rested on valuing both nature and black and indigenous peoples, inspired this book. Coined in the 1980s, the term *biodiversity* soon came to dominate the science and policy of conservation.[2] In that context, the works of botanist Alwyn Gentry, and a few others, which brought to light the remarkable variety of living organisms in the forests of Chocó, helped to recast the long-held view of the lowlands from naturally exuberant to biologically rich. Gentry had pointed out that the outstanding level of rainfall and the absence of dry periods could explain why Chocó seemed to have as much diversity as those parts in the upper Amazon recognized for being the most biologically diverse on the planet. The Upper Chocó receives over 8,000 millimeters of rain a year, while most of the lowlands receive over 4,000 millimeters, well above the 2,000 millimeters that the Amazon rainforest receives on average.[3] Gentry also indicated that the region had an outstanding level of endemism. For example, in terms of birds, the organisms best known by scientists, the southern part of the lowlands had been signaled as having perhaps the highest level of endemism in the entire world. Gentry stressed the need for more research by pointing out that innumerable species living here were still unknown to science. His position as senior curator of the Missouri Botanical Garden and as a leading authority on the botany of tropical America added weight to his words.[4] As a result, in 1992, when Colombia presented a proposal for the Global Environment Fund (GEF) for biodiversity conservation, it turned to the Pacific lowlands, and following scientific parlance referred to it pompously as *Chocó Biogeográfico*.

The resulting project, which came to be known as Biopacífico (1993–98), sought to contribute to formulate a biodiversity conservation strategy for the region. Biopacífico represented a novel way of thinking about conservation. Until then, protected areas and natural scientists dominated conservation efforts in the country. In Biopacífico, biologists stood alongside a varied staff focused on knowing biodiversity and understanding people's use and conceptions of the environment.[5] An experienced sociologist, Enrique Sánchez, worked by himself in the socioeconomic area, and the project's director thought that a senior economist, an expert on environmental issues capable of influencing government officials, should join him. Fortunately, that sort of economist was hard to come by, so the director settled on hiring me, who besides having an undergraduate degree in economics could only show interest and knowledge of environmental issues by having lived for a few months in the Amazon.[6]

Biopacífico took off when black rural people of the Pacific littoral were beginning to be officially recognized as *ethnic* by Colombian law. Following a Latin American trend, the 1991 Colombian constitution redefined the nation as multiethnic, primarily as a way of acknowledging the rights and symbolic importance of indigenous groups.[7] Cultural difference was assimilated to ethnicity, a concept that in Colombia and Latin America has been used since the early twentieth century almost exclusively to designate indigenous groups. Therefore, in this context, ethnicity has not been a universal classificatory system. According to the 1993 census, Colombia had 532,000 indigenous people. By 2005, largely due to processes set in motion by the constitution, the indigenous population had grown to 1,393,000, forming about 87 different ethnicities and representing 3.4 percent of the population. Ethnicity has a geographical dimension, for ethnic groups are often identified according to their place of origin or habitation. Communal land rights have been correspondingly a fundamental aspect of this kind of identity. By 2005, the 313 *resguardos* (officially recognized indigenous territories) existing in 1993 had multiplied to 710 and occupied about 30 percent of the national territory.[8] Following this tradition, and thanks to the lobby of an incipient black movement supported by a few academics and allies, the Constitutional Assembly included a transitory article stating that within two years a special commission would draft "a law that recognizes the collective property rights of black communities that have inhabited the public lands (*tierras baldías*) in the rural riparian zones of the Pacific coast, in accordance with their traditional production practices."[9]

Law 70 of 1993, which established the mechanisms for collective titling, brought much attention to the dwellers of the lowland jungles and generated excitement and optimism. It explicitly defined "black community" as an ethnic group with its own history, culture, traditions, and customs; and it defined "traditional productive practices" as activities used customarily "to guarantee the conservation of life and self-sustainable development."[10] Just as what had happened with indigenous ethnicity, black ethnicity was predicated upon the assumption of ecological stewardship.[11] With the legitimacy added by environmental arguments, the black social movement grew as local leaders, priests, activists, and state officials brought the law to every corner of the region and fostered the creation of organizations in each river and community. Various public institutions at the national level, such as the institutes of anthropology and geography, contributed to the process of titling.[12] Through various exchanges, meetings, and casual encounters, a network of people from inside and outside the region, with veterans and many newcomers, formed and strengthened. We believed in the need for inaugurating a new era for the region, one that did justice to long neglected peoples and put the environment at the forefront.

These agitated years strongly shaped a group of scholars, who have produced important works on this region. Many of them focused on ethnicity and the black social movement, either using cultural difference as a way of understanding black people or explaining the conceptual changes and novel forms of collective action that took place at the time. The works of Arturo Escobar, Eduardo Restrepo, Kiran Asher, Ulrich Oslender, and Odile Hoffmann stand out.[13] These scholars, who like me are not from the region, shared the fascination I felt with this place, a fascination that has roots in my childhood and that curiously also builds on an idea of difference (although not the same one that guided these anthropologists and geographers).

The Pacific coast loomed large in my imagination because my dad enjoyed reminiscing about the times he spent there during the 1950s working on a geodetic survey. Engineers at the Agustín Codazzi Geographical Institute avoided places deemed too difficult, so soldiers and officers of the Military Geodetic Commission—like my dad—had to take over. I recall bits and pieces of what he told us, which together built a hazy image of a strange and alluring place. He once returned to Buenaventura, after just a few days absence, to find his shoes ruined by mold, while in swampy Sanquianga he spent several hours every evening in the 25-meter metal tower used to carry out his work, for the breeze helped protect him from being bitten by swarms of mosquitoes. Meanwhile, a black peasant living nearby hunted for rodents and game fowl at night while being very lightly dressed. In Gorgona Island, he and his men were forced to slide down the hill they used for their measurements; they did not dare to hold onto any branch, as it might be one of the snakes that, as the island's name suggests, dominate the place. Perhaps most striking to him was running into an Indian, in the jungles close to Panama, dressed with a loincloth and dexterously hunting with bow and arrow.

Other travelers also perceived the difference that my dad identified between the people and the environment of the lowlands and what he was used to. An anthropologist friend of mine once expressed plainly and with conscious irony his odd feeling of unfamiliarity by saying that in Chocó he had felt transported to "deepest Africa." The connotations of backwardness and exoticism this view entails leave some repulsed and others captivated. Among the latter, my dad decided to share his experience by organizing a trip, in December 1969, for his wife and friends. In 1988, when I was eighteen, our family went back to that same spot, Playa Blanca, a tiny island at the mouth of the Ensenada de Utría. I observed with great pleasure how the luxuriant vegetation crept all the way to the edge of the beach and was shocked by the subservient position I perceived indigenous people had, and also by hearing Quiteria, an aged woman in the neighboring town of Jurubidá, explain that she had been given a little girl, which sounded like a hand-me-down to me. We spent New Year's Eve there and celebrated with *sancocho de guagua* (wild-meat soup), which seemed less appetizing after someone came rushing past the guests with a baby mouse that had fallen from a roof beam into the pot, while everyone laughed. I had been transported to an unfamiliar world and felt bewitched.

I could not have known that my first job would take me back. As I learned about mangroves, timber extraction, and production practices, I also read everything I could about the history of the lowlands to understand how this place came to be what it was. Works concentrated on slavery and colonial times, but conceptualizing black people in a new manner, as was happening in those days, highlighted the need to recognize that they have a history as free people and not just as slaves, and that the jungle and the rain have a place in that past. So I decided I would fill that void with a PhD dissertation and ended up in the University of California, Berkeley's Department of Geography. The result is this book, which explains how a postemancipation society emerged in the most humid of the rainforests in the Western Hemisphere.

As I worked on my dissertation, the optimism that inspired it gave way to deep concern. The change has been in part a return to older and ever present worries centered on the region's poverty. My encounter with doña Eleuteria Candelo Castillo reminds me of the harsh realities of the lowlands. I ran into her in Buenaventura while visiting with my friend Eduardo, who had spent time with her in a logging camp. She was on her way to buy candles for the wake of her granddaughter. The little girl was still alive, but doña Eleuteria wanted to be prepared. A place with one of the highest infant mortality rates in the country made me cautious about getting swept away by a romantic tide that, by focusing on the assumed harmonious relationship people had with the environment, obscured the hardships of life in those jungles. Even more, the lowlands have been swept by a wave of violence associated with coca growing and cocaine trafficking.[14] Local peoples have endured much suffering, while the social movement weakened and environmental concerns receded to the background. Yet, by 2005, more than five million hectares had been titled to black communities across the entire lowlands. It has been a momentous yet bittersweet victory that unfortunately does not by itself guarantee the lowlands a promising future.

INTELLECTUAL WANDERINGS

Between 1850 and 1930, free black people in the Pacific lowlands of Colombia fully appropriated the rainforest environment, and in so doing built a unique postemancipation society in which they enjoyed much more autonomy than their peers elsewhere. By dominating the very humid jungles of the last northern stretch of South America's Pacific coast, blacks came to constitute a peasantry. In most agrarian economies slavery gave way to the formation of a rural working class, and in the few places where black peasantries emerged, they mostly had family farms that produced foodstuffs for the regional market. Here peasants extracted gold, platinum, rubber, and vegetable-ivory nuts and sold them to a few local white merchants who shipped these products overseas. Throughout much of the nineteenth and twentieth centuries, taking nature's treasures and turning them into commodities to supply distant markets mediated people's relationships to tropical jungles. But extraction can be colored with many hues: in the eighteenth century, when the Spanish dominated the Pacific lowlands, gold extraction led to enslavement rather than autonomy. The latter significance grew out of blacks' use of a vast territory, where they procured the materials they sold as well as many of the resources they needed to survive, such as food and construction materials, reducing their dependence on the market. The independent fashion in which ex-slaves and the descendants of slaves lived their lives gave a concrete and deep meaning to the legal condition of freedom.

This book employs an environmental approach to contribute to our understanding of a crucial aspect of the building of modern Latin America: the transition from slavery to freedom, which was integral to the construction of a new political republican order. Although black people are at the center of this narrative, the numerous archives I consulted, as well as the surprisingly prolific press of the time and traveler's accounts, only allow us to hear a very faint echo of their voices. Conscious that their perspectives and the detailed textures of their daily lives are missing, I examine the experience of freedom by turning to the political economy of resource use and by interpreting writings whose authors deliberately distanced themselves from free blacks. By exploring the transformation of a rainforest *extractive economy*, which depended on extracting minerals and vegetable products rather than harvesting crops, this book weaves together social and environmental history to not just add a missing case study to the historical map of Afro-Latin America, but to reconstruct a postemancipation trajectory that has not hitherto been examined. It also explores the building of *racialized landscapes*, which entailed both the material transformations of the forested environment and the meanings ascribed to them by those who left a written record. Black people experienced their freedom in these very concrete spaces and in a milieu tainted by a strongly racialized ideology that overlooked their achievements.

First enslaved and then free, blacks supplied manual labor within the extractive economy that developed in the Pacific lowlands. Extraction is a form of production that depends on the supply of materials from environments not primarily the product of human labor, such as subsoils, forests, or oceans. Mining is the quintessential extractive activity; fishing and forest gathering constitute other prominent examples. The emphasis on the initial absence of human labor does not imply that people cannot play a role in the availability of some of these resources, in particular those from the forests, as for instance, by encouraging the growth of certain plants. Yet extractive economies differ sharply from agriculture, which is based squarely on planting. Extractive economies also differ from extractive practices geared for subsistence. For centuries, indigenous groups have used countless plants for a wide array of purposes, including food, medicine, and rituals. These extractive activities mainly produced things to be used rather than traded; even when trade was involved, its ultimate goal was not to generate profit. Conversely, extractive economies are formed by activities that turn elements of nature into *commodities*—for instance, Hevea latex, the fluid that keeps these trees alive, into rubber, a raw material for making tires. The ultimate purpose of trading this natural resource was to accumulate wealth. In rainforests, this sort of extraction has assumed a leading role—and thus generated extractive economies—mostly when supplying extra-regional markets, since internal markets tend to be too small to generate a strong extractive sector.[15]

In Latin American rainforests, as the notable case of the Amazon rubber boom shows, extractive economies often formed or strengthened during the period of export-led growth (1850–1930). Large forested areas, marginal or unincorporated during colonial times, were integrated into the global economy.[16] In the Pacific lowlands, the extractive economy developed in earnest earlier, in the eighteenth century, when the Spaniards finally conquered the region and began producing gold. The native population had dwindled, due to war and disease, and gold miners decided to follow a course already developed in other mining regions of New Granada: bringing blacks, Africans, and some creoles to work the placer deposits as slaves. The most prominent slave owners never lived in the lowlands; they remained in western Andean cities, close to their haciendas. Had they been able to produce sugar cane and grass for cattle on a wide scale on the coast, this history would have been quite different. But given the paucity of agricultural soils and the excessive humidity, slaves lived in itinerant mining camps in the middle of the jungle, supervised by just one or two white overseers. Under such conditions, and given that this economy produced a means of exchange, extensive self-purchase was the most outstanding outcome of the tacit negotiation between slaves and masters over the conditions of enslavement. As chapter 1 explains, spaces for freedom opened within an extractive economy that rested on an extreme form of coerced labor.

After emancipation, chapter 2 shows, lowland blacks achieved a level of control over the means of production hardly matched by any other sizeable group of rural Afro-descendants. Absentee slave owners lost their most important asset—the slaves themselves—and for the most part abandoned the mines, whose most productive placers had been depleted. A few smaller ex-slave owners remained in the region, and joined by a few newcomers formed a small white elite devoted to trade in natural commodities. The social relations of extraction changed for merchants, and independent producers replaced masters and slaves. Blacks gained access to mines (through rent, purchase, or simply occupation) and to the wider forested territory, partly through migration from the mining areas to the rest of the region. And they expanded commercial extraction beyond gold to include rubber and vegetable ivory (the seed of a palm tree used to make buttons), as well as platinum. By selling natural products, free men and women bought goods, such as cloth, salt, and metal tools, needed to survive. Their independent lifestyles hinged to a large extent upon subsistence practices: cultivating plantains, corn, sugarcane, and other crops; fishing and hunting wild animals; and procuring materials to build and thatch their houses and to make canoes and other useful objects. All of these activities revolved around access to fertile soils, forests, wetlands (*ciénagas* and mangroves), rivers, and oceans. Black people's dominance of this diverse environment, and thus of extraction, freed merchants from having to engage in onerous production costs. As free men and women working on their own terms, they constituted what we could call a *rainforest peasantry*. Like other peasantries, this one was made up of families who controlled the labor processes geared both to fulfill their own subsistence needs and to supply marketable commodities.[17]

The formation of a peasantry indicates that black people in the Pacific lowlands achieved what researchers on postemancipation societies identify as their highest aspiration: autonomy—the capacity to decide, as much as possible, how to use their bodies, their time, and the spaces they lived in without having to follow orders.[18] This literature has also signaled *land* as the key for fulfilling this dream; according to Woodville K. Marshall, who examined the West Indies, free people's "land-hunger was enormous and evident."[19] In the same vein, Ralph-Michel Trouillot noted of Saint Domingue that "the acquisition of family land and the laborers' right to the product of the labor on such land were the terms under which freedom was first formulated." He referred to the garden plots to which plantation slaves were entitled, where they grew food for themselves and for the market. The significance of these plots for slaves eager to increase their degree of autonomy can be inferred by the main demand in the 1791 rebellion: to have more days to work them.[20] However, in places with prosperous plantation economies—such as Cuba, Brazil, and Puerto Rico—free blacks had a hard time finding land, for their previous masters exercised a tight control over it. In these situations, ex-slaves tended to become proletarians rather than form peasant families.[21] Even in the Colombian Caribbean and Cauca, whose economies were not as buoyant as export-oriented plantation areas, haciendas eventually encroached upon black peasants.[22] This also holds true for peasantries that did not emerge from slavery. In many parts of Colombia, as Catherine LeGrand explained, the competition for land between entrepreneurs and peasants resulted in a highly unequal land tenure pattern with thousands of hectares titled mostly to large landowners.[23]

However, some ex-slaves and their descendants continued to keep provision grounds within plantations, while others managed to have access to, or sometimes even buy, a piece of land outside, but usually near, plantations. Even though those fortunate enough to work their plots almost invariably labored seasonally on the estates, these plots should not be overlooked, for lots of different sizes gave a minimum base for survival, and thus for security, as well as a physical space in which to ground new identities.[24] Most opportunities for black people to have access to land, though, arose far from or on the peripheries of the plantation world. In burgeoning São Paulo, "free people successfully established themselves in economically declining or insignificant localities, which were not coveted by the dominant sectors."[25] Similarly, on the fringes of the coffee plantation economy of Rio de Janeiro, the availability of land enabled the formation of a peasantry, which included Afro-descendants, producing for the local market.[26] In the impoverished Brazilian northeast, ex-slaves and Afro-descendants occupied plots of land within large estates in exchange for labor, or they migrated inland to the *agreste* (the dry, hilly, and narrow zone located between the coastal forest area and the semiarid *sertão*).[27]

Scholars who mention these physical spaces of freedom acknowledge their economic marginality but seldom remark on their environmental features. To expand, plantations required particular natural conditions: not just land but soils covered by forests that when burned provided fertilizer to produce future harvests, and in the case of sugarcane, *flat* land. When those conditions were not met, as in Cuba's eastern *mountains*, free blacks had better chances of joining the peasant route.[28] In Jamaica, a place known for the emergence of a black peasantry, the existence of *rugged* lands strengthened black food production since the times of slavery. Later, peasants who also produced coffee for export went from being 11 percent of the population in 1860 to around 18 percent from 1890 to 1930. This development owed much to the decline of the sugar economy, which made marginal lands more available.[29] Similarly, in Haiti, after the revolution caused the collapse of the world's most prosperous sugar economy, a large peasant class sustained both the state and the most powerful social group, merchants, through the production of coffee. The availability of (again) mountainous land in the interior played an important role in this process.[30]

Patterns of land access *within* plantations further reinforces the relevance of environmental attributes, as it was usually "waste" or "refuse" land that free blacks managed to buy or at least live on without the security offered by titles. As Rebecca Scott and Michael Zeuske, writing of Cienfuegos, Cuba, suggest, it was on "the *edges* of and in the *interstices* of [the] plantation world, [that] former slaves and other rural people [. . .] planted subsistence and market crops, grazed animals, and built lives."[31] By ruining the environment, plantations could paradoxically create spaces for the formation of peasantries, as Philippe I. Bourgeois recounts for West Indian migrants in the border between Costa Rica and Panama. In the early twentieth century, "The company often leased its depleted, infected lands [by Panama disease] to former workers and then purchased the bananas or cacao that these newly reconstituted peasants were able to squeeze out of the formerly productive farms. Ironically, therefore, disease and the depletion of soil fertility promoted the consolidation of a peasantry."[32]

Obsessed with land, researchers have seldom explored how access to rivers or woodlands, where to fish, hunt, or gather firewood, made a difference for free blacks. Scott E. Giltner, a notable exception, has shown how, in the American South, "along with independent hunting and fishing came better control of subsistence, freer use of guns and dogs, and the ability to more easily avoid permanent labor in the service of whites."[33] The best evidence of how access to resources other than land was important for developing autonomous lifestyles comes from rainforests. In the lower Amazon (present states of Pará and Maranhão), the forest itself, as well as a location close to imperial borderlands, facilitated the formation of communities of runaway plantation slaves.[34] To this day, these Amazonian communities have combined agriculture with small-scale mining, as well as other extractive activities such as collecting Brazil nuts and *coco de babaçu*.[35] Not too far away from them, the so-called Bush Negroes of Suriname, as Richard Price has emphasized, have been "the most highly developed *independent* societies and cultures in the history of Afro-America."[36] Formed by massive flight from coastal plantations, these maroons established peace treaties with the Dutch colonial government after the 1760s, guaranteeing their free status and living in the interior jungles, far from the plantation complex of the coast.[37]

Contrary to what these examples suggest, coercion could also develop within rainforest extractive economies. Free black people in Belize remained indebted to logging companies, which owned most of the land in the colony and exercised much influence over the state, and faced imprisonment whenever they fled from the mahogany camps.[38] Therefore, control over the environment that blacks in the Pacific coast of Colombia enjoyed cannot be taken for granted. To fully explain the level of autonomy that these people achieved it is crucial to understand the competition for resources they faced and the ways they withstood or coped with it, a task undertaken in chapter 3. The economic marginality of this region limited competition. After emancipation, mine productivity continued to decline, following a trend that began decades before as the richest and most accessible placers became exhausted, while new forest exports never achieved much significance on a national scale. However, struggles did erupt, not over land but over access to extractive resources: vegetable ivory and precious minerals. With the support of local elites and officials, black peasants successfully confronted entrepreneurs interested in acquiring monopolies over vegetable ivory, for the existing economic arrangements ultimately benefitted everybody. Regarding mines, lowlanders had to cope with powerful companies in the San Juan and Timbiquí river basins. Yet modern mining did not touch most of the region, and even where it did locals were able to defend some of their rights, limiting the impact on their autonomy. The reconstruction of these historical conflicts takes inspiration from the burgeoning field of political ecology, which from its inception signaled that in agrarian contexts struggles revolve around soils, forests, water, and a wide variety of natural elements that political economy often packed—and left unexamined—under the conceptual abstraction of land.[39]

After examining, in the first part, the transformations and inner workings of the lowland extractive economy in relation to freedom, this book uses, in the second part, another concept—racialized landscapes—to delve into the production of rural and urban landscapes in an ideological context that tempered the principle of equality by legitimizing blacks' alleged inferiority. In the second half of the nineteenth and the first decades of the twentieth century, race reigned as the leading concept to (hierarchically) conceive social groups, with science serving to advance and legitimize it.[40] The sharp racial divide that characterized the lowland economy—with blacks toiling to produce commodities in the natural environment and whites trading with them in urban settings—allowed for blacks to have a fulfilling experience of freedom, but it also fit prejudiced ideas of society's purported natural order. Moreover, this spatial division of labor facilitated literate contemporaries' association of the rural landscape with blacks and, particularly in the case of the local elite, the emerging urban landscape with whites. The spatial dimensions of the division of labor led to spatialized manifestations of racial prejudice.

Geographers have understood and used the concept of landscape in two very different ways: as a material reality to study the physical aspects of place building and as an idea to reflect upon the implications of portraying the world as a commanding and pleasing view, for instance, through landscape painting.[41] I draw from both of these understandings to emphasize the material construction of humanized environments, as well as the readings of those spaces—that is, I explore both the views and the viewers. Adding "racialized" to this classic term emphasizes the social and ideological context in which the Pacific coastal landscape was built and interpreted. The extractive economy physically shaped the coast both by leaving human imprints on the forests and by starting the conscious construction of urban areas with the proceeds of the trade in minerals and vegetable ivory. As blacks migrated from the mining areas and settled most of the region, they built wooden houses, grew native and exotic staples, and planted breadfruit trees, all of which came to characterize the most conspicuous lowland view: that of the levees seen while navigating along a river. Small towns and the canoes that slid through the waterways enlivened these scenes. This rural landscape that signaled blacks' full appropriation of the region constituted the material evidence of their freedom.

While the rainforest stood out as a conspicuous feature of this landscape, plantation agriculture expanded in other parts of Latin America, eliminating forests. Certain environments facilitated the development of certain export economies, which in turn transformed those environments. Sugarcane production fared well in the flat lands of Cuba, which ended up denuded, while the existence of palm trees with seeds resembling ivory contributed to the development of an extractive economy in the lowland forests, which remain standing. Neither mining nor gathering produced dramatic environmental transformations. Traditional placer mining does imply removing all forest cover, but only in relatively small spaces. And when a mine is abandoned, the vegetation recovers. Similarly, the impact of cutting down black rubber trees to collect their sap was limited because these trees grow scattered throughout the forest, and when felled new plants invade the opened gaps. Vegetable ivory palms, in contrast, grow in clusters, and gatherers simply collected their nuts from the forest floors without harming the palm populations. Due to the extraordinary high humidity of the lowlands, peasants practiced, in the small strips of fertile land along river levees, slash-and-mulch agriculture: they cut patches of vegetation and let it rot over the planted seeds; later they allowed the forest to grow back.

As chapter 4 expounds, writings of the time show little appreciation for lowlanders' environmental knowledge and rather subtle imprint on their surroundings. Infused by the racial ideology and environmental determinism of the day, travelers and local elites coupled what they considered semisavage peoples with the alleged inhospitable jungle. It was fate and nature, not hard work after the vileness and misfortunes of slavery, that best accounted for blacks' place in the lowlands. Contemporaries construed blacks—as they did with indigenous groups in other rainforest settings—as a people without history. Environmental historians of Latin America tended to leave these less transformed environments without a history too. The deforestation brought about by plantations, especially in the days of export-led growth, in places like Cuba, Brazil, and the coast of Honduras led scholars, such as Warren Dean, Reinaldo Funes, and John

Soluri, to produce some of the most outstanding works in the field.[42] This book shows that outside plantation settings both free blacks and tropical forests have a history that needs to be told.

The building of the lowland landscape also involved erecting incipient cities, as the final chapter reminds. Some blacks moved into the emerging ports of Quibdó and Tumaco and contributed to the development of urban environments. For local whites, cities represented the opposite of the jungles that ultimately produced the resources to build them. They took pains to erect public buildings, construct handsome houses, and battle against water in the form of sea erosion, marshes, and creeks to prove that, like civilized people elsewhere, they too inhabited a suitable space. In their view, each race had its place, as José María Samper—one of Colombia's leading intellectuals—concluded in the 1860s.[43] They considered that black culture was contrary to urban life, so they scorned, but ultimately could not do much against, blacks' most conspicuous cultural manifestation: marimba music. Blacks made up most of the population of these ports and, for the first time, lived in relatively large numbers alongside a minuscule white elite. Ideas of the proper place for black people, as well as the evident power imbalance between the majority of blacks and the most privileged whites, contradicted the egalitarian republican ideals that had been taking hold in Latin America for several decades. The racial tensions that such contradictions provoked led to the imposition of the capital punishment on a former black judge, highlighting the difficulties Afro-descendants faced in the process of becoming citizens.[44]

The construction of postemancipation societies, such as the one that developed in the Pacific lowlands of Colombia, is not an obvious topic for environmental history. But this field has been demonstrating that an environmental perspective serves as an "angle of attack" to tackle long-standing historical questions, an approach that ultimately rests on the blurring of academic boundaries.[45] Latin American environmental history has been walking in this direction by moving beyond an exclusive focus on the fate of environments to examine histories of working peoples.[46] Karl Zimmerer has explained the persistence of agrodiversity in the Peruvian Andes, Angus Wright has denounced the effects of modern agriculture on workers' health and lives, and Myrna Santiago and Alejandro Tortolero have linked environmental laboring conditions with labor and peasant unrest.[47] Other authors, such as Chris Boyer and Thomas Miller Klubock, writing about the temperate forests of Mexico and Chile, have followed in the steps of histories of South Asia's forests by exploring the fights between local communities and state institutions for control over forest resources, but in a national rather than imperial setting.[48] This book follows in their steps, but it does not look at proletarians working with health hazards, nor at peasants struggling against state institutions or landowners; rather it examines an economically marginal but biologically rich rainforest where black people gave concrete shape to the republican ideal of freedom.

A GUIDED TOUR

In the century that followed independence, a few government officials—the members of the Chorographic Commission in charge of drafting a map of the country, priests, naturalists, explorers in search of an interoceanic canal route, and fortune-seekers, among others—visited the lowlands. However, most travelers never set foot on this coast. Since colonial times, the territory that became Colombia faced north toward the Atlantic. Colombian elites returning from Europe or New York, as well as foreigners entering the country, usually endured a month-long trip along the Magdalena River connecting the Caribbean ports with the interior. They complained bitterly about the rowboats and the "naked" *bogas* that conducted them in the heat of the tropics.[49] They ended their journey by ascending the Andes through a mule trail up to Bogota at 2,600 meters. Not until the last decades of the nineteenth century could they expect to enjoy the comfort brought by steamboat navigation, and until 1909 to complete their trip by train.[50]

Visitors crossing Colombia's paths noted how sparsely populated it was. In the mid-nineteenth century, Colombia, which has an area roughly about the size of California, Nevada, Oregon, and Washington combined, had just over two million people. Population grew rapidly during the following decades to 2.7 million in 1870 and to almost 5.5 million in 1912.[51] Other Latin American countries experienced the same phenomenon as population recovery finally picked up pace after the dramatic decline that followed the arrival of Europeans. One by one, and mostly after 1870, those countries joined the tide of export-led growth by providing Europe and the United States with raw materials and foodstuffs for their industries and workers. Colombia lagged behind. The export of tobacco in the 1850s and 1860s and of cinchona bark (*quina*, used for making quinine to cure malaria) in the 1870s and 1880s did not last. By the end of the century, coffee gave temporary hope, but a downturn in prices toppled by the last, longest, and bloodiest civil war since independence—the War of the Thousand Days (1899–1902)—did away with optimism.[52] The separation of Panama in 1903 added to the general gloom. The twentieth century inaugurated a new peaceful era. Coffee exports finally took off in the 1910s and helped create favorable conditions for expanding the state and developing infrastructure.

The difficulties of reaching the Pacific lowlands exemplify the challenges of bringing the country together. Most travelers visited Chocó, the northern half of the region, and typically went to the mining zone—the upper basins of the San Juan and Atrato Rivers, known as Upper Chocó—where most people lived. Some followed, for a week or more, one of the three trails that led from the adjacent Andes, through steep slopes, into the lowlands. Travelers going to Quibdó, the capital city located on the Atrato, could enter from Urrao or Bolívar, in Antioquia. Those heading to Nóvita, in the San Juan basin, left from Anserma, in the southern province of Cauca. Men descending these trails did not enjoy the experience. One referred to the northern route, in 1931, as "precarious and tedious", while almost forty years earlier another one bluntly stated that the trip among "mires and bogs" was simply "dreadful."[53] A traveler using the southern route clarified, "Trail there is none, but a footpath"; yet another—after spending the journey drenched by endless rains, sliding from root to root, navigating quagmires, and exhausting himself in endless gymnastics—condemned all the "horrifying paths" and "Dantean trails" that went into Chocó.[54] Since these paths were impassable for pack animals, Santiago Pérez, a renowned Colombian politician and educator, sought to ease his descent by hiring a human porter. From the wooden seat on the porter's back he observed "uninhabitable wastelands," as well as the path itself, which he described as: "a deep and tortuous line, [. . .] almost always boxed in by walls formed by the water . . . usually so narrow that no more than one porter can fit at a time. . . . There are spots where the light barely penetrates because of the intertwined branches extending from one side to the other."[55] No wonder many travelers identified with the one who "promised himself never to return to those jungles."[56]

The tough conditions of the trails owed much to the fact that these men were crossing into one of the rainiest areas of the planet through steep trails with minimum upkeep. All travelers remarked upon the extraordinary levels of precipitation as well as the humidity of the air. The observations of a Colombian engineer are thus just one variation on a constant lament:

> Everything gets ruined because of the humidity that corrodes iron objects in a few days, that rots leather and decomposes wool and cotton cloth. In two or three days, shoes sheltered from the drizzle, inside a hut and close to the fire, become covered by a thick layer of mold. To smoke a cigarette, it must first be dried out by the fire and hermetically sealed containers are needed to preserve salt. [. . .] the only way of making a fire is to find a particular, essentially resinous tree that burns despite being covered by a thick layer of rotting moss.[57]

By departing from the city of Cartagena in the Caribbean, travelers avoided trails but not rainfall. This route entailed following the coast and then ascending the Atrato, which had been closed to navigation for most of the eighteenth century to control contraband. The increasing importance of this route illustrates how, in the nineteenth century, the region shifted from being mostly oriented toward the Andes, from where much of the slave mining was controlled, to having an outward look consistent with its coastal location and export economy. From Quibdó to the Caribbean, the Atrato stretches over 250 kilometers while barely descending 43 meters. Some have, quite tellingly, referred to this river as a large lake in slow motion. In 1819, a young Italian officer who later became a renowned geographer took fourteen days to travel from the river mouth to Quibdó. He felt tormented by the torrential rains and the unbearable insects. Yet like other travelers of the day, he found solace in the wonders of tropical nature: "So much hardship was compensated by the contemplation of the grand and admirable works of Nature, the quantity of trees and palms found at each step and the infinite number of animals whose sight causes either terror or pleasure but always surprise."[58] On the lower Atrato, he had to sleep in the *bongo* or *barquetona* (large thatched canoe) poled upriver by Indian bogas, because since the river banks there are submerged most of the year, no towns or even huts were found. By the 1850s, Riosucio, a trading post made up of just a few houses, had emerged in this part of the river.[59] After the 1860s, lucky travelers could board a steamship and cut travel time to just eight days from Cartagena to Quibdó, but for many decades large canoes continued to be the norm (taking passengers downriver in just five days).[60]

Within the Upper Chocó, as throughout most of the region, transport was carried out on smaller canoes and by foot. Going from Quibdó to Nóvita took about five days and involved crossing the most famous of the many land-passes of the lowlands: the *istmo de San Pablo*, which connects the Atrato and the San Juan basins. Because it joins waters flowing into the Pacific with waters flowing into the Atlantic, some thought, following Humboldt and quite mistakenly, this could be the place to build an interoceanic canal.[61] On these istmos, people left their canoes on one side and took another craft after walking from half an hour to six hours.[62] However, these passes seldom appear in the written records because only local people crossed most of them, just as other descriptions of areas beyond the main routes are hard to come by. Some of those who spent more time in the region, such as missionaries or the French engineer Jorge Brisson, give us glimpses of areas less frequented by visitors, thus filling in obscure areas for our mental map of the lowlands—a map still delineated by people foreign to the region. Brisson, for instance, had a positive impression of the Andágueda River (a tributary of the Atrato), which apparently was the most populated basin in Chocó. He wrote that the river "offers . . . an enchanting view: the banks, as far as the eye can see, are planted with plantains, sugarcane, peach-palm, etc., and all the little houses are inhabited by black families."[63]

Travelers rarely referred to indigenous peoples, even in Chocó where they constituted a sizeable population, because outsiders rarely ventured into their territories.[64] Known as Chocó then and as Embera and Wounaan today, indigenous peoples lived in the upper reaches of some of the Atrato tributaries, the Baudó Mountains, and the lower San Juan. On reporting on his excursion to the upper Atrato, a missionary touched upon two issues frequently brought up when referring to Indians, namely their isolation and their iconic houses:

> The Indian of Chocó . . . [l]ives at the headwaters of the rivers, withdrawn from relating with those that he calls the rationals, that is the blacks and the whites. The only way to reach his dwellings is by climbing over the rocks and through the brush of the rivers with light boats, which preclude both luggage and company. Their houses are like all those of the rivers, thatched, and simply constructed. What distinguishes them is their semi-circular shape, sometimes closed, sometimes open, and their roof that, shaped like a cone, extends down until it almost touches the floor. . . . The floor tends to be quite elevated; one enters by climbing up an inclined log in which carved notches serve as footholds. . . . Entire families live in them, a single roof sheltering all the forebears and descendants. Rooms or storage spaces are unknown; [. . .] and everything is in plain sight. They sleep on the hard ground, or on *jamaguas*, a kind of cloth obtained from the bark of a tree.[65]

Travelers did not talk much either about the Chocó coast or the adjacent Baudó Mountains. This westernmost area was sparsely populated, had little economic importance, and remained rather remote. Partly on account of the ocean currents, even though navigation was risky and expensive, coastal people traded with Panama rather than Buenaventura, the port that sits in the middle of the Colombian portion of the Pacific coast.[66] The rocky Chocó coast has high cliffs and beaches that at low tide can span up to 100 meters. This shore differs enormously from the impressive mangrove forests that grow to the south of Buenaventura, which are dominated by tall red mangrove trees whose arching roots help retain sediments and provide nursing grounds for many species. The sediments are brought by rivers that run down the western slope of the Andes one after the other. The brackish waters of the *esteros* (channels) that crisscross mangroves permit secure inland navigation from Buenaventura pretty much all the way to Ecuador.

Buenaventura sits right where the littoral narrows the most, providing the shortest way to cross the Andes. In 1935, due to the increase in coffee exports, Buenaventura surpassed Barranquilla, located in the Caribbean, as the main port of the country. It gained national prominence but shared the profits of international commerce with Cali, the up-and-coming city of the interandean Cauca Valley. Buenaventura also became the place bringing together the Colombian Pacific coast. Before that could happen, Tumaco, in the southern end of the coast, and Quibdó, in the Atrato River, emerged as small aspiring subregional centers. Buenaventura lagged behind owing its growth more to maritime commerce than to a strategic role within the region itself. And on that count it developed slowly. Not until 1923 did it acquire its first wharf, and even then it could only accommodate one relatively small steamship at a time. Furthermore, efficient transport to the Andes proved to be a longtime challenge.

For most of the nineteenth century, commodities and passengers came and left Buenaventura through a mule path and by navigating in small canoes the fast Dagua River. One French visitor, leaving the country through this port in the early 1820s, took two days to travel by horse from Cali to Juntas, in the Dagua River, and two more on a canoe all the way to the ocean. He described the beginning of his adventurous river trip with the following words:

> An expert pilot: the black man brandishing the pole skillfully avoided the overly swift current; daring, he ventured between the turbulent waters formed by rocks and, without fear of crashing the canoe, made it glide through those narrow passages. But sometimes a rock held us up while descending, and the water that

> bubbled up against this new obstacle threatened to sink us. Those were the critical moments. It was then that the two men jumped into the water and, holding tightly onto the canoe, thus lightened it and prevented it from being sucked into the whirlpool.
>
> These new kinds of dangers make an impression on the traveler who, trapped in the center of the canoe and not even daring to blink, to prevent causing a shipwreck, unintentionally breaths a sigh of relief each time that an obstacle is avoided or rapids crossed. This happens to me too, and the black men, taking my sighs of happiness for laments, asked me with ironic tranquility:
>
> Did Mister get wet?
>
> And effectively I was soaked. The rain came down in torrents, and the sailor, always alert to avoid the rocks, constantly kicked in order to bail out the water that filled the canoe.[67]

The construction of a railroad went through many ordeals. By 1882, passengers could traverse the first 20 kilometers from Buenaventura to Córdoba on a train wagon, but only until 1909 could they reach Caldas, 82 kilometers from the coast and close to the Andean summit. Finally, in 1915, the trip from Cali to Buenaventura was reduced to just one day by train.[68]

The narrow littoral south of Buenaventura has eight medium-sized rivers crossing it from east to west, and then it widens halfway between the port and Ecuador. The Micay River is the largest, while the Yurumanguí has the most beautiful name. Travelers seldom talk about them, as they mostly went further south to visit Barbacoas, in the large Patía River basin, or the port of Tumaco. Nested inland 70 kilometers from the coast, Barbacoas was the only colonial city in the lowlands with a local elite that lived off the gold extracted by slaves in its rich surroundings. Throughout the nineteenth century, it slowly declined, while the port of Tumaco increased in importance. Barbacoas could be reached by a trail that connected it to Túquerres in the Andes, and then to Pasto. Descriptions of the route are reminiscent of those referring to the descent into Chocó. However, this trail stood out for its heavy traffic, as much of what was consumed in Barbacoas—cheese, eggs, hens, and vegetables—came from the highlands. In 1853, it was "a curious sight to see: Every day at three in the afternoon, between fifty and a hundred Indians, both men and women, enter with a basket on their backs, a staff in their hands, and a felt hat unfailingly on their heads. The police only let the *güisas*, for that is how they are called, enter the city at one time."[69] A proper trail was built from 1888 to 1893 and allowed mules to slowly replace porters, who returned carrying salt for the highland market. Even in 1907, it would take seven days for a visitor to climb the mountains all the way to Túquerres.[70]

The ocean stood closer. In the early twentieth century, once the steamboat service began operating, it took two days to travel from Tumaco to Barbacoas, much less than the ten days people had to spend a century before. Downstream the trip was somewhat faster.[71] Some steamers, including a few of the Pacific Steam Navigation Company, stopped at Tumaco as well as Buenaventura, connecting the region to the outside world. However, lack of facilities and a lively commerce made the bustling life associated with maritime ports absent.[72]

In the late nineteenth century, the Pacific coast stood in the western margin of Colombia, tied to the Andes through difficult and uncomfortable trails. It had started to break off the colonial forced enclosure by establishing ties through the oceans with Panama, Peru, and the Caribbean. Its inhabitants, mostly black but also indigenous peoples, lived in the forests and used canoes and paths to travel largely through areas close to their own homes. They, as well as the foreign travelers who visited the place, did not have a sense of sharing a region. Yet seen from afar, key processes that made this coast—its postemancipation condition and the relation local peoples established with the environment—give unity to the area and allow for a common historical study.

PART I

AN EXTRACTIVE ECONOMY

1

SLAVE MINING AND EMANCIPATION

THROUGHOUT COLONIAL TIMES, Latin American extensive rainforests typically remained outside imperial control. The most humid of them, located on the Pacific coast of New Granada (now Colombia), constituted an exception. In the eighteenth century, they contributed much of the sole product exported from this colony: gold. Mining here initiated a trend that all rainforests would follow in the nineteenth century: the development of extractive economies—that is, the large-scale extraction of natural resources for the market. The lower Amazon also began this trend relatively early exporting the so-called *drogas do sertão*—spices, cocoa, and other vegetable and animal products. Colonial and republican societies largely based their relationship with jungles on taking advantage of their diversity by converting elements of nature into commodities. The most common path has been using parts of plants—tree trunks for timber, sap for making chewing gum, mangrove bark for its tannins—yet in the Pacific coast, the colonizers found the riches in the subsoil. Still, the logic mediating their use of the environment remained the same: harvesting whatever could be sold profitably.

Extractive economies not only produce different commodities, they also vary in duration, techniques of extraction, environmental impact, and, quite importantly, the types of societies they contribute to build. Colonial mining lasted a good century and stripped small areas of forest cover to access the subsoil and obtain gold. But decades later prospectors failed to find some of these mines because the forest had grown back. Bringing blacks to work as slaves had more noticeable and lasting consequences: it developed New Granada's most productive slave-based economy and laid the basis for the creation of the largest area of Spanish America where black people make up the overwhelming majority of the population.[1]

In this jungle, extracting a shiny metal that served as means of exchange led to a form of slavery that opened inroads for freedom through self-purchase. Slaves mined for gold in camps scattered throughout the jungle. Although mining here fulfilled a crucial economic role within the colony, it was subservient to the interests of the largest slave owners who lived in the nearby Andean region. There, they developed haciendas, something almost impossible in the Pacific lowlands due to environmental conditions. The few whites living on the coast and the lack of cities attest to the absence of important agents and symbols of European colonialism, and ultimately to tenuous state control. Masters' weak position and slaves' limitations to permanently run away for lack of an open frontier, led to an understanding in which slaves had days and spaces to mine gold freely and use it to purchase their freedom. In other slave societies, self-purchase occurred mostly in urban settings offering diverse economic opportunities. Thus the lowlands' unique form of slavery laid the first building blocks of the postemancipation society that developed in the second half of the nineteenth century. Based on works mostly published between the mid-1970s and today, this chapter offers the first general overview of the particular form slavery took in this region.

ENSLAVEMENT FOR GOLD

Colonial economy and society in the lowlands were organized around the extraction of gold. The existence of gold dust along the western flank of the Andes structured the process of occupation and the colonial geography of the place. Gold deposits formed a long and narrow strip parallel to the mountains within which three large mining areas could be discerned. Upper Chocó and Barbacoas were the main ones (see map 2).

Chocó comprised the entire northern half of the lowlands, but gold was only found in the Upper Chocó—that is, the upper San Juan and Atrato River basins. Beyond there (mainly in the lower Atrato and Baudó basins) the Crown had little to no control.[2] For this reason, and in order to avoid contraband, the

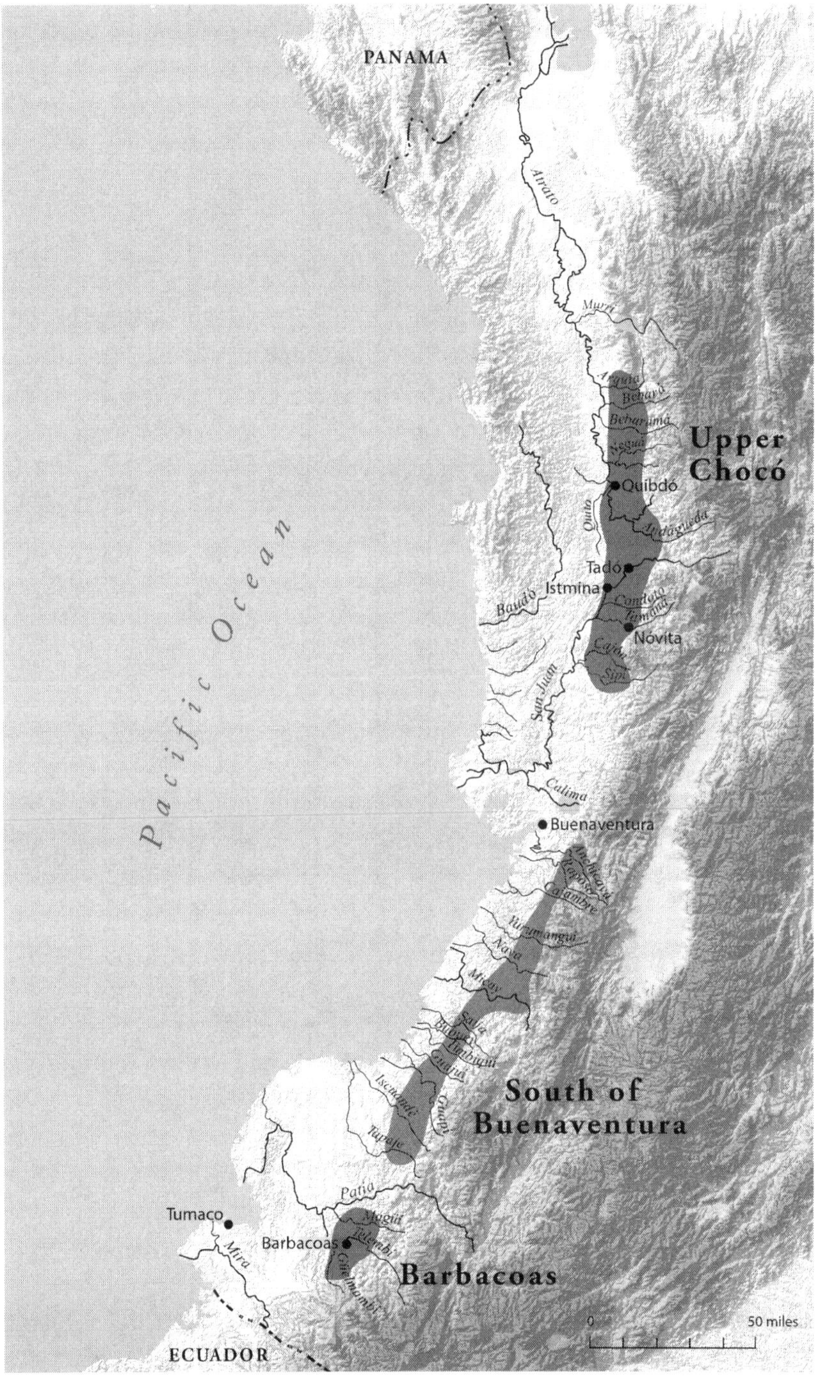

MAP 2 Mining districts of the Pacific lowlands. Map by Paola Luna, Cartography Lab, Universidad de los Andes, Bogotá.

Atrato was officially closed to maritime traffic from the end of the seventeenth century to 1782. A fortress (*vigía*), which signaled the limit of state control, unsuccessfully attempted to enforce this regulation. Contraband persisted along the Atrato, as well as the San Juan, whose traffic was in theory severely restricted but without effective enforcement.[3]

In 1726, given its rising economic importance, Chocó became an independent province (*gobernación*) with two main administrative divisions. The San Juan basin made up Nóvita, which historian Orián Jiménez dubbed "the country of gold" for its outstanding mining productivity. He referred to Citará, the other division corresponding to the Atrato basin, as "the country of agriculture," given the role of its Indian population in producing foodstuffs.[4] Surprisingly, Chocó was a gobernación without cities. The town of Nóvita, where the governor resided, had barely twenty houses in 1731, and almost a century later still only had one street.[5] The dearth of cities was largely due to the predominance of absentee mine owners from the Andes, who invested their profits far from the lowlands.

Barbacoas, the second mining area, formed part of the very large province of Popayán, and of the Audiencia de Quito. The name was used to refer to two, or even three, different mining areas—a matter that causes much confusion. First, there was Barbacoas proper, a relatively small area surrounding the city of Santa María del Puerto de las Barbacoas that included part of the Telembí and adjacent rivers. Barbacoas stood out for having the only settlement in the lowlands that despite its shortcomings could be called a city. With about sixty houses in the 1760s (most of which burned down in the 1783 fire), it was larger than any other town. Most importantly, it had a working town council (*cabildo*), presided by a local slave-owning elite.[6] This elite derived from the times of conquest and had ties with the Andean city of Pasto, as well as with Popayán and Quito.[7] It is to this core area that I refer to as Barbacoas throughout this book.

The name Barbacoas has also been used to designate a larger area over which the city had some influence, stretching to the north either up to the Micay River or all the way to Chocó. Robert West carefully drafted this extension of Barbacoas in a map that shows a narrower littoral traversed by various rivers descending from the Andes to the Pacific Ocean (see map 3). The northern part of the area depicted on the map was referred to at the time as Raposo—so historians often use this designation, but then sometimes they encompass this district within a broadly conceived Barbacoas. Raposo was largely controlled from the city of Cali. The rest of this intermediate area,

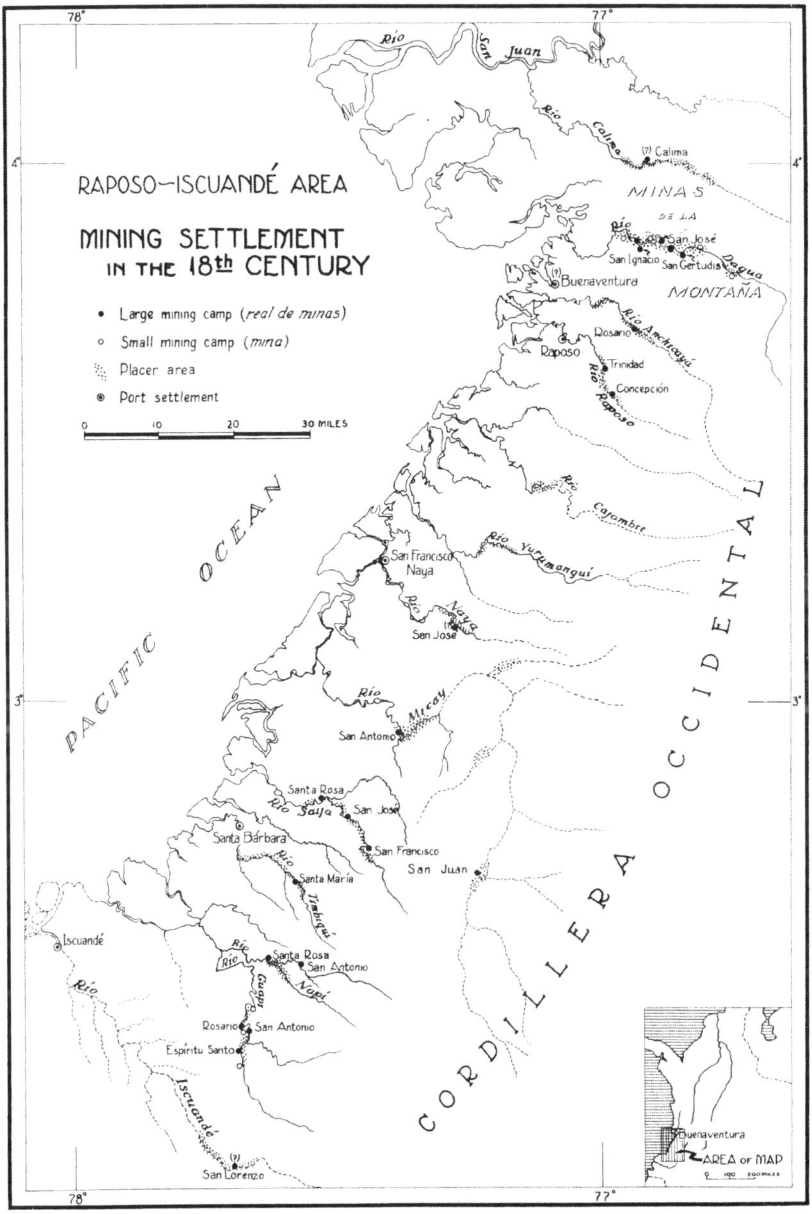

MAP 3 Raposo-Iscuandé area, mining settlement in the eighteenth century. From Robert West, *Colonial Placer Mining in Colombia* (Baton Rouge: Louisiana State University Press, 1952).

in which the larger Micay River stands out, is frequently overlooked in the historical record.

All mining areas were in production by the early eighteenth century, but efforts to take over the placers started much earlier. From 1512 to 1540, expeditions up the Atrato and along the coastline brought news of gold riches and fierce native groups. The first experiment at colonizing and extracting gold—in the upper San Juan—began in 1573, but it failed completely by the mid-1590s.[8] Permanent control over parts of the lowlands began in the seventeenth century. Barbacoas was conquered first, but it took more than thirty years of warfare for the Spanish to establish "a shaky outpost at Santa Maria del Puerto" in the 1630s.[9] As with the rest of Spanish America, the surviving population was "entrusted" to the invasion leaders who would benefit from its labor for two generations. But unlike other *encomiendas*, Indians here were not forced to form villages; instead they lived in scattered family dwellings and worked the mines. In the 1630s and 1640s, the most productive gold fields were in production as the colonizers brought in African slaves, mostly from the highland mines of Popayán, to join the Indians at the placers. Lacking official control, the encomienda in Barbacoas came to resemble a form of slavery. Indians responded with massive temporary flight but could not stop their numbers from diminishing.[10]

Gold deposits dwindled to the south of Barbacoas, something that must have helped the province of Esmeraldas (today in northern Ecuador) to remain semiautonomous through most of the colonial period. Beginning in the 1780s, miners from Barbacoas and Chocó moved in with experienced slaves to work its placers.[11] Much earlier, the town of Barbacoas and its subsidiary, Iscuandé, served as posts for launching expeditions to the north.[12] By 1640, mines in the Timbiquí basin were in production, and evidence exists of a small encomienda there in 1680.[13] Miners from Popayán eventually dominated this area revolving around the Micay River.[14] Further north, the Raposo district came under colonial control through efforts that originated in Cali; by the early eighteenth century, several small slave gangs worked its placers.[15] However, a detailed explanation of the incorporation of this large territory stretching between Barbacoas and Chocó is unavailable.

The Spaniards attempted to conquer Chocó throughout the seventeenth century, especially the Atrato mining area. Violent expeditions between 1638 and 1640 that concentrated on the Atrato served mostly to alienate indigenous peoples; many were killed, captured, and forced to migrate. In the 1660s, and probably earlier in the San Juan, efforts by a few priests and adventurers who favored peaceful methods allowed the development of mining on a very small scale.[16] In the early 1670s, following royal instructions to pacify the populations of Chocó without creating encomiendas, Franciscan friars arrived in the Atrato to convert the indigenous peoples and congregate them in permanent settlements. By then, the native population had been largely decimated. In 1678, a priest estimated the population of the San Juan and upper and middle Atrato to be just 3,850 people, while Kathleen Romoli calculated that only a century earlier the Upper Chocó had over 35,000 inhabitants.[17] They lived in scattered and temporary settlements composed of a few houses. Spaniards wanted to resettle them in villages close to the mines, so that they could produce foodstuffs to feed the slave gangs. The friars were met with resistance and had no one to negotiate with because these groups lacked political leadership. However, by the end of the decade, three permanent Indian settlements had been established.

But control over the local population remained tenuous, as indicated by the attack launched on Spaniards from these settlements. In 1684, Indians killed almost all Spaniards in the Atrato, along with their servants, between 112 and 126 people. As a response, three expeditions, totaling 750 men, came to Chocó between 1684 and 1687 and killed the leaders of the rebellion, subduing the Indian population. However, it took at least a decade more to restore some sense of normalcy, and for mining to resume.[18] Developments in the San Juan basin are unclear. Yet the fact that by 1690 only twenty slaves worked the Tadó mines suggests that a thorough appropriation of the area by the Spaniards did not occur until the eighteenth century.[19] In the meantime, in Barbacoas at least twenty-eight camps were operating, and Santa María del Puerto already had a cabildo, a smeltery, and a jail.[20]

The mines of the Pacific littoral sustained what Germán Colmenares termed the second gold cycle of New Granada.[21] New Granada, which since 1739 was permanently elevated to the status of viceroyalty, exported gold almost exclusively. From 1550 to 1620, mining districts mostly in the vast Andean region kept gold production up, but for over half a century afterwards mining fell into a deep crisis. From the 1680s onward, after the Chocó placers started to produce gold, a second gold cycle began that lasted until Independence. Between 1735 and 1799, the period for which we have better data, the Pacific lowlands produced somewhere between 45 percent and 70 percent of the total official gold output of New Granada (see graph 1).[22]

Gold production figures are based on tax collections that do not account for contraband, which was widely extended over the region. They ultimately

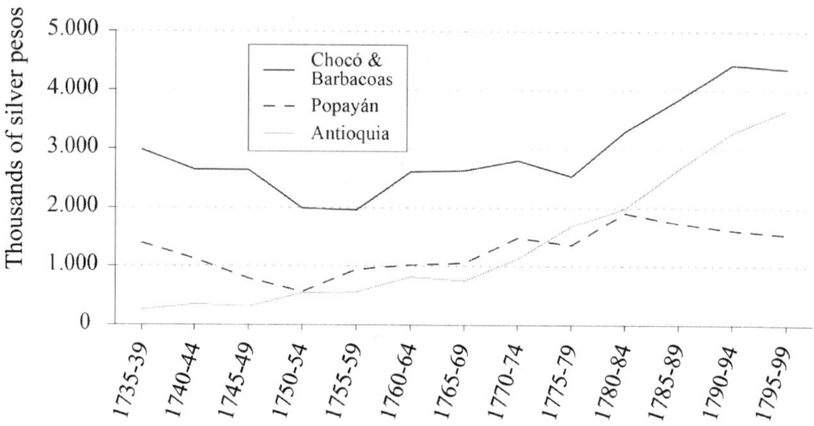

GRAPH 1 New Granada gold production, eighteenth century. Graph based on data from Jorge Orlando Melo, "Producción minera y crecimiento económico en la Nueva Granada durante el siglo XVIII," *Revista Universidad del Valle* 3–4 (1977): 29–46.

show trends rather than precisely account for output. Chocó serves as a good example. After 1721 and before the establishment of a smeltery in Nóvita in 1782, miners were supposed to send their gold dust to Nóvita or Quibdó to pay the *quinto* (fifth). As its name suggests, this tax began as a 20 percent duty but by 1777 had diminished to 3 percent. After the smeltery began operations, all gold had to be taken to Nóvita to be turned into ingots, a process in which it lost 8 percent of its weight (twice as much as in other smelteries). Many miners did not follow these regulations. They used the gold dust to buy illegal imports (among them slaves) or took it to Popayán where they registered it as coming from a different mining district. In 1789, an observer estimated that "more than half of the gold mined in the Chocó was fraudulently transported from the region"; therefore production must have been considerably higher than what the records show.[23] The difficulties in estimating gold production in Chocó can be seen in the differences portrayed by the two authors—William Sharp and Jorge Orlando Melo—who have estimated its production. While Sharp argues that gold output peaked in the second quarter of the eighteenth century and remained relatively stable throughout the rest of the century, Melo reports a second peak in output toward the end of the century (see graphs 2 and 3).[24] Fortunately, the two authors concur that Nóvita produced about 50 percent more gold than Citará throughout the period.

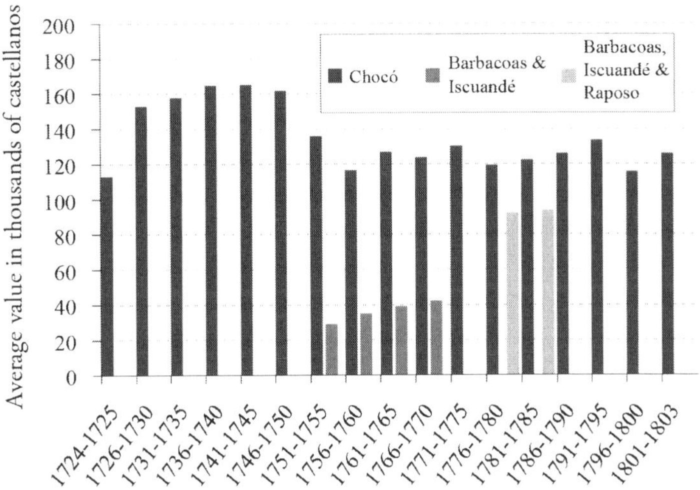

GRAPH 2 Registered gold production, eighteenth century. Graph based on data from William Sharp, *Slavery on the Spanish Frontier: The Colombian Chocó 1680–1810* (Norman: University of Oklahoma Press, 1976), and Kris Lane, "The Transition from Encomienda to Slavery in Seventeenth-Century Barbacoas (Colombia)," *Slavery & Abolition* 21, no. 1 (2000): 73–95.

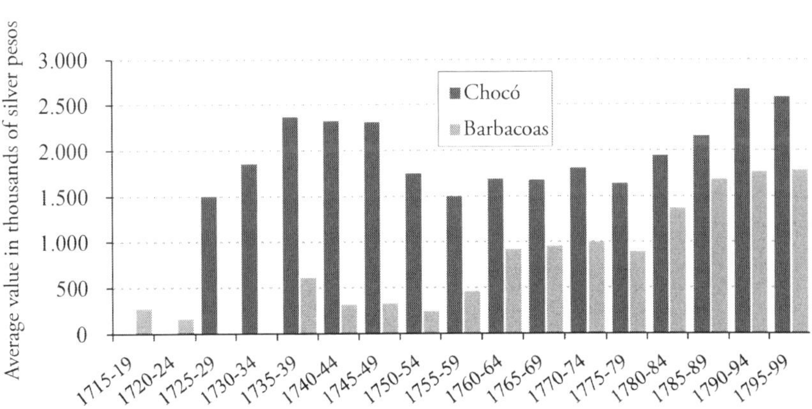

GRAPH 3 Registered gold production, eighteenth century. Graph based on data from Jorge Orlando Melo, "Producción minera y crecimiento económico en la Nueva Granada durante el siglo XVIII," *Revista Universidad del Valle* 3–4 (1977): 29–46.

In any case, Chocó was the most productive district; but by the end of the century Barbacoas' rising output was coming close. Lane estimated that in the late 1670s, when the mines in Barbacoas had been in production for twenty or thirty years, their annual output was between 15,000 and 20,000 castellanos, while the few records from the 1680s show wide variations, from 5,475 castellanos in 1683 to 20,442 in 1684.[25] Between 1700 and 1708, Barbacoas' production contracted to a yearly average of 12,560 castellanos. Yet as both Melo and Lane reveal, the wide gap in production with respect to Chocó diminished notably after midcentury. Registered output in Barbacoas increased from an annual average of about 30,000 castellanos in the 1750s to about 40,000 in the 1760s, before rising close to 100,000 castellanos per year in the 1780s.[26]

All that gold, removed from the lowland subsoil, enriched slave owners who managed their assets from the Andean region, where they invested their profits. Elites of the cities of the gobernación de Popayán—not only the more prosperous Popayán and Cali but also smaller ones such as Cartago, Toro, and Buga—played an important role in conquering the lowlands and putting its placers to work. As a consequence, they owned a sizeable part of the slaves and the mines there. Chocó in the early eighteenth century illustrates this point: "In 1711, fourteen owners from Popayán, many of them absentee, owned a little less than half the slaves working in Chocó (356 of 821, that is, 43.4 percent). Slave owners from Cali, Cartago, Anserma, Toro, and Santa Fe, as well as permanent residents in the province, owned the rest. Two families stood out among the owners from Popayán, the Mosquera and Arboleda, who owned close to a quarter of all the slaves."[27] Likewise, the Raposo mining district gave rise to the largest fortunes from Cali. A few members of this city's elite also had mines further south, in Micay, Timbiquí, and Iscuandé, and north in Nóvita.[28]

Slave owners' choice of residence stemmed partly from the difficulties for developing haciendas in the lowlands. Despite the growth of the slave population, the lowlands represented a relatively small market; plus it was more profitable to have slaves mine rather than cultivate crops. But most importantly, there were serious constraints on agriculture in the lowlands: constant cloud cover reduces luminosity and therefore crop productivity. The predominantly acidic and highly leached soils further curb the development of commercial agriculture. The levees and low river terraces that are enriched by occasional flooding and are suitable for growing crops occupy an extremely small area, less than 5 percent according to Mario Mejía. Swamp soils, which have high organic content, are also scarce and poorly drained.[29]

As a result, Andean elites' interest in the lowlands was limited to mining. In contrast, older mining districts closer to their hometowns, whose lands were partly used for cattle ranching, were converted into proper haciendas. In the late seventeenth century, these families invested the surpluses from mining and commerce in buildings, slaves, and agricultural production, mainly sugar cane. The resulting haciendas were the most reliable investments and the ultimate source of prestige and influence. As Colmenares aptly explained, these families mortgaged haciendas to the Catholic Church for credit and used it to expand their mining operations—often on the coast.[30] If these entrepreneurs wanted the highest possible return on borrowed capital, they invested it in long and risky trips to Cartagena to purchase imported merchandise. Mining encouraged this long distance trade by maintaining a wealthy group that could afford conspicuous consumption, and by demanding slaves, who accounted for up to 75 percent of total investments in this sector. Mines by themselves were worth little; enslaved black people made them valuable by extracting gold, and in this manner they guaranteed elites' economic and social position. To emphasize the point: commercial proceeds were in turn invested in mining ventures. The strategy came full circle as elites used gold mining profits to continue building their haciendas, so that ultimately the Andes consumed the wealth generated in the lowlands. Mining also supported the development of haciendas by sustaining a small but lucrative trade in liquor and salted meat—and perhaps a few other provisions—produced in the Andes.[31]

Barbacoas deviates from this model, however, as its mine-owners resided locally and apparently did not own Andean haciendas. Nonetheless, haciendas around Pasto supplied the mines with cereal and dried beef, which arrived daily in town transported by highland Indians.[32] One way or another, the relations between the Andes and the coast contributed to the creation of a slave society with long-lasting consequences in the lowlands. The heavy investment in slaves, coupled with the decimation of Amerindians, led the population of the region to "change from one almost exclusively Indian to one predominantly black."[33] In the 1710s, around 1,350 slaves lived in the lowlands, 60 percent in Chocó and the rest in the south.[34] At the close of the century, the number of slaves reached its all-time peak at around 15,000 (see table 1). By that time, the proportions were inverted as mining in Barbacoas was booming and apparently generating an influx of slaves from other provinces. In the southern lowlands, in those years, slaves accounted for between one-third and one-half of all inhabitants, and in Chocó close to 40 percent. Nowhere else in present-day Colombia were

TABLE 1 Lowland slave population in the eighteenth century

	CHOCÓ	SOUTH
1711	821 (a)	
1717		530 (c)
1759	4,237 (a) 3,919 (b)	
1772	4,231 (e)	
1778	5,756 (b,d)	
1782	7,088 (b,d)	
1788		4,407 (d)
1797		9,179 (d)
1808	4,968 (b)	

Table based on data taken from: (a) Germán Colmenares, *Historia económica y social de Colombia, Tomo II: Popayán, una sociedad esclavista, 1680–1800* (Medellín: La Carreta, 1979), 73–74; (b) William Sharp, *Slavery on the Spanish Frontier: The Colombian Chocó 1680–1810* (Norman: University of Oklahoma Press, 1976), 115, 117, 123, 124, 199; (c) Kris Lane, "The Transition from Encomienda to Slavery in Seventeenth-Century Barbacoas (Colombia)," *Slavery & Abolition* 21, no. 1 (2000): 73–95, 87; (d) Hermes Tovar, Jorge Andrés Tovar Mora, and Camilo Ernesto Tovar Mora, *Convocatoria al poder del número. Censos y estadísticas de la Nueva Granada (1750–1830)* (Bogotá: Archivo General de la Nación, 1994), 88, 316, 321–22. 365–66; (e) Oscar Almario, "Territorio, etnicidad y poder en el Pacífico sur colombiano, 1780–1930" (PhD diss., Universidad de Sevilla, 2007), 133.

enslaved people such a sizeable part of the population; in other provinces they accounted for less than one-fifth of all residents. Yet due to the extremely low population density in the lowlands, slaves living there made only between one-sixth and one-fifth of the total slave population of present-day Colombia.[35] Perhaps more important for the racialized geography that developed in the nineteenth century, slaves plus free blacks, mulattos, and zambos made up over two-thirds of the people inhabiting the lowlands.[36]

The black population derived from slave gangs, called *cuadrillas*, which grew larger with time and evolved into the basic social unit in the lowlands. In 1711, owners had on average seventeen slaves in their mines in Chocó and, in 1717, had twenty-one in their mines in the south.[37] In the next half-century, gangs, particularly in Chocó, grew larger by importing slaves, which could only be done legally in Cartagena (or in Guayaquil, via Lima). Although the Atrato and San Juan Rivers were closed to trade, miners often used these prohibited water routes because the overland trek was costly and time-consuming, plus more than

20 percent of the slaves could perish. Bringing slaves into Barbacoas was likely more expensive, for owners could not bring their highland slaves since they had none, and location meant longer and riskier routes.[38]

Just how big slave gangs were is somewhat unclear. The confusion stems to a great extent from the ambiguity of the term *cuadrilla*, which authors define as a "labor gang" while also using the term to refer to the number of slaves per owner.[39] For instance, referring to Nóvita, which had the largest groups of slaves in the lowlands, Sharp mentions that in 1759 the wealthiest slave owners had cuadrillas of 567, 192, and 125 slaves working in their mines (in plural). He implies that the largest groups of slaves were split between various mines (that could be hours if not days apart), and they thus formed several working units.[40] Therefore, we cannot assume that all the slaves belonging to the largest slave owners labored together to form immense gangs. Furthermore, slaves were classified as *útiles* (literally, useful) and *chusma*—that is, children, the infirm, and those too old to work. In this sense, defining cuadrilla solely as a working unit is somewhat misleading. Yet authors stress the large size of slave gangs and give the impression that it was fairly common to find very sizeable groups of slaves working together. Referring to the entire lowlands plus the Andes close to Cali and Popayán, Colmenares wrote, "Eighteenth century mining . . . was based on the existence of large work groups [cuadrillas] of slaves—between 50 and 500."[41] Based mainly on Sharp, George Reid Andrews asserted that "in the Chocó [. . .] cuadrillas of 100 or 150 were not uncommon, and some slave owners assembled corps of 300 to 500 slaves to work on their holdings."[42]

A careful reading of works on slavery in the lowlands suggests that working units in general were smaller. According to Colmenares, in 1759, owners had an average of 75.6 slaves in their mines in Chocó. He also affirmed that 63.2 percent of slaves were owned by someone who had more than one hundred slaves in the area; Sharp lowers this number to 51.4 percent.[43] A different picture emerges when looking only at working slaves. A Chocó report reveals that while around 1753 sixty-one mines had an average of 43.4 working slaves, only two had more than one hundred working slaves, while eleven had ten or less. Small gangs were common, and the very large ones somewhat atypical (see table 2 and graph 4).[44] An 1807 report on Chocó permits the conclusion that fifty years later very large slave gangs continued to exist, while most mines had a smaller labor force. That year, 73 percent of all slaves lived in mines with more than one hundred slaves, but 62.5 percent of the mines had less than one hundred slaves, and for the most part less than fifty adult slaves.[45] Looking beyond Nóvita to include the whole

TABLE 2 Working slaves per mine, Chocó c. 1753

WORKING SLAVES PER MINE	MINES	TOTAL NUMBER OF SLAVES	PERCENT OF TOTAL NUMBER OF SLAVES
1–10	11	83	3.1
11–40	26	600	22.6
41–70	12	644	24.3
71–100	10	844	31.8
101–214	2	344	13.0
Total	61	2.650	100

Table based on data taken from Caroline A. Williams, *Between Resistance and Adaptation: Indigenous Peoples and the Colonisation of the Chocó, 1510–1753* (Liverpool: Liverpool University Press, 2005), 228–32.

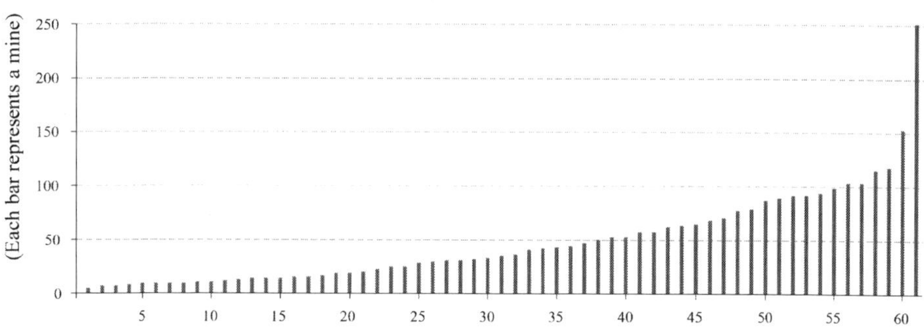

GRAPH 4 Working slaves per mine, Chocó c. 1753. Graph based on data taken from Caroline A. Williams, *Between Resistance and Adaptation: Indigenous Peoples and the Colonisation of the Chocó, 1510–1753* (Liverpool: Liverpool University Press, 2005), 228–32.

region, and having in mind the entire century, the existence of very sizeable cuadrillas is more the exception than the rule. In the late eighteenth century, the two largest cuadrillas in Barbacoas had more than two hundred slaves, but most were smaller, with thirty-one members on average.[46]

Slave gangs went from being relatively small work gangs composed of mostly young men to becoming larger social units made up of families, including numerous women and children. In the early eighteenth century, cuadrillas in Chocó were dominated by African-born (*bozales*), male slaves. As they had few women, for several decades these units grew mostly through purchases.[47] By midcentury there were a little less than two men for every woman among working slaves, but three decades later, taking children into account, women constituted more than 45 percent of all slaves, and by the time of independence there were almost as many slave women as there were men. As the ratio between sexes evened out, the proportion of children grew and native-born slaves replaced those born in Africa. By 1759, the African-born comprised about 30 percent of all slaves, and children accounted for a somewhat larger percentage. By the end of the century, children came to represent almost half the total number of slaves in most cuadrillas.[48] These children belonged to families, sometimes with married parents and others—as Mario Diego Romero has pointed out—formed around single women.[49] In the south, this demographic change probably occurred earlier, as mining has a longer history there. That in 1717 minors comprised 32 percent of the slaves in Barbacoas seems to confirm this assumption.[50]

Cuadrillas' shared history and family groups gave them cohesion, forming building blocks for life in freedom. Even as early as 1725 a mine inventory in Chocó listed the slaves as follows:

> Item the captain named Francisco of *casta Arara*
> Item the wife of said captain named María de la candelaria of *casta popo*
> Item two children of said captain, one girl about 10 years old called Dominga and the other, a boy, called Bicente, also criollo, and about 6 years old
> Item a little mulata girl named Geronima, daughter of the captain's wife, about 12 years old
> Item the black *contracapitan* called Bernabe of *casta mina*
> Item the wife of said *contracapitan* called Maria teresa of *casta lucumi*
> Item three children of said pair, a girl called Juana about eight years old, and a boy named Martin about five years old, and a baby in arms called Nicolas.[51]

Families appear in order of importance: first were those of the *capitán* and the *contracapitán*. The former was the most important slave, in charge of organizing labor and supervising the washing of clays to obtain gold. Always a man, either young or mature, this slave worked close with the *minero*, or mine administrator, who was usually the only white person around. If the cuadrilla was large, one or several *contracapitanes* or *capitanejos* would help him.[52]

Cuadrillas' identity stemmed also from their association with a place—or a *real de minas*. While in other parts of Latin America this term meant "a large mining *town* based on vein deposits," in the lowlands large mines merited this designation.[53] A single *real de minas* could occupy a whole basin and thus included—apart from a settlement—mining works, forest, and plantain and corn fields.[54] The mining camps themselves formed the primordial settlement unit in the lowlands: apart from a few huts, some had a blacksmith shop, a storehouse for food and tools, and perhaps a very basic chapel. For the most part, miners abandoned these camps after the deposits were depleted.[55] In Barbacoas (and probably in a few other parts of the south), some camps were not transient. Mine owners had a house in town and—as recounted by Fray Juan de Santa Gertrudis—"they have another house by the river where they have the mine, and . . . they continually come and go between the mine and Barbacoas . . . so only for Easter and Holy Week do all the people gather in the city."[56]

In these reales de minas, slaves used mostly Native American techniques to mine the placers. The mines consisted of deposits of gold dust and small grains that were separated from underground veins located in the Andes thousands of years ago through physical and chemical weathering and water erosion. Streams transported gold particles that, due to their higher weight, eventually settled in places where the water slows down. In this manner, gravels particularly rich in gold—or placer mines—formed. These deposits are found both in present riverbeds and in ancient ones—that is, in the alluvial terrains that surround rivers. Ground sluicing, which the Spaniards learned from Amerindians, was the most common method used to mine ancient gravels in high terraces. As its name indicates, this technique's most obvious trait was a sluice or ditch (*canalón*) dug along a terrace just deep enough to access the richest deposits. Slaves excavated the terrace and dumped the gravel into the sluice, which they later washed with water. They took out the cobbles with concave wooden plates (*cachos*) and washed out the sand and gravel. Gold mixed with clay settled in the bottom of the channel. Laborers scraped off this material using hooked metal blades with wooden handles (*almocafres*). They then washed it in round, shallow, wooden bowls called *bateas* and obtained a black mixture (*jagua*), to which they added the glutinous sap of several plants. The sap attracted the iron oxide flakes and left the gold behind. Mercury was seldom used, probably due to high costs. Ten to fifteen workers carried out the whole operation within about two weeks.[57]

The lowland environment provided gold and also much needed water that made mining possible. The omnipresent jungle was more of a nuisance; although it was rich in timber for building houses, canoes, and bateas, slaves had to cut it down and remove it (often without fire due to humidity) in order to work the gravels. Obtaining water, no matter how abundant, implied onerous investments. Because high deposits are located above stream channels, an adequate supply of water had to be secured first to successfully wash gravels in a ground sluice. For this purpose slaves built reservoirs (*pilas*) on hilltops and canals (*acequias*) to bring water to the mines. The heavy rains that fall throughout the lowlands almost every night, except in the dry months of January and February, filled the reservoirs and allowed the workers to proceed without major interruptions. This infrastructure, referred to as *entables*, could take months to build and was what made the mines themselves valuable. Miners needed to buy costly iron tools and maintain slaves over a long period of time before reaping any benefits.[58]

Besides building ground sluices, slaves also constructed pits and dived in the rivers to obtain gold. On flood plains, river bars, and low terraces adjacent to streams, slaves dug pits (*hoyos*) to reach the gold-bearing sands. These pits were probably 12 to 14 feet square, and from 10 to 15 feet deep. Larger pits had steps so that a human chain could pass bateas full of sand. Workers had to cover the walls with logs for reinforcement—which they did not always do—and to bail out water that seeped in. Gold is also found in the streambeds, especially beneath boulders and wherever the current slows. To mine that gold, workers built several small wing dams (*burros*) from the bank some four feet into the stream. In the quiet spaces between them, they extracted the cobbles and then scooped the sand to be washed in bateas. During the dry season, they also dived with a heavy stone tied to their waist to scrape gravel from the bottom, a technique referred to as *zambullidero*.[59]

Slaves also cultivated plantain and corn, either on groves that belonged to the mine or on small plots of their own. The larger agricultural fields, which usually included a few pigs and cattle, were frequently located one or two days away from the mines because they needed well drained soil.[60] These units were pretentiously called *haciendas de minas*. Masters preferred to devote slaves to mining but engaged in cultivation to secure food given its scarcity. They would purchase food produced by Indians whenever possible, especially in Chocó, given its sizeable Indian population.

In the 1780s, Chocó's 6,552 Indians greatly outnumbered the thousand who lived in the entire south. More than two-thirds of those in Chocó lived in Citará, which meant that around 59 percent of the Indian population in the entire lowlands resided in the Atrato basin.[61] These people were known as *Citaraes* at the time and are known as *Embera* today, while their peers from the lower San Juan are called Wounaan. As a Crown official put it in 1713, "Indians

[were] not . . . employed in the extraction of gold . . . but they assist[ed] and contribute[d] to all [other] activities conducive to this end."[62] For this purpose, their ways of life had been greatly transformed: They lived part of the year in villages, worked for the colonizers, and had an elite of *indios mandones*.[63] The towns of Quibdó (San Francisco de Atrato), Neguá, and Lloró were established in the 1670s, and three more—Bevará, Murrí, and Beté—were founded further down the Atrato between 1690 and 1720 (plus Chamí and Tatamá, which lie in Chocó's limits).[64] In 1782, Quibdó, the largest town, had seventy-five huts, while the three smaller ones had just six each. As Eric Werner Cantor has shown, Indian towns in Citará were erected close to the gold fields and each had assigned agricultural lands comprising the *resguardo*, mostly in the nonmining western tributaries of the Atrato. Indians only lived half of the year in town, and in the remaining half they worked in their fields.[65]

Each town had a Spanish *corregidor* in charge of overseeing Christian instruction—a mission in which they largely failed—and regulating access to Indian labor by collecting tribute and assigning tasks. These colonial officials bought the Indian produce, mostly corn, and resold it. They also rented Indians to miners to work as canoemen, help with building slave huts or houses for the Spanish, and engage in agriculture. A few Indians did domestic service or served in the Atrato fortress. Those from Chamí, the town at the foothills of the Andes, also worked as carriers. Plus Indians constructed most of the canoes necessary for transportation. Corregidores greatly relied on *caciques* and *gobernadores* initially appointed by the Spanish. In the eighteenth century, this hereditary elite was firmly established partly because their role as intermediaries between the communities and the colonizers also took the form of protecting their people from different forms of abuse. Most of their grievances centered on corregidores not respecting the privileges of the Indian elite (such as exemption from labor, taxation, and corporal punishment), not allowing Indians time to work for themselves, paying them in kind, and conducing them to indebtedness. They seem to have been apt at exploiting tensions between the Spanish, complaining to the governor of Chocó and on occasion even traveling to Santa Fe to file complaints with the Audiencia.[66]

The important presence of Indians in Chocó sets the experience of lowland slavery apart from the case that most closely resembles it—that of Minas Gerais. This Brazilian region also began producing placer gold with slave labor in the late seventeenth century, but the scale of mining there, as of the region itself, was much larger. The present state of Minas Gerais, which does not include mining areas in Matto Grosso and Goias, is five times larger than the Pacific lowlands. The biggest mines or *lavras* in Minas surpassed the largest operations in the lowlands in terms of number of slaves, hydraulic works, and output. But the economy in both places opened avenues for slaves to purchase their freedom. The urban culture that flourished in Minas allowed slaves various ways to earn a living and save money; on the frontier, slaves called *faiscadores* (about a quarter of the total number of slaves) prospected and mined autonomously, and then brought gold to their owners. In both extremes of the mining economy, slaves enjoyed much autonomy and had the possibility of attaining freedom by paying for it. By 1776, free people of color already made up 41 percent of the Afro-descendant population, slightly less than in the Pacific lowlands of Colombia around that same time (43.3 percent in 1779).[67] But the history of how slaves achieved freedom differs, as the Pacific coast of Colombia had neither urban life nor an open frontier in which to discover new deposits.

FREEDOM

Slavery, which turned people into commodities and subjected them to the designs of their owners, often benefited from opening spaces of freedom within it.[68] The rights some slaves had to provision grounds or to celebrate parties were fundamental to slavery, for they made it more tolerable, and contributed to the perpetuation of bondage. Slaves frequently fought for enlarging those spaces of freedom or for achieving the ultimate goal of freeing themselves altogether from the ignominious condition of enslavement. In the Pacific lowlands, these two goals came together in the right slaves had to work for themselves, which often led to self-purchase. For this reason, the Pacific coast of Colombia stands out for being—in all likelihood—the place in the Americas where self-purchase accounts for the largest percentage of manumissions. A combination of factors, including the particular nature of the frontier and the presence of gold mining, explains this outcome. As elsewhere, the independence struggles, together with the gradual process of abolition that they initiated, brought an end to the institution of slavery. Yet freedom did not commence suddenly in 1852 when the last slaves were liberated; it developed within the slave system itself, first as spaces of autonomy and then in the increasing free population of color.

The frontier condition of the lowlands, mentioned by many authors, suggests that slaves had relatively favorable circumstances for attaining freedom by fleeing and rebelling.[69] Overseers lived surrounded by slaves in relatively isolated mining camps where the state could not guarantee assistance in case of trouble. No army or police force existed in the lowlands, and the Andean forces were stationed many days away. Furthermore, the mines were located amidst a vast forested territory that would have provided many hideaway places. One could easily envision a phenomenon similar to that of the maroon communities in the forests of Surinam and Jamaica that successfully resisted the Dutch and the British; or a situation akin to that of many regions in Brazil where *quilombos* of different sizes cropped up around areas signaled by slavery.[70] Yet rebellions seldom occurred and maroon communities did not develop, although temporary flight was common. Unraveling this apparent contradiction requires an understanding the type of frontier that this place was.

Unlike Minas Gerais in Brazil or the American West, the lowlands did not have an open frontier to explore, conquer, and colonize. On the contrary, this littoral was and still is tightly bound by the Pacific Ocean to the west and the Andes to the east. While true that the mining districts did not include extensive parts of the region, areas suitable for habitation were restricted to the narrow levees where cultivation was possible; the rest tended to be hilly and swampy forested land. Those levees stood along the same rivers that had to be navigated to reach the mines (or, in the case of the western tributaries of the Atrato River, in places already occupied by Indian crops). Therefore, much of the land suitable for agriculture was in use and any community nested in the lowlands was always within reach. Furthermore, no cities existed where maroons could blend in among other residents, and low population numbers contributed to everyone being easily identifiable.

This geography did not lend itself to the creation and maintenance of maroon communities. That is perhaps why the sole *palenque* that survived was located on the fringes of the lowlands, in a deep depression within the Andean mountains formed by the Patía river. Information on El Castigo, as it was called (which means punishment), is scant. It was probably formed in the early eighteenth century by free people of color, as well as by runaway slaves from both the southern lowlands and the Andean haciendas and mines. To join this community, slaves from Barbacoas had to trek several days inland from the last mines in the Telembí, through thick, forested, and rugged territory. A priest who visited in 1732 reported that a population of freemen and slaves of about one hundred lived in two towns (with the capacity of housing three hundred people), which they abandoned for half the year in order to mine for gold. Yet Lane estimates that its population probably did not exceed fifty inhabitants.[71] Other small palenques might have formed but did not live long.[72]

In the north, slaves could seek a new life in the Baudó Mountains and the coast adjacent to Panama, an area beyond Spanish control for most of the eighteenth century. For this reason, Jiménez has termed this area "the country of freedom and refuge." The Baudó was officially, but tenuously, incorporated into the colony in 1776, when those living there were granted pardon for escaping state control. A census taken that year reveals that only 265 people inhabited the area, and that over two-fifths of them were Indians. The three Indian women married to *libres*, plus the thirty-two zambos, attest to the close relation between Indians and at least some of the Afro-descendant men who came to live here. Other sources suggest that people in Baudó lived mostly dispersed, but did form three hamlets, at least one of which seems to have been primarily inhabited by Indians. No one at the time apparently referred to the existence of palenques there, but rather to "dispersed" and "fugitive" peoples, and no existing record provides information on raids aimed specifically at disciplining those living here.[73]

Just as palenques were conspicuously absent, slaves rarely rebelled collectively. The lowlands defy the idea expressed by Herbert S. Klein and Ben Vinson III that "[i]solated mining communities were particularly prone to slave rebellious activity."[74] Jean-Pierre Minaudier informs that between 1750 and 1810 there was only one slave revolt in Barbacoas, which ended in the death of two mineros.[75] In Chocó, the sole major rebellion, which aimed at killing all white men, was promptly suffocated. It occurred relatively early—in 1728—and in Nóvita, the area with the largest cuadrillas. Slaves from several cuadrillas working along the Mungarrá River (close to the Indian town of Tadó) and belonging mostly to the same owner killed about fourteen mineros (a large number considering that in 1778 only sixty-four whites lived in the entire Tadó area).[76] The leaders, mostly African-born, apparently had been in Jamaica, a colony with ample experience in maroonage. Within a few days, before the requested troops from Popayán even took off, the rebellion was quelled and its leaders killed. Apparently several cuadrillas acting independently put an end to the revolt.[77] If this is so, some slaves might have considered that the system offered better options for improving their lives than rebelling. Or perhaps they assumed that the uprising would be eventually crushed, like the Indian one that occurred four decades before, or internal divisions between slaves might have surfaced when this unique opportunity to ingratiate themselves with their masters emerged. In any case, rebellions did not seem to be a very attractive option. The privileges a few slaves enjoyed—mainly being *capitán de cuadrilla*—might have helped deter violent collective action.

As pointed out by Bernardo Leal, documents about the Tadó rebellion tell us more about the anxiety of colonizers than about how the uprising unfolded.[78] As soon as he was informed of the killings, the maximum authority in Chocó at the time wrote to Popayán requesting troops. His letter did not contain many details about what happened but rather emphasized that the purported 120 rebel slaves could potentially join with others working in a nearby river to form a powerful force of one thousand. Although the latter figure is without doubt an exaggeration, it does neatly illustrate the crux of whites' fears. Another local authority echoed this concern by referring to its flipside when he explained that slaves "know and observe how few or no white people live in the whole of the province."[79] Whites knew all too well that they hardly had any force at hand to use if necessary. News of this uprising took twelve days to arrive in Popayán and a detachment sent from Barbacoas took a month and a half to get to Nóvita.

Masters' and overseers' limited power to impose the conditions of labor can be observed in the recorded occurrences of slave flight. The difficulties of establishing communities and the personal bonds created within the cuadrillas constituted strong disincentives for escaping permanently. But slaves could and some did flee, as shown in a few court cases, letters, wills, and mine inventories. They did so mostly temporarily and for the purpose of negotiating better working and living conditions. Masters had a hard time forcing them to come back even if they knew their whereabouts. Unlike in Brazil, no permanent official or hired force existed to catch runaway slaves; each master had to figure out for himself how to get his slaves back.[80]

The difficulty of controlling slaves, on the one hand, and their inability to escape permanently, on the other, coupled with an economy organized around procuring a means of exchange, led to an arrangement by which slaves sought to liberate themselves principally by purchasing their freedom. However, since most manumission letters for the lowlands have been lost in fires that consumed the colonial records in places such as Quibdó and Nóvita, we cannot reconstruct how many slaves obtained their own freedom and calculate the precise share of self-purchases versus freedom granted by owners.[81] Yet given the way slavery operated in the lowlands, only extensive self-purchase can explain the high relative number of free Afro-descendants. As we will see, while data for other slave societies shows that granted manumissions almost always exceeded purchases, the available evidence in the lowlands suggests that more than 60 percent of manumissions were purchased. This massive communal undertaking is still unrecognized by both studies of slavery and emancipation in Latin America and the Caribbean and mainstream Colombian history.[82]

The puzzle of how slaves attained freedom in the lowlands begins with evidence of the substantial number of people included in the category *libres de todos los colores* (free people of all colors) in colonial censuses. This group could be conceived as an anomaly in a system strictly divided into colonizers of European origin (whites), colonized (Indians), and slaves of African origin. Some influential Colombian historians have interpreted libres as consisting of the mixed-blood population (and thus of evidence of extensive early miscegenation in the country).[83] Since they assume that *libres* is synonymous with *mestizos*, or mixed-bloods, *slave* ends up implicitly translating into *black* and, what is worse, *black* becomes coupled with *slave*.[84] So the free black population falls through the cracks. Referring to the Colombian Caribbean, Alfonso Múnera has pointed out that free blacks were counted as libres, thus breaking the commonly held assumption that black equals slave.[85] While this is a much-needed clarification, it is nonetheless true that in Caribbean Colombia most libres were Afro-descendants with different degrees of mixtures with whites and Indians. On the contrary, in the Pacific lowlands libres were mostly blacks with a smaller percentage of mulattos and zambos. The existence of very few whites in the context of a slave economy that boomed relatively late in the colonial period, added to a relatively strict division between slaves and Indians in Chocó, deterred the emergence of a robust mixed population.[86]

In the last two decades of the eighteenth century, libres went from comprising almost one-third of the total population of the Pacific lowlands to—most likely—surpassing the number of slaves. In 1779, the sole year for which figures exist for the entire region, libres already accounted for 29 percent of the population, and 43.3 percent of Afro-descendants (see table 3). This means that for every slave there were 0.7 libres. Just three years later, another census for Chocó indicated that out of a total of 17,900 inhabitants, libres represented a smaller share of 21.8 percent (and slaves 39.6 percent, a ratio of 1:0.55). Chocó's situation is partly explained by its larger Indian population, which represented 36.6 percent of the total (while whites made up a negligible 2 percent). In the south, the number of libres increased from 3,351 in 1779 to 6,284 in 1797—that is, it almost doubled in eighteen years. However, libres decreased as a percentage of the total population as the number of slaves increased even more.[87]

TABLE 3 Population of the Pacific lowlands, 1779

	CHOCÓ		SOUTH		TOTAL	
Whites	336	2%	810	10%	1,146	5%
Indians	5,693	37%	1,084	13%	6,777	29%
Free	3,342	22%	3,351	41%	6,693	29%
Slaves	5,816	38%	2,950	36%	8,766	37%
Total	15,187	100%	8,195	100%	23,382	100%

Table based on data taken from Hermes Tovar, Jorge Andrés Tovar Mora, and Camilo Ernesto Tovar Mora, *Convocatoria al poder del número. Censos y estadísticas de la Nueva Granada (1750–1830)* (Bogotá: Archivo General de la Nación, 1994).

Although these figures indicate that libres grew in number while representing a smaller share of lowland inhabitants, the 1808 census for Chocó (that had two-thirds of the lowland population) suggests that libres became the largest population group in the region. But this census generates serious questions (see table 4). The population in Chocó increased to 25,002 (that is, grew 3.4 percent annually since 1782). Whites remained about the same minuscule percentage, while Indians decreased to 4,450 (to make up 17.8 percent of Chocó's population), slaves decreased to 4,968 (19.9 percent), and libres increased to 15,184 (60.7 percent). This means that the Afro-descendant population (slaves plus libres) increased from 61.4 percent of the total to 80.6 percent, while Indians decreased from 36.6 percent to 17.8 percent. The extraordinary rise in the number of libres is hard to explain. It could be justified if slaves and Indians changed categories to libres with the same rates of their decrease in numbers. The purchase of freedom could explain how some individuals moved from slaves to libres, but no similar explanation exists for Indians becoming libres.[88] Given this enigma, we should take these numbers as reflecting tendencies, the most important of which, according to anecdotal evidence, is that the free black population was increasing rapidly. Documents from Chocó refer to houses and families of free people, as well as to free mulattoes.[89] Minaudier adds that Barbacoan slave owners were anxious, not for fear of a slave rebellion, but because "the free black population seemed to be expanding."[90]

Slaves purchasing their freedom is the only explanation for the expansion of the free black population. As there was no immigration to the lowlands, free blacks and mulattoes originated in the slave population. They were either manumitted slaves or the offspring of women of color who were already free.

TABLE 4 Chocó population, 1782 and 1808

	1782		1808		CHANGE
Whites	359	2%	400	1.6%	−11.4%
Indians	6,552	36.6%	4,450	17.8%	−32.1%
Slaves	7,090	39.6%	4,968	19.9%	−29.9%
Free	3,899	21.8%	15,184	60.7%	289.4%
Total	17,900	100%	25,002	100%	39.7%

Table based on data taken from William Sharp, *Slavery on the Spanish Frontier: The Colombian Chocó 1680–1810* (Norman: University of Oklahoma Press, 1976), 199.

As elsewhere, slaves could legally obtain freedom as a gift from their owners for the services rendered, or they could purchase it with their own resources or with those provided by a third party. It is very unlikely that granted manumissions accounted for the large numbers of free people in the lowlands. Studies on other slave societies demonstrate that proximity to slaves was important for masters to grant freedom. As Stuart Schwartz has shown, manumission was granted to masters' lovers, offspring, and godchildren, as well as to those who worked as nannies or took care of the masters in times of sickness.[91] This sort of situation was less common in the lowlands, since the largest masters lived elsewhere and domestic service was rare.[92] Granted, manumissions in the lowlands did occur, but infrequently, and tended to benefit capitanes.[93]

Available evidence backs the claim that self-purchase was much more frequent than granted manumissions (with or without conditions). Colmenares found that in most cases in which manumission letters from Popayán mentioned slaves working in mines (either in the lowlands or in the Andes) from 1720 through 1800, freedom was paid for rather than granted.[94] The information provided by Bernardo Leal is more conclusive: he found twenty-four manumission letters for slaves from Chocó in Popayán for the period 1720–81, 58.3 percent of which were purchases. He also reported that 68.3 percent of the 104 manumission letters in the notary of Quibdó from 1808 to 1814 corresponded to purchases.[95] According to Klein and Vinson III's overview of slavery in Latin America and the Caribbean, purchased manumissions oscillated from a quarter to a half of all manumissions.[96] Only in a few regions of Brazil was self-purchase dominant, and in just one case did it exceed 50 percent of all manumissions.[97] Since self-purchase was less common in North America, the Pacific lowlands were perhaps the place in the Americas where the largest percentage of manumissions were bought rather than granted by the owner. Furthermore, widespread self-purchase in the Pacific lowlands frontier runs counter to the historical experience by which "manumission occurred more frequently in urban rather than the rural settings [for] urban slaves had more opportunities to gain income than rural slaves and were seemingly more cognizant of their rights than the more isolated plantation slaves."[98]

The existence of legislation that allowed self-purchase, coupled with the particular conditions of slavery in the lowlands, made this option an escape-valve that permitted this economy and society to operate. Unlike almost everywhere else in Spanish and Portuguese America, whites were greatly outnumbered from the beginning of colonization until the end of slavery. Under this situation, whites had to, as one concerned slave owner put it, "observe a degree of tolerance not at all fitting of their station."[99] Self-purchase should be understood here, as Mariana Dantas mentioned for manumission in general, as part of a negotiation between masters and slaves over the organization and control of labor.[100] Just as quilombos in Minas Gerais served as an outlet for the most rebellious slaves to foresee and achieve a life out of bondage, so too did self-purchase serve as way for keeping slaves in check by allowing them to envision an end to their opprobrious condition.[101] William Sharp explained that owners also had an incentive for allowing and even encouraging self-purchase, at least for Chocó since the late eighteenth century, as it provided them with a way to recuperate their investment as the profitability of gold mining declined.[102]

It was precisely gold mining that made it possible for slaves to procure the means to buy their freedom. Long-term geologic processes endowed the lowlands with a mineral that had great intrinsic value and, thus, could be used as a means of exchange. Slaves had access to it by having free days in which they could mine for themselves. As a slave from Raposo explained in 1773, "masters give them Saturdays for themselves, and Sundays are non-working days [but it is possible to attend religious services or rent oneself out]."[103] Sundays were in theory days for resting, while Saturdays, and sometimes even other days of the week, were meant for slaves to contribute to procuring the means for their own reproduction. They could have their own plots to produce food, but more often they mined gold to buy what they needed, or hired out themselves for other services. Especially in smaller mines, owners would lower slaves' rations and give them extra time to procure food for themselves. When productivity was low and demand for labor diminished in a given mine, slaves worked independently, paid the owner a daily wage, and could keep any extra gold they managed to procure. Although mines belonged to slave owners, customary arrangements determined that gold mined by slaves in their free time belonged to the slaves. Rather than working in the principal mine, slaves had to find their own deposits; this helped owners find new productive deposits. With the gold earned in their free time, slaves could purchase food, cloth, tobacco, liquor, or eventually their freedom.[104]

Slaves commanded high prices, and saving such large amounts of money was extremely hard. Fray Juan de Santa Gertrudis, who visited the mines in Barbacoas in the 1760s, retold the story of a mulatto who managed to purchase himself, his family, and even buy slaves of his own. I will cite this entire testimony given that it is the only one available of its kind. Santa Gertrudis learned that this man had an exceptional story from the beginning: his father was white, a friend of the owner, but lived far away and did not recognize him as his son. Although raised as a slave, he learned how to read and write. With this skill he helped his owners, who married him to an enslaved mulatta at age fifteen. Of the way he achieved freedom, Santa Gertrudis reconstructed the following words as if they were the former slave's:

> [I]n Barbacoas the men who have slaves do not give them more than one pound of beef jerky each for the week, and five plantains per day. Everything else, clothing, salt, lard, chewing tobacco, etc., the slave has to procure himself, and for this they allow them, on Sundays and holidays, to prospect in some area that they designate within the lands that comprise their master's mining claim.
>
> Once I had a wife and two children, and I saw that we were always hungry and ragged, I opened my eyes and decided, through hard work, to try and get out of this unhappiness. With my wife, I opened a little mine, and every Sunday and holiday, well before sunrise, we were already at work. Usually, after working all day, we would return to the mine after dinner and work until midnight. I kept working like that for an entire year [. . .]. After a year, I washed it and saved all the gold that I had uncovered. I kept working like that for three full years, by which time I had collected three hundred pesos, which I used first to ransom the two creatures that my wife had borne, since they were not worth more than one hundred and fifty pesos still so small, and so I got these two free children. My wife and I continued working until I had amassed five hundred more pesos, which I next rescued my wife. And after returning to work like this, I managed to rescue myself. In the meantime, my wife bore me two other children, and since she was free, they were born free.

> After I had liberated my entire family, my master's main foreman died, so he picked me to take his place, with the agreement to maintain my whole family and to pay me four reales per day in wages. Sometime later my master died, and his wife added four more reales to my daily wages. With this money, little by little I bought the slaves that I have, and with my two sons I set them up with a mine.[105]

Like this man, other slaves and ex-slaves worked hard to buy their freedom and that of family members, and in some rare cases went on to become small slave owners themselves. There were exceptional opportunities, such as a mine with succession problems, in which all slaves purchased their freedom and even the mine and formed a community of libres.[106] But mostly, as Sergio Mosquera has stated, these were "family manumission endeavors." In the manumission letters from Quibdó from 1808 to 1849, Mosquera found many parents, as well as some siblings, uncles, cousins, and husbands, among other relatives, paying for the freedom of their loved ones.[107] These cases have some overlap with those examined by Leal, and referred to above, in which 29 percent of the purchases were made by the slave who became free, 13 percent by a group of slaves paying collectively, and 45 percent by other family members.[108] When slaves themselves paid, they often gave their gold to their masters little by little, since they often did not have a place to hide it, and masters registered these advances in their wills.[109] At least in Chocó, by the 1780s some slaves made arrangements with their owners to pay for their freedom in installments, in a manner reminiscent of Cuban and Brazilian *coartación*.[110] After paying between 20 and 50 percent of their value, they were free to seek their own employment and continue paying their debt.[111]

The few existing judicial cases in which slaves demanded that their freedom be upheld suggest that owners accepted manumission reluctantly and even tried to prevent slaves from legally attaining their freedom. Equally interesting is the fact that in these cases the courts always ruled in favor of the plaintiffs by endorsing their free status. When other issues were at stake, such as demanding payment for work done while illegally held captive, the courts tended to side with the masters. But more importantly, these cases confirm what ample self-purchase indicates, that even in this distant territory slaves knew their rights and were willing to use the law to defend them against the much more powerful mineros and masters.[112]

The independence struggles (1808–25) brought a heightened awareness of slaves' right to freedom, new opportunities for attaining it, and the beginning of the definite demise of this colonial institution through the legal process of abolition.[113] Scholars have examined the role of slaves during the struggle for independence in the southern part of the Pacific lowlands, but not in Chocó, largely because they have found telling sources in one place and not the other. Although evidence is scarce and the picture that emerges somewhat murky, they have shown that slaves were political actors in their own right who took advantage of the changing situation to increase their autonomy and thus materialize the ideal of freedom.[114] Their activism took the form of rebelling against their masters by taking control of the mines rather than joining the armies as happened elsewhere, partly because these did not form locally.[115] That most slave owners became renowned patriots contributed immensely, as Marcela Echeverri has argued, to slaves embracing royalism, for they saw their masters as interfering with the measure of protection they enjoyed from monarchical justice.[116]

In 1810, Iscuandé, Citará, and Nóvita joined the creation of government juntas, adhering to the patriot side along with the city of Cali, while Popayán, Pasto, and Barbacoas remained royalist. The following year, slaves living in the region of the Raposo, Yurumanguí, and Micay Rivers refused to obey orders. Slaves from Yurumanguí revolted after learning that their masters participated in the patriot uprising, for it was the king who "guaranteed [them] protection against excessive violence and cruel treatment."[117] Slave actions suggest that these early acts of defiance were not only aimed at sustaining monarchical rule by confronting those who attacked it but at undermining the condition of enslavement. That seems to be the interpretation of the patriot junta in Cali, which decided to send two priests to Raposo to "let it be known to these cuadrillas the mistake of their *feigned freedom*."[118] Moreover, in Micay slaves "became unruly" because they heard that governor Miguel Tacón had freed the slaves—although the offer only referred to slaves who took up arms to defend the King and was never formally announced.[119] These slaves had already rebelled the year prior for a similar reason: according to them, a black queen had come to the Americas bringing freedom, and the slave owners were hiding her. In both cases, almighty rulers channeled and made crystal clear their ultimate desire, which was so hard to attain by established and well-known means.

That achieving autonomy was—or became—their ultimate goal is also suggested by other events. In 1812, after being defeated in the Andes, royalist commander Tacón took his army to the Pacific lowlands to be defeated once again in Iscuandé.[120] According to the patriot leader, Tacón tried to attract slaves to his cause by "disingenuously offering them freedom," so they came massively ("in 17 canoes"), but having arrived late, returned to their mines. A Spanish official later recalled that "all blacks from the mines [. . .] were addicted to the true cause" as four hundred or five hundred of them had come "to wait for orders." Yet as Oscar Almario points out, this same official added that fighting the "insurgents" had since become difficult because "the blacks have become defensive."[121] Slaves did not come to Tacón's aid as mere obedient subjects wanting to help the cause, but as enslaved human beings tempted by the promise of freedom—a promise that patriots shunned away from.[122]

The Micay mine rebels mentioned above provide the strongest evidence of slaves' fight for autonomy. They continued, at least until the end of the decade, to control the mine, or rather the territory encompassed by the mine, by extracting gold (as they wore out the tools), caring for their plantings, and hunting in the forests.[123] Something similar could have happened in Barbacoas and elsewhere, where cultivation might have taken precedence over mining.[124] Yet the scant evidence provided by historical documents does not allow us to assert widespread black domination of the lowlands at the time.[125] The strategy of one member of the powerful Arboleda family seems to prove the point, for it implies control over his slaves and mine. For fear of having his Andean slaves recruited, he moved them to his mine in Timbiquí in 1816. Only nine were recruited, and in 1820, when he perceived the situation had calmed down, he moved them back to his Andean haciendas.[126]

The autonomous Micay slaves knew all too well that they remained legally enslaved. Self-manumission and the existence of a sizeable black free population taught them the difference between exercising freedom and being legally free. So, in 1816, after the Spanish regained control of the colony, they requested freedom for the twenty-three men involved in exchange for their services, which included twice denying passage to patriot troops and aiding royalists. Their petition was probably denied under the argument that such behavior was expected from subjects and therefore did not deserve a prize, and because paying for their freedom was onerous for an impoverished government. Unable to secure legal freedom, they continued to defend their autonomy. When the mine owner himself traveled to the mine in 1819, they rejected returning to their subservient position, even under the promise of much better working conditions. Disheartened, the owner admitted the failure of having "buried himself [for eleven months] in that horrendous and hellish mine." His world had been turned upside down as most of these slaves "conducted themselves *as if they were freemen*."[127] Other slaves also assumed belligerent attitudes. That same year, rebel slaves in the neighboring Saija River received a Spanish expedition with poisoned darts, while in 1822, the leaders of a slave revolt in a Barbacoas' mine renamed themselves after the most renowned independence generals—Bolívar, Sucre, and Santander.[128] This gesture sought to legitimize their own struggle by assimilating it to the wider national fight and borrowing the prestige of its heroes.

The independence wars greatly transformed the Pacific lowlands by increasing slaves' opportunities for autonomy and by ruining many mines. The mining infrastructure—reservoirs and canals—belonging to absentee owners must have deteriorated, and with their Andean properties impoverished it became almost impossible for these investors to return the mines to their former conditions.[129] Smaller mine owners who resided locally suffered similarly from the disruptions caused by the war, as did one from Chocó who lost pretty much all he had: in 1816, the Spanish army took away his most valuable possessions—thirty heads of cattle, five canoes, seventeen slaves, and iron tools—and plundered his plantain groves. By 1821, having been left with a few female slaves, their babies, and ten old men, he could not put the mine back into production.[130] Many other mine owners were left broke after paying contributions on top of having their properties pillaged and their mining infrastructure destroyed.[131]

Mine dilapidation contributed to the multiplication, albeit temporarily, of local and small slave owners. The case of the Olayas, studied by Almario, reveals a general trend despite its exceptional nature. Manuel de Olaya rose as a patriot leader in Iscuandé in 1810 and apparently used his standing to buy mines that had been expropriated from the Spanish governor of Micay. Manuel, who died in the 1830s, and his son Carlos are remembered as the masters of the Tapaje and Iscuandé Rivers, who owned the unlikely quantity of one thousand slaves.[132] Other local masters behind slave ownership were becoming more widespread and less concentrated. Between 1850 and 1852, the richest 53 percent of slave owners in Chocó owned 73 percent of the remaining slaves. A century earlier, the richest 53 percent of masters owned 83.7 percent of working slaves. More telling still, in that lapse of time slave owners in Chocó multiplied from 61 to 220.[133] Nonetheless, the largest slave owners (fewer and less powerful) continued to be based in Popayán.[134]

Their fate as slave owners was sealed in 1821 when, as the Gran Colombia emerged, the Congress of Cúcuta passed the law of free birth. The representatives adopted the text of the 1814 Constitution of Antioquia, which determined that all children born of slave mothers were in theory free but in practice had to serve their masters until the age of eighteen. In this manner, a gradual process was put in motion, one that should have freed the first slaves in 1839. But the War of the Supremes (1839–42) stood in the way, and when the war ended, slave-masters' opposition to freeing slaves resulted in a new law that determined that these young people should continue to work for their masters (as concertados, a euphemism) until age twenty-five. This measure effectively delayed until 1846 the freeing of the children of slaves born after 1821. At last, in 1851, the law of final abolition passed granting freedom to all remaining slaves on January 1, 1852. Masters were paid with government bonds that the state apparently redeemed with much effort.[135]

Although the 1821 law allowed for the early liberation of slaves by paying for them with state collected funds, this provision had little effect on the lowlands. *Juntas de manumisión* were formed for collecting money and selecting the beneficiaries, among other functions, and thus contributed to grant freedom to 15 percent of slaves who were liberated by the law. In cities such as Cali and Cartagena, slaves received their freedom in public ceremonies, enlivened with strong republican language, which contributed "to reinforce the idea that emancipation would be a liberal accomplishment."[136] In the lowlands, the juntas rarely operated. In 1843, the governor of Chocó wrote that not a single slave had been manumitted in this manner due to lack of funds.[137] The absence of these rituals, related to the lack of an urban culture, attests to the difficulties for developing a political culture in this region.

In the lowlands, almost all slave liberations that resulted from the abolition laws took place after 1850; therefore the previous decrease of the slave population has to be explained in other ways. According to census data, the number of slaves in Chocó, the place for which we have more reliable information, diminished from 4,968 in 1808 to 1,725 in 1851 (see table 5). The latter figure corresponds roughly with the number of slaves manumitted by the law. The data from 1835 onwards does not include the children born after 1821, who in theory were free and thus obtained their freedom without payment to the masters. If we include them, following the estimates by Tovar and Tovar and given that they effectively lived as slaves, we would have a slave population in 1851 of 2,937.[138] The drop from the beginning of the century would then seem less impressive (41 percent vs. 65 percent). However we look at these numbers, there are 3,243 slaves who disappeared from the statistical record. Based on Mosquera's findings for Citará, I estimate that 1,212 purchased their freedom.[139] That would leave us with around 2,000 slaves that still have to be accounted for. Some of them died, others might have been taken away from the region to the Andean haciendas or included in the groups that were sold to Peru in the 1840s or before.[140] Unfortunately, the data does not provide a clear answer.

We do know that in the last decades of slavery, the remaining slave population concentrated more heavily in the southwest, and within it, in the Pacific coast (see table 6). Toward the mid-nineteenth century, this broader region (which besides the coast includes the southern Andes) had about 60 percent of the nation's slave population; the Caribbean and the rest of the Andes each had about 20 percent. In 1778, the southwest accounted for 41.3 percent of the total number of slaves in what is present-day Colombia, and the coast alone accounted for 16 percent.[141] By 1851, this last percentage had risen to 45 percent, corresponding to about 7,600 slaves.[142]

TABLE 5 Chocó's slave and total population

	SLAVES	%	TOTAL
1808	4,968	20%	25,002
1825	4,843	28%	17,250
1835	3,260	15%	21,194
1843	2,496	9%	27,360
1848	1,741	—	—
1849	1,276	—	—
1850	1,381	—	—
1851	1,725	4%	43,649

Table based on data taken from William Sharp, *Slavery on the Spanish Frontier: The Colombian Chocó 1680–1810* (Norman: University of Oklahoma Press, 1976), 199; Jorge Andrés Tovar and Hermes Tovar, *El oscuro camino de la libertad. Los esclavos en Colombia, 1821–1851* (Bogotá: Universidad de Los Andes, 2009), 79.

TABLE 6 National distribution of the slave population

	1843	1851
Southwest	57%	64%
Andes	21%	17%
Caribbean	21%	20%
Total	99%	101%

Table based on data taken from Jorge Andrés Tovar and Hermes Tovar, *El oscuro camino de la libertad. Los esclavos en Colombia, 1821–1851* (Bogotá: Universidad de Los Andes, 2009), 79.

Gold extraction and slavery signaled the eighteenth-century colonial experience of the Pacific lowlands of Colombia. Slavery eroded over many decades, avoiding open confrontation because self-purchase developed as a successful outlet to bondage. Several natural factors contribute to this unique turn of affairs: master control was weak in part because owners could not establish haciendas here and lived at a distance in the Andes; the region's geography made permanent flight unlikely favoring other means for slaves to attain autonomy; and the existence of gold—which led to slavery in the first place—also opened the possibility for slaves to save enough to pay for their freedom. In this manner, free Afro-descendant people grew to eventually become the vast majority of the regional population. Although freedom did not begin at midcentury, something important did change in 1852. From that year onwards, nobody in this vast forested region had to bear the opprobrium of slavery. No longer were there freedmen in a slave society; just free men and women who continued to live off bits and pieces of nature to sell to other people far away to enjoy. The extractive economy outlived the demise of slavery, but it expanded from the subsoil to the forest and operated differently as two new social classes came into being: black independent producers and white local merchants. The persistence of extraction and a racial division of labor underlie the dramatic changes that took place in the second half of the nineteenth century and first decades of the twentieth.

2

FREEDOM AND THE PERSISTENCE OF EXTRACTION

IN COLONIAL TIMES, gold mining by slaves made extraction of natural resources the backbone of the economy of the Pacific coast of Colombia. Since then, dependence on nature's treasures has continued to be a major defining trait of this region, although the social relations underlying it changed dramatically. After the final manumission law (1851) allowed the lowlands to move beyond colonial institutions, an organization based on independent producers and a tiny merchant export group developed. Most free blacks continued to live in the mining areas and to extract gold, so mining remained the principal sector of the regional economy. Nonetheless, it declined because miners continued to use the same techniques in largely exhausted deposits, with dilapidated infrastructure. The lowlands ceased to be Colombia's main gold producer as gold ceased to be the nation's main export. Therefore, for this coast, departing from its colonial past involved losing its economic standing. It also involved blacks gaining access to mines by renting them out, buying them, or seeking unclaimed placers, which allowed them to choose how and when to mine—free from the commands of a master but not bound to the tight schedules of wage laborers.

Some free people migrated to areas without precious metal deposits. Many of them collected latex from rubber trees and the seeds of vegetable ivory palms (used to manufacture buttons and known as *tagua* in Spanish). The extraction of forest products diversified the regional economy without changing its underlying logic of turning bits and pieces of the environment into commodities. Furthermore, it allowed natural resource extraction to expand beyond the mining areas and become a truly regional phenomenon. Those who migrated collected these novel products in public forests and, like miners, had no supervision. As the cases of both gatherers and miners indicate, blacks continued providing manual labor but they did not form a rural proletariat. Rather, they constituted a rainforest peasantry that since then has been an integral part of Colombia's Pacific coast.

Blacks' peasant status rested on their access to the forests and the subsoil, just as rural dwellers elsewhere are peasants because they have access to land where to grow the crops that they sell. Peasants here and everywhere use family labor to produce both for the market and for their own consumption. Therefore, in the lowlands, their independent status did not solely rest on being able to mine gold or collect rubber and vegetable ivory seeds but on controlling a broad territory that provided materials for building houses, canoes, and tools, as well as soils in which to grow food and animals they could hunt and fish for their tables. Their use of land, mines, forests, rivers, and even the ocean—that is, the relevant means of production in the lowlands—guaranteed their reproduction and autonomy. Free blacks' management of the environment was part of a new political economy of extraction, in which they carried out the physical work in the jungle, while white merchants living in incipient cities bought and exported the commodities they produced. The formation and role of this merchant class is the subject of chapter 3; this one examines the production of gold, rubber, and vegetable ivory that underlied black peasants' experience of freedom.

This lived experience meant that freedom was more than a legal status long fought for. It was the center of a public identity built in opposition to slavery, as indicated by the word—libres (free people)—that in the lowlands designated blacks. In colonial times, libres de todos los colores (free people of all colors) was a census category that included everyone that did not fit the three foundational population groups of Spanish colonialism: whites, Indians, and black slaves. In other places of New Granada, this official category did not have much effect on ordinary classifications, but in the lowlands libres served to designate the very people whose past was tied to bondage. This label with colonial roots carried on well after the end of slavery when blacks decided how to use their time and invest their living space with meaning, within the options and constraints of a rainforest economy.[1]

SMALL INDEPENDENT MINERS

The formation of a rainforest peasantry began with mining and took place in the context of economic decline. In the eighteenth century, slaves brought by Spaniards to work in previously unexploited placers turned the region into the main supplier of New Granada's gold exports. Toward the end of the century, the richest and most accessible placers were exhausted, so gold output began to diminish, and with the Independence Wars decreased even more. After midcentury, lowland gold became unimportant for national gold production, as gold's share of national exports declined from three-fourths between 1834 and 1845, to one-third between 1854 and 1870, to around one-fifth between 1870 and 1898.[2]

As mining weakened, slaves obtained their freedom mainly through self-purchase and, for the most part, remained as free people in the mining areas. As explained in chapter 1, more than working groups, slave gangs became social units organized by families, whose members made enormous efforts to save gold with which to liberate themselves and their kin. Personal bonds between free men and women and those who remained enslaved, plus better opportunities, kept the former in the mining areas. Those opportunities lay largely in procuring gold, the trade ex-slaves knew best. Evidence from the late eighteenth century and the first half of the nineteenth century shows how Afro-descendants continued mining after becoming free, often close to the mines where they had toiled as slaves.[3] In 1822, for instance, the governor of Chocó asserted that "the slaves that have liberated themselves from the mines [. . .] retain their habits and spend their time panning for gold."[4] A mine in the Atrato in which, in 1845, forty slaves worked alongside seventy freed blacks corroborates the governor's appreciation.[5]

Legal disputes by three libres over the possession of gold deposits confirm that many remained devoted to mining and attest to the early formation of communities of free blacks. The first case refers to a group of twenty-six people known as the libres de Belén, who worked on a mine they apparently bought in the 1760s. Besides the deposits, the property included plantain groves, houses, a forge, and a trapiche (sugar cane mill). The second community, which had ties to the first and was also located on the Guapi River basin, was established around 1790 by Pedro Antonio Ibargüen and his two sisters, who worked a mine belonging to a slave owner. The siblings were joined by other libres and a decade later the community had twenty-two members. Both Ibargüen and Manuel de Hinestroza, the leader of Belén, became small slave owners themselves.[6] So did

Tiburcio Ortiz, a libre from Barbacoas, who also had to fight in court in the late eighteenth century to defend his right to mine ownership.[7]

The Ibargüen lawsuit, studied by historian Oscar Almario, gives interesting clues about the problems libres had in accessing gold deposits. In his deposition in 1793 he complained, "There are many of us freemen here who have no place to work, and much land that remains unoccupied on account of having been claimed by miners." He further added, "When permission is requested to one of those individuals to work [in a mining claim], some of them grant it, but once a *mazamorrero* has broken ground and discovered a mine he is dispossessed, often losing the product of his labor."[8] It seems then that libres played a similar role that slaves did when they worked for themselves in their free time: serving as prospectors for mine and slave owners. They could certainly mine, but seldom in the best deposits.

As lowland mining declined, initially in Chocó and then everywhere else, opportunities increased for the growing population of color to have access to gold deposits. Large absentee owners lost interest in their dilapidated mines, but due to the general economic downturn could not sell them easily and were often forced to abandon them. Some small and medium-sized owners sought a life outside of the lowlands, and like their more powerful counterparts, relinquished their possessions. Isidro Mosquera, for instance, abandoned, after 1876, a mine in the San Juan River that he bought in 1820 from Francisco Hurtado y Pontón, who had owned it since 1773.[9] A few wealthy families, like the Mosquera and Arboleda from Popayán, kept overseers; others found a buyer. In 1845, the owners of the large mine of Tutunendo, in the Atrato River basin, sold it to the Fernández, who later divided and sold the property.[10] As explained in chapter 1, the number of slave owners in the first half of the nineteenth century, at least in Chocó, greatly increased. Several of them, having few slaves and lacking other alternatives, held onto their mines but settled in small towns such as Nóvita or Quibdó. In Barbacoas, which posed an exception to the pattern of large absentee slave owners, many local miners stayed.[11]

Rent, not wages, was the standard way by which mine owners who kept their properties continued to profit from mining after the end of slavery. Capital-starved owners could afford to pay neither the relatively high wage rate nor the management and supervision costs that hiring workers entailed.[12] The prevalence of rent over wages partly reflected the scarcity of labor, and therefore the bargaining power of free blacks, who gained control over mining.[13] They formed their own working teams and set their own rules without having to obey a master or a boss. Furthermore, they decided how to use their time, combining mining with tending crops or hunting.[14] Leased mines operated in a context of low-mining productivity caused by the depletion of the best deposits and the lack of much-needed investments in reservoirs, canals, pumps, and tools. As a result, rent left owners with meager profits, hindering further investments that could lead to a recovery of gold production.

Rent took different forms in the two main mining areas of the lowlands: in Chocó, black miners paid a fixed amount, while in Barbacoas workers split their proceeds in half with mine owners. A Colombian lawyer, in a 1821 report on Chocó, stated, "In almost every place and spot of this province there is gold: there is no river nor stream, for small that it may be, where there is no multitude of men occupied in extracting it; they are called *mazamorreros*. They pay annually four pesos for the right to *mazamorrear*."[15] This information suggests that toward the end of the Independence Wars, rent was already a widespread feature of mining in Chocó. However, it could also indicate that the state established a tax on independent miners, as it did in the 1780s in the province of Antioquia.[16] With no further evidence of such a tax, and other documents corroborating the existence of rent, the former interpretation seems more plausible. In the San Juan area, in 1898, a local official referred to independent miners as renters, while in the late 1910s, a report stated that miners had "to pay the owners of the mines a small amount, usually half a castellano (equivalent to about 35 grains troy) per man per month."[17]

Inspired by the way they managed their Andean haciendas, the Mosquera family from Popayán requested that rent in the Timbiquí basin be paid with labor time. Based on rights upheld by colonial titles, in 1858 and again in 1864, the family established a set of rules by which inhabitants of the basin needed to work for one day a week for an overseer to avoid eviction. Thus while governing the country as president for four times between 1845 and 1867, Tomás Cipriano de Mosquera tried to improve the family's finances by tapping into the labor of the descendants of the slaves that had belonged to his parents. Yet repeated drafting of the rules and the fact that the second draft took the form of a decree by the district's mayor suggest that the president was not being very successful.[18] Absentee owners in an area with an extremely weak state had a hard time enforcing such regulations. The fixed rent paid by miners in Chocó suggests that mine owners living there had better chances with collecting payment for the use of their properties.

The local elite in Barbacoas, which had presided over a relatively small mining district since the seventeenth century, had a somewhat stronger position. In this southern district, miners and owners formed partnerships in which the former contributed their labor while the latter contributed the mines. The two parties then divided the proceeds equally. Since miners continued to work in gangs, they divided their part among the group, with the foreman typically receiving a larger share. Miners only had to work half the time for the partnership and could choose any other part of the claim to work for themselves.[19] In the 1890s, for example, José Alberto Valverde established a partnership with Cándido Angulo, a mine owner, to work part of Las Peñas mine. Besides working for the partnership, Valverde used his right to test any part of the claim and found a good spot. Given that the site chosen for the company did not prove very productive, the mine owner decided to take over Valverde's independent work. However, a judge stopped him after Valverde sued.[20] Even if Barbacoas' white mine owners had more leverage than their peers elsewhere in the lowlands, they still had limited powers vis-à-vis small Afro-descendant miners.

Many independent miners did not pay rent at all. As seen above, a small number of former slaves became slave owners and acquired mines, which their descendants inherited and worked. Other free blacks bought land from their former masters, often through informal transactions that did not entail an exchange of titles, or simply worked abandoned properties.[21] Since most mine owners did not live in the mines and did not keep overseers, local residents could work apparently unclaimed deposits. That happened, for instance, in the Naya River basin, which was granted to the University of Cauca in the early nineteenth century, and where locals made use of the mines and developed their own property rights.[22] Another way for miners to avoid paying rent was to refuse to pay whenever they could get away with it.[23] Black peasants also mined freely the riverbeds, which belonged in the public domain.

Free blacks, working autonomously, took over lowland gold production during a period of diminishing mining productivity. In part for this reason, observers at the time and historians alike failed to acknowledge the importance, and sometimes even the existence, of independent miners in the lowlands. In this way, free black miners from the littoral fell out of history, and the unique postemancipation trajectory of lowland society has since gone unrecognized. The strengthening of Antioquia's gold economy throughout the nineteenth century served to accentuate the neglect and misinterpretation of lowland history. Located in the northwestern Andes, this province gained historians' attention largely for its role in the flourishing of coffee production and for the industries of its capital city, Medellín. At the close of the eighteenth century, Antioquia's production accounted for almost 40 percent of the colony's gold exports, up from 16 percent four decades earlier. At midcentury, Antioquia became the nation's leading gold producer, and after 1870 it produced more than two-thirds of the nation's gold exports.[24] Readings of the opposite trajectories of these two regions have contrasted slave-based mining in the Pacific coast and Cauca with antioqueño independent miners called mazamorreros. Such view, for instance, led Robert B. White to observe in the 1870s that "[Chocó] would be rich today . . . if emancipation had not severed the vital nerve of the gold question, and left the district with its wealth buried. . . . This mortal blow to large mine exploitation . . . happened in 1851."[25] White assumed that only slaves carried out mining on the coast, and that abolition was the sole culprit for the decline of mining. He overlooked the protracted demise of slavery and ignored the key role slaves and free blacks played in extracting gold to pay for their freedom and that of other family members. A decade later, in his seminal book on Colombian gold and silver mining, Vicente Restrepo referred to the flip side of this view of Colombian gold production by attributing the rise of Antioqueño mining to the hard-working ethos of mazamorreros.[26]

More recently, researchers have continued to stress the importance of independent miners in Antioquia, while virtually ignoring their presence in the lowlands. The predominance of economic history, particularly in the 1970s and 1980s, has been instrumental in forging this view. Not only does it focus on prosperous areas while overlooking depressed ones, but it also tends to consider blacks (at least in the littoral) only as slaves. A recent book on antioqueño mining recognizes the key role played by mazamorreros in the following manner: "Alluvial mining in Antioquia was very important in [the 1870s] since it represented about 70 percent of annual gold production. A large proportion of alluvial gold was extracted by mazamorreros, who mined the accessible deposits of the Cauca, Porce and Nechí rivers with rudimentary techniques."[27] In contrast, an influential article on nineteenth century Colombian economic history asserted that in Cauca and the Pacific coast "production could have been maintained . . . if the former slaves had devoted their time to mining, but various factors made this unlikely. The [mining] titles . . . remained in the hands of the old owners . . . additionally, the slave population largely preferred to work in subsistence agriculture and fishing, leaving panning for gold as an occasional occupation."[28] This reading misses the fact that many free blacks continued mining more than just "ocassionally" and uses the term "slave population" when referring to free people, bluntly demonstrating that in these accounts black people mattered only as enslaved workers. Although not all accounts ignore independent miners in this region, none makes more than a quick mention to them.[29]

Not only did many lowlanders mine independently, a close look at Antioqueño history suggests that slaves might have also been somewhat more important there than most researchers recognize. Evidence of mazamorreros' early significance comes from Ann Twinam's study of late colonial Antioquia, which estimates gold production through the records of the Casa de Fundición. It assumes that the gold declared by merchants (around 81.5 percent between 1670 and 1801) was produced by mazamorreros, while the rest, declared by large mine owners, was produced by slaves. Germán Colmenares pointed out that this assumption is problematic, for some of the gold declared by merchants could have resulted from payments by mine owners for slaves. Furthermore, he stressed that according to this account, slave-based production oddly diminished as the slave gangs were being reconstituted.[30] Other fragmentary evidence further suggests that we should be more cautious. In the Valle de los Osos, one of Antioquia's leading gold-producing regions, the 1779 census counted 662 slaves, while between 1792 and 1808 only 552 mazamorreros were registered.[31] A more nuanced view that recognizes the importance of slavery and independent mining in both places, while acknowledging regional differences, is needed to understand fully the various trajectories of the transition from servitude to freedom in Colombia.

Even in the mining areas, this transition implied a diversification of productive activities. In some cases Afro-descendants gave up gold extraction altogether. Before the end of slavery, limited access to mines in Barbacoas, combined with local scarcity of provisions, encouraged libres to produce food. They had small plots in the river levees where they cultivated plantain, sugar cane, and tobacco, and had a few head of cattle. Others worked as itinerant traders visiting the mines, as well as in transportation, fishing, and as craftsmen. Libres on the Dagua River worked as bogas, transporting people and affairs between Cali and Buenaventura, and as intermediaries in the liquor trade.[32] Since the late eighteenth century, some libres moved to the towns built for congregating the Indian population in the Atrato River basin, while further south their peers created new ones in the Raposo, Naya, Cajambre, and Timbiquí Rivers, which quite tellingly became known as *pueblos de libres*. Others moved to Barbacoas, the only city in the lowlands, where they could operate as goldsmiths and employ themselves in other trades.[33]

Some Afro-descendants did not remain in the mining areas; they left partly attracted by the opportunities opened by a new form of extraction—that of forest products. Around midcentury, precisely when slavery ended, rubber and vegetable ivory began to be traded in the world market. Black rubber trees grow all around the lowlands, while vegetable ivory palms grow close to the coasts. Like miners, those who migrated extracted latex and collected vegetable ivory seeds in an independent fashion, without having to obey orders, plus they did not pay rent because they used public lands over which the state had very little control. The gathering and exporting of rubber and vegetable ivory gave lowlanders new opportunities to obtain income by tapping into nature's resources. In this manner, the extractive economy was strengthened through its expansion from the subsoil to the forest, and from the mining areas to the rest of the region.

BLACK RUBBER

The extraction of wild rubber in the Pacific lowlands of Colombia lasted only about three decades, ending before the height of the boom that opened the Amazon basin to the world economy. The rubber boom, the largest and best-known effort to supply industrial economies with a raw material from tropical forests, neatly illustrates the pervasiveness of extractive economies in these environments. Furthermore, the early end of the wild rubber trade in the lowlands paradoxically underscores the difficulties of breaking away from extractive economies. After virtually all rubber trees had been felled to extract their latex, lowlanders en masse attempted to cultivate rubber. However, the drop in prices that put an end to the wild rubber boom elsewhere in the 1910s also did away with efforts at planting new trees. Despite this notable experiment with commercial agriculture, the region remained dependent on natural resource extraction.

The trade of rubber and vegetable ivory resulted from global developments that opened markets for rainforest products, greatly affecting the Pacific lowlands and other tropical areas. Technological innovations associated with the industrial revolution created new uses for many natural products, turning them into coveted commodities. Rain forests attracted attention because of the great variety of plants and animals found there, which scientists dreamt of classifying, understanding, and marketing. Naturalist Charles Stuart Cochrane, who visited the lowlands in the early 1820s, noted for instance that the "milk" of the rubber tree, when just extracted, was used to make "roanas, boots, and hats . . . perfectly impervious to water," and predicted that "this milk [would] some day be in great repute."[34] At the time, no one had yet figured how to solve the problem posed by rubber's natural characteristics. Because it is stiff when cold, and sticky when hot, the consistency of any product made with this material varied with temperature changes. In 1839, Charles Goodyear developed the vulcanization process that made rubber resistant to these changes. Soon after, a rubber industry flourished, fabricating waterproof boots and shoes, as well as tubes, hoses, inflatable lifesavers, balls, tires, and many other products.

In the mid-nineteenth century, the milky sap from a variety of tropical plants was the only available source for rubber. These plants found in the tropical forests of Africa and Latin America resulted from different evolutionary paths, as evidenced by their classification into different botanical families. A vine and a tree from the Apocinaceae family produced the rubber exported from Africa, while *Hevea brasiliensis*, from the Euphorbiaceae family, produced most of the Amazon basin's supply.[35] Some species of Sapium, another genus of the Euphorbiaceae family that yields a different kind of white rubber, were exploited in parts of the Amazon and in central Colombia, and probably also in the Pacific lowlands.[36] Mexico, Central America, and the Pacific coast of Colombia and Ecuador exported black rubber produced by three subspecies of *Castilla elastica* from the Moraceae family (see map 4).[37] Although its latex is also white, it rapidly darkens upon exposure to air and dries into a black color, hence its name. It is easily confused with *C. tunu*, which yields a yellowish latex but does not produce rubber. For this reason, *C. tunu* is known as *ule macho* or *caucho macho*, a "male" unproductive relative of the real caucho. *Castilla ulei*, a species practically identical to *C. elastica*, produced a small percentage of the Amazonian supply.

The rubber boom that developed by procuring the sap of these species led to the formation or strengthening of extractive economies in different parts of the tropical world, most notably in the Amazon basin. Extraction of natural resources for the market was already happening on a limited scope in the lower Amazon since the seventeenth century, when the Portuguese sought "turtle oil, spices, hardwoods, vegetable oils, and cacao beans."[38] In the second half of the nineteenth century, the extraction of rubber led to the integration of the entire basin into the global economy. Amazonian exports increased steadily from 2,197 tons in 1855 to 5,434 tons in 1866 and 10,136 tons in 1879. However, demand increased even faster: it picked up in the 1890s mainly due to bicycle production and in the 1900s due to the manufacture of tires for the burgeoning

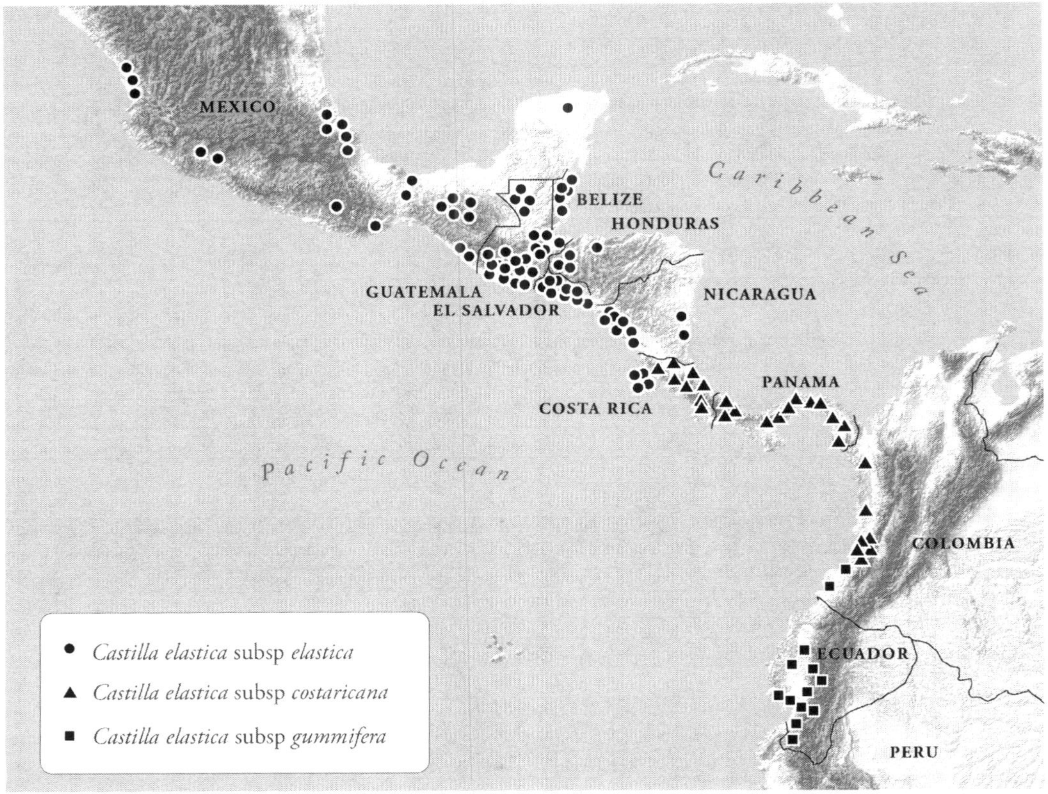

MAP 4 Distribution of *Castilla elastica* in Central America and the Pacific coast of South America by subspecies. Map by Paola Luna, Cartography Lab, Universidad de los Andes, Bogotá. Based on C. C. Berg, "Olmedieae, Brosimeae (Moraceae)," *Flora Neotropica* 7 (July 1972): 1–228.

car industry. Brazil's exports grew to 26,750 tons in 1900, and in 1909 reached their maximum of 42,000 tons.[39]

Extractive activities are distinct because their location is determined by natural supply, a condition that often increases transportation costs. Until the successful development of plantations in the twentieth century, the rubber economy grew by companies and tappers pushing ever deeper into the forests. The expansion of the extractive frontier rested on the steady increase in prices, and was also made possible by the relatively low investments associated with rainforest extractive activities at the time. However, since extraction costs can increase with time, as the distance to which resources have to be sought expands, a decrease in price can have dramatic effects. In the 1910s, rubber prices dropped sharply when Asian plantation rubber flooded the market and extraction became unprofitable in most wild rubber producing areas (see graph 5). The Dutch and the British governments had spent decades and significant resources trying to determine which rubber species produced more and better quality latex, as well as the conditions under which each species grew best, how to transport seeds, and the planting and tapping methods that should be implemented. By 1911, plantations in Malaya, the Netherlands East Indies (Indonesia), and Ceylon (Sri Lanka) produced 20 percent of the world's rubber supply. By 1915, they exported 68 percent of the total, and by 1919, 90 percent.[40] Other rainforest extractive economies, such as vegetable ivory or chicle, also ended or were severely weakened as plantations or chemical products replaced wild sources.

Lowland rubber supply began in the 1850s but ended well before the height of the boom, for gatherers cut down these trees, as opposed to tapping them (as with Hevea) because their physiognomy allows only a moderate flow of latex when the bark is cut. The earliest evidence of rubber exports from the region is found in the Gulf of Urabá, on the Caribbean coast, far from the Upper Chocó mining area where slaves used to live. In 1852, before ascending the Atrato River in search of a transoceanic canal route, John Cresson Trautwine stopped at the small village of Turbo, where he found "a factory for preparing the rubber from the milk of the tree . . . established . . . by a New York house." He noted that the business was "on a very limited . . . scale."[41] A year later, the Chorographic Commission that toured the country did not come across the factory but observed that Turbo's inhabitants collected rubber, as did the Cuna Indians who lived in the gulf.[42] In 1857, another explorer of canal routes, Lieutenant Michler, remarked that "about eighty tons [of rubber] per year [were] col-

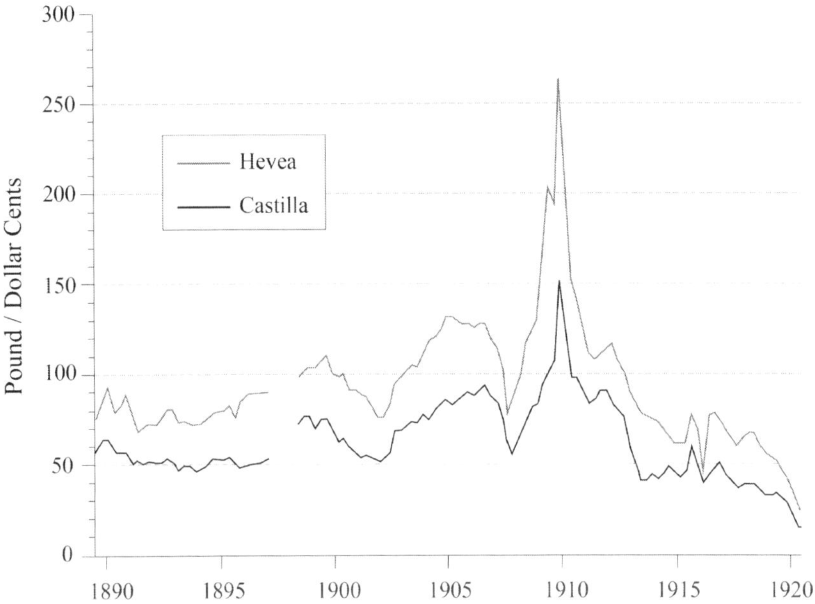

GRAPH 5 Rubber prices, 1890–1920. Note: Hevea prices correspond to the most expensive kind of Hevea in the market, labeled Para Upper River Fine, while Castilla corresponds to the kind labeled Esmeralda Sausage (probably from Esmeraldas, Ecuador). Other kinds of black rubber had very similar prices. Graph based on data taken from *India Rubber World*, various numbers, 1890–1920.

lected and brought to Turbo."[43] He observed that Riosucio, a hamlet located on the lower Atrato, was a collection post where merchants bought and stored rubber from such rivers as the Sucio and Truandó. This area had been controlled by indigenous peoples, but by this time black people had started establishing themselves there, surely aided by income from rubber, as well as the abundant fish and game resources. In the 1850s, the rubber trade was also taking hold nearby in Darien in Panama.[44]

Soon after, the upper Atrato followed the example of the lower part of the basin and began shipping rubber to Cartagena. In 1870, when Thomas Oliver Selfridge, yet another canal explorer, visited Quibdó, merchants bought rubber along with gold dust.[45] As recognized by the U.S. business agent in Cartagena, by the early 1870s rubber gathering had become a widespread activity in Chocó and the Caribbean coastal jungles around the Sinú River.[46] It is very likely that the rubber trade reached its peak in Chocó during this decade; the Statistical

Yearbook of 1875 mentions rubber as its main export, well above gold.[47] Rubber extraction in the southern part of the Pacific lowlands must have started around the same time. Official statistics, available only for 1865 to 1873, indicate that during those years both Buenaventura and Tumaco exported rubber.[48] A newspaper from Barbacoas published an article in 1867 intending to help those who collected rubber or were considering entering the business, so the trade must have been alive there as well.[49] Yet in 1874, the U.S. consul at Buenaventura reported "that rubber and quina exports had declined along the Colombian Pacific Coast because extraction of these products involved killing the trees."[50]

Rubber gatherers from Ecuador to Mexico, and also in the Amazon, felled black rubber trees to collect their latex.[51] They organized excursions that could last several months, in which they "hunted" the trees from high spots. The height of *Castilla elastica*—more than one hundred feet—and the fresh light green of its hairy leaves make this species easily recognizable. Trees grow scattered within the forest, in well-drained soils up to 2,800 feet above sea level, in clearings, along streams, and at forest margins, often in the company of Cecropia, a conspicuous colonizer known in Colombia as *yarumo*. After spotting their targets, gatherers cleared a path through the jungle. Once felled, the trees were "bled to the branches. Latex [was] gathered in kerosene cans, or holes in the ground, and [was] brought to market in solid cakes."[52] It took three or four days to gather all the rubber from a single tree. Underneath the fallen trunk collectors put big leaves or simply cleaned the soil and then collected the rubber, letting it dry and coagulate in the heat for two or three nights.[53] Gatherers used different substances to coagulate the latex or "separate" the rubber; the following method was used in Panama: "Coagulation is done in a hole in the ground, or in a trough cut out of a balsa log. When there is sufficient milk for coagulation, a bunch of amole vines are pounded, the mass washed, and the water that comes out poured into the trough. As the rubber begins to coagulate at the top, it is gently pressed down, until the rubber forms one piece. Then it is kneaded to remove much of its water. A week later the mass will be black, and about half its weight."[54]

Gatherers of various origins scoured pretty much the entire Pacific lowlands in search for *Castilla elastica*. Rubber must have enticed and helped the migration process of Afro-descendants outside the mining areas. They most likely searched for rubber almost everywhere they went: in the forests of the south, in the Baudó Mountains, and in the lower Atrato valley. In the latter place, they joined other migrants of mixed Indian, black, and Spanish ancestry coming from the Caribbean plains to the east, as explained in a 1911 report: "when the price of rubber rose in the mid-nineteenth century, a great population from the Caribbean coast and the upper Atrato invaded this area, and explored and exploited the basins of the Salaquí, Juradó, and Cacarica rivers, whose jungles yielded fabulous quantities of elastic gum."[55] The Cuna Indians of Urabá, as well as the Embera, who still inhabit some of the upper reaches of the Atrato tributaries, also supplied rubber.[56] Antioqueños ventured occasionally from the Andes into the lowlands for the same purpose, but they did not settle in the region.[57]

Little information exists about the actual ways in which these gatherers organized themselves to work. However, a hint suggests that, as men who extract timber today, caucheros formed partnerships whose members agreed to assume the costs of extraction in equal parts and distribute the resulting profits or losses in the same fashion.[58] A traveler in 1893 learned from a cauchero who was returning from selling rubber in Quibdó that "in three months he . . . made $799 from . . . rubber along with his gang of eight, their expenses amounted to $383; so they were left with $416 of benefits, which yielded $52 for each one of them." With that money, they could buy a small rural property along one of the rivers in Chocó or purchase two barrels of flour or two quintals (hundred pounds) of either coffee or sugar in Quibdó.[59] Gatherers like this one depleted wild rubber fairly rapidly, leading to an early decline of the trade.

By the mid-1870s, the rubber business was waning in Buenaventura, the lower Atrato, and Panama; afterwards only small quantities continued to be collected and sold.[60] Although the jungles of western Colombia supplied rubber for almost three decades, the region was a fairly small player in the international rubber trade. Cartagena, which exported rubber from the Chocó and the Sinú jungles, was by far the most important rubber exporting port in the country. Its exports for the period 1865/6–1875/6 averaged 74 percent of the national total.[61] In 1875, the Amazon basin exported thirty-seven times more rubber than Cartagena, but from a much larger area.

As the rubber market continued to expand after the depletion of mature rubber trees in the Pacific coast of Colombia, the only way for lowlanders to benefit from the burgeoning rubber market was to domesticate the native *Castilla elastica*. The enthusiasm for rubber planting led some entrepreneurs to write, in 1905, that "[t]he future of the Chocó is to be found in the cultivation and exploitation of rubber trees on a large scale."[62] Just a year later, a visitor to the southern tip of the region expressed a similar opinion when he anticipated that the town of Tumaco "[would] become a city if to its present growth one adds what the future has reserved to the rubber that [was] being planted in the nearby public lands."[63] The intendant of Chocó joined the generalized optimism and, in 1907, issued a decree that favored and stimulated the cultivation of rubber.[64]

By 1914, locals had planted more than one and a half million rubber trees in Chocó alone.[65] Peasants planted the majority of them, a development with no recorded parallel elsewhere in the tropics. According to the consular agent in Quibdó, blacks in Chocó started to plant rubber around 1895, and by 1905, every peasant had "at least a few dozen trees."[66] Evidence for small rubber plantings in Chocó is abundant and covers the mid-Atrato valley, the Baudó River basin, the Munguidó River in the San Juan basin, the Pacific littoral, and extends to the Gulf of Urabá.[67] For the southern part of the region, archives and newspapers mention the existence of small rubber plantings along the Mira River, on the border with Ecuador, and on the littoral as far north as the Timbiquí River.[68] Some even had small plantations of as many as a couple thousand trees.[69]

Local entrepreneurs joined peasants by establishing at least thirteen relatively large plantations, all except one in Chocó.[70] The largest one had around eighty thousand trees, but most had fewer than fifty thousand.[71] Elsewhere in Colombia, similar efforts started as early as 1875, leading to the development of a few scattered plantations, none of which used black rubber.[72] By contrast, in Central America and Mexico planters experimented with *Castilla elastica*. In 1905, Nicaragua had five large plantations with about four hundred thousand trees, and a few plantations also existed in Panama.[73] These enterprises, however, paled in comparison to rubber cultivation in Mexico, where American, British, and Mexican companies established plantations in the states of Veracruz, Oaxaca, and Chiapas. *India Rubber World* estimated in 1912 that Mexico had one hundred thousand acres planted in rubber, the most significant cultivation effort outside of Asia.[74] With six million trees, the largest block of Castilla made efforts in the lowlands look irrelevant.[75]

Those efforts, however, were quite impressive for peasants and entrepreneurs who relied solely on their own ingenuity and limited resources. Unlike the Asian enterprise, no major research backed these experiments. The Colombian government tried, in a very modest manner, to encourage rubber cultivation through an 1884 law that gave tax exemptions to planters. While news of this law did not reach or affect Chocó, some local entrepreneurs did request titles to their lands after President Rafael Reyes decreed, in 1905, that rubber and cacao planters could request one thousand hectares of public land for every twenty thousand trees they planted.[76] But such incentives did not provide the planters with any indication of how to securely proceed. On their own, locals planted both seeds and seedlings in the forest understory where plants required little weeding, or in cleared land to allow the sun to accelerate plant growth. After about eight years, the trees were ready to be milked.[77] Lowlanders did not cut down planted trees as they had previously done with wild Castillas. According to an observer, collectors cut "the bark with machetes at intervals of a few inches, as far as a man could reach. The cultivated trees . . . [gave] a thick latex which [ran] but a short distance down the trunk, and [was] gathered, when dry, by tearing off the strips and rolling them into balls."[78] Rubber obtained from dried strips was known as chaza rubber.[79] Planters apparently did not collect latex regularly; Miguel Abuchar, a member of Quibdó's commercial elite who experimented with rubber, milked the trees every two or three months.[80]

The successful domestication of white rubber in several Asian colonies put an end to experiments in both the lowlands and the rest of Latin America.[81] The ultimate aim of European colonial powers was to undercut the market by replacing wild rubber with planted rubber; by contrast, cultivators in Latin America did not intend to alter the market but rather to profit from its extraordinary conditions. Due to these differences, rubber domestication in Asia started in the 1870s, while planters in the New World waited until the 1890s, when prices were much higher. Rubber prices plummeted as planted trees in the Pacific lowlands reached maturity. By 1908, none of the Chocó plantations had started producing; the first harvests weren't expected until 1910.[82] Peasant production must have begun before, as exports from the Atrato decreased from almost thirty thousand kilos in 1908 to about nineteen thousand in 1913.[83] A newspaper captured the mood around Tumaco in 1914 when it stated: "Why—peasants ask—should we tap into our trees, when the product is practically given away?"[84] Nominal prices paid for Tumaco's rubber had decreased 68 percent in the previous four years. So even if the amount of rubber exported in 1909 and 1915 remained the same, its value had greatly diminished. Rubber continued to be exported in small quantities, but expectations about its potential ended.[85]

Some lowlanders then turned once again to extraction, this time of a rather inelastic gum useful for machine belting, referred to locally as *níspero* or *caimitillo* but known as balata in the international market.[86] Balata prices fell below rubber prices but in 1915 began to increase, creating a considerable price differential (see graph 6). Consequently, in the 1910s and into the 1920s, lowlanders sought balata in various parts of the region and exported it from Tumaco, Buenaventura, and Cartagena.[87] According to a Tumaco newspaper, balata gathering

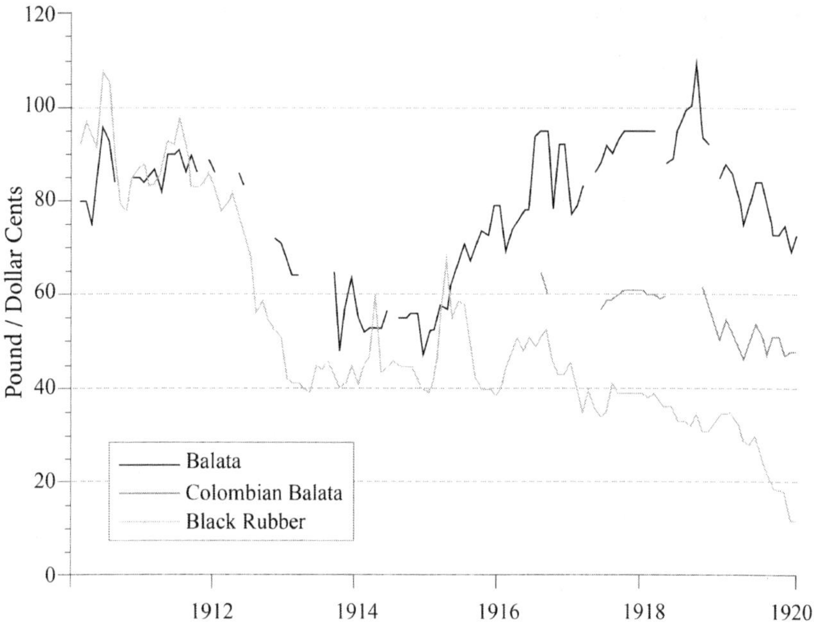

GRAPH 6 Balata prices, 1910–20. Graph based on data taken from *India Rubber World*, various numbers, 1910–20.

in that area began in 1915 after a rural dweller named Lorenzo Solís learned the extraction process in Panama and other peasants embraced the new activity, especially in the Mejicano, Colorado, and Gualajo Rivers, where the tree abounded.[88] Gatherers also collected balata in the Gulf of Urabá, the Pacific littoral of Chocó, and the San Juan basin. But since they cut down the trees for their latex, just as they had done with black rubber, they once again exhausted the supply fairly rapidly.[89] During those years, lowlanders also gathered chicle, another gum used to make chewing gum.[90]

VEGETABLE IVORY

Unlike balata and rubber gathering, the vegetable ivory trade did not lead to the depletion of palm stands and therefore lasted longer. For just a few decades, rubber gathering made forest resource extraction pervasive across the entire region; vegetable ivory collection, in turn, made this new kind of extraction the backbone of a few local economies, most notably that of Tumaco. This difference stems largely from the distribution and biology of each species. While individual rubber trees were found scattered all over the region, vegetable ivory palms form large clusters in just a few places. These vegetable ivory groves can withstand intense harvesting, whereas the limited flow of latex from black rubber trees encouraged felling them. Gathering seeds was also a much simpler affair: no need for long excursions or felling trees; instead gatherers picked up seeds from the forest floor.

The characteristics of the seeds (or "nuts") of vegetable ivory palms made them ideal for manufacturing buttons. Like ivory, mature seeds are hard and have a cream color underneath a brown coating. But they are not as durable and will dissolve if left very long in water. They become shiny when polished and absorb dye easily. Only small objects could be made from them, because they are hollow in the center and roughly resemble a hen's egg in shape and size. Although primarily used for manufacturing buttons until the 1940s, they were also used to carve out umbrella handles and chess pieces. A modest craft industry has developed recently around the fabrication of colorful jewelry and, to a lesser extent, decorative figurines in the form of parrots or hummingbirds.

Three palm species that inhabit the rainforests of Panama and the Pacific coast of Colombia and Ecuador provided the majority of seeds that ended up being manufactured into buttons. A smaller percentage came from the mid-Magdalena valley.[91] Vegetable ivory palms form the genus Phytelephas, a name that stems from the Greek words for plant and elephant.[92] *Phytelephas tumacana*, found in the coastal plain of Nariño in southern Colombia, and *Phytelephas aequatorialis*, which grows in the coastal plain of Ecuador, fit the stereotypical image of a palm tree: They are tall, have only one stem, and are topped by large pinnate leaves. *P. aequatorialis* is much taller, growing up to fifty feet and its leaves averaging twenty feet long. *P. tumacana*, by contrast, grows up to sixteen feet and has smaller leaves (see map 5 and fig. 1). *Phytelephas seemannii*, which is distributed throughout Panama and in the northern part of the Pacific lowlands of Colombia, is a bit different. Most of its stem lies on the ground while only the tip is erect, usually rising up to 6.5 feet. Over this height, the stem cannot support the palm's weight and breaks or slowly subsides. The tip of the palm tree continues to grow erect even after being broken because roots grow along the stem (see map 5 and fig. 2).[93] These three species often grow in alluvial river plains subject to brief flooding, where they form large dark green stands known as taguales. Vegetable ivory palms also grow in the forest along with other species.

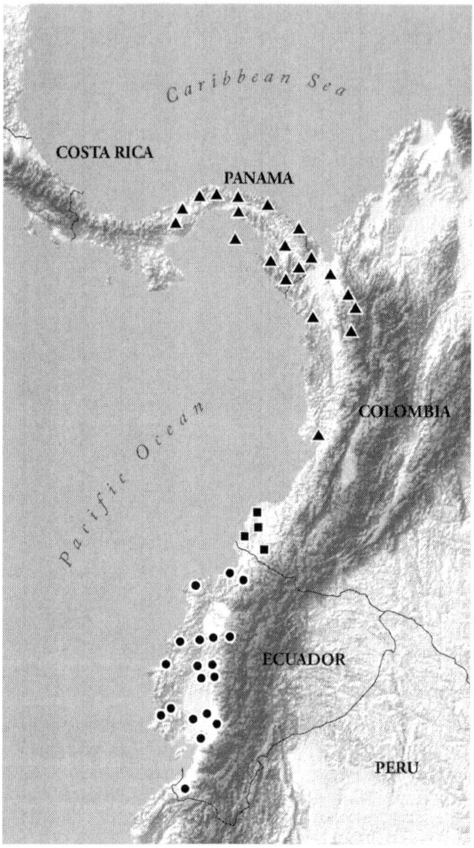

MAP 5 Distribution of three vegetable ivory species. Map by Paola Luna, Cartography Lab, Universidad de los Andes, Bogotá. Source: Anders S. Barfod, "A Monographic Study of the Subfamily Phytelephantoideae (Araceae)," *Opera Botanica* 105 (1991).

Each palm tree has usually close to twenty large fruit clusters covered by a woody, dark, spiky shell. The round form and rugged surface give the palm the common name by which it is known in the southern Colombian coast: *cabecinegro*, which means black man's head. Clusters contain several fruits formed by radially arranged groups of four to eight seeds, each seed enveloped by a shell and covered by oily flesh. The process of maturation from flower to ripe fruit takes about three years. During that time, young seeds, which are initially liquid, become creamy and gelatinous, and finally hard. When ripe, the shell cracks and falls, and the fruit release a smell that attracts rodents. These animals eat the flesh and help disperse the seeds, something water cannot do easily because the seeds do not float.[94]

FIGURE 1 *Phytelepas tumacana* and *Phytelepas aequatorialis*. Source: Anders S. Barfod, "A Monographic Study of the Subfamily Phytelephantoideae (Araceae)," *Opera Botanica* 105 (1991).

FIGURE 2 Florentino Valencia in vegetable ivory grove, Boroboro River, Chocó. Photograph by Rodrigo Bernal.

The collection of vegetable ivory for export started before the mid-nineteenth century and ended a hundred years later. According to Seemann, in the late 1840s "the 'nuts' of this beautiful palm-like plant [were] extensively used by turners, and converted into knobs for walking-sticks, buttons, toys, and various other articles." However, he also mentioned that at the time Panama and the Ecuadorian port of Esmeraldas still did not export vegetable ivory.[95] The earliest reported exports from Colombia date from the period 1839–49, but the quantities are insignificant. Available export data shows that in the 1850s Colombia had an incipient trade with England, France, and the United States, which increased considerably from the 1860s on. This data, however, is incomplete: it does not include imports from Italy or Germany before the 1890s, which until World War I accounted for most of the trade worldwide. In the 1890s and 1900s, U.S. imports of Colombian vegetable ivory grew, and after World War I this country became the main importer.[96] Demand from the United States came mostly from some forty button manufacturers concentrated in New York, New Jersey, and Massachusetts. Many of these factories closed in the early 1930s, probably due to the Great Depression and the increasing competition from

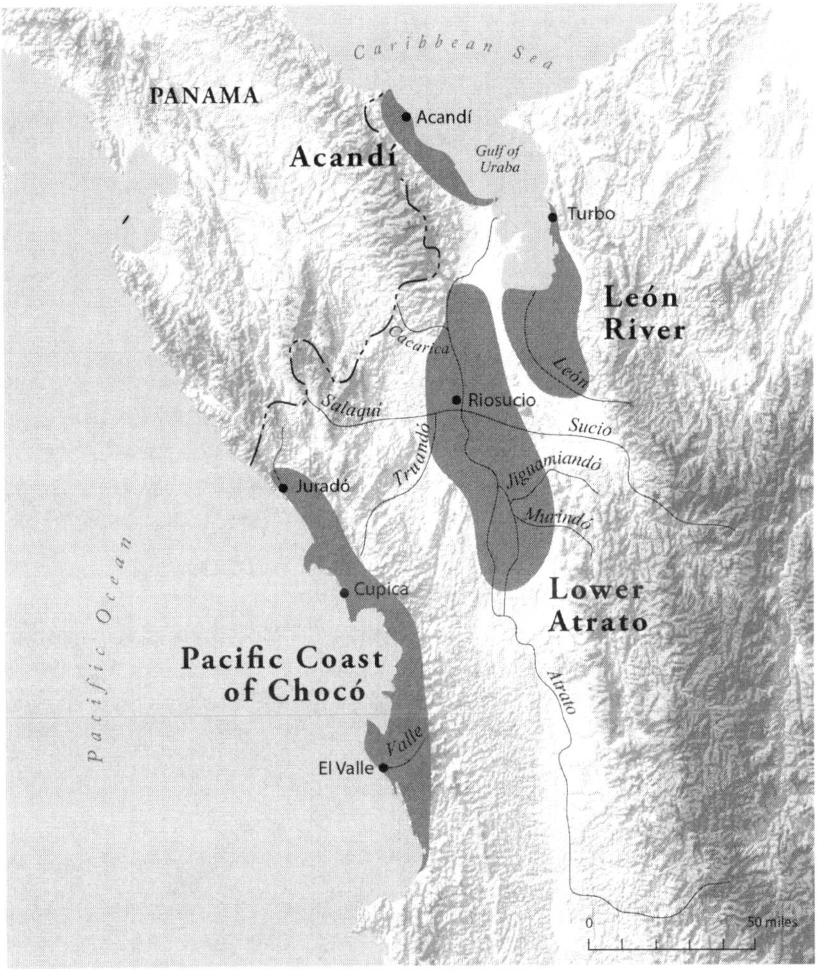

MAP 6 Northern vegetable ivory collection areas. Map by Paola Luna, Cartography Lab, Universidad de los Andes, Bogotá.

plastic buttons. The trade suffered considerably but managed to survive until World War II.[97]

In the northernmost part of the lowlands, migrants hailing from the Caribbean and the upper Atrato collected vegetable ivory from the Gulf of Urabá and the lower Atrato valley, which merchants exported from Cartagena (see map 6). The León River, which drains into the gulf, was the most productive of these areas. Gatherers also picked up nuts in Acandí, the district located on the western side of the gulf, but its production was much smaller. According to the U.S. consul in Quibdó in 1913, Acandí produced only seven hundred tons annually, while the León River produced eight thousand tons. In these two areas the majority of gatherers came from Bolívar, that is, the Caribbean plains to the east. These settlers—with Spanish, Indian, and African ancestry—also migrated further west into Panama, which at the time was part of Colombia.[98] Meanwhile, the production of the lower Atrato, the third gathering area of the northern lowlands, fell in between the above-mentioned areas at three thousand tons.[99] Migrants from the Upper Chocó mining area collected this amount in the Jiguamiandó, Murindó, and Sucio Rivers.[100] The same holds true for the nearby coast of the Pacific Ocean, where vegetable ivory nuts were for many decades the main and often only export product.[101] The area best known for vegetable ivory nut gathering there was the Valle River, but forests from the Baudó River further south and Cupica and Juradó near the Panamanian border also supplied some seeds. Coastal dwellers took most of their output to Panama for export. Perhaps the small production of the Baudó basin accounts for the scant exports from Buenaventura.[102]

The abundant groves near Tumaco, in the southern end of the lowlands, made it the main vegetable ivory shipping port in the country (see map 7). As noted in a 1912 newspaper article, "vegetable ivory forests are found in all [the municipality's] territory, except in a few places."[103] Gathering areas included the rivers that drain into the Ensenada de Tumaco, just north of the port, and the Mira and Mataje Rivers to the south.[104] The location of vegetable ivory groves coupled with the demand for their seeds generated one of the most important migration streams in the lowlands, from the mining district of Barbacoas down to the coast. "All workers collect vegetable ivory," observed a local entrepreneur in 1878.[105] They turned Tumaco into an exporter of these nuts: vegetable ivory was one of its principal exports and the most important one among those produced locally. In 1875 and 1877, although it comprised about a quarter of total exports—the most valuable products being gold from Barbacoas and cinchona bark from the Andes, also known as quina and used to make quinine—vegetable ivory accounted for more than 50 percent of local exports.[106] This situation did not change in the twentieth century: available data between 1909 and 1915 shows that vegetable ivory oscillated between 14 and 30 percent of the port's total exports, and between 32 percent and 57 percent of local exports.[107] Around that time this port shipped more than 50 percent of national vegetable ivory exports in terms of value.[108]

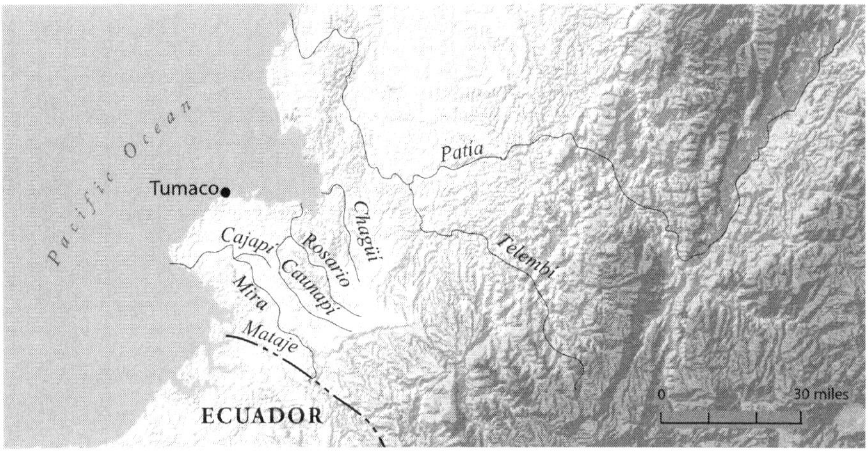

MAP 7 Southern vegetable ivory collection areas. Map by Paola Luna, Cartography Lab, Universidad de los Andes, Bogotá.

Gathering vegetable ivory nuts was a fairly simple affair. Men and women who usually lived relatively close to the stands collected them from the ground in large baskets and occasionally in sacks and returned home after the day's work. Nuts were available—and thus collected—all year round. However, vegetable ivory gathering was more seasonal in the Valle River than elsewhere in the lowlands. As it rains more there, collection intensified during the first months of the year when the forest floors were dry. Local inhabitants remember that vegetable ivory was sometimes collected at night with torches or lamps, probably to make the most out of the harvest season.[109] Gatherers sometimes knocked off the fruits from the palm trees before they fell, then matured them by burying and covering them with leaves. When ready, the shell was cracked open by mallet (*mazo*) blows—for this reason the collection of unripe nuts was called *maceo* or *maceado*.[110]

Button manufacturing made seeds the most valued part of vegetable ivory palms, but black people did more with these species than make commodities. They ocassionally drank young seeds, like the water of a coconut, or ate them before their flesh became hard.[111] More importantly, people used the leaves for thatching, especially in kitchens, since they harden with smoke.[112] These leaves were preferred over more durable ones of other palms because their smaller size made them easier to handle, and because vegetable ivory grew in accessible places close to rivers and streams.[113] People also ate the young male flower clusters when the tissues were still soft, made brooms with the leaf base and petiole fibers, and ate the palm hearts.[114] All these subsistence uses happened in the stands themselves or in the homes, while heavy mature seeds needed to be transported to collection centers or ports of export. Gatherers often took them in canoes, although sometimes the merchants or their agents would travel through the production areas purchasing the seeds.[115] Dwellers of the Pacific coast of Chocó employed larger canoes or small boats to take the seeds to Panama.[116] When transportation became problematic due to navigation constraints, as what happened in the Salaquí River due to excessive woody debris, no one collected the seeds.[117]

Unlike the case of rubber, the abundance of these palms and their high tolerance to harvesting eliminated incentives for cultivation. However, there are some indications that vegetable ivory palms might have been planted on a small scale. According to Misael Acosta Solís, an Ecuadorian botanist who wrote about vegetable ivory in the 1940s, this palm tree was cultivated in the Santiago River in Ecuador.[118] Colombian archives and newspapers contain only a few inconclusive hints. In 1912, a worker in a property in the lower Atrato estimated the number of palm trees there from the size of the containers used to carry the seeds for four plantings.[119] Since the species that grows in the lower Atrato needs about twenty-four years to mature and the property had been developed only eight years before, the palms in production could not have been planted. If successful, the planted palms would have begun producing when the trade was about to end.[120] Announcements in Tumaco newspapers often read that a given farm was cultivated with or had plantations of rubber, cacao, and vegetable ivory.[121] Wild vegetable ivory was probably just listed along with crops as one of the properties' assets, for elsewhere I have found the expression natural plantations to refer to vegetable ivory stands.[122] Besides, the U.S. consul in Quibdó and a U.S. trade commissioner stated in 1913 and 1921 that "no attempt [had] been done to cultivate the vegetable ivory palm."[123] Even if some attempts at planting were actually made, it remains true that practically all nuts were collected from wild stands. Vegetable ivory gathering was, therefore, an extractive activity.

As the vegetable ivory trade flourished, logging slowly developed, and after the trade ended, timber replaced vegetable ivory nuts as Tumaco's main export.[124] Since colonial times, visitors had noted the abundance of timber and thought that with adequate transportation it could provide a good source of income. Locals recognized dozens of tree species and knew where to find them. They also knew the properties of their wood and thus used them to build houses, carve out canoes, and make bateas, paddles, and drums. As small markets developed in the larger lowland towns, a few merchants took advantage of this knowledge and included timber among the many commodities sold in their stores.[125] The construction of the first section of the railroads connecting Buenaventura and Tumaco with the interior, in the 1880s, opened temporary markets for lumber for crossties. Local entrepreneurs also started selling timber outside the region. Although export data is scarce and scattered, it shows that Tumaco and Buenaventura, and even Quibdó, occasionally shipped timber from at least the 1850s.[126] Additionally, logs left the region through nonofficial ports.[127]

The installation of sawmills in the first decades of the twentieth century best illustrates the early stages of a regional logging industry, which developed most rigorously in Tumaco than anywhere else in the lowlands. The first sawmill of this port was installed as early as 1870—probably the one known as *Máquina de aserrar* (the sawing machine), which gave one of the port's neighborhoods its name.[128] By 1916, Tumaco had three sawmills, and in 1923 Francisco J. Márquez, a local merchant, constructed a large one that became a city landmark. At least three others sprang up along the coast north of this port in the following decade.[129] In the 1910s, local entrepreneurs also established at least three sawmills relatively close to Buenaventura.[130] The lower Atrato had a sizable mill, established in 1903, which sold its timber in Barranquilla. By 1914, two more sawmills existed in the area.[131] Local businessmen installed a few other mills in Timbiquí, Barbacoas, and Quibdó at the turn of the century, the latter two geared to the local market.[132]

Timber extraction eventually gained strength all over the lowlands to become the most widespread extractive activity in the history of the region. Prior to 1930, the lowlands had fewer than twenty sawmills, and probably only around ten operated simultaneously. By the 1960s, this number had grown to more than one hundred. In the 1920s, electrical plants began to replace the steam engines supplying power to the first sawmills. As years passed, loggers sought timber in virtually every corner of the region almost exclusively for Colombia's domestic market.[133] Other forest resources—most notably mangrove bark used in the tanning industry and palm hearts, a delicacy—were also extracted from the lowlands in the twentieth century.[134] All these resources kept alive the extractive model that began developing in the lowlands in the seventeenth century and contributed to the independent character of black people's lives.

Although extraction of natural resources for profit had signified society's relation with the rainforest since colonial times, only after the mid-nineteenth century—when it expanded to incorporate new products and areas—did it come to encompass practically the entire Pacific coast of Colombia. The most important transformation, however, revolved around the social relations of extraction. Masters, overseers, and slaves gave way to black peasants, the most conspicuous trait of the lowlands' social fabric, and a few white merchants who for the first time in the region's history formed a local elite. These merchants, as the next chapter explains, benefited from a division of labor in which peasants alone were in charge of procuring natural resources: it cemented their privileged status and allowed them to make profits, although not without risk. Despite their efforts to break away from their dependence on extraction by engaging in plantation agriculture and other ventures, they remained traders in natural commodities.

3

TRADERS IN NATURAL COMMODITIES

AFTER THE END OF SLAVERY, rainforest peasants worked in tandem with merchants who purchased natural resources for export. The few white mine owners who stayed in the region made small profits by renting out their mines to free blacks; buying precious metals from these newly independent miners, and then exporting them, proved to be for most a better deal. A few newcomers, among them some foreigners, joined this business and devoted themselves to importing merchandise in exchange for gold or other valuable products, notably rubber and vegetable ivory but also animal skins and anything else that they might sell outside the region. In this manner, a very small merchant class formed in Quibdó, the largest lowland town, like the one living in Tumaco, the southern maritime port.

Black peasants, who enjoyed unusual levels of autonomy by living in the forests and controlling the extraction of natural commodities, obtained tools, cloth, salt, and other basic goods through this trade that connected them with whites, while keeping them hierarchically separated. Merchants formed the tip of a new local elite imbued with a sense of superiority stemming from their alleged whiteness and strengthened by the shelter and distance that cities and nonmanual labor provided them from the jungle. Searching to increase their profits, they invested in other ventures, such as steam navigation and commercial agriculture, but as we shall see, their gains ultimately rested on the trade in natural resources. Those trading in vegetable ivory let gatherers run endless debts with them, something that seems to undermine the notion of peasants' autonomy. Although at first sight debts may seem a means to oblige lowlanders to work, a close examination suggests that they served primarily as incentives offered by merchants competing for scarce labor. Therefore the exchange in forest products and precious metals made commerce between direct extractors and local merchants—not the subjection of the former by the latter—the most prominent relationship of the lowland economy.

This new political economy of extraction overcame the lack of capital that afflicted the region. Despite their poverty, miners and gatherers could be in charge of the labor-intensive and technologically simple processes of extraction. Rubber gatherers needed supplies for a few weeks and adequate tools to cut down the trees, while vegetable ivory collectors simply used baskets and canoes to carry the product. Merchants, on their part, could keep costs to a minimum. They set up a shop in town and perhaps had a canoe for purchasing natural products directly in the producing areas, and they did not have to engage in much processing. Gold was sold as purchased, and vegetable ivory nuts were just dried and rarely shelled and sorted.[1] Although drying nuts in the sun could take up to three or four months because of the humid and rainy climate of the lowlands, and merchants needed to establish relations with buyers overseas, they did not have to pay salaries or supervise labor, nor spend money for securing access to vegetable ivory or acquiring specialized technology (see fig. 3). Furthermore, because gatherers and miners also worked for their own subsistence, they sold natural products at prices that did not fully account for their reproduction needs. In other words, they subsidized the trade in natural resources with their subsistence labor, a characteristic feature of peasant economies. It should also be noted that nature subsidized these trades, because no one had planted or tended the trees and palms, much less fabricated the mineral deposits.

This merchant class developed in tandem with trading centers. In colonial times, mining camps, not towns, constituted the principal settlement units in the lowlands. Towns such as Nóvita, and even the small city of Barbacoas, were mostly administrative centers with relatively little commerce. Merchants came from distant places to sell a variety of wares, and then they left rather than making these places their homes. More importantly, most of the merchandise "went directly to the mines."[2] Mine owners monopolized gold output, which they could not trade freely because the Crown mandated it to be sent to the official smelting houses. Commerce was further hindered in a large part of the lowlands because the most powerful mine owners procured part of their inputs,

FIGURE 3 Vegetable ivory nuts drying in Tumaco, early twentieth century.

such as beef jerky, from their Andean haciendas. With independence, the disruption of the links between mines and haciendas, and the growing population of free miners, commerce began to pick up. The end of slavery and the demand for forest products gave further impetus for commerce.

The vegetable ivory trade provided opportunities for some men in the Pacific coast of Chocó to become small traders; in Tumaco, it created a merchant class. Inhabitants from the small town of El Valle remembered that José Llorente, Casino Bermúdez, Damián Murillo, and Cristóbal Sanclemente took the largest quantities of vegetable ivory to sell to exporters in Panama.[3] Margarito Secaida, a native of Juradó and dweller of Coredó further down the coast, was another such intermediary.[4] Larger trade centered in Tumaco, leading an elite to form. Although the port also shipped other commodities such as gold, hats, rubber, cacao, and hides, from the 1860s through the 1930s, trade in vegetable ivory was by far the most important local economic activity. Referring to one of the port's leading merchants, a local newspaper made clear how he made his money from natural resource extraction: "[H]e fought in the forests against wild nature; he extracted their natural wealth and laid the foundation of his fortune."[5] But the wording was only a form of rhetorical aggrandizement, as these merchants were proud of having their businesses organized around commercial houses—as far as possible from the forests off which they lived. Each house took its name from its owner and had a store and a warehouse with a pier. Merchants received vegetable ivory seeds on the piers and stored them in the warehouses along with the merchandise they imported.[6] The stores were always well located in town—ideally by the pier—and the merchant's family usually lived in the second floor. These commercial houses, as well as their owners, became one of the most conspicuous traits of Tumaco at the turn of the century (see figs. 4 and 5).

Tumaco's commercial sector was constantly being reconstituted, except for a few core houses that managed to survive for a long time (see table 7). The trade in vegetable ivory took off in the 1860s. A decade later, the port had a strong commercial establishment capable of joining forces to repeal a tax on vegetable ivory exports.[7] Many of the early small export businesses vanished from Tumaco before the turn of the century. Commercial houses continued to open from 1880 to the 1910s, but again only a handful survived for more than a few years.[8] The persistent creation and disappearance of firms indicates that business could be unstable. Anecdotal evidence indicates that the price of vegetable ivory fluctuated widely. In 1891, for instance, a traveler passing through Tumaco remarked

FIGURE 4 Max Heimann's commercial house, Tumaco.

FIGURE 5 Advertisement for the commercial house F. J. Márquez, *El Litoral Pacífico*, Tumaco, November 1909.

TABLE 7 Tumaco's main merchants

NAME OF MERCHANT OR COMMERCIAL HOUSE	DATE OF ESTABLISHMENT	NUMBER OF WAREHOUSES IN 1911
Gaminara y Leeder	1867	4
Marcos A. del Castillo	Before 1877	—
Pedro Alcides Douat	Before 1877	—
Delio Delgado	Before 1877	—
Francisco Benítez / Amelia D. v. de Benítez	Early 1880s	4
Thomas Clark	1884	—
Gabriel Manzi	1889	1
Max Heimann	1897	2
Stanley Woodcock	1899	2
Manuel S. Benítez	Before 1906	2
Manuel José Díez Colunje	Before 1906	—
Alejandro Nahar C.	Before 1906	2
Jorge Mercado	Before 1909	2
Francisco J. Márquez	Before 1910	2
Escrucería Hermanos	1910	2
Dumarest Bros. & Co.	1910	2
Delfín Martínez	—	2

Sources: *El Vapor*, Tumaco, No. 5, December 10, 1877; *El Tumaqueño*, Tumaco, No. 1, June 28, 1878, and No. 4, August 31, 1878; *El Litoral Pacífico*, Tumaco, No. 5, November 13, 1909; No. 10, January 22, 1910; No. 14, February 23, 1910, No. 18, April 2, 1910; No. 39, October 29, 1910; No. 42, November 19, 1910; *El Eco del Pacífico*, Tumaco, No. 65, November 10, 1917; *La Estrella*, Tumaco, No. 1, March 11, 1906.; No. 11, January 29, 1910; *Gaceta Departamental*, Tumaco, No. 14, February 29, 1909; AGN, *Baldíos*, t. 33, ff. 38–47; *El Concejal*, Tumaco, Nos. 96, 97, and 98, January 31, 1911.

that "the price of vegetable ivory [had] greatly diminished; a quintal, which before was worth from 25 to 30 francs, [was no longer worth] more than 13 or 14 francs."[9] Prices also plummeted in 1908 and during World War I.[10] Once again in 1922, Tumaco's merchants grew worried about low vegetable ivory prices, while a priest reported on its devastating effects on the Pacific coast of Chocó.[11] Besides price variation, merchants were subject to other liabilities. Francisco Benítez, for instance, lost most of his property twice: once in a fire, a common problem in lowland towns, and then due to war.

By 1910, some of the first merchants began to pass away; their heirs continued their businesses, turning the families into local commercial dynasties. For instance, Amelia Duclerq de Benítez kept the house started by her late husband Francisco Benítez, while their son established an independent commercial business.[12] In a similar fashion, Marcos A. del Castillo continued operating the house founded by his father.[13] When Escrucería Hnos. was dissolved in the 1920s, several members of the family kept independent firms, while other long-established houses changed ownership.[14]

The commercial establishment was rather small. In 1911, a group of twelve merchants dominated the export business, each owning at least a shop and a warehouse. They were the town's richest people, the most prominent members of its white elite. A few went to Europe and the United States for business and sometimes turned the trips into family vacations.[15] Their origins were diverse. Some, like Francisco Benítez and Marcos A. del Castillo, came from Barbacoas. The former was of humble birth, while the latter belonged to one of the most important families of the Telembí River. Others came from abroad: F. J. Márquez's father was Spanish, Max Heimann was German, apparently Manzi and the Escrucería were Italian, and William Jarvis and Thomas Clark were British. A few probably came from other parts of Colombia or from the Ecuadorian coast.

Just as Tumaco concentrated commerce in the southern Pacific coast, Quibdó centralized the commerce of the Upper Chocó, a very important mining area in the lowlands. Barbacoas, located among rich placers, could have been just another commercial center, but in this town a strong local mine-owning class that formed in colonial times remained throughout the nineteenth century. In other mining areas, buying and exporting gold and later platinum became the main business, well above renting mines. In this manner, minor trading centers developed, such as Istmina, in the upper San Juan, and Guapi, El Charco, and Iscuandé on the southern Pacific coast.[16]

Quibdó also achieved its position largely due to its strategic location. Built on the banks of the Atrato, a river that drains into the Caribbean, Quibdó had a direct connection to Cartagena, the only authorized port of New Granada. As mentioned in chapter 1, the Spanish Crown prohibited navigation on the Atrato throughout most of the eighteenth century in an attempt to halt contraband. This measure severely restricted commerce, although smuggling never stopped. In 1782, however, the Crown reopened the river, seeking to stimulate gold production by diminishing the cost of imported commodities. Although free navigation on the Atrato did not revive the decaying mining sector, it did lead to more dynamic commercial activity. In 1819, Agustín Codazzi remarked on the importance trade had achieved in Quibdó—a trade that revolved around gold:

> Some creoles . . . devoted themselves to trade with the interior of Cauca and Cartagena. But the difficulties of traversing the Andes, where mules could only pass three months in the year . . . limited commerce with Cauca to only foodstuffs. . . . Commerce with Cartagena was easier. Small ships left that city and came up the Atrato . . . with the help of Indians . . . who sometimes transferred the cargo to canoes and transported it to the capital. They brought fabric and all things necessary to dress the creole population, given that blacks and Indians do not need much. Quibdó also received all that is useful for mechanical arts and foodstuffs in general, such as bizcocho, flour, rice, beans, salted and dry meats of all sorts, and salted fish; they are exchanged for gold dust.[17]

Around that time, renewed commercial activity and the ever-alluring power of gold brought to the port a handful of Englishmen who established trade connections with Jamaica. Although some married local women, they soon made their homes in other parts of the country.[18] Cartageneros, not Englishmen, gave Quibdó's commerce its strongest impetus.

The same is true for Turbo, a smaller settlement on the Gulf of Urabá. Commerce there received its initial momentum from rubber. In 1857, "Mr. Dean, an Englishman by birth, but for many years a resident of New Granada," was one of the main rubber traders of this small settlement. The principal person in Riosucio, "Señor de la Rosa, a Spaniard by birth, [was an] agent of Mr. Dean in the caoutchouc trade."[19] The vegetable ivory economy, which lasted longer and depended on Cartagena, enriched and empowered a few merchants. Paradoxically, Cartagena's steep decline after independence helped spur business on the Atrato. Besides losing its colonial monopoly on overseas trade, Cartagena was hit particularly hard by the Independence Wars. Between 1809 and 1851, its population declined by 46 percent. In the 1840s, it also lost its role as the nation's port to Barranquilla, which is strategically located at the mouth of the Magdalena River, the country's main thoroughfare. Some of Cartagena's merchants turned to the Sinú and Atrato Rivers in search of local products in demand in the world market.[20] A few settled in Turbo, and as far as Panama, and profited from the trade in vegetable ivory. Eusebio Campillo, who in the early twentieth century became known as the "vegetable ivory king," was the most prominent of them. Since Turbo was not an export port, Campillo sold his vegetable ivory to export houses in Cartagena, as did his peers.[21]

The merchant elite of Cartagena included foreigners, among them some Italians, several of who tried their luck in Chocó.[22] Mr. Bonolli, for instance, owned a house in Quibdó, in which he probably installed a shop to trade in metals and other products between the late 1840s and late 1870s.[23] The most prominent businessman to have lived in Chocó at the time was Juan Bautista Mainero y Trucco. Born in Italy, Mainero settled in Cartagena before mid-century, and by the time of his death he was probably the richest man in the city. He built his fortune working in several parts of the country, Chocó being one of the first. In the 1850s, he settled in Quibdó temporarily with his wife, where they "mounted . . . agencies to buy gold and several shops in the two main streets of the commercial sector and in the calle del puerto. They supplied them with goods sent by their agent in Cartagena. . . ."[24] It is also very likely that Cartageneros who did not settle in Chocó made trips up the Atrato for the purpose of trading.[25]

Former slave-holding families who moved to Quibdó further stimulated commerce. Unlike merchants from Cartagena who only settled in the Atrato temporarily, slave-mining families from the Upper Chocó came to stay.[26] Such was the case of the Valdés, Rey, Barbosa, and Carrasco families, who came from the San Juan, and the Abadía, Valencia, and Ferrer families, who came from the tributaries of the Atrato.[27] These newcomers joined a small influential group who had been living there since colonial times, which included the Contos, Castros, Arrunáteguis, Argaez, and Ulloas.[28] Most of these families continued to own mines, but many also engaged in commerce. They imported a few luxury items for well-to-do residents and basic goods for the town's population and people who lived along the rivers. They sent gold to Cartagena, as well as rubber, timber, and hides. In the Caribbean port, they hired agents to deal with large exporting houses.[29] In the last two decades of the nineteenth century, a few men from Quibdó started to form partnerships for the purpose of trading. They joined capital and alternated tending the shop with traveling to the rivers to purchase gold. Eventually, some of these Quibdoseños established businesses with branches both in Quibdó and Cartagena to directly manage overseas trade.[30] This was the beginning of the commercial houses that flourished in Quibdó in the first decades of the twentieth century.

Enrique Escobar & Cia, one of the few commercial houses of the early 1890s, resulted from the association of a man living in Quibdó with firms from Medellín and Cartagena. It had branches in all three cities. Apart from the usual business of exporting natural products and selling consumer goods in Quibdó, it also brought imports to Medellín and probably also introduced foodstuffs from Antioquia to the Atrato.[31] Antioqueños from the southeast sold pigs and a few other items in Quibdó. However, the difficult trail, even after it was improved in the 1860s, limited the extent of both the goods sent to Quibdó and the imported merchandise carried up the Andes for the Antioqueño market.[32] Although a few Antioqueños traded in Chocó, real business depended on gold and the route to Cartagena.[33]

The heyday of Quibdó's commercial houses came about with the arrival of several Syrio-Lebanese merchants, who established import-export businesses with branches in both the capital of Chocó and Cartagena. The migration to Colombia of people from the Middle East, known as "Turks," was part of a larger exodus of Christian families that started in the 1880s and extended through the first decades of the twentieth century. Those who came to Colombia settled initially in the Caribbean.[34] Starting in the late 1890s, a few of them, attracted by the prospects of the mining economy, made their way up the Atrato. The cousins Miguel Abuchar and Tufik Meluk were the first to arrive (see fig. 6). In 1895, they rented a house in Quibdó.[35] Two years later, Miguel created Abuchar Hermanos with his five brothers; the following year, Tufik formed A & T Meluk with his brother Amín, who remained in Cartagena.[36] Another cousin, Bychir Meluk, also came to Chocó and settled in Neguá, while his brother and partner Kalil, lived in the Caribbean.[37] Of this pioneer group, A & T Meluk, who arrived with resources, quickly rose to become the principal commercial house in Quibdó, keeping this leading position well into the 1930s. In the first decade of the twentieth century, other Syrians joined these traders. First came the Malluk brothers in 1903.[38] In 1909 and 1910, arrived the Rumié, Dualiby, Chamat, and Cudsi brothers, all of whom established commercial houses.[39] The Syrian traders integrated themselves to the local society by marrying local women and

FIGURE 6 Miguel Abuchar, from the commercial house Abuchar Hermanos. On the left, the day he married Isabel Lemos in Cali, 1910. (Courtesy of Alberto Abouchar Lemos.)

participating in the port's life in various ways. They organized parties, joined local festivities, and even donated monuments to the city.[40] Above all, they dominated the commercial scene of Quibdó in the early twentieth century.[41]

While merchants from the Middle East positioned themselves in Chocó, locals continued to create commercial partnerships. The Ferrer family remained prominent by founding three firms between 1905 and 1908.[42] Gonzalo Zúñiga, a man from Popayán who apparently arrived in Quibdó as a schoolteacher and was already in business in the 1890s, also remained a leading figure throughout the first decade of the century. The same held true for Delfino Díaz, his main partner since 1899.[43] E & A Rey, Lucindo Posso & Cia, and Angel Piñeres & Co stand out among several other firms.[44] Although a few of the older merchants died in the 1910s, the commercial elite that formed between 1895 and 1910 continued to dominate the port's commerce throughout the 1920s.[45]

Quibdó's commercial houses received merchandise from Cartagena to sell in Quibdó and other towns of the Atrato and the San Juan basins. The largest ones opened branches in towns surrounded by mines, where they could trade their merchandise for precious metals. Bychir Meluk, mentioned above, settled in Neguá, a town in the upper Atrato not far from Quibdó. The Malluk, Meluk, and Rumié houses opened branches in Istmina, Condoto, and Tadó, especially when platinum prices soared.[46] They either had one of the partners running the branches or they established a new partnership with another merchant who received a monthly salary and a percentage of the value of the sales.[47] Commercial houses usually operated on credit and frequently had properties mortgaged to their name to back debts.[48] They also served as a kind of bank that occasionally lent large sums of money to trustworthy clients, or smaller sums to residents who brought in valuable items.[49] Additionally, they offered wire service.[50]

Commercial houses in Quibdó and Tumaco represented the power of local merchants. As the most conspicuous business establishments in the lowlands, they clearly showed that money was made through commerce in natural products. Yet their owners, as well as the rural folk who supplied them, attempted to complement the extractive economy with other kinds of income-generating activities. They tried their luck by growing crops for the market and, in the case of merchants, sought to benefit from the introduction of steam navigation. However, they either failed or developed only small-scale ventures that ultimately depended on the extractive economy.

FUTILE EFFORTS AT DIVERSIFICATION

Despite the constraints posed by the region's climate and soils, lowlanders tried to develop commercial agriculture. In the lowlands, the areas suitable to plant crops are for the most part restricted to narrow river levees, and these areas often have drainage problems. Endless cloud cover poses additional limitations to large-scale agriculture, as well as high transportation costs and the small size of the local market. Besides attending to their own needs, rural inhabitants supplied towns with local produce, especially plantains, the most important lowland crop; but this was a small-scale trade. Some grew sugarcane and distilled their own aguardiente or supplied the state "monopoly."[51] Selling cattle in local towns was yet another option for lowlanders. Although some cattle grazed near Tumaco, the largest efforts at cattle ranching developed in Chocó.[52] As early as 1903, Abdo Abuchar set up a farm for this purpose on the Arquía River, yet in 1914 most cattle slaughtered in Quibdó were brought from the Sinú. In 1923, the Arquía ranch grew to have four hundred hectares of grass with a grazing capacity for five hundred cattle.[53]

Real hope for developing commercial agriculture rested on supplying markets outside of the lowlands. As explained in chapter 2, the extraordinary high prices of rubber led some members of Quibdó's elite to establish plantations, an experiment that ended when prices for rubber dropped. The Meluk brothers owned the largest one, in the Baudó Mountains, with 80,000 trees in 1913. Although Gonzalo Zúñiga estimated that his plantation had as many as 150,000 trees, a local bureaucrat claimed it had just 40,000. The Abuchars developed a plantation in the lower Atrato, while Francisco de B. Carrasco, a member of Istmina's elite, established the only one along the San Juan River. Even Henry Granger, an unrelenting American mining speculator, had rubber on his property, probably inherited from his brother Rene.[54]

Cacao growing, always on a limited scale, both preceded and outlived rubber planting. In the second half of the nineteenth century, the Atrato basin and Buenaventura exported cacao in small quantities.[55] However, historical sources do not reveal whether some of the cacao trees that produced those exports were found in forests rather than planted.[56] In both the lower Atrato and in Baudó, local entrepreneurs, mirroring timid efforts carried out in the Sinú Valley, tried to develop cacao plantations in the 1880s and 1890s, but by the turn of the century some of them abandoned cacao to pursue rubber cultivation.[57] Yet by 1914, the Baudó district alone had 190,000 trees, while the entire Chocó had about 600,000.[58] Peasants around Tumaco had also cultivated cacao since at least the late nineteenth century.[59] Data from 1909 to 1915 show that cacao amounted to between 3.4 percent and 11.4 percent of Tumaco's total exports.[60] When the rubber and vegetable ivory markets declined, as in 1914 and 1922, local merchants hoped that cacao would become a pillar of the economy, as it was in Ecuador.[61] However, as cacao cultivated in the African British colonies swamped the market and drove down prices in the 1910s, the great expansion of Ecuadorian cacao exports that began in the 1870s reached its end.[62] Furthermore, disease plagued the formerly lucrative Ecuadorian plantations. Such developments worried Tumaco merchants and might have also limited the expansion of cacao cultivation in Chocó.[63]

War, not disease, ended the first attempt at banana cultivation on the fringes of the lowlands. Based on developments in neighboring areas, this crop grabbed the attention of Chocoanos and the national government in the early twentieth century.[64] Panama had been exporting bananas since the 1890s, while Santa Marta's shipments increased rapidly in the first decade of the twentieth century after the formation of the United Fruit Company.[65] In 1909, the Colombian state gave a German company a 4,945-hectare concession on the Gulf of Urabá near the mouth of the León River to establish a banana plantation. The government's decision was in part motivated by the desire to counteract the perceived threat of American influence in the region after the secession of Panama. The Americans reacted in 1913 by sending a consular agent to Quibdó to check on the Germans.[66] However, due to lack of credit during World War I, among other reasons, the company had to abandon the area, leaving behind a half-built railroad and wharf as well as a few banana trees.[67] Half a century later, the United Fruit Company moved its business from Santa Marta to Urabá and greatly transformed the area.[68] Rainfall decreasing to below 3,000 mm a year must have contributed to the belated success of commercial agriculture.[69]

Hacienda Sautatá, the single largest agricultural enterprise of the lowlands in the first decades of the twentieth century, developed near the failed banana plantation on the other side of the Atrato. Owned by the Abuchar and Meluk brothers, the hacienda became best known for its production of sugar in the 1920s and 1930s. In 1993, the centenarian Eliseo Mena, who used to work there, remembered the place with nostalgia:

> Sautatá . . . that was a beautiful place, I tell you: a sugar mill, a sawmill, a chicken incubator . . . There was a port in the river, but the buildings were located inland. It took half an hour to get from the port to the sugar mill using the railroad. Gangs of workers from Buenaventura and elsewhere came to cut sugar cane. Cativo logs, cedar logs, güino logs, abarco logs . . . came from upriver to be sawed. Sawn-wood then went to Barranquilla. Sautatá: that was a real farm, no kidding. You make me remember that and I get sad. I promise you, that was a life of angels. They killed two cows . . . they could kill them every day because there were lots and lots and lots of cattle. I promise you, had Sautatá not failed, it would be a city.[70]

The dream of creating an agricultural emporium began at the turn of the nineteenth century. In 1899, a few years after their arrival in Chocó, the Abuchar brothers purchased a farm with cacao and rubber trees located in the lower Atrato.[71] A year later, they bought a nearby property developed by Juan C. Olier, a Cartagenero who lived in Riosucio. The 400-hectare farm called Las Delicias, located in "the point named Sautatá," had 15,000 cacao trees; 6,000 coffee trees; 1,000 coconut palms; 10,000 rubber trees; 12,000 tobacco trees; 5 hectares of sugar cane; abundant plantain, manioc, *ñame*, rice, corn, and fruit trees; 150 cattle; 200 hectares of planted grass; a trapiche; 5 houses; 2 warehouses; 12 cabins for workers; a horse; 3 donkeys; a tobacco press; and all the tools necessary for a farm.[72] Miguel Abuchar tried to improve the hacienda in various ways. He built a nursery with more than 100,000 rubber plants for cultivation; introduced 50 more cattle and 100 hogs; cleared 1,800 more hectares of jungle, then planted 800 of them with pasture; bought 10 miles of barbed wire; acquired 100 hens; installed a sawmill at the port;

and built 1 kilometer of railroad.[73] Then the Abuchar brothers requested title over their property, estimated at 5,000 hectares of land, since not even the initial hacienda bought from Olier had been titled.[74]

Despite financial difficulties early on, the Abuchars managed to develop an agribusiness. In 1905, they sold 20 percent of Sautatá to their cousins Amín and Tufik Meluk.[75] A few years later, the fall in rubber prices ended their rubber planting efforts; Sautatá became best known for its lumber mill. In the following years, the Abuchar brothers sold the remaining 80 percent of the hacienda to their cousins. In 1919, they convinced their cousins to sell them back Sautatá in order to produce sugar. Since they did not have the money to pay for the property, the Abuchars mortgaged the hacienda, promising to pay its full value in four years. They then proceeded to plant sugarcane and contracted Puerto Ricans to install a mill. Sautatá had its first harvest in 1920 or 1921.[76] By 1924, the hacienda had 500 hectares of sugarcane, 10 km of railroad, and a still. It produced less than two thousand tons of sugar per year, plus aguardiente for Chocó and the Caribbean. Sautatá developed into a small settlement, leaving a strong imprint on an area with a low and fairly dispersed population. It often had more than seven hundred workers at a time, for whom it had a general store and schools for boys and girls. Also the intendancy created a police station.[77] The 1924 intendant called Sautatá "a great effort by hard workers to implant in the solitary jungles of Chocó a prosperous enterprise" (see figs. 7 and 8).[78]

FIGURE 7 Sautatá in the late 1920s: steamboat loading sugar at the port.

FIGURE 8 Sautatá: aerial view, 1929.

Although Sautatá's prosperity was more apparent than real, in the minds of some it remained the quintessential example of the economic potential of the lowlands. A 1991 account, for instance, blamed the end of the enterprise on a catastrophic accident: "Everything was going smoothly until the tragedy struck. A huge fire devastated the fields. The columns of smoke could be seen from the mouth of the Atrato. Losses were substantial. More than three million gallons of alcohol burned until they left buildings, installations, and houses in ashes."[79] But even before the distillery burned in 1929, things were not going smoothly.[80] The plantation and the railroad continued to expand in the late 1920s, but by the early 1930s Sautatá had accumulated an onerous debt. Because the Chocó market was too small, it sold its production to the Colombian Caribbean, where it had to compete with the mills of the coast—Sincerín, which started producing in 1909, and Berástegui, which was established in 1928—with the disadvantage of having smaller production and higher transportation costs.[81] Although state aid allowed it to survive for a couple more years, it eventually ceased operations in the early 1940s. It is therefore a mistake to cite Sautatá as proof of the possibilities for commercial agriculture in the Pacific lowlands.[82]

Eager to diversify their portfolios, local entrepreneurs also turned to steam navigation. In a region where almost all transport occurred by water, this option seemed an obvious opportunity for investment. Nonetheless, navigation on the Pacific Ocean was beyond their means. The British Pacific Steam Navigation Company covered the route from Panama to Chile and ocassionally stopped in Buenaventura and Tumaco.[83] In addtion, movement of cargo and people between the few small coastal villages was rather limited for business purposes. The opportunities, then, were in equipping boats for the two routes with the most traffic: from Cartagena to Quibdó on the Atrato River and from Tumaco to Barbacoas on the Patía and Telembí Rivers. Traffic to Barbacoas had the advantage of including commodities that continued their voyage along the trail, later turned into a road, which led up the Andes to Túquerres and Pasto. By contrast, shipments from Barbacoas to Tumaco were limited to gold, some rubber, and occasionally timber and produce.[84] Boats traveling upstream on the Atrato River to Quibdó carried mostly commodities to supply the small local market, cheese and even cattle from the Caribbean coast, and imported merchandise for the poor and the rich alike. Quibdó and other localities along the Atrato exported more merchandise than Barbacoas, and passenger transportation was also more important.

Commercial capital financed steam navigation along both routes.[85] Merchants from Cartagena, and then from Quibdó, owned most of the steamboats used on the Atrato. Antioqueños and foreign capital also participated in this business. Juan Bautista Mainero y Trucco, the Italian merchant who started his career in Quibdó, offered such a service for the first time in the late 1860s with a steamship called Bolívar.[86] A decade later, the steamboat Albión, which belonged to the Cartagenero Nicolás de Zubiría, covered this route.[87] These must have been rather erratic attempts, for months or years could go by between the appearance of a boat navigating the Atrato River waters.[88] By virtue of its name, the Colombian Navigation and Commercial Company, which operated the steamship Atrato from the late 1880s to at least 1895, suggests the presence of foreign investment.[89] Diego Martínez and Cia, again from Cartagena, signed a five-year contract with the government in 1905 and began using a boat named after its owner, which in 1914 belonged to the Colombian Steamboat Company.[90] Around that time, the Compañía Antioqueña de Vapores operated two more boats—Ilse and Kate—along this route.[91] Finally, in the 1920s, A & T Meluk and Rumié Brothers, Syrian merchants with commercial houses in Quibdó, joined this business.[92] The Abuchar brothers also had steamboats associated with their sawmill and sugar mill in Sautatá.[93]

Three merchants doing business along the southern Pacific coast owned most of the boats that reached Barbacoas. Steady steam navigation to this port began in 1870 with a boat named Telembí, which worked for at least eight years.[94] Marcos A. del Castillo, who owned a commercial house in Tumaco, served as its agent, as well as captain for El Morro, a boat operating irregularly in the 1890s.[95] In 1912, his son, who had inherited his business, had a boat built to cover the same route.[96] The Englishman Thomas Clark, another local merchant, began as an agent for the Pacific Steam Navigation Company and in the twentieth century expanded into the steam navigation business. He imported the steamboat Tumaco that operated in the first decade of the century, and in 1907 launched a new vessel—La República—that he had built in San Francisco, California. Then in 1912, he bought yet another boat called La Palomita.[97] The main entrepreneur behind steam navigation in the Patía and Telembí Rivers, however, was Jorge Mercado, a merchant from Buenaventura acting as an agent for the Pacific Steam Navigation Company in both Tumaco and Buenaventura. He owned a shipyard and founded the Línea Costanera Fluvial de Vapores (Coastal and Riverine Steamship Line), which in 1914 operated three boats along the Telembí route, the first of which was introduced in 1906.[98] He also had a boat that traveled from Buenaventura up the San Juan River and along the coast to the Micay and Guapi Rivers.[99] His service along the San Juan had some competition from the mining companies (see next chapter), which operated their own steamboats.[100]

By the early twentieth century, several vessels covered both routes, but this business operated on a small scale and faced several drawbacks. Customers sometimes criticized the food or the sleeping arrangements, but above all they complained about the lack of a schedule.[101] In Quibdó, for instance, steamboats had to wait until they fully filled their cargo before leaving the port, which impeded having the much-desired regularity.[102] Furthermore, boats suffered various mechanical and maintenance problems and thus ceased navigating for weeks or months at a time.[103] The relatively dry months from June to August posed additional trouble in the Telembí, since the waters could recede to the point that boats risked running aground.[104] This hazard existed even though all steamboats operating in the lowlands were fairly small; contemporaries frequently referred to them as *vaporcitos*.[105] Although the condition of the boats probably improved with time, several shipwrecks confirm the risky nature of the business.[106] Yet steam navigation served to complement the business portfolio of mostly local entrepreneurs. Additionally, it gave temporary work to small crews, firewood suppliers, and carriers. Nonetheless, its contribution to the economy along the rivers and in the ports was ultimately minor. Furthermore, steam navigation was sustained by extractive activities; like commercial agriculture, transport did not constitute an alternative to commodity extraction, which remained the center of the region's economy.

INDEBTEDNESS

An extractive economy in which merchants did not interfere with black peasants' procurement of natural commodities characterized the lowlands, and ultimately guaranteed free blacks' a significant degree of freedom.[107] However, in the case of vegetable ivory, merchants advanced goods to gatherers who then paid with nuts, and invariably ended up indebted. If these debts constituted a form of coercion by which merchants forced gatherers to work, it would undermine the notion of the latters' autonomy. A careful assessment of the available evidence and of variations in the historical trajectories of the two main places where this occurred, as well as the literature on the topic, suggest that in the Gulf of Urabá debts were onerous for gatherers, while in Tumaco they acted more as incentives offered by merchants to guarantee a voluntary supply of vegetable ivory. Of the two, Tumaco has more relevance than Urabá to the discussion about the transition from slavery to freedom in the lowlands, for gatherers in this area had their origins in the slave mining camps of the southern littoral, while in Urabá they came from the Caribbean coast further east. Since indebtedness continued to be a prevailing situation in the lowlands after the end of the vegetable ivory trade—most notably in the logging economy—understanding its history and rationale has significance to comprehending labor relations in the Pacific coast throughout the twentieth century.[108]

Evidence for Urabá is more prevalent than it is for Tumaco. Accounts about the preceding rubber trade in neighboring Panama are very explicit about the existence and oppressive character of debt relations, while visitors to Turbo, the main town on the gulf, also emphasized the subjection of vegetable ivory gatherers through debt and the heavy-handedness of merchants. In 1877, Napoleon Wyse remarked how the "bosses" charged very high prices for basic goods, thus increasing the debt of the workers and keeping them in debt-bondage.[109] More than thirty years later, the U.S. consul to Quibdó emphasized how merchants sought to maintain debts—and thus keep laborers—endlessly: "The [vegetable ivory] nuts are gathered by peons who are paid from $2.40 up to $5 per 320 pounds, varying with the market price. I am informed that this payment usually consists of provisions, whereby the peons are usually badly cheated. It is customary to advance supplies to the peon who binds himself to obtain his outfit and provisions from the store of his employer. Thus the laborer is induced to contract debts which his employer manages to continue indefinitely, supposedly paying off part of the amount charged against the peon's account, when the nuts are brought in."[110]

Debt relations in Turbo and the Gulf of Urabá were more complicated than what this quote suggests. Merchants usually paid for the trip of men who came from the Caribbean plains to the east to gather rubber or vegetable ivory. Hence, these men arrived already in debt. Settlers who migrated to Acandí, on the western side of the gulf, told a similar story. In 1910, one of them explained: "I came . . . in the service of José María del Real, from . . . the department of Bolívar, and Manuel Rengifo, from the Chocó, to found this town and extract rubber as well as vegetable ivory."[111] Just as the workers were indebted to local merchants, these merchants were indebted to exporters in Cartagena, as a 1914 report by Turbo's mayor suggests: "Four or six multimillionaires from Cartagena give to sixteen or twenty individuals of lesser means sufficient money to hire in several parts of the region enough workers to exploit vegetable ivory."[112] The same was true for Acandí; the intendant of Chocó wrote in 1907 that the commercial sector from Cartagena "venture[d] capital there just as it did in the León River."[113]

For the rest of the region, evidence of indebtedness is harder to come by and what exists has no trace of the criticisms that characterized descriptions of natural resource trade in the Caribbean. There is no mention of debts related to the rubber trade beyond the northern tip of the region. Although this could be due to a paucity of sources, that a canal route explorer who referred to indebtedness in Darien only mentioned the barter of basic consumer goods for rubber (and gold) in Quibdó, weakens this suspicion.[114] The same is the case with references to merchants' abuses that fail to mention debts, as with the following one from 1907: "[With the education of blacks and Indians] whites would lose the better part of their fat profits, which consist in the pounds of rubber and the gold and platinum that they take from those unfortunate ignorants, giving them in exchange, low quality fabrics and food at exorbitant prices."[115] But when it comes to vegetable ivory, debts become discernible.

Apparently merchants from Panama gave credit to gatherers living (considerably far) on the Pacific coast of Chocó. After receiving "provisions for the return trip, a shotgun, some gunpowder, a box of soap, a gallon of kerosene, some lard, a pack of matches, an outfit, a dress for the wife and a shirt for a kid," they ended up in debt, agreeing to pay later with more vegetable ivory.[116] For Tumaco, a local newspaper provided the sole albeit rich and satirical piece of information that I found. An unnamed local, who could have vested interests but also familiarity with how the trade worked, wrote it:

> It used to be that by 11 a.m. a peasant had gathered a quintal of vegetable ivory [. . .]. Moreover, working the whole day, alone or with his naked woman, he could gather three quintals. With that he came to Tumaco where he found free shelter in the merchant's pier. The merchant pampered him, asked him about his kids, and offered to be the godfather when the next one was born. Provided that the peasant brought more vegetable ivory, the merchant gave him booze and . . . sold to him on credit fabric, groceries, etc. A week of dancing, drunkenness and all debauchery followed this trip [. . .]. Two weeks later the peasant dedicated another day to gather vegetable ivory and returned to Tumaco. Since he owed the boss an amount equivalent to the three quintals of vegetable ivory he brought, he went to another boss, sold to him two quintals, and gave in partial payment of his debt just one to the previous boss, who was now the godfather of one of his kids. Trapped this way, merchants gave out large sums of money which are now lost.[117]

Given the disdain with which the author treats this imagined peasant, as a freeloader drunkard, who more than an individual person stands for all of those of his class, one is tempted to dismiss this prejudiced testimony. Yet an examination of migration patterns and the literature on the topic suggests more caution. While, as explained in chapter 5, entire families moved from Barbacoas toward the coast as part of a larger wave of migration originated in various mining areas of the Pacific lowlands, in the Caribbean single men migrated alone with the explicit purpose of collecting rubber or vegetable ivory and arrived in Urabá indebted to a *patrón* from the outset.[118] Those in Tumaco also came from a place that seemed closer, as the port had historical ties to Barbacoas, and did not arrive tied to a merchant. Furthermore, in Tumaco, everyone had relatives and friends on whom to rely for everyday needs or in times of difficulty; while in Urabá, settlers took longer to build a community with similar bonds. These divergent histories made Caribbean settlers much more dependent on gathering, leading them to devote more time to this activity than their peers around Tumaco, who "dedicated half the week to their small property, and the other half to vegetable ivory collection."[119] Gatherers in Urabá, it is safe to assume, had a weaker position vis-à-vis merchants than those in Tumaco.

Historical studies of debt relations give further hints for this analysis, as they have stressed that more often than not debt served as enticements to attract voluntary labor rather than as means of compulsion. Most of this literature is based on haciendas with resident indebted workers or, perhaps more often, where debts served to attract seasonal labor.[120] An example from the Colombian Caribbean illustrates how owners fought against advancing money and thus establishing debts, often to no avail. The manager of one hacienda informed its owners: "I have tried to avoid giving advances on wages since they cause us to lose a good deal of money and especially because individuals who receive such advances work poorly. But I'm afraid that to obtain the number of workers we are going to need, we will have to hand out advances. I have offered to pay 25 cents without an advance (five cents more than the going daily wage) but nobody shows up, so engrained is this custom to pawn oneself before working." When this hacienda managed, in 1925, to end this practice, it still needed to recuperate $1,500 pesos in monies advanced to laborers.[121]

In the context of labor scarcity, haciendas frequently and unwillingly gave money or products in advance as ways to secure labor. Extractive economies could operate in a similar fashion, but not always. This same literature recognizes that in some extreme cases, such as the logging camps of Chiapas and Tabasco in Mexico and rubber extraction in Putumayo, debts were quite coercive and led to forms of servitude. O. Nigel Bolland provides another example by explaining the functioning of Belize's logging industry, where debts contributed to the oppression of black workers in the context of another rainforest extractive economy:

> Laborers were given advances on their wages when they signed contracts at the beginning of the season, around Christmas time. Ostensibly, the advances were intended to enable the labourer to purchase supplies prior to going to the forests for the season, but the money was generally spent "keeping Christmas" with his family and friends in Belize Town. The result was that labourers had to purchase their supplies on credit and at exorbitant prices from the employers' truck shops at the camps in the forest. Often, the balance of the wages a worker received was insufficient to meet his expenses and he would end his season in debt to his employer. To work off his debt, the labourer would have to sign another contract with that employer the next season, with the result that the advance and truck systems effectively bound the labourers to their employers in a form of debt servitude.[122]

The Amazon rubber boom constitutes a counterexample that bears more resemblance to the vegetable ivory trade in Tumaco. In Belize, the companies owned most of the land in the colony and paid wages to loggers. Furthermore, the state enforced through the judicial system the compliance of contracts between workers and the companies, ruling always in favor of the latter when problems arose. Free black people faced imprisonment whenever they fled from the mahogany camps or failed to comply in any other way. On the contrary, in the Amazon, as in Tumaco, gatherers sold a natural product to merchants, rather than their labor to employers. Furthermore, discount prices for rubber and high prices for consumer goods were conspicuous. One study points out that merchants did their best to entrap newly arrived workers in debt. Nonetheless, "[i]t seems that the tappers had come to expect an advance in kind and treated it as a bonus that they did not have to repay." In the rare cases in which entrepreneurs did not offer advances, workers were hard to secure.[123] Through this relation, workers got access to the resources they needed for work, as well as basic consumer goods, and merchants guaranteed themselves a supply of the commodity they were interested in. Therefore, within the most extensive extractive economy that developed in Latin America, debt served, as in the case of Mexican peonage, mostly as a perk rather than a bond, to borrow an expression of historian Alan Knight.[124]

In Tumaco, as elsewhere in Latin America, debt developed in a context of labor scarcity. A few merchants thought to benefit from the market in vegetable ivory in a region inhabited by relatively few people. In 1870, the municipality of Tumaco had only 2,391 people, equivalent to 17.5 percent of the entire population of the southern lowlands.[125] More importantly, rural dwellers spent part of their time working to fulfill their own subsistence needs, reducing the time they devoted to gathering vegetable ivory. In this context, merchants whose profits depended on the amount of vegetable ivory they traded needed to guarantee a steady supply of nuts. For debt to have been a coercive mechanism to achieve this end, merchants needed a way to enforce debt payment. The newspaper cited above suggests that they did not have any, and the general weakness of the Colombian state—which at the local level must have lacked adequate personnel and had a negligible police force—backs this suggestion.[126]

However, there is a hint that the judiciary might have been able to enforce debt payments at least for a few years. Several newspapers from 1913 to 1916 published court orders to confiscate land without giving information on the processes. The orders favored some of Tumaco's merchants and the places in question were almost always located in areas where vegetable ivory collection was prevalent.[127] Merchants might have sued some of the collectors for failing to pay their debts, but those debts could be unrelated to vegetable ivory—resulting, for instance, from cacao cultivation. The dilatory debtors could also have been city dwellers with rural properties, since it is very likely that merchants were the town's lenders.[128] Furthermore, judiciary orders are insufficient proof of enforcement since they could have been disobeyed. Therefore, these orders do not indicate with any certainty that the state enforced the debts acquired by collectors; they could even indicate a belated effort by merchants to put an end to debts. In any case, the situation in Tumaco most likely resembled that of the Amazon, where "legal prosecution for debt evasion was virtually unknown, and violent retaliation was often difficult to implement."[129]

Not only was the use of force virtually impossible, it was unnecessary. Rural dwellers had strong incentives to supply vegetable ivory. Although control of the means of production allowed them to provide for themselves much of what they needed to survive, they still required certain goods that could only be bought. To secure an income, they had few alternatives for producing marketable commodities. Planted rubber proved futile, disease limited cacao production, and plantains or fish had only tiny local markets. Besides, transportation costs diminished the economic viability of some of these products. Collecting vegetable ivory was relatively easy and more importantly could be carried out along with gatherers' other productive practices. The need for certain articles tied rural dwellers to urban merchants much more than did debt. Similarly, for resident "debt" peons in northern Mexico, a "relatively secure standard of living [that they could not find otherwise] was the principal factor tying them to the estate." Lowlanders were "voluntary" gatherers in the same sense that these were "voluntary" peons and "proletarians are 'voluntary' wage workers."[130] They all chose these kinds of work within the limits of their living situations.

Debt existed, and did so for a long time, because it brought benefits to both parties, however unequal the conditions between them. For gatherers, indebtedness brought the added advantage of having a patrón; a long-lasting relation with a merchant provided more than just a source of credit. As the sardonic quote above suggests, it offered the sort of security involved in patron-client relations: a place to sleep when in town, someone affluent to turn to in case of misfortune, perhaps even a better price for the extractive products. Each merchant, for his part, sought faithful gatherers who would provide him and not his competitors with nuts; by exchanging vegetable ivory for merchandise, they

FIGURE 9 Token used by the Benítez commercial house.

kept the cost of credit in check. The making of tokens by at least one vegetable ivory merchant extended this strategy (see fig. 9). The relation therefore had advantages for both merchants living comfortably in town and gatherers toiling in the jungles and enjoying a measure of freedom within the constraints of poverty.

Legal freedom here came hand-in-hand with an autonomous lifestyle based on the dominion of the rainforest environment. However, blacks' control of the key natural resources that sustained the lowland economy did not go uncontested. Small entrepreneurs foreign to the region, local merchants turned speculators, and large mining companies all attempted in various ways to gain exclusive access to vegetable ivory groves or mining deposits. Their aspirations run against black rural people's interests and autonomy. Therefore, to explain the strength of the arrangement between merchants and peasants, and blacks' territorial control, we need to understand why many of these attempts at monopolizing mines and vegetable ivory groves failed, or at least did not succeed in significantly impinging upon Afro-descendants' autonomy.

4

THE POLITICS OF NATURAL RESOURCE ACCESS

THE CHOCÓ PACÍFICO MINING COMPANY formed in 1916 to mine with dredges the deposits of the platinum-rich Condoto River. For the next fourteen years, as the price of this metal soared, it successfully accomplished this task, and for several decades afterwards continued dredging the neighboring rivers. The Chocó Pacífico is the most outstanding manifestation of the competition black rural dwellers faced for the control of the natural resources that sustained the lowland economy. While many other attempts at developing modern mining failed, the New Timbiquí Gold Mines Ltd.—which brought horizontal tunneling to the Pacific lowlands—also succeeded. Their stories, and those of the many entrepreneurs who hoped to acquire exclusive rights to coveted parts of the lowland environment, contribute to explain fully the two main themes of part I of this book: the workings of the extractive economy and the autonomy achieved by free blacks.

Conflict over natural resource access characterizes extractive economies and defines how they function. Disputes in these places tend not to revolve around land but around the specific natural elements considered valuable, in this case the seeds of certain palm trees and precious mineral dust. These elements possess a concrete materiality that affects the struggles for them, just as soil and water—so important in agrarian economies—do. But agrarian studies often treat land as an abstraction, even if the land that peasants eagerly desire and fight for has specific traits and might actually include marshes or forests valuable for reasons different than their capacity to sustain crops. By forcing us to look beyond land, extractive economies invite us to acknowledge the environment's role in history.

In the lowlands, gold is found scattered throughout the mining areas in riverbeds and alluvial terraces, and at different depths. Within those areas it takes the form of small particles mixed up with the rest of the subsoil. Traditional mining methods allowed accessing superficial deposits, but others lay too deep to be reached in this manner. By the mid-nineteenth century, profitable mining depended on using expensive technology—mainly but not exclusively dredges—invented and used in other parts of the gold-mining world. Only big players, with access to large-scale capital and mining knowledge, could transform lowland mining and earn good profits. For this reason, lowland elites and many mining prospectors did not stand a chance. They bet on partaking in the bounty by acquiring mining titles to every inch of the vast mining areas; thus, whenever investors looked for deposits, they would have to negotiate with these title holders for access to the mines. Their strategy was twofold: using the law to secure rights of access—mining titles and concessions—and covering as much ground as possible given the scattered nature of gold particles. Vegetable ivory seeds are also found scattered over large expanses of forest but are much less valuable, and because they fall on muddy soils, no machines were needed to collect them. In this case, too, the strategy of those who wanted exclusive rights to nut collection involved using the law to acquire formal rights to the forests—initially through land titles and then through forest concessions—in the hope of forcing gatherers to sell them the nuts.

Clashes between these small businessmen and vegetable ivory gatherers offer insights into the defense of an autonomous way of life that gave meaning to legal freedom. In alliance with local politicians, rural people defended customary access to forested commons rather than resort to private legal appropriation. In this manner, the political economy of extraction that supported peasant gatherers and merchants survived. A similar story lies behind the determined continuation of mining practices sanctioned by customary regulations against the policies of powerful foreign companies. Whenever threatened, lowlanders strove to maintain access to the diverse environment that allowed them to survive. They were largely successful not only because they knew how to live in this place and had in some bureaucrats partners for their battles but also because, even when powerful, these businesses were interested in very specific resources, whose exploitation was determined by the technology of choice. Dredges only serve to mine gold in riverbeds. Local miners exploited rivers and creeks too small for dredges and areas removed from levees that heavy machines could not reach. As we shall see, even where the dredges worked, local people managed to assert their customary rights. Although the companies effectively restricted local people's access to gold and platinum within their areas of influence, they never eliminated the autonomy Afro-descendants gained after leaving slavery behind.

These struggles and their implications for the history of rainforests and black people have largely remained unrecognized. Because these conflicts did not involve peasants fighting over land with large landowners or land speculators and did not lead to land titling, as happened in other parts of the country, they escaped the radar of agrarian historians who have tried to explain the unequal land distribution of Latin America. Catherine LeGrand's classic book *Frontier Expansion and Peasant Protest in Colombia, 1850–1936* aptly explains how clashes over land in the republican era generated the land tenure pattern that still predominates in the country today. In the late nineteenth and early twentieth centuries, settlers migrated from the densely populated Andean highlands to the lowlands, frequently attracted by new economic opportunities opened by export markets. In the process, they encountered land speculators eager to benefit from the incorporation of new lands into the national economy. Despite the existence of laws aimed to protect settlers' rights, relatively few peasants managed to benefit from them. Entrepreneurs were much better prepared for legal maneuvering and paying the costs associated with land titling. Thus they amassed large properties; so much so that three-quarters of the land titled between 1827 and 1931 were given in portions larger than a thousand hectares.[1] Meanwhile, lowland forests remained public. However, as this chapter shows, this does not mean that the lowland environment and people do not have a history of their own—even if it is not one of extensive dispossession and deforestation.

THE FAILURE OF VEGETABLE IVORY MONOPOLIES

Between the 1870s and the 1910s, black gatherers in alliance with merchants and state officials successfully opposed attempts to monopolize access to vegetable ivory in Tumaco and the Pacific coast of Chocó. Vegetable ivory palms tend to form homogenous stands within coastal forests covering very large areas. Their seeds fall on the ground and have to be sought for in the muddy forest floors, which are sometimes subject to flooding. The hardship involves finding the seeds, even if they are fairly large, bending constantly to pick them up, and transporting them. No capital is needed for that, no fancy machine could facilitate collection; but someone had to do the job. As seen in chapter 3, merchants competed amongst themselves for labor by establishing personal relations with collectors and giving them credit. Those who wanted to undercut merchants faced the problem of finding another way to cheaply control labor, for expensive undertakings could easily undermine uncertain profits; they attempted to do so by controlling space. In the late nineteenth century, these monopolizers tried to claim ownership of vegetable ivory stands through land titles. Requesting forest concessions became an alternative strategy after 1907, when the government regulated the use of natural resources in public forests. Opposition centered on the defense of "free access" to vegetable ivory, which implied keeping the region's forests in the public domain and did not envision obtaining any specific rights for black rural dwellers over the lands they cultivated or the forests they used. However, it did guarantee that business could proceed as usual.

Struggles over vegetable ivory first appear in the historical records in 1878, when José María Reinel and Manuel Velasco requested title from the Ministry of Public Works for more than sixty hectares of land located along the Caunapí River, in the Tumaco area. These men expressed their intentions of developing a large-scale and much-needed agricultural project. Because everyone in Tumaco collected vegetable ivory, they argued that plantains, the basic lowland staple, were very expensive. However, they forgot to indicate that the desired property lay in a very prolific vegetable ivory producing area, and that five gatherers (probably along with their families) lived within the proposed limits of the title. Lack of similar agricultural initiatives and the overwhelming importance of the vegetable ivory trade in Tumaco suggest that the main objective of these men was to secure access to the nuts. Reinel and Velasco were eventually forced to accept the existence of five huts in the solicited area, but they also accused their owners of being nomads, of not cultivating the soils, of destroying the vegetable ivory stands, and of not allowing the solicitors to work and fence the lands. On those grounds they restated their petition.[2]

Merchants and gatherers came together and resorted to land legislation to stop this scheme. The names Reinel and Velasco, as well as the nature of their request, suggest they were locals. The latter tried his luck with commerce and probably was trying to undercut competitors, who found out about his ploy and teamed up with the gatherers to stop him. Solicitors complained that four men who bought vegetable ivory from the gatherers supported them in their claim of having the right to use the forests. Unnamed "Tumaco residents" requested an inquiry on the situation in Cajapí that led authorities in Cauca to recommend denying granting the title to those lands. The authorities based their recommendation on the national legislation that since 1874 protected peasants by establishing occupation and cultivation as main criteria for granting titles to land.[3] And they did so after the "Tumaco residents" made it clear—because they knew the spirit of the law, I assume—that the area was inhabited. The Ministry of Treasury followed the advice from Cauca and rejected the petition.[4] The alliance between merchants and gatherers avoided the privatization of the resource over which the former derived their profits and position, and the latter part of their autonomy.

A few years later, in the neighboring Cajapí River area, a larger conflict erupted when Nicolás Arias and Gervasio Vallecilla tried to appropriate five thousand hectares of terrain rich in vegetable ivory that supported numerous gatherers. They claimed that, in 1804, the colonial state had granted this property to two individuals and that they had later purchased it from the heirs. Since a market in untitled land existed all around the country, the issue for the alleged owners did not concern validating the purchase but rather demonstrating that the terrain in question had effectively been severed from the public domain by relevant authorities. To prove this issue, Arias and Vallecilla provided a dubious copy of a copy of the original title. In 1884, authorities in Barbacoas refrained from accepting such evidence. However, four years later, based on that same document, the judge from the small town of Bocagrande granted these men possession of the property. With such endorsement, Arias and Vallecilla proceeded to accuse gatherers of stealing their nuts and, with the support of the mayor, confiscated some of the nuts. In this and other ways they disrupted the local vegetable ivory trade. For this reason, twenty-seven illiterate gatherers undertook a daylong journey to Tumaco, where they found help with writing a lengthy and complex petition to the Treasury Department requesting that the area be declared public so they could continue "practicing [their] trade." They were backed by the municipal ombudsman, who additionally accused the mayor of having vested interests because his wife sold part of the property to the controversial owners in 1875.[5] The Treasury Department demanded to see the title, but it seems the title was never produced or, if it was, did not convince officials that it was legitimate.[6] In 1897, another group of gatherers facing a similar problem referred to the actions of the Treasury Department as having "stopped the abuse."[7]

Gatherers and their allies managed to guarantee the "free exploitation" of vegetable ivory by questioning the validity of the title and requesting that the area remain in the public domain. Their most outspoken supporter, the municipal ombudsman, argued that valuable forest resources should not be privatized and humble people should not be deprived of their means of subsistence. He informed national authorities that the area had about one million vegetable ivory palms and stressed that they "have always been freely exploited by poor families and from them many poor families have earned their livelihood."[8] Other influential people, merchants I presume, must have helped the men who traveled to Tumaco to compose the letter they sent to the nation's capital. In that letter, the gatherers and their collaborators stated that the "immense vegetable ivory grove had *always been part of the commons*," and they requested that the area remain public land.[9] Nobody suggested that agricultural plots, much less the forests, be titled to rural dwellers. The petitions argued that their well-being depended on the consuetudinary right to collect vegetable ivory, without mentioning that merchants' prosperity was also at stake.

Attempts to gain exclusive rights over vegetable ivory by claiming land persisted around Tumaco in the 1890s, and also happened in the lower Atrato in the early twentieth century.[10] The most egregious case in this latter region dealt once again with the validation of old titles. In 1896 and 1897, Próspero and Hortensio Ferrer, members of a leading merchant family in Quibdó, bought the entire Murindó River basin from the heirs of Plácida Colón, who based her rights to the land on some declarations, registered in Quibdó's notary in 1848, stating that her late husband was the owner of the basin.[11] The Ferrers placed an overseer in Murindó in charge of buying vegetable ivory. Rather than a manager of a rural property, this man should be regarded as a commercial agent. The Ferrers had sought to use land rights as a strategy to outcompete merchants from coastal Turbo, who purchased vegetable ivory for exporters in Cartagena. However, competition must not have been too intense because this was not a very productive area. Yet in 1922, the "overseer," Lisímaco Andrade, obtained a concession contract for the exploitation of forest resources in the Murindó basin, which provided a more solid legal basis for control over the basin's commercial resources. Both the Ferrer brothers' claim and Andrade's contract were opposed by local and regional officials. The dispute apparently ended in 1925 with Andrade's sudden death.[12]

Andrade's stratagem of requesting a concession contract from the government followed regulations on access to forest resources established during the administration of Rafael Reyes (1905–1909). This president took charge of a poor and unruly country shortly after the end of the last nineteenth-century civil war (the War of a Thousand Days, 1899–1902). Following the example of Porfirio Díaz in Mexico, Reyes strove to achieve material progress for Colombia by encouraging railroad construction and foreign investment. In order to pass his reforms, he closed congress and in 1905 convoked a national assembly, which extended his powers. His government prohibited the free exploitation of resources in "national forests," explicitly including those forests containing vegetable ivory, and determined that these terrains could not be privatized.[13] This legislation followed previous attempts at separating the regimes of forest and land tenures.[14] After independence, public lands constituted a large portion of the Colombian territory and one of the few assets of the impoverished state. As a consequence, the state attempted to use land legislation and distribution as a means to contribute to its meager finances (as well as to foster the "progress" of the nation). As the trade in cinchona bark (*quina*) picked up after midcentury, and then boomed in the late 1870s and early 1880s, officials realized that part of the public wealth lay in the forests that covered public lands. Such recognition gained force with the subsequent rubber boom. Therefore extractive economies prompted the establishment of rules meant to guarantee that the nation would retain some of the profits derived from them. Disparate logic inspired land and forest legislation. In places where agriculture seemed promising, land was privatized for owners to securely develop it by clearing the forests and planting the soils. Conversely, where forest extraction proved more profitable, the state retained ownership and granted concessions in exchange for a percentage of the value of the resources extracted.

The national government did not grant concessions in the forests around Tumaco because it had ceded the rights to their use to the municipality. Tumaco's city council maintained open access to the forests and charged a tax on exports that amounted to a collection fee. As we will see in chapter 6, this money proved crucial for the development of the port. Yet soon after the new legislation was passed, rumors spread about the risk of privatizing forest rights. Inhabitants in the principal collection areas sent letters to the Ministry of Public Works demanding that no concessions be given and their rights be protected.[15] Even Vicente Micolta, a prominent citizen, wrote to the ministry saying that it would be harmful to public finances and for the tranquility of the region if the lower classes were deprived of their right to collect vegetable ivory.[16] However, nothing much happened, even after several well-known men from Tumaco formed a commercial company to request concessions to exploit the vegetable ivory stands.[17]

On the coast of Chocó, the national government granted the first and last concession in the Pacific lowlands proper. In 1910, General Tomás Quintero became concessionaire of the Valle River basin and lowered vegetable ivory prices. In response, many settlers moved to Panama, where they normally sold the nuts. The coast was sparsely populated: about one thousand inhabitants lived in the Valle River basin and along the coast all the way to the border with Panama.[18] Thus it is plausible that a local bureaucrat did not exaggerate when he said that 75 percent of the basin's inhabitants (some fifty families), had left the area.[19] Those who stayed argued that as settlers of public lands, they had the right to continue making a living through vegetable ivory nut collection, and they used the threat to leave as their main leverage. In a letter addressed to the president, they likened their situation to slavery and, using nationalist language spurred by the loss of Panama, said that it was painful for them "to emigrate to the rebel department."[20] Local and regional authorities sided with the settlers by accusing Quintero of abusing the gatherers and asking the national government to rescind the contract. An ex-governor of the short-lived department of Quibdó, the intendant, the local mayor, the special commissioner to Juradó, and even a special commission sent by the Ministry of War to explore the border with Panama all expressed concern over the abandonment of the area and recommended that free access to the forests of the Valle River be reinstated.[21] Complaints were ultimately heard; in 1912 the commissioner to Juradó wrote: "Fortunately, the present government, in an act of justice and reparation, dashed to the ground the ominous contract, giving back to their true owners what nature has given them."[22] In 1913, he was happy to inform that many of those who left had returned.[23]

Gatherers strove to keep access to vegetable ivory groves within the terms they were used to, not to gain explicit recognition of their rights, largely because the existing legislation had no provision to protect the collective use of extractive resources. Gatherers who participated in these struggles combined tending small plots and gardens with collecting forest products. Habitation areas and crops were still considered for private use, while collection areas had common but regulated access. Only members of the neighboring communities could partake in the so-called free access provision. Furthermore, labor confers right over specific resources. For instance, clearing the way to haul logs gives those involved the right to trees in a given area, but it does not grant them ownership of the place and all its resources.[24] Similarly, in the Arias and Vallecilla case, gatherers indicated that their rights to gather vegetable ivory were derived from having plots nearby and from clearing the vegetation that obstructed canoe navigation in the streams leading to the groves. Their foes knew these rules well, so they cultivated a small plot and claimed that they "cleaned" the waterways.[25] However, neither the land legislation that intended to protect settlers nor the forest legislation recognized the right to the collective use of forest resources. On the contrary, republican elites strove to eliminate all forms of collective property, represented in commons (*terrenos ejidales*), indigenous *resguardos*, and Church lands.[26] Therefore the best strategy for gatherers interested in maintaining access to vegetable ivory, as well as the benefits derived from patron-client relations, was to strive to keep the groves in the public domain and to oppose concessions.

However, the numerous concessions granted in the Gulf of Urabá were apparently not met with much resistance. As explained in chapter 3, this area, located in the Caribbean, differed in this and other ways from lowland patterns, and thus could be thought of as a transition zone. Its settlers came mostly from the plains to the east rather than the lowland mining areas, and it depended heavily on Cartagena. An initial concession granted in 1907 over both sides of the Gulf of Urabá did prompt protests from settlers. They stressed that the forests should not be given away to private interests because they were settled and argued, strategically, that they would be forced to return to Bolívar if the concession was granted, thus leaving the border with recently seceded Panama deserted.[27] Merchants from Cartagena, who bought the vegetable ivory and financed the gatherers, also objected to the contract, suggesting that this concession posed a threat to the way business was conducted.[28] Still an avalanche of concessions followed in the ensuing two decades. In the eastern and richer side of the gulf, almost thirty concessions were established over about four thousand hectares.[29] Little opposition erupted apparently because some of the most powerful local vegetable ivory merchants received concessions, while most grantees never used theirs.[30] Therefore it seems that in Urabá, effective concessions largely legitimized the state of affairs.[31]

This history of disputes over access to vegetable ivory shows how conflict in the lowlands erupted over forest resources—not over land—and demonstrates the resilience of the exchange between gatherers and merchants that guaranteed blacks' autonomous lifestyles and the continuous flow of nature's marketable products out of the jungle. Vegetable ivory only grew in a few areas within the lowlands, mostly along the coasts. Other areas further inland had a much more valuable resource—gold—but the mining economy had been sluggish for decades. Expectations about a technological revolution that would reinvigorate gold extraction generated a speculation frenzy in the late nineteenth and early twentieth centuries. The issue here, again, centered on access to natural resources different from land—not forests but the subsoil. The local elite and a few outsiders created several mining companies and requested mining titles, but few investors seemed willing to engage in costly and systematic prospecting and mine development. For this reason, the struggles over access to precious metals did not generate as much conflict as what might have been expected. Yet in two places in the lowlands, foreign companies did bring new technologies and created enclave economies. Grave conflicts erupted as these companies imposed their power locally, but even in these places lowlanders did not completely lose the autonomy achieved in the transition from slavery to freedom.

GREAT EXPECTATIONS

When Agustín Codazzi visited Barbacoas in 1853, he found the place impoverished but its elite hopeful for happier days: "Barbacoas' sole source of wealth is its abundant gold; if it is not exploited . . . this city will disappear. Its inhabitants console themselves with the hope for a better future if they can make foreigners come to work their mines."[32] Since the mid-nineteenth century, mine owners throughout the Pacific lowlands remained convinced that only foreign investment in mining could revive the depressed regional economy. They depended on descendants of slaves to extract gold with colonial techniques and thus achieve modest earnings, while they wanted to strike it big. This desire became entrenched with the development of new placer mining technologies and the world boom in gold production during the 1850s and 1860s.[33] Hydraulic mining emerged during the Gold Rush in California and was perfected in the 1850s and 1860s; it consists of using a jet of water at high pressure to excavate rich banks. Dredges, devised and used for the first time in New Zealand in the 1860s, operate quite differently: these are boats with machines equipped with scooping or suction devices to dig material from the river beds and banks. Mine owners agreed that only foreigners had the capital and expertise necessary to import and operate such equipment. A few foreigners did come, attracted by mining prospects, but most of them contributed little or nothing to the great transformation that the lowland elite was hoping for.

Rumors and a few laudatory publications convinced some adventurers to try their luck in the lowlands. An 1883 report by mining engineer Robert B. White, for instance, greatly exaggerated the productivity of some lowland mines.[34] Success stories, though scarce and probably embellished, also fueled adventurers' fancies. In the 1850s, according to one such account, a California miner "took some $50,000 by working four years in the Andagueda with a pump."[35] Encouraged by these tales, a few fortune hunters arrived without capital, mining experience, or knowledge of the region, thinking they could easily make themselves rich.[36] People in Barbacoas recounted that "[i]n 1866 there was a big immigration of miners from California . . . , but they had to go back because they did not bring resources. They thought they had arrived to an Eden where they would only need to bend down and gather gold."[37] By that time, miners had been working the rich alluvial gravels for well over a century. The shallow placers, equivalent to those that sustained the very first years of the California Gold Rush, had disappeared. The issue in the lowlands was how to profitably mine the ancient placers buried beneath more recent deposits. An 1899 article in a U.S. mining journal explained why so many miners blatantly failed in this land of plenty: "The new-comers to the Choco . . . are . . . mostly, entirely ignorant and inexperienced in mining of any kind. They are apparently imbued with the idea that the inhabitants of the locality are not rich solely because they do not know that gold is yellow. The early Spaniards having cleaned out all the easy work in the rich creeks and gulches, and there being no established mines where they can gain experience while making a living, they are soon reduced to a sad plight."[38]

Others did try, albeit without luck, to change the history of mining in the lowlands by introducing new technology. Benjamin S. Pray and his associates provide the best example.[39] A businessman from Boston, Pray promoted the exploitation of mines in the upper Atrato in the 1880s by founding two mining companies—the Atrato Mining and Development Company and the Chocó Hydraulic and Mining Company—both equally starved for capital. The desperate circumstances of these developers even led them into a scheme that blurred the distinction between promising prospectors and river peddlers. In 1885, the promoters of one of these companies purchased a *barquetona* (large canoe), loaded it with goods, and sold them along the way up the Atrato to Quibdó.[40] Not surprisingly, raising capital was the companies' most urgent task. Pray and his associates tried to lure investors by boasting about the "great [gold rush] from all parts of the world" that they believed would flood the district. They also referred to the Andágueda River, where they had secured access to deposits, as "the richest river of Colombia and undoubtedly of the world."[41]

Technology was the companies' road to success, or so their promoters believed. The Atrato Mining and Development Company intended to use dredges, as suggested by the drawing that adorned its letterhead.[42] In 1883, the company raised enough money to import a dredge that sank before arriving to Quibdó because its wooden hull got worm-eaten.[43] Two years later, a second dredge reached its destiny but shut down soon after being put to work. Two more dredges imported to Chocó in the late 1890s also failed.[44] One of Pray's associates brought one of them, which only worked for a month on the Quito River.[45] At the time, dredging technology still needed major improvements. This method only flourished in the early twentieth century after the bucket elevator dredge, created in 1881 in New Zealand, was perfected in the United States.[46] Pray also bet on hydraulicking, a more reliable method at the time: in 1889, the Chocó Hydraulic and Mining Company, his second enterprise, worked at least one of its mines using this kind of equipment, but only for a month.[47] Although the company blamed a decrease in rainfall for the failure, according to another version the problem lay in "a hasty prospect" and limited capital.[48] Whatever the reason, the endeavor was a complete fiasco, as expressed by one of the company's organizers: "I feel so terribly depressed by the turn that affairs have taken that I am in no condition to write. I shall have to look for some other business, and begin life all over again."[49]

All the nineteenth-century enterprises were long shots rather than carefully planned undertakings. Besides Pray and his partners, other miners that used hydraulic equipment either failed or constituted rare and short-lived exceptions in a place where colonial methods prevailed.[50] Difficulties in collecting water, despite abundant rainfall, help explain the scant use of hydraulic equipment in the lowlands. Building tanks in sizeable catchment areas and high enough to guarantee good water pressure proved to be a difficult challenge to overcome.[51] However, other technical problems, lack of research, and poor investment contributed even more to the unsatisfactory results of the latest placer mining technologies.

Decades of failed attempts only confirmed the ideas that took shape in the 1850s: foreign investment and imported technology would sooner or later produce a breakthrough in mining. The persistence of such expectations led to an unprecedented wave of speculation. Joined by a few foreigners, many locals procured mining rights with the hope of acquiring rich deposits that they could later sell to foreign firms. In this manner, they appropriated on paper the totality of the mining areas, where most black people lived and which they recognized as theirs. Although speculators trod over the rights of rural dwellers, clashes with them were surprisingly rare, because most never attempted to develop the mines. Instead, they confronted one another over their alleged rights while they waited to make a deal with foreign investors.

Colombian laws facilitated the speculation frenzy by making mine acquisition cheap and easy, and by allowing mines to stay idle indefinitely. Antioquia's mining code, adopted nationally in 1887, served as the legal basis for acquiring mines.[52] Claimants had to make their requests to the mayor's office of the corresponding district, specifying the exact location and size of the mines. Each titled mine could not exceed 10 square kilometers. Until 1909, when the government forbade titling of navigable rivers, they also claimed riverbeds in portions of 5 kilometers.[53] When the entire lowlands formed part of the department of Cauca, all mayors mailed requests to the governor in Popayán. Later, requests from Chocó went to Quibdó (1907), requests from Valle to Cali (1910), and requests from Nariño to Pasto (1904). Regional authorities returned the documents to the mayor's office declaring possession. The mayor then posted the documents for three weeks outside his office. If someone opposed the title, the case had to be tried in court. If not, the mayor formally granted possession of the mine and the paperwork went again to the capital, where the regional authorities issued the title. This whole process, although straightforward, could take several months. A small initial fee and an equally small annual tax did not deter claimants who had no intention of exploiting the mines. If the owner failed to pay the annual tax, others could claim the mine; but if he paid, he could keep the mine even without working it. Furthermore, if the owner paid the equivalent of forty years' taxes at once, he did not need to make any further payments.[54]

The speculation boom began in Chocó, with U.S. citizens leading the way. Not surprisingly, Benjamin S. Pray and his friends took the first steps. Between 1888 and 1904, they obtained titles to forty-six mines in the districts of Lloró and Bagadó. Those titles included 45 km of the Andágueda River, 28 km of the Quito River, and 11 km of its tributary, the San Pablo River. Although by 1908 the energetic Pray had formed his third company, called the Boston Colombian and Dredging Company, no evidence exists that he succeeded in working any mine after the failed attempts referred to above. Other foreigners joined Pray and his associates by acquiring twenty-four more mines in the area in those same years.[55] Henry Granger beat them all by claiming more mines than anyone else in the entire lowlands. He settled in Colombia in 1894 when he was in his early twenties and acquired a farm called Yankolombia in the lower Atrato. He soon realized the promises of mining and between 1897 and 1899 obtained titles to no fewer than seventy-six mines located throughout Chocó's gold-bearing basins. For the next eight years he acted as American consular agent in Quibdó, although apparently did little work in such capacity, and instead promoted mining in Colombia.[56]

After the secession of Panama in 1903, the government feared further losses of national territory, particularly in areas close to the new border, and for that reason issued Law 19 of 1904 prohibiting the adjudication of mines and public lands in Chocó to foreigners. Granger had been given possession of additional mines without having yet received the titles. So he wrote to the government expressing that since the law was not retroactive, he should still be allowed to obtain his titles. When he received a negative response, he requested that the mines be transferred to his wife, Adelaida Cervera, a Cartagenera with whom he had five children.[57] The government gave her title over thirty-seven mines in 1906. As it turned out, Granger's worry about Law 19 was premature: in 1906, Legislative Decree 12 repealed it on grounds that it was "indispensable that foreigners bring their science and capital for the progress of the country."[58]

In the twentieth century, speculation spread to the rest of the lowlands and involved local residents, notably merchants and regional authorities. In this more intense phase of speculation, several companies, divided by law into twenty-four shares, were created to stake out mining claims. These companies allowed the sharing of expenses and thus made it cheaper to partake in the mining frenzy. By buying shares, speculators could acquire mining rights faster than by claiming mines, and thus have access to deposits that had already been titled. In this way, they diversified their mining portfolios more readily to increase their chances of making a deal with foreign investors.

In Chocó, speculation reached its highest point between 1909 and 1914, with 2,148 mines claimed. Although the intendancy (an independent political unit created in 1907) issued only 866 titles, this figure amounts to an average of 128 mines per year.[59] In 1911, a local newspaper alarmingly reported on the mining frenzy, noting that someone had claimed forty-eight mines all at once and that only a few mining companies were responsible for most of the claims.[60] Among the dozens of speculators, a few merchants from Quibdó figured prominently. Cicerón Angel, for instance, created three companies between 1909 and 1916. The Malluk brothers for their part concentrated for fifteen years on buying mines and created at least one company.[61] However, it seems that Félix Meluk, Quibdó's largest merchant, was also the town's main speculator: by 1910 he had claimed more than one hundred mines through his various mining companies, among them El Progreso Minero del Chocó and Sindicato Minero de Cartagena.[62] Colombians from Antioquia and Caldas in the adjacent Andes also joined the quest for Chocoano mines. Perhaps the event most revealing of their mining interests in Chocó is the appointment as intendants of two Antioqueños involved in mining: Justiniano Jaramillo (1910–12) and Rubén Santacoloma (1914–16).[63]

The most prominent speculators in the southern part of the lowlands were based in Buenaventura. However, most merchants with businesses there lived in Cali, had little interest on the coast, and did not participate in the frenzy. Jorge Mercado was a special case: he lived all his life in the port, operated a steam navigation service between Buenaventura and Tumaco, and had stores in Tumaco and Barbacoas. Between 1911 and 1914, Mercado acquired shares of forty-two mines in six of the rivers that drain into the Pacific Ocean south of Buenaventura. He also claimed fifty-one mines in Chocó.[64] A couple of foreigners based in Buenaventura joined Mercado. In 1910, Alexander G. Davidson, the one New Zealander who came to this port, claimed forty-seven mines in the Saija River and its tributaries, and the Frenchman Louis Chedé obtained titles to forty-six mines in the Dagua, Raposo, and Calima Rivers.[65] A few entrepreneurs who lived south of Buenaventura also acquired mining property in the area. In 1910, Theodore Vanin, a French citizen from Martinique, formed a company with two associates to work the eighteen mines it acquired in the Bubuey River.[66] Ramón Payán, from the small town of Guapi, obtained, in 1914 and 1915, titles to seventeen mines in the Guapi River and its tributaries.[67] Other speculators preceded him: in August 1911, the mayor of Guapi informed the Ministry of Public Works that 368 claims to mines had been registered since May.[68]

Barbacoas apparently experienced a milder version of the frenzy. Surviving records from 1896 to 1898 show that mines were being titled there but not to foreigners, and at least half of them to people who already possessed other mines and, for the most part, worked them. It seems then that rather than speculating, Barbacoanos were legalizing their properties.[69] Yet in 1915 a Tumaco newspaper mentioned that mining companies had claimed huge mineral areas in Barbacoas that encompassed the works of many honest and hardworking miners.[70] Barbacoas had for a long time deviated from certain regional patterns: in colonial times, most slave owners were local, and after independence and manumission at least some members of each family remained in town and monopolized much land through their never-abandoned colonial titles.[71] This situation might have limited the number of mines available for speculation.

Limited mining development reduced potential conflicts caused by the wave in titling. In 1920, the intendant of Chocó stated that more than half of the intendancy's territory had been titled to companies as mines, but that 90 percent of the mines were not being worked.[72] Yet speculation did produce disputes, notably among the speculators themselves. Conflicts between them first arose during the titling process. Only 37 percent of the mine claims filed in Chocó between 1907 and 1927 ended in the issuing of titles; legal objections by competing speculators often halted the process.[73] The issuing of a title did not prevent further problems, for mine boundaries were usually ill-defined and claims could overlap. Furthermore, mines usually lay idle, so it became possible to reclaim a mine under a different name.[74] Actual exploitation and the involvement of influential individuals complicated matters. In 1911, when El Progreso Minero del Chocó started work in a mine in Bagadó, another company accused it of invading its property. After the judiciary ruled in favor of El Progreso, the prefect and the intendant, who happened to be partners of the plaintiff company, tried to prevent a judge from granting possession of the mine to their competitors.[75] Although it was probably the best-known case, it was by no means the only one in which intendant Jaramillo took advantage of his position to promote his mining interests.[76]

In the restless competition for mining rights, speculators not only stepped on one another but also impinged on the rights of local dwellers. In 1906, Tadó's priest wrote to the president demanding protection for the local miners who were being dispossessed by speculators. He wrote that some mine claimants "were able to appropriate what has been a special inheritance of social groups . . . passed on from generation to generation." Miners resisted attempts to turn them into tenants, but "their efforts foundered by the almost connivance of authorities."[77] Officeholders did not always facilitate these abuses. The governor of Cauca, for example, backed Indians in the Saija River who requested protection against Davidson, the New Zealander.[78]

Bureaucrats also protested against speculators who used mining claims to acquire agricultural lands and thus extract rent from peasants who lacked titles to their lands, an abuse particularly common in the San Juan mining district. In 1911, for example, the procurator of Istmina wrote to Bogotá saying: "In this municipality some people are claiming mines not only in those places where there really are mines, but also in those used for agriculture and cattle raising, with the only purpose of claiming property over a parcel of land and in this simple manner exploit the miserable and ignorant farmers who work them."[79] Similar things happened in the Atrato: in a letter in which signatures occupied two entire pages, inhabitants of the Tutunendo River accused two men of claiming nonexistent mines.[80] Speculators also appropriated agricultural land by claiming mines in several nonmining areas across the lowlands. The mayor of Baudó, for instance, wrote to the intendant in 1911: "I have got full knowledge that many of the mine claimants in this district are claiming terrains . . . where common sense indicates that there cannot be any mineral wealth."[81] Mercado, the Buenaventura merchant, claimed ten mines north of Buenaventura in rivers that did not contain precious metals. Someone even tried—to the dismay of local journalists and the thirty-two settlers of the place—to gain ownership over the Isla-del-Gallo, a coastal settlement north of Tumaco.[82]

Although speculators were hoping to profit from selling mines to foreign investors, a few settled for lowly goals. They decided to cash in rent from local residents, most of whom possessed neither mining nor land titles. The latter could have protected them, for the mining code determined that mines located on private lands could only be titled to their owners or with their authorization. The disputes that ensued lasted a few years and were scant in relation to the amount of titles issued. Speculators probably did not have the muscle to extract rent or lacked interest in such petty business. Most of the mines titled were never exploited with advanced mining technology. Their owners must have stopped paying the annual tax, and the titles eventually expired. Consequently, disputes caused by mining speculation alone paled in comparison to those that arose when a technological revolution in mining effectively broke out.

MUDDY WATERS

A mining revolution involved more than just mastering modern technologies—it implied successfully navigating the muddy waters of overlapping property regimes. The colonial state had granted rights over large areas conceived of as mines, rights that included access to both land and the subsoil. The republican state upheld colonial rights and also set norms of its own. As seen above, in 1887 it adopted the mining code of Antioquia, according to which precious metal deposits belonged to the nation but could be titled in exchange for a fee.

Additionally, based on the same principle of public ownership, the state issued concessions to dredge riverbeds. All these regimes were defined by authorities far from the lowlands and consigned on paper. Meanwhile, local people developed their own rights regulating access to the region's resources. These coincided with the principle of grounding the right to land ownership on occupation defended by the national state. The existence of overlapping regimes opened various ways for speculators and investors to obtain mining rights, but made it difficult to secure them, for the state somehow upheld all of them without solving the underlying legal contradictions.

As hopes for a mining revolution intensified, a few mine owners with titles that were issued in colonial times tried selling their mines or finding capital to operate them. In the 1870s and 1880s, Pablo Reynel, a man from Barbacoas, apparently sold three mines to companies in San Francisco, New York, and Philadelphia, but nothing much came out of those deals.[83] A similar operation did lead to the first major breakthrough in lowland mining. The Mosquera and Arboleda families from Popayán, who had been the largest slave owners in the lowlands, never gave up hope of benefiting from their colonial possessions. On behalf of these families, in the 1890s, Reginald Paris persuaded a French engineer living in New York to visit the Micay River. The engineer returned dissatisfied by what he saw and Mr. Paris died soon after without closing a deal.[84] Just a few years later, the families had better luck. Perhaps its most precious property in the lowlands lay in the Timbiquí River; these families owned the entire basin except for the San José mine, which belonged to Liborio Lemos, a resident of Barbacoas. The Mosqueras and Arboledas never completely abandoned the Timbiquí mines, since they kept an administrator to collect rent.[85] His presence most likely contributed to giving legitimacy to their rights, a strategy that eventually paid off. In 1898, a German merchant acting on behalf of the family sold the Timbiquí River basin to a fellow countryman named Leon Vogt. The merchant was married to María Josefa Mosquera Arboleda, granddaughter of Tomás Cipriano de Mosquera, who was four times president in the 1840s and 1860s.[86]

In 1899, after obtaining the rights to the basin from his brother (who in turn obtained them from Vogt), an Englishman formed the Timbiquí Gold Mines Limited in London.[87] The New Timbiquí Gold Mines Ltd. (NTGM), a British company with French capital and French personnel, was formed in 1902 to replace its predecessor.[88] The company started operations in 1907 and after Liborio Lemos died, in 1912, it purchased the San José mine from his heirs, gaining ownership over the entire basin.[89] The company's possessions encompassed an estimated 250 km^2, inhabited by about two thousand people living in four towns and along the river levees.[90] Its technological innovation had nothing to do with dredging or hydraulic mining; it consisted of building—for the first time in this region—horizontal drifts or tunnels in high terraces, which miners from neighboring rivers have imitated ever since.[91] By 1913, NTGM had been "obtaining a steady, though not very large yield"—a better result than could be claimed by any previous foreign investor in lowland mining.[92] The company closed down around 1928 but reopened in 1936 for a second phase that lasted until the beginning of World War II.[93]

The technological revolution in mining developed timidly in Timbiquí after 1907 and arrived with full force a decade later in the Condoto River. Between 1916 and 1930, the Chocó Pacífico Mining Company dredged this river, and in so doing firmly established the world's leading placer technology in the region. Its success followed at least ten abortive attempts to work with dredges carried out over the preceding thirty years. Besides the five disasters in the Atrato recounted above, three experiments in Barbacoas also failed.[94] The fate of the machinery brought to dredge the Nulpe River, on the border with Ecuador, remains unknown, and a dredge launched by a French company in the Guajuí River in 1914 capsized. Even the rival British Gold and Platinum Company, which introduced a dredge to the Condoto, failed in 1927.[95] In stark contrast to this long history of frustration, the Chocó Pacífico worked, in 1930, not just one but three dredges.[96] This achievement resulted from more than mastering technical difficulties and overcoming the financial constraints that had previously led to disappointment. The existence of overlapping property rights created a situation that required much maneuvering. Confidential negotiations, years of litigation, and sheer bullying allowed dredging to succeed. Modern mining in the lowlands was therefore as much a political as it was a technical accomplishment.

The history of the infamous Chocó Pacífico starts with yet another form of mining speculation. As part of his broader program of economic development, President Rafael Reyes devised concessions not only for forest resource extraction but also for large-scale mining. Decree 34 of 1905, one among the 4,742 issued by Reyes during his five-year presidency, allowed the granting of concessions to exploit mineral and oil deposits in exchange for a percentage of the value of the resources extracted.[97] This decree targeted oil development and led to renowned and controversial oil concessions, but it also considered precious minerals, for the golden age of dredging was in full swing in California and New Zealand, and the successful launching of a dredge in Antioquia in 1887 suggested that this technology had great potential for Colombia.[98] Opposition to Reyes, in part a response to his quasi-dictatorial powers, drove him out of office in 1909. The new administration dismantled some of Reyes's reforms, among them the granting of mining concessions with Law 4 of 1909.

The Ministry of Public Works, created by President Reyes to deal with mining and other issues, granted concessions quickly and carelessly. In four years, it granted eight concessions to dredge ten lowland rivers to Colombians who invariably wanted to transfer these to foreigners, but most had not even contacted potential investors (see table 8).[99] So in most of these rivers work never even started. Although concessionaires risked losing their privileges if they failed to begin dredging within two years, the government did not enforce this clause. Thus, although they could request to extend that deadline, most concessionaires did not bother to do so. As early as 1908, a commission appointed by the government recommended that the threat of terminating concessions be used as an incentive to jump-start works.[100] It was not until 1933 that the Ministry of Industry, which in 1924 replaced the Ministry of Public Works, revised the files to declare the contracts expired.

The government either did not know or blatantly ignored the fact that some lowland riverbeds had been titled as private property. Therefore the granting of concessions led to a few serious disputes. As we have seen, in the late nineteenth century, the Cauca government titled some riverbeds in the Atrato basin to Benjamin S. Pray and others. The last of Pray's companies held those titles, among them several covering the Quito riverbed.[101] Yet in 1908, the Ministry of Public Works granted a concession to dredge this river to a Colombian lawyer, who immediately transferred it to the Cértegui Mines Dredging Company. Despite the protests of Pray's group, the company brought a dredge in 1909, which only worked an equivalent of thirty days of eight hours between August and December 1912 before a freshet destroyed it. After the failure, both companies continued for many years to assert their rights over the Quito River but failed to restart operations.

High platinum prices greatly contributed to the bitterness of the struggles over the Condoto River, where the gravel had particularly high concentrations of this metal (three-to-one to gold). Miners in Chocó identified *platina* early on and initially considered it an "unripe" form of gold, an undesirable intruder that debased the valuable precious metal. Although they threw away considerable amounts, they also sold it surreptitiously intermixed with gold dust. The unusually hard platina attracted scientists' attention and experiments paid out in 1786 when a French

TABLE 8 Riverbed dredging concessions, Pacific lowlands, 1906–13

RIVER	YEAR	CONCESSIONAIRE	EXTENSIONS	TRANSFERS	EXPIRED
Andágueda	1907	Justiniano Jaramillo and Antonio Nuñez	1910, 1912		1933
Quito and tributaries	1908	Antonio Olano		1908: The Cértegui Mines Dredging Co.	1933
				1919: Quito River and Dredging Co.	
San Juan	1906	Juan Jacobo Restrepo		1907: Francisco Restrepo Hermanos	1926
				1913: Anglo Colombian Development Co.	
Iró	1908	Leopoldo Cajiao	1910, 1912	1908: Compañía Minera del río Iró	1933
				1914: Anglo Colombian Development Co.	
Condoto	1907	Cicerón Castillo		1912: Anglo Colombian Development Co.	1933
Dagua and Micay	1906	César Sánchez			
Naya	1909	Universidad del Cauca			
Patía and Telembí	1906				
Munguidó	1913*	Guillermo O. Hurtado			

Table based on data from AGN, *Ministerio de Minas*, t. 9, ff. 1–62, 195–267; t. 10, t. 12; *Baldíos*, t. 25, f. 529; t. 29, ff. 623, 672; Ministerio de Industrias, "Memorandum sobre la propiedad minera en la intendencia nacional del Chocó," in *Boletín de Minas y Petróleos* t. 10, n. 55–60, Bogotá (julio-diciembre, 1933).

* This contract was not approved by Congress because granting concessions was illegal since 1909.

chemist working in Spain was able to purify platinum from the platina mixture, rendering it workable. From then on the king declared this rare metal—only known to come from New Granada—as his exclusive property and purchased it at very low prices to hand it out in its purified form as gifts. In the meantime, scientists created uses that spurred some demand and a minor contraband trade emerged.[102] This metal acquired more importance in the 1820s with the discovery of platinum in the Ural Mountains, leading Russia to become the world's main and practically exclusive producer, consuming much of its own supply for coinage. In the 1860s, the chemical, electrical, and dental manufacturing industries found new uses for this highly malleable metal, which can resist oxidation and corrosion caused by high temperatures and chemical elements. Platinum also conducts electricity and is a powerful catalyzing agent. Increased demand led to the steady growth of Russian production, particularly between the mid-1870s and the end of the century. The development of new processing techniques further augmented its applications, most noticeably for jewelry. All these developments drove up the price of platinum, which in 1905 surpassed that of gold. At that point Russia was still practically the only source of platinum. Colombia exported a negligible quantity equivalent to 3.2 percent of Russia's exports.[103]

When the government granted the rights to dredge the Condoto riverbed to General José Cicerón Castillo in 1907, the price of platinum was high and increasing.[104] The promising prospects of platinum extraction must have prompted the interest in this particular river of the Anglo Colombian Development Company (ACDC), a subsidiary of the renowned Consolidated Gold Fields of South Africa Ltd.[105] Founded by Cecil Rhodes in 1887 to mine gold in the Transvaal, this British company had ample experience with placer mining. In 1912, Castillo transferred the concession to the ACDC, which carried out for two full years the most thorough prospecting job ever done in the lowlands. To gather accurate information on the mineral content of the Condoto River basin, the ACDC built shafts that intersected the river every 1,200 feet. As it proceeded with its research, the ACDC purchased considerable mining rights and land in the area. It also obtained, through transfer from the original grantee, the concessions to dredge parts of the San Juan and the Iró Rivers. The ACDC maintained a strong local presence through a staff of ten to thirty foreigners and a group of 150 to 300 workers. It also imported a small steamer that carried cargo along the San Juan River and built two camps along the Condoto River, which had a general store and the only hospital in the entire San Juan River basin. By 1914, the ACDC planned on moving both camps to the river mouth and setting up a machine shop, a lumber mill, and employees' quarters. It even planned on building a hydroelectric plant nearby. Most importantly, it ordered a dredge to start mining.[106]

All that expertise, planning, and investment did not guarantee the success of dredging because the company did not have secure property rights over the riverbed. In the late 1890s, Henry Granger claimed, among dozens of mines, the last 10 km of the Condoto riverbed. Registered as René and Lincoln, these mines comprised two-thirds of the portion of the Condoto River that could be dredged. When the ACDC brought a dredge in 1915, Granger sued the company. He demanded formal possession of the René mine, which the ACDC had begun exploiting. Even though the company knew about Granger's titles, it did not consider him a serious threat. After all, eager to attract foreign investment, the central state stood behind the concession. However, just as the state failed to clearly define guidelines for resource access, it proved unable to fulfill its role as mediator when the confusion led to open conflict. In this manner, it effectively ceded control over the most important platinum deposits of the country. While the Ministry of Public Works issued a resolution denying the validity of Granger's rights over the René mine in September 1913, it had to retract the resolution when government lawyers pointed out that such an action lay outside the ministry's jurisdiction. It then issued a second resolution declaring that it would protect the ACDC's rights as grantee, but would also respect the rights acquired previously by third parties. Thus the ministry tacitly acknowledged the existence of two overlapping property regimes that came into conflict. By recognizing both the rights of the concession grantee and the titleholder, the government left the matter in the hands of the courts. This reluctance to end the legal chaos led two foreign companies to decide the fate of the nation's richest platinum riverbed at a time when prices for this metal soared.

The competing claimants resolved the problem of conflicting property rights over the Condoto riverbed by creating the Chocó Pacífico Mining Company. After the ruling in favor of Granger, the ACDC had to suspend dredging. Prompted by his success, Granger sued again. This time he accused the ACDC of operating a clandestine dredge and asked for a large sum of money to compensate for damages. The company risked losing its dredge and its other investments and having to pay for reparations. To make matters worse, Granger secured the backing from the General Development Company (GDC) of New York, whose principal shareholder was Adolph Lewisohn, a powerful entrepreneur of German origin with extensive investments in mining.[107] Cornered, the

ACDC accepted a second offer of negotiation with Granger and the GDC. Negotiations led to the creation of the Chocó Pacífico, an entity that operated in the name of the two companies behind it. The Chocó Pacífico was registered in the Notary of Istmina in July 1916.[108] In October, rumors that the parties involved had met to work out an agreement reached the Ministry of Public Works. The news came as a blessing. If the parties solved the problem by themselves, the government would not have to get involved. So the ministry decided to wait—and it waited forever. The companies never formally informed the Colombian government about their negotiations. Because neither the government files nor the notarial deed provide any details on the agreement, its exact terms remain unclear.

The creation of the Chocó Pacífico paved the way for dredging to begin, but problems related to mine ownership persisted. The new company owned the last 10 km of the riverbed and also had the concession rights to dredge the entire river. For two years it worked within those 10 km unchallenged, but new conflicts arose in 1918, when it began dredging the portion of the riverbed that it did not own.[109] José A. Mayolo and the heirs of his former partner claimed ownership over this 5 km stretch, known as El Salto mine.[110] In order to exploit the entire Condoto River and guarantee the long-term survival of its dredging works, the Chocó Pacífico had to engage in endless litigation in Istmina, Cali, and Bogotá. After eight years of legal battles, the Chocó Pacífico secured the last of the three portions of the riverbed that could be dredged. It then focused on the last clash over this riverbed. In 1925, Antonio Asprilla, a distinguished man from Istmina, obtained a mining title over the four-hectare Bazán Island, which was barely separated from the river levee within the part of the riverbed known as Lincoln mine.[111] Asprilla, as Mayolo before him, made arrangements with the British Platinum and Gold Corporation to mine his property. However, by 1926 the Chocó Pacífico had already dredged half of the island, which was eroding at a rapid pace. The few clues available in the archives suggest that the Chocó Pacífico's strategy for ending the dispute by destroying the island proved successful.

Between 1916 and 1930, when platinum prices reached their highest levels, the Chocó Pacífico dredged the richest platinum riverbed in Colombia (see graph 7). Prices for this precious metal skyrocketed because of disruptions brought about by the First World War and the Russian Revolution. Russian production decreased by 84 percent between 1914 and 1918. Platinum prices rose and remained exceptionally high between 1916 and 1929. During most of that period (1916–24), Colombia was the main world producer (see graph 8).

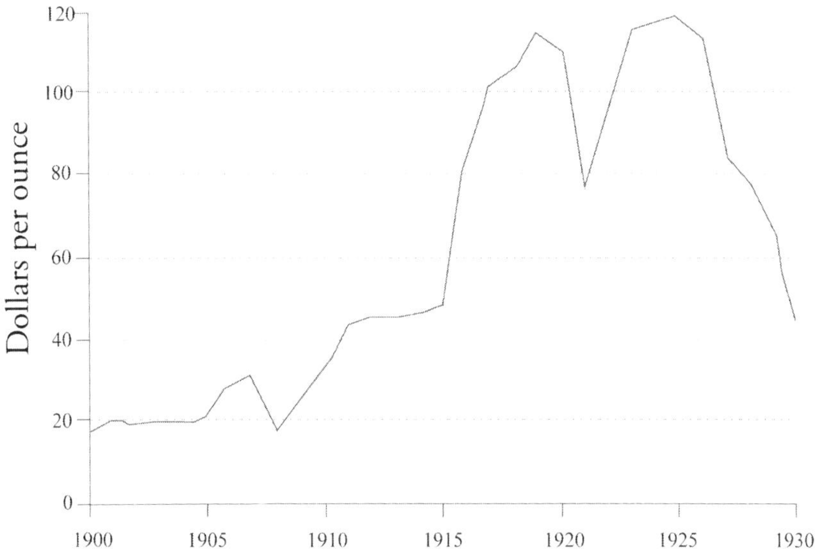

GRAPH 7 Platinum prices, 1900–30. Graph based on data from Roberto Wokittel, "Apuntes sobre el platino," *Minería* 28 (1934): 1876–78.

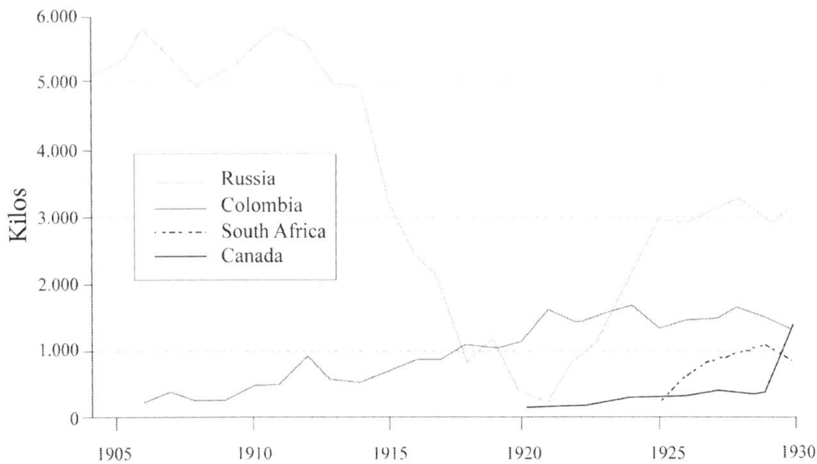

GRAPH 8 World platinum production, 1906–30. Graph based on data from Roberto Wokittel, "Apuntes sobre el platino," *Minería* 28 (1934): 1876–78.

Colombian exports, which came almost exclusively from Chocó, rose steadily from 211 kilos in 1906 to 1,586 kilos in 1921 and remained at an average of 1,460 kilos until 1930. Prices began to drop in 1925 mainly due to the recovery of Russian production and the discovery of substitutes for platinum. By 1930 they reached pre-boom levels, and by 1934 the price of platinum fell below that of gold.[112] The drop in platinum prices did not deter the Chocó Pacífico. After completing works in the Condoto River, it continued to exploit the upper San Juan area for more than forty years and started dredging in Barbacoas through a subsidiary, the Compañía Minera de Nariño—but that is another story. The one recounted here ends with the conflicts that emerged from the establishment in the early twentieth century of the two most powerful players in a marginal rainforest region.

DISCONTENT IN REVOLUTION

The long-awaited technological revolution in mining finally occurred, but it did not bring the benefits imagined by the numerous men who had so avidly anticipated its arrival. They expected to make themselves rich either through speculation or by the general transformation of the economy set in motion by modernization. The New Timbiquí Gold Mines Ltd. and the Chocó Pacífico operated as powerful enclaves, generating little subsidiary activities. In a region with an impoverished local population and a very weak state, these companies excelled for their capacity to extract precious metals and affect local lives. Their attempts to monopolize gold and platinum were met with resistance from local people who defended their customary rights to mine. The violence and broad participation in the conflicts that erupted demonstrates the extent of the discontent generated by these concerns. Paradoxically, these fights also underscore the limits of these companies' power. In so doing, they show that Afro-descendants did not completely lose the autonomy achieved in the postemancipation years.

Despite being a much smaller concern, the New Timbiquí Gold Mines had something its peer in San Juan did not: a colonial title that granted it ownership of an entire basin. Such wide-ranging rights led it to consider the place an immense mining camp and its population as tenants, putting in jeopardy Timbiquireños' autonomy.[113] For making effective its alleged monopoly over gold, the NTGM sought to exercise control over both the mines and labor. It prohibited mining by natives, considering it an act of theft, and in a place where illiteracy was the norm, it forced heads of households to sign tenancy contracts. These documents obliged those living near the mines to work for the NTGM two weeks every month for the "usual daily wage." Other men had to provide the company with timber.[114] Local people responded by defending customary rights built over decades of occupation. Many refused to both sign the contracts and fulfill their work quotas. Exploiting the mines by themselves, even when paying rent, had been a long established right. Even slaves had been able to mine gold autonomously to purchase their freedom.

As an additional measure to control access to gold, the NTGM prohibited the purchase of this metal within the basin. Given the persistence of small mining, commerce seemed (as it did elsewhere in the lowlands) a key way to capture the profits of the extractive economy. The company had its own stores and its own money—tokens known as *cachaloas*. By paying its workers with its own currency, the company forced them to buy everything they needed from its own stores. The NTGM justified this measure on the grounds that it needed to provide a means of exchange given the scarcity of money. This arrangement echoed the indebted relations established between merchants and vegetable ivory gatherers in Tumaco discussed in chapter 3—except miners had little to gain, for the company did not act as a trustworthy *patrón*. The company also fiercely opposed efforts by local authorities to have the areas of the upriver settlements designated as public land. It argued that if local authorities could rule within the confines of the towns, they would allow people to trade gold freely.

Local inhabitants could not easily accept the rules set by eight Frenchmen who acted as owners of everything that surrounded the Timbiquí River between the Pacific Ocean and the Andes. The tension between the NTGM and local dwellers led to a confrontation that ultimately signaled the powerlessness of the state at the local level and the erratic interventions of regional and national institutions. In October 1909, Timbiquireños reacted against their mayor, who apparently sided with the company, leading him to take refuge in the NTGM's headquarters. When the company complained to the Colombian government, the Ministry of War and the state of Cauca sent a commissioner to mediate the dispute. His visit resulted in the signing of an agreement, in November 1909, between him and the directors of the company. This agreement sought to legitimize the company's demands and assure their enforcement with a police force paid in part by the NTGM itself. The agreement referred to local dwellers as tenants and established that they had to work a given number of days per month for the company. The NTGM ceded almost nothing, granting a few mining permits in places far removed from its own works. The beneficiaries of these permits had to sell their gold to the company and comply with a labor quota. Not surprisingly, the conflict persisted, for the agreement did not include local dwellers.

National and regional institutions went from completely backing the company by trying to keep local people in check, to upholding local people's rights to mine, to finally settling for an intermediate "solution." Enduring clashes must have prompted the state of Cauca, in 1914, to issue a resolution backing dwellers' rights to mine. However, the company appealed to the Ministry of Public Works, which responded that same year by issuing another resolution that settled the matter legally. It established that poor river dwellers only had the right to mine the beaches and riverbeds that the company did not occupy.[115] The resolution legalized the rights of locals to mine areas that could not be reached by the NTGM, given that it worked with drifts dug into high terraces. Small miners still had to negotiate with the company if they wanted to exploit their terrace mines. In those cases, just as what happened with mines in Barbacoas owned by the elite, local miners had to give half of their product to the company. They also risked losing access to the mine if the NTGM considered it productive enough to exploit itself.[116]

Lacking both legitimacy and repressive power (there is no available information about the police force after the agreement), the NTGM could not easily impose its will.[117] It never had a monopoly over the mines. Furthermore, it exerted complete control over neither commerce nor landed property in the basin. As a compromise with some of the most influential locals, the NTGM licensed a few merchants (three in 1911).[118] That was probably the case of Clímaco Martínez, a black man and the river's most important merchant, who had his main store in Santa Bárbara with branches in San José, Coteje, and Santa María. He even had a boat to carry merchandise from Buenaventura.[119] The existence of a parallel property regime further exemplifies the limits of the company's power. People in the basin bought and sold land (if not mines) and urban property, and they notarized all those transactions. In theory, such a market could not have existed because the entire basin's land belonged to the company.[120] Twenty years of foreign presence could not erase the ways by which Timbiquireños regulated what they were sure belonged to them.

Although condoteños faced similar problems, dredging was a different story. It implied a much larger investment and generated an unparalleled power display. The Chocó Pacífico, for instance, had a steamer, not to make profits by providing public transportation, as was the case of the very few steamers used in the lowlands at the time, but for the company's own needs—an unheard-of luxury in the area. Much more striking was the building of a hydroelectric plant to operate the dredges. The plant embodied modernity and its transformative power while blatantly exposing how the local state's capacities could not match those of the foreign company. In an area with virtually no public services, the Chocó Pacífico eventually generated electricity for the main towns in the upper San Juan basin. Andagoya, the company's headquarters, provides further evidence of the Chocó Pacífico's striking presence and ability to create radically new realities. Located in the heart of the mining area at the confluence of the Condoto and San Juan Rivers, it differed from all other settlements in the region. Shortly after its establishment, a journalist described it as follows:

> [In Andagoya] one finds the living quarters of the manager, superintendent, doctor, and employees and the offices, stores, and workshops of the company, as well as the restaurant, hospital, and some workers' dwellings. All located in comfortable buildings, cleaned with care, protected against mosquitos, supplied with water, ice, telephones, electricity, and all that civilized life, hygiene, and morals demand. The main buildings look like the structures that are made in England and the United States *for the tropics*, as they say there: serious aspect, simple lines, gray color with white moldings and cornices as sole decoration or amenity, and lots of air in the interior.[121]

With its distinct layout, architecture, and amenities, Andagoya looked and felt unique (see fig. 10). Most settlements in the region had a few long streets parallel to the river, with rows of houses adjacent to one another. In Andagoya, houses that stood separated from each other introduced a Caribbean architectural style to the Pacific coast. They only had one floor, in contrast to the two-story houses of the well-off in nearby towns, and were surrounded by spacious porches. Services such as electricity and the only hospital in the area contributed to making the Chocó Pacífico's headquarters an exceptional place. Andagoya's inhabitants also differed from those of other lowland settlements. Instead of extended families with slave ancestors, company employees, most of them foreigners, lived in town. Whites occupied the nicer houses, as in Quibdó and Istmina, but whites here spoke Spanish with an accent and considered Andagoya as a temporary home. They came to fulfill the company's specialized tasks and worked, among other occupations, as mechanics, electricians,

FIGURE 10 Andagoya, 1929.

mining technicians, and accountants. In 1920, twenty of the 266 employees on the Chocó Pacífico's payroll came from the United States, eight from England, and seven from other European and Latin American countries. They received the highest salaries, most likely in addition to benefits such as "Caribbean" housing. The largest group of foreigners, which received the lowest pay among the non-Colombian employees, consisted of forty-two Jamaicans, most likely black men also living in Andagoya.[122]

More than the comfortable and hygienic mining camp or the hydroelectric plant's quasi-magical powers, the dredges themselves best symbolized the Chocó Pacífico's power (see fig. 11). They stood along the main thoroughfare as constant reminders of the company's influence. Moreover, dredges created new labor relations and transformed the landscape at a rate never experienced before. The river levees provided the most common shared landscape in an area that is fairly flat and thus devoid of vistas, and where people travel by canoes. Their lush green vegetation mimicked the jungle, while crops and houses gave them a distinct rural character. However, for dredges to operate, all that needed to go. Workers cleared the way for the machines to do their business. Unlike small mining operations, most company workers were male and many came from other localities within the lowlands—the Atrato and some southern rivers such

FIGURE 11 Condoto, dredge no. 2. "Informe que rinde el señor alcalde del municipio de Condoto al señor alcalde provincial correspondiente al año 1932 y los meses de Enero a Abril de 1933, sobre la marcha de la administración pública en este Distrito." Source: Archivo General de la Nación, Colombia, Sección República, Fondo Ministerio de Gobierno Sección 1ª, Tomo 1050, Folio 398.

as the Timbiquí, Guapi, and Micay.[123] A few acted as foremen, instructing others to cut the vegetation; remove tree trunks, branches, and foliage to burn them when the weather allowed; and loosen the roots to ease the dredges' work.[124] Then the dredges excavated the levees and turned what was left into piles of gravel. Dredging also altered the river itself. Beaches emerged in new places, as did eddies and pools.[125] Local people, who knew their river, had to keep adapting to the new ways of the current as they went up and downstream in their canoes.

Many disputes arose from the destruction caused by the dredges and the cables used to secure them. Local inhabitants filed myriad of complaints to Condoto's mayor regarding loss of crops and houses and difficulties with canoe navigation. They also took advantage of visits by high officials to accuse the company of wrongdoing. Although bureaucrats recognized the negative effects of dredging, local authorities did not effectively mediate between the company and the plaintiffs. Sometimes the Chocó Pacífico paid compensation; however, plaintiffs argued that the company had a standard rate that did not necessarily account for the damages, a charge that the company denied. As in Timbiquí, the persistence of these problems led to the signing of an agreement between the company and a government commission in 1923. The company agreed to pay compensations for verifiable claims. It also committed itself to redress the damages caused to the riverbed and river levees, and to ease navigation by canoes.[126] However, the resource-starved local government was in no capacity to enforce the agreement, given the widespread nature of the problems and the power of the company.

The Chocó Pacífico's accumulation of extensive property rights in the Condoto and San Juan area affected local people's claims. This company managed the concessions to dredge the Condoto, Iró, and San Juan Rivers, as well as the titles to two mines in the Condoto riverbed, five in the Iró, and sixteen in the San Juan. The latter extended for 80 km from Negría to Tadó along the second largest river in Chocó. The company also owned extensive mining lands: three mines in the Tamaná River and 59 percent of Condoto's municipal area.[127] Some plaintiffs stood in a weak position since they had sold their plots to the company; the words of a local official signal their double-cause of distress, besides losing their land they were left discredited. "Who is right?" he asked, "The natives who sold their mining properties to foreigners or the foreigners who bought those properties?"[128] The company's concentration of mining rights and its sheer power of destruction generated much resentment and provoked resistance against it, to the point that at one critical moment the government took the most unusual decision for this region: to send in troops.

Violence and the temporary halting of dredging signaled the worst hour in the long-term tensions generated around La Lozana mine. The wide participation of local people in the skirmish against the company expressed the antagonism they felt toward the encroaching foreign power. In 1909, a company formed primarily by members of the prestigious Lozano family, who had ceded the area where the town of Condoto lies, claimed this strategically located mine (on both sides of the Condoto River, along several miles upstream from the river mouth, see map 8). The principal partner, Francisco Carrasco, a merchant and journalist from Istmina who held 11.5 percent of the shares, filed the claim. The intendancy granted the title in 1911.[129] The company formed in the midst of the speculation frenzy most likely to legitimize the consuetudinary rights of the Lozano family with the idea of profiting from the much-expected technological revolution. By 1912, the Anglo Colombian Development Company (ACDC) had acquired more than half of La Lozana's shares, and by 1920, the Chocó Pacífico owned 75 percent of them. Most partners sold their shares before dredging began and before the prices of platinum skyrocketed. When they realized what they had lost, many of them felt tricked, a feeling echoed in the stories

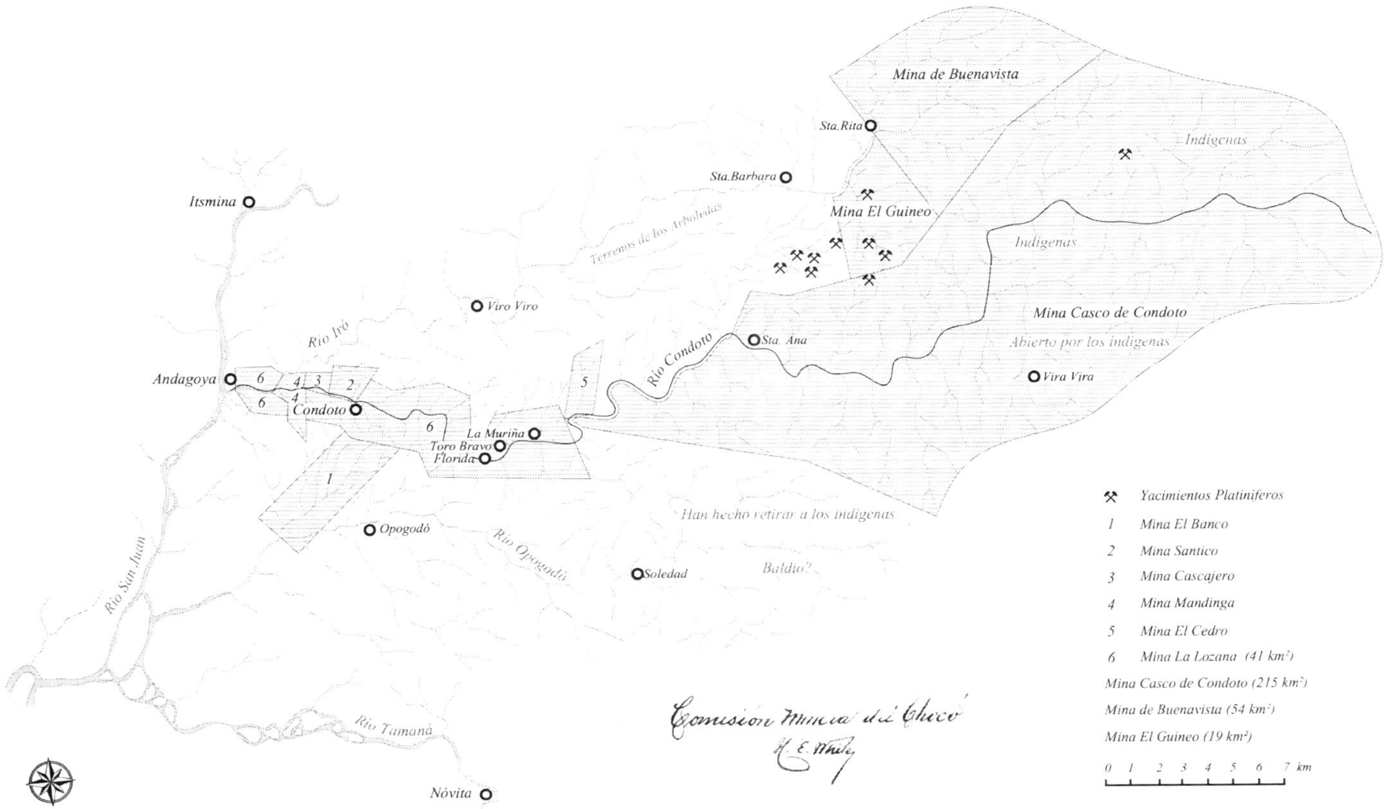

MAP 8 Condoto district. Map by Paola Luna, Cartography Lab, Universidad de los Andes, Bogotá. Based on a 1931 map by H. E. White, Comisión Minera del Chocó, Archivo General de la Nación.

that for decades circulated among locals. These recounted how the company used dubious methods to convince owners to sell their shares at bargain prices.[130]

Those who remained in possession of their shares also felt abused. As soon as the ACDC gained control of La Lozana's board, in 1912, it created new fees that clashed with partners' customary mining practices. It first decided to charge half a *castellano* (2.3 grams of gold) a month to every person who worked the mine. It stipulated that those partners who did not pay their dues would lose their shares and therefore their right to mine; but partners who did not follow the board's provisions continued to assert their rights by mining La Lozana. Whenever they did, the board requested the mayor to evict them, but torn between two ways of understanding mining rights he refrained from evicting co-owners from their property and sent the cases to the "expedient" judiciary. The board charged an additional fee to every partner in order to finance the preparations to exploit the mine with modern technology, although the ACDC was not ready to begin dredging works at the time.[131]

The hostility between the remaining initial shareholders and the board intensified after the creation of the Chocó Pacífico. This company worked in parts of La Lozana as early as 1919.[132] Major problems erupted in 1926 when the intendant overturned the mayor's order to suspend the dredge's works on account of the damages they were causing. Some of the shareholders protested, plainly exposing the rift between them and the company. The conflict spilled beyond these two parties, involving a large part of the local population who threatened to use force to stop the dredge. The situation worsened when the dispute ended in murder. Honorio Lozano shot an employee of the Chocó Pacífico who got in a fight with Carlos Lozano, a shareholder, killing them both. The deaths exacerbated the ill feelings against the company and its substantial power, generating a great commotion and prompting the government to send in troops. The company stopped all dredging, and for a while the Chocó Pacífico's foreign employees stayed away from the town of Condoto.[133] Under arrest, the murderer left town as a hero with a diatribe against the company and its abuses.

Although, in the end, the company finished mining La Lozana, its power had limits.[134] Dredging transformed the Condoto basin, but not always in ways the company anticipated or accepted. Local miners, primarily women, had traditionally dived to scrape the sands from the river bottoms, a practice known as *zambullidero*. Lowlanders considered riverbeds communal areas where everybody could work; exclusive rights over them were a late nineteenth-century development. But owners and concessionaires did not enforce those rights and only after

FIGURE 12 Dredge no. 1 and divers. Source: "Informe que rinde el señor alcalde del municipio de Condoto al señor alcalde provincial correspondiente al año 1932 y los meses de Enero a Abril de 1933, sobre la marcha de la administración pública en este Distrito." Source: Archivo General de la Nación, Colombia, Sección República, Fondo Ministerio de Gobierno Sección 1ª, Tomo 1050, Folio 401.

dredging succeeded did disputes arise. Because dredges dug deep, reaching the pay streak or concentrating mineral in one spot, divers tended to work next to them (see fig. 12). They were making use of their communal rights, whose limits they understood all too well. When the dredges exploited someone's mine on a riverbank, local dwellers restrained from diving for only the minerals of the riverbeds were communal. However, the company considered itself sole owner of those deposits; in its view, diving by the dredges was utter theft.

The Chocó Pacífico tried hard but could not stop this practice. The central government adamantly argued for small miners' rights, claiming that the subsistence of poor people rested upon them. Historical and practical reasons help explain the government's position. The Mining Code had been drafted in Antioquia, where small independent miners played an important role in making this province the country's major gold producer. For this reason, the law guaranteed their rights with a provision allowing mining with traditional methods (*derechos de mazamorreo*). Moreover, all concession contracts stipulated that the rights of small miners should be respected, and a 1912 resolution by the Ministry of Public Works reiterated these rights. At the local level, both bureaucrats and merchants defended small miners, since the local economy depended on their production. Irritated by the persistence of diving by the dredges, the Chocó Pacífico argued in 1927 that the resolution issued in 1914 for the Timbiquí River should also apply to their case. As mentioned above, this resolution limited small miners' rights to working the areas (riverbeds and levees) that the New Timbiquí Gold Mines Ltd. did not occupy. After some hesitation, the Ministry of Industry tried to reconcile both interests by issuing a resolution that limited the right of divers to areas outside the range of action of the dredges. This resolution, however, did little to stop the divers. The state had different interests at the local level and no real way of enforcing such regulations.[135]

The state's incapacity to mediate conflict in both the Condoto and the Timbiquí Rivers stemmed from more than its historical weakness in the region; it was also due to the lack of resources it derived from the extractive economy. Since the NTGM mined private property instead of a state concession, it did not pay royalties to the Colombian state. A similar situation occurred with the Chocó Pacífico, even though it dredged the platinum-rich Condoto basin as the prices for this metal soared. The national government attempted, a bit late, to collect the 10 percent of the value of the metals extracted that, according to the concession contract, corresponded to the state as administrator of public resources. In 1925, it appointed a platinum inspector to collect these royalties. The inspector arrived in Andagoya and soon found out what had been evident for almost ten years: the company had been dredging the René and Lincoln mines as private property and, therefore, had not paid a penny to the state. The company paid the 10 percent share regularly starting in April 1926, when it began dredging the El Salto mine, to which it lacked titles. The nation only received income from the boom, which ended in 1926, by charging a 5 percent export tax on platinum starting in 1919.[136]

Although for about fifteen years the economy of Chocó depended on platinum extraction, the region benefited little from the funneling of resources to the local and regional administrations or from the direct impact of the company. The regional government received even fewer resources from the boom than the national government. Only between 1921 and 1923 did the intendancy derive income directly from platinum production, in the form of a percentage of the export tax.[137] The boom increased the intendancy's meager revenue in indirect ways, mostly through a rise in the proceeds from the liquor tax and, to a lesser extent, from the property tax. Because the Chocó Pacífico operated as an enclave and imported most of its supplies, it had a relatively small effect on the local economy. Although purchases by the company and its employees channeled a little money into local hands, this demand did not generate subsidiary economic activities. The increased revenue received by both small miners and merchants during the platinum boom probably outstripped the direct benefits provided by the company.

When big capital reached the lowlands it stayed squarely within the extractive model that the Spanish colonizers started when they began mining gold. Investors still looked at the place as one in which nature had produced something valuable that they could take away to enrich themselves. The Spanish brought enslaved human beings, while Americans and Frenchmen introduced mining technology. Dredges and shafts, previously unknown in the region, allowed these foreigners to make use of the rights they had acquired by navigating the murky waters of Colombian mining law. They amassed colonial titles over soil and subsoil, republican mining titles, and even concessions to dredge rivers, and used them all. This strategy of investing capital in securing legal rights and importing technology created a new political economy of extraction that coexisted with the most pervasive one, described in chapters 2 and 3, which rested upon two social classes that developed after 1850: black peasants and white merchants. The new technologies allowed for the expansion of the mining frontier: dredges dug deeper in the riverbeds than any experienced diver ever could, while shafts penetrated the subsoil creating a novel underground geography. Because of their larger scale, they also caused greater environmental impact than traditional mining methods did. Dredges in particular completely altered the riverbed, changing water flow and thus navigation patterns. Black residents resented this rather brutal creation of an unfamiliar landscape, especially when the riverbanks—where they had crops and dwellings—became piles of boulders. Over the years, however, the rivers replenished the levees with sediments, the vegetation grew back, and people rebuilt their homes. Seen from the distance of time, it is the company's impact on the local society that stands out.

Although capital and the technological revolution it spurred greatly affected Afro-descendants' lives, it did not annihilate the autonomy that they associated with freedom. This autonomy rested on their access to the means of production. In the mining areas, mines were the most important productive assets, but forests, rivers, and small patches of cultivable land also contributed to people's subsistence. In the Atrato and most of the southern mining rivers, local people were able to maintain their productive practices because the technological revolution never arrived. Until 1930, dredges operated only in the upper San Juan, while shafts were restricted to the Timbiquí basin. By contrast, free miners, as slaves had before them, worked all the region's placers. Even in the areas where the companies established themselves, they forcefully developed alongside traditional mining and without ever eliminating the local trade in gold and platinum. In the San Juan, small miners continued to produce a very important share, about 50 percent, of the gold and platinum exported.[138]

In the places where companies established themselves, small mining persisted largely because the new technologies were not as versatile as traditional mining methods. Drifts worked only in high terraces while dredges functioned on riverbeds and levees. Moreover, companies could not simultaneously work all deposits suitable to exploitation with those methods. Therefore, local people still had many available deposits to continue working in the ways they knew well. Although in many cases the companies tried to forbid such works, they could not enforce their rules. Despite their tremendous local power, they had neither legitimate means nor sufficient state support to achieve those ends. Having access to the mines and forests, local people were not compelled to seek wages by working for the company. Some did, but as part of a broader subsistence strategy that involved large families. Lowlanders coming from other basins joined them. In 1911, the director of the NTGM undoubtedly exaggerated but still pointed to a new reality when he wrote that "[i]n our exploitations labor is abundant and not only do our tenants come to work more frequently than they are supposed to, but dwellers of the nearby rivers—Saija, Napi, Guafi—come in larger numbers each day. While two years ago we could only bring together from 15 to 20 men, we now have regularly about 150 to 200, and the total number of workers, men and women, varies around 300 and 400."[139] The platinum boom also generated a wave of immigration to the richest platinum territory, but here the existence of platinum attracted more people than did the salaries offered by the Chocó Pacífico. In 1923, during the height of the boom, a traveler observed that since the price of platinum was eleven times greater than that of gold, "[e]verybody . . . migrated from Nóvita, Sipí, Tamaná, and the lower San Juan to Opogodó and Condoto."[140] In those days the Church estimated the growing population of Condoto to one thousand inhabitants, a large number for lowland standards.[141] Although some of these people must have joined the company's workforce, independent work rather than wage labor remained the rule in the Pacific coast.

The access to the means of production that guaranteed lowlanders' autonomy lacked legal protection. Therefore, even if people's rights were recognized by consuetudinary regulations, their situation remained precarious. During these fundamental years the government began drafting legislation to regulate access to forest resources. However, forest peoples were far from being a central concern; the goal was to secure the state a share of the value of the exploitation of renewable resources. Forests with valuable products became *national*. This meant they could not be titled and that their exploitation needed special permits and fee payments. What started at this time went full fledge in 1959 with the declaration of seven national forest reserves (one of which comprised the entire Pacific lowlands). Mines also had their special legislation. Mining rights could and did eventually expire, rendering both subsoil and forests part of the public domain. No legal regime accommodated the particular use of the surrounding environment by rural lowlanders. Land titles did not take into account access to the forest and even depended on forest clearing. Furthermore, they were extremely hard to obtain for poor and illiterate peasants living far from administrative centers, or even impossible in the case of national forests. Peasants also had difficulties acquiring and keeping mining rights. In the absence of a tenure regime that worked for them, lowlanders remained squatters in public lands.

Black peasants' rights were not recognized in the constitution or in legal codes; instead, they were written in the landscape. Part II of this book now turns to the building of rural and urban landscapes and the ways in which white literate men interpreted them. Blacks appropriated most of the region, leaving their imprint wherever they went. They also helped to turn the profits of the trade in natural commodities into buildings and public works that made the ports of Tumaco and Quibdó into small cities. Yet the sharp racial division of labor of the lowland extractive economy, with its spatial underpinnings, facilitated commentators' coupling of the jungle with blacks and the urban environments with whites. Racial prejudice manifested itself spatially in the way literati underplayed blacks' management of the rainforest, erasing their accomplishments, and denied them a respectable place in urban settings. A historical view of both the lowland environment and the creation of a rainforest postemancipation society, in the decades between 1850 and 1930, would not be complete without examining the building of cultural landscapes and the ideological context in which blacks came to endow freedom with meaning.

PART II

RACIALIZED LANDSCAPES

5

BLACKNESS, FORESTS, AND NATION

THE FORMATION OF A postemancipation society in the rainforests of the Pacific coast of Colombia involved fully appropriating the region—that is, expanding beyond the mining areas and transforming the landscape. Colonial times had meant the death or relocation of many of the aboriginal inhabitants; the seasonal concentration of most of those who survived in Indian towns along the upper Atrato basin; the creation of mostly temporary camps for enslaved blacks; and later, the emergence of communities of free blacks near the gold mines. After the mid-nineteenth century, the diversification of the extractive economy, and its dependence on blacks' procurement of their own subsistence, contributed to the building of a distinct rainforest landscape. The scant black population increased and dispersed as it explored all environmental niches. Free blacks traversed the forests in search of rubber and vegetable ivory, which they exchanged for salt, gunpowder, and other basic goods. They also sought places that provided good timber, hunting and fishing grounds, and fertile soils, where they could produce much of their food, tools, and shelter. In the process, houses and crops appeared more readily along the river levees, not only in the upper parts where gold was found, but also in the middle sections favored for agriculture, and even in the lower parts where fishing in *ciénagas*, mangroves, and the sea provided alternative livelihoods. Along with the houses, crops multiplied, and so did canoes, all of which ultimately embodied black people's autonomy. As indigenous peoples abandoned the settlements that had been theirs in colonial times, blacks moved in; they also formed new towns around churches and schools. Others settled in the two most dynamic regional ports—Tumaco and Quibdó—and contributed to turn them into small cities.

Landscape building rested on the physical labor that allowed blacks to make a living and also on their freedom of movement. For ex-slaves and descendants of slaves everywhere, moving about without restrictions was a fundamental aspect of living in freedom: not just being able to go to places without consent from owners or overseers but also choosing where to live. In Cuba, for instance, some ex-slaves moved away from the plantations and into town or migrated to Oriente, which "offered improvement for the impoverished, opportunity for the oppressed . . . land to the landless and livelihood to the unemployed."[1] Like free blacks in Cuba, so too did many other landless peasants migrate throughout Latin America. This region had low population densities and many areas where native ecosystems thrived, notably forests. Building nation states in the nineteenth and twentieth centuries involved settling and nationalizing frontiers, often with atrocious consequences for indigenous populations. In Colombia, scholars have recognized the importance of the movement of highland peasants into lowland areas.[2] Environmental historians have introduced a novel approach by examining the environmental consequences of migrations, particularly the destruction of the Atlantic forest in the Brazilian south.[3] The significance of free black migrations in the lowlands does not reside in its environmental costs but rather on the way in which blacks contributed to the republican ideal of freedom and to build the largest region in the Americas where black people predominate.[4]

This significance had no place in the worldview of commentators who at the time appropriated the lowlands by writing about it. As happened in other rainforest areas, most of the men who wrote about this place underplayed the human management and transformation of the environment, emphasizing the wild presence of nature rather than the dear civilizing powers of culture. Furthermore, they equated black rural dwellers with an environment deemed unhealthy but prolific, suited for savage beings and conductive to laziness. The racial ideology and environmental determinism that guided learned thinking in those days came together to produce and legitimize this reading of the landscape and its people, which assumed that blacks were misusing the freedom that enlightened elites had generously granted to them. Because racial prejudice colored the interpretation of a landscape forged within an economy defined by a racial division of labor, this was—both materially and ideologically—a profoundly racialized landscape. In the decades after the end of slavery, literate men conceived those who shaped the landscape as obstacles rather than assets for nation-building in the frontier. Blacks' fight for freedom and their efforts in settling the fringes of the national territory did not seem to deserve recognition, much less praise. These writers thought of themselves as the bearers of civilization and progress: they—not blacks—had the duty and powers to improve the place; and for that purpose, they fostered missions and schools to educate and congregate a disperse population. Through these means they sought to control and guide the exercise of freedom.

SETTLING AND THE MAKING OF A LANDSCAPE

Libres or free blacks created the basic traits of the rural landscape as they spread throughout the region and grew in number to become the dominant social group of the lowlands. Living dispersed and beyond the areas formally controlled by the colonial state was a product of liberation: slaves could not have left the gold-bearing levees where they lived in mining camps. As explained in chapter 1, these camps were built along streams and consisted of a few huts, a store-house for food and equipment, and perhaps also a chapel and a blacksmith shop. Most of the camps moved as miners abandoned depleted deposits in search for more gold. The Spanish colonizers created another form of settlement—the so-called Indian villages—to congregate the indigenous population (which survived mainly in Chocó). However, for most of the year the Embera people tended their often distant corn fields and worked as canoemen. A new landscape began to form within the mining areas as the Embera abandoned the villages and opted for a dispersed way of habitation, and libres enriched the place with their houses, hamlets, and crops. They remained close to their families and at the center of lowland economic life, working the placers of their former masters and even their own or making a living in activities such as rowing, serving as carriers, and producing food and liquor. The complete end of slavery coincided with the opening of new economic opportunities that encouraged migrating. The rubber trade motivated some to scour the forests in search of *Castilla elastica* trees, while the gathering of vegetable ivory seeds provided a way to make a living in several places where there was no gold to be found.

Migrations originated from the three mining districts: Upper Chocó, the long belt south of Buenaventura, and Barbacoas (see map 9). The Upper Chocó had several particularities: its population was double that of the other two combined;

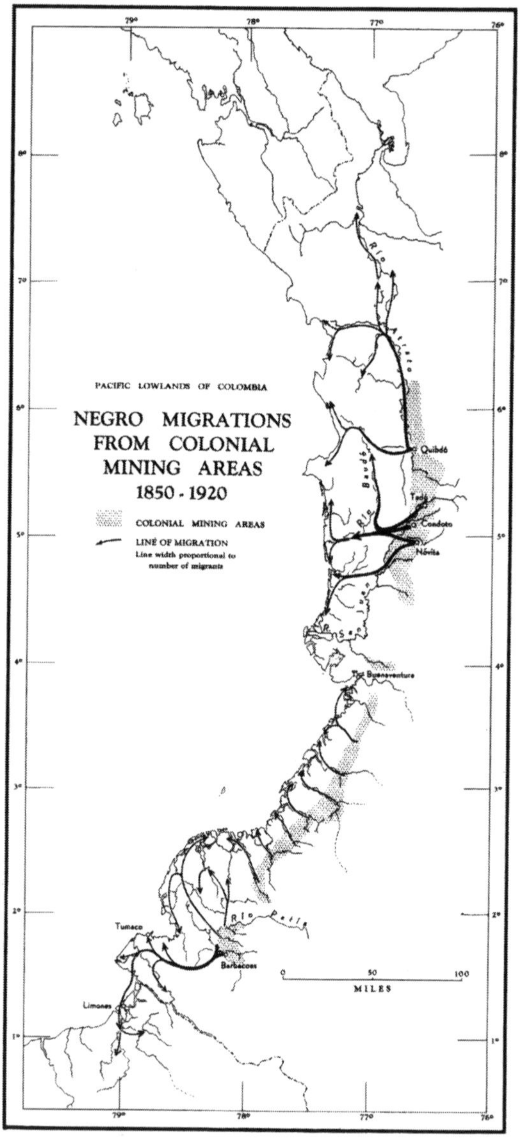

MAP 9 Nineteenth-century migrations of black people. Source: Robert West, *The Pacific Lowlands of Colombia* (Baton Rouge: Louisiana State University Press, 1957).

it was the home of most of the regional indigenous population; and it was close to Baudó and the lower Atrato, two vast areas with extremely low population densities and weak state control. Settlers headed in these directions: west to Baudó and the Pacific coast and northwards, down the Atrato River and to the Caribbean coast.[5] Colonial dominion over the Atrato River stopped at the *Vigía*, or lookout, which was initially located near the mouth of the Bojayá River. Cuna Indians, never subdued by the Spanish, reigned beyond that point. In the late eighteenth century, the Crown sought to extend its dominion by moving the Vigía further north. Yet around 1820, travelers ascending the Atrato noticed that houses along the river edges only became frequent upstream from the original location of the Vigía.[6] By midcentury, visitors saw houses extending further north, up to the mouth of the Sucio River, where the village of Riosucio had emerged. They also mentioned another newly created settlement, Turbo, in the Gulf of Urabá, which also traded in rubber and cacao. The production of dried fish, especially in the months of January and February, supplemented livelihoods in this swampy area.[7] After midcentury, free blacks from the Upper Chocó migrated more readily to these areas; in the Gulf of Urabá they were outnumbered by settlers from Bolívar (in the Caribbean lowlands to the east), who succeeded in establishing, in the 1870s, the town of Acandí along the western side.[8]

Migrations in Chocó had a very strong effect over Indigenous peoples, both those of the Chocó family who had lived under colonial rule and the rebellious Cuna. By around 1930, Indians accounted for less than 6 percent of the region's population, down from 30 percent at the end of the eighteenth century.[9] Not only had their relative numbers decreased but their territories had diminished. As black settlers moved into the nonauriferous eastern Atrato tributaries, even before 1850, Indians migrated upstream to the headwaters. Along the Munguidó River, for instance, black residents grew crops for sale in the 1920s; Indians from the villages of Lloró and Quibdó had worked there in colonial times.[10] The Embera abandoned most of the San Juan mining area as well. Their Wounaan cousins continued to occupy the lower San Juan and extended into the short Docampadó River to the north. The largest group of Chocó people, 2,500 in 1929, remained in the Chamí country, which was annexed by the Andean department of Caldas and had served as a haven since the seventeenth century. The Embera also occupied large stretches of the Baudó Mountains, which they came to share with blacks.[11]

According to officials from Chocó, settlers continued to encroach upon Indian lands in the early twentieth century.[12] However, I only found one case in the archives (corresponding to 1924) in which Indians directly accused blacks of invading their lands: ninety Embera from the Docampadó River claimed that at least five men had recently come from the San Juan area to back the incursion orchestrated by a certain Hipólito Tamayo.[13] Situations of this sort must have encouraged regional authorities to back Law 60 of 1916, which established procedures for creating *resguardos*, or granting communal land titles, to indigenous groups. With the exception of the Chamí people, whose *resguardo* was created under Law 89 of 1890, other groups did not have secure titles to the areas they inhabited. In 1920, the intendant informed the national government that the regional authorities had approved a resguardo in the abovementioned Docampadó basin, and that they expected to do the same in Docordó (lower San Juan), Tadocito (upper San Juan), and Acandí (Urabá). But as the case of the Cuna Indians illustrates, the authorities were overoptimistic.[14]

In the nineteenth century, the Cuna from Baudó, the Pacific coast, and the lower Atrato, left these areas and joined those living in Urabá.[15] Caribbean and Chocoano newcomers increasingly occupied territory previously controlled by the Cuna, as a missionary explained in 1927: "It will be hard to satisfy these poor Indians because they want something impossible, to have the town of Unguía . . . This town belonged to the Indians not long ago, [until] a smallpox epidemic depopulated the place. . . . In the meantime black rubber gatherers took possession of the lots . . . today there are about 30 houses. . . ."[16] The Cuna from the eastern side of the Gulf of Urabá fought most tenaciously for legal recognition of what remained of their territory. Chiefs repeatedly wrote to the intendant and the Ministry of Public Works demanding the demarcation of their lands, but in 1919 the ministry responded that it lacked the resources to pay a surveyor, and the following year regional authorities complained about the difficulties of finding an engineer. Although the intendant resolved to simply go ahead and grant the lands, for a resguardo to form, the ministry had to give its approval based on a map establishing clear boundaries. In 1922, an indigenous delegation traveled to Bogotá, taking with it a detailed agricultural census, to demand definite titles. By 1930 they still lacked legal recognition of their territory, even though the intendancy had supposedly hired an engineer the previous year to draft the required map.[17]

South of Buenaventura, blacks moved to the middle and lower parts of the basins, and in the Micay and Saija Rivers they joined the descendants of indigenous migrants who came from Chocó in the eighteenth century; by 1920 they numbered around eight hundred.[18] Rivers from the Dagua to the Tapaje traverse a mostly narrow alluvial plain and then split into many mouths to form islands covered by mangrove forests. Blacks living in the upper parts of these basins moved downstream to seek better lands for cultivation and to fish in the sea. They also made ties for the construction of the railroad from Buenaventura to Cali, which began in 1878. This migration changed the settlement pattern from one dominated by mining camps located in the upper reaches to one characterized by dispersed dwellings built along the entire river courses. The 1870 census data indicates that settlers were quite young: 85 percent of them were less than forty years old, and of these, 35 percent had not reached their eighth birthday. Barbacoanos moved toward Tumaco and Esmeraldas to occupy forests with vegetable ivory groves, such as those of the Mira and Rosario River basins.[19]

As they settled the lowlands, free blacks erected hundreds of houses, sprinkling the landscape with one of its most conspicuous traits. These dwellings, built on stilts, usually stood alone and had split-palm floors and thatched roofs. Square instead of round like most Indian huts, black people's houses also differed from Indian dwellings in that they had walls (see fig. 13). To the dismay of visitors, blacks kept very few things inside their houses, sometimes not even a table or a bench. They slept on beds over a piece of *damagua*, a bark used to

FIGURE 13 Black family dwelling, lower San Juan. Photograph by Robert C. West (R32 N13), Archivo Fotográfico Robert West, Las Tierras Bajas del Pacífico Colombiano. Biblioteca Luis Angel Arango and Biblioteca Universidad de los Andes. https://robertwest.uniandes.edu.co.

make a kind of cloth. Black settlers made and had baskets around the house to store food and hold their scant belongings. They often kept pigs underneath the house and, on very rare occasions, had cows roaming around. Many also owned hunting dogs—in the case of Chocó, mutts brought from Antioquia. Free blacks wore far too few clothes for the prudish travelers and walked barefoot. Women might simply wrap a cloth around their waists, although often they wore shirts or handkerchiefs to cover their breasts. Men wore short pants or just tissues to cover the bare minimum. Yet when visiting town, they put on pants and shirts, while the women liked to dress up. Blacks also made and wore hats sometimes, while Indians never did.[20]

Black rural dwellers further transformed the landscape through agriculture. They cultivated food around the house, usually plantains, the region's staple since the Spanish introduced it to feed the slaves. Additionally, each family had plots where they cultivated other kinds of plantains and bananas, as well as a variety of corn that has small ears and grains and is endemic to the lowlands. They grew sugarcane, and many families had *trapiches* to squeeze its sweet juices to make molasses and alcohol. Visitors also saw cacao, rice, coconuts, and a few fruit trees, such as *almirajó* (*Patinoa almirajó*) and *borojó* (*Borojoa patinoi*), native from Chocó. The tall and spiny peach palms (*Bactris gasipaes*), domesticated for their rich oily fruit, adorned the riverine landscape. So did the breadfruit trees, introduced to Colombia in the early nineteenth century. The small coco yam plant (*papachina*, *achín*, or *rascadera*, *Xanthosoma sagittifolium* (L.) Schott.) also formed part of the cultivars that blacks carried with them as they colonized the lowlands (see fig. 14). Close to their houses, blacks built square platforms (*azoteas*), or simply used an old canoe, for growing annuals, such as onions, tomatoes, coriander, and a variety of medicinal plants, protected from leaf-cutter ants, rodents, and excessive humidity.[21]

Blacks helped build the national territory by physically occupying frontier lands, but also by turning to the state to guarantee their property rights. Increasing the occupation of sparsely populated lands was one of the main tenets of republican projects in Latin America. By the end of the colonial period, Colombia's population inhabited mostly a few Andean areas; vast expanses of land such as most of the Amazon and Eastern Plains had very few people living there and were not under any form of state control. By making the Pacific lowlands productive, blacks quietly carried out a republican ideal and in a few cases attempted to make this contribution official by requesting land titles. Between 1920 and 1922, for example, the intendancy of Chocó granted thirty-four titles

FIGURE 14 Agriculture, Saija River. Photograph by Robert C. West (R15 N28), Archivo Fotográfico Robert West, Las Tierras Bajas del Pacífico Colombiano. Biblioteca Luis Angel Arango and Biblioteca Universidad de los Andes. https://robertwest.uniandes.edu.co.

of twenty hectares or less to peasants, mostly in Baudó, while the Public Lands correspondence shows evidence of other small plots of land granted in Chocó.[22] Yet most lowlanders never requested titles. Even though Colombian laws gave settlers rights to the land they occupied, in some places within the region—the Naya, Timbiquí, Jiguamiandó, Murindó, Cértegui, and Dagua River basins—peasants could not claim their lands due to the existence of large land titles or mining concessions.[23] Perhaps more importantly, they did not consider this procedure necessary because they knew of a more expedient way to achieve legal recognition of their plots.

Settlers from all over the region turned to the state by registering their lands in the public notaries. The notary books of Quibdó, Buenaventura, Guapi, and Timbiquí contain many examples of these transactions. Despite being largely illiterate, blacks were well acquainted with written procedures. When they purchased their freedom, the transaction was notarized and they received copies of their *cartas de libertad* (freedom certificates) to prove their new status.[24] Some bought their land from holders of old colonial titles, and these transactions were also frequently registered in the closest notary.[25] Therefore when blacks sold or purchased land, they also notarized those contracts. Most needed to find a literate person to draft the deeds. The reference to a single *literario* in the 1870 census of the Anchicayá, Cajambre, Calima, Micay, and Timbiquí Rivers attests to the importance of such knowledge.[26] Notarizing land sales and purchases presented other difficulties. Since most settlers lived far from the towns that housed the notary offices, they had to make trips over many days to secure their properties or request someone else, usually a person who lived in town, to have the transaction notarized.

Lowland oral tradition presents further evidence of the importance blacks gave to state sanctioning of their properties. A priest who, in the early 1960s, recovered the history of Las Mercedes, a town in the Chagüí River north of Tumaco, heard that the first settler, who arrived in 1907, found out that someone else had already claimed ownership of the area. In hearing the news, he headed to the notary in Tumaco to check if it was true. Finding no evidence of such claim, he securely acquired the land where the town later developed.[27] The story of the Tapaje River basin deed, collected and analyzed by historian Oscar Almario, also attests to the power of state endorsed papers. After the death of the last slave owner of the Tapaje River (which occurred in 1866), a boy found a piece of bamboo that contained the basin's deed and a member of the community carefully kept it. Soon after, a company came looking for gold mines. According to the story, two ambassadors of the local inhabitants showed the company's representative the papers that proved that both sides of the river were titled. The miners corroborated their validity in Pasto and Bogotá, and with this irrefutable proof local dwellers were able to retain their possession.[28]

The existence of customary property rights did not exclude the adoption of an external regulatory entity. Rural dwellers also sought the state's recognition of their rights as settlers by writing to local, regional, and national authorities when someone violated those rights. As illustrated in part I, blacks protested attempts by speculators to acquire titles to their agricultural lands through mining claims and opposed the granting of concessions to extract forest resources. In their letters they often specified how long they had occupied the disputed area and how they had worked it, either by planting crops or gathering vegetable ivory. They used these arguments based on national legislation that recognized settlers' rights to their land through extended occupation and labor. Lowlanders turned to the state both in times of trouble and in normal times. In recognizing its power, they helped strengthen a weak state and integrate the region to the nation.

AGAINST DISPERSION

In the first decades of the twentieth century, after black people had reached almost every corner of the lowlands, the state tried to exert a somewhat stronger grip over the region, encouraging, along with the Catholic Church, the formation of villages. Both civil and ecclesiastical authorities could best control and influence the population under their jurisdiction if it lived congregated rather than scattered throughout the region. A priest clearly expressed this point of view by saying that blacks needed to form small settlements "where they could be indoctrinated, taught, and corrected. Disseminated throughout the forests and rivers they would never learn the science of the Christian duties."[29] The Church and the state thus promoted the creation of towns, sometimes against peasants' will, by erecting temples and, as we will see later in the chapter, primary schools.

Authorities followed the logic of those who ruled the lowlands in the eighteenth century and attempted to keep slaves and Indians under control in mining camps and Indian villages. Some former Indian villages survived into the twentieth century as black towns. Many declined, such as Bebará, which had about thirty-five houses in 1852 and just fifteen ruined dwellings in 1924.[30] Even Lloró, which fared better, had just twenty houses in 1893 and twice as many in 1924 (see fig. 15).[31] A few mining camps became hamlets; such was the case of Barco, in the upper Cajambre River, whose church bells have the year 1786 inscribed in them.[32] But by the twentieth century, many of these old mining settlements had fallen into disrepair; Father Merizalde described San Juan, one such place in the upper Micay River, as a "village formed by miserable shacks and a run-down chapel."[33]

The involvement of the Church in the lowland settlement process followed the return of religious orders to the region. With independence, the decay of the mines, and, after the mid-nineteenth century, the promotion of anticlerical measures by liberals, the Church presence in the lowlands greatly diminished. According to a missionary, during this time "[t]he devil took hold of the Pacific coast; the works of the missionaries fell to the ground, and the burning simoon [hot sand-laden wind of the Sahara] of vice withered the fields in which virtue could have flourished."[34] Missionaries only returned to the coast fifteen years after the 1886 Constitution and the 1887 Concordat, signed with the Vatican, assigned a renewed role to the Church. In returning to power, the conservatives sought support by the Church to help organize a poor country weakened by

FIGURE 15 Liquor stand, Lloró, Chocó, 1853. Watercolor by Manuel María Paz, 1853. Láminas de la Comisión Corográfica, Biblioteca Nacional de Colombia.

extreme federalism and other liberal excesses. Among other things, the Church had the mission to help "civilize" frontier Indians and—why not—blacks too. After losing most of their influence in the country in 1861, the Augustinian Recollects regained forces in 1890 with the arrival from Spain of Fray Ezequiel Moreno. As bishop of Pasto, Moreno promoted the creation of the Apostolic Prefecture of Tumaco in 1899 and the mission in Guapi in 1902.[35] The Claretians, a congregation formed in Spain in the mid-nineteenth century, established themselves in Quibdó in 1909 to create the Prefecture of Chocó.[36]

Augustinian and Claretian missionaries alike erected churches that helped strengthen lowland villages (see fig. 16 and table 9). They trekked to the rural

FIGURE 16 Church and house for priests, Yuto, Chocó. Source: Francisco Gutiérrez, editor. *Relación de algunas excursiones apostólicas en la misión del Chocó.* Bogotá, Imprenta Nacional, 1924.

areas to baptize, marry, and confess the many souls who lived without the sacraments of the Catholic Church, and they spent a good part of their energies and resources directing the construction of chapels and dwellings where priests could stay when they visited. They complained about people's lack of support for their projects; as illustrated by one comment that settlers "[did] not move a finger to benefit the construction of chapels, unless the priest gets the works started, directs them, and even toils in them. . . . [Furthermore, settlers] often [felt] entitled to borrow, and not return, the materials assembled for the construction of the chapels."[37] The houses of God served to bring the Church back into the center of the lives of rural black folks. Chapels, as well as cemeteries, provided people with a place to gather and elevated the status of settlements. When, in 1917, Father Belarra noticed that a village was forming downstream from Quibdó, he organized the building of a chapel for the virgin of Las Mercedes, which gave the town its new name.[38] The seventeen chapels built by missionaries in Chocó between 1919 and 1923 accounted for more than half of the temples in the thirty Chocó villages that had more than eight houses and attest to the zeal with which these religious men performed their duty.[39]

The role of priests in creating towns became part of the region's memory. In the mid-1960s, for instance, the inhabitants of Santa María, in the Rosario River basin, north of Tumaco, remembered how Father Hilario created a town after the tsunami of 1906 and chose the Virgin of the Rosary as its patron saint.[40]

TABLE 9 Settlements, churches, and schools from the Micay River to the Mira River, 1921 (not counting the Barbacoas area)

RIVER	SETTLEMENTS, CHURCHES AND SCHOOLS
Micay	Seven villages, six with chapels, and four schools
Saija	Two villages, one with chapel, and one school
Bubuey	No villages
Timbiquí	Four villages, at least three with chapels, and four schools
Guafui	Two villages with chapels and one school
Guapi	Eleven villages, ten with chapels, and five schools, plus the town of Guapi
Iscuandé	Three small villages without chapels, plus the town of Iscuandé
Tapaje	Two villages with chapels plus the town of El Charco
La Tola	Two villages with chapels and schools
Sanquianga	Three villages with chapels and schools
Patía	Three villages with chapels
Mira	Seven villages with chapels
Coast	At least six villages, two with chapels and schools

Table based on data from Bernardo Merizalde del Carmen, *Estudio de la costa colombiana del Pacífico*. Bogotá: Imprenta del Estado Mayor General, 1921.
Note: According to another priest working in Tumaco, by 1928 the number of settlements on the Mira River had increased from seven to nine, and in the Tapaje River from two to six. The Chilví, Caunapí, and Chagüí Rivers had two, three, and two settlements, respectively. Settlements in the Guapi basin had decreased from eleven to five. Teodoro Maetzu, "Prefectura Apostólica de Tumaco. Bellezas de la costa del Pacífico," *Revista de Misiones* Year 4, no. 34 (1928).

Similarly, in the late 1970s, an inhabitant of Jella, in the Pacific coast of Chocó, explained that "an agreement existed between the Spanish Dominicans and the Marroquín administration by which the government would give 60,000 pesos to the [missionaries] for each town they founded. Thus Father Onetti cleared all this area where Jella is located."[41]

The Church also sought to congregate Indians. The Claretian missionaries took it upon themselves to "reduce" to settlements the Indians living in the Andágueda basin. In 1917, with the consent and some financial support from the intendancy, they created four villages, which started off with only three to eight houses each, and housed a total of 415 people.[42] Partially to encourage families to live together, missionaries created schools, mostly in the Chamí region, and hired policemen to force parents to send their children.[43] The regional state would have liked to see all Indians living in towns. In 1912, it instructed the special commissioner to the northern Pacific coast to "reduce" the Indians of the western Baudó Mountains, but the commissioner lamented the impracticability of that goal given the vast area that these families occupied, their alleged natural laziness, and their tendency to solitude and isolation.[44]

Small villages also formed by initiative of rural folk, as happened on the beaches along the northern rocky Pacific coast and amidst the mangroves to the south. The scarcity of space available to settle along the coast encouraged people, usually extended families, to cluster in a few spots.[45] In 1922, Octávira, with its twenty houses, was one of the largest villages on the northern edge of the Pacific coast. In the south, near the Iscuandé River mouth, several white families colonized the available beaches from the late 1700s on, forming an exception to the black colonization of the lowlands.[46] Coastal villages tended to disappear or relocate because of the erosion caused by marine currents and tides; such was the fate of Pantajoná in the northern Pacific coast, the hamlets formed in the Pichimá River and Docampadó River mouths, and Usmal in the south. The tsunami that struck the southern coast in 1906, which destroyed the town of Santa Rosa and severely affected San Juan, best exemplifies the unstable nature of such settlements. Yet a relatively large town like Pizarro, in the Baudó River mouth, managed to survive despite the erosion caused by both sea and river.[47]

Lowland towns were fairly small, especially those in the south, and often consisted of a single row of houses along a river or the ocean. Jacques Aprile and Gilma Mosquera, who have studied the development of lowland settlements, show how, as these settlements grew, they opened a street behind the first row of houses for a second row to form.[48] In 1923, the missionaries listed thirty towns in Chocó having between eight and forty houses. Larger towns across the region, like Neguá and Iscuandé, grew to have around fifty houses. Opogodó, a boom town in the Condoto basin, stood out with eighty houses. Most people, however, still lived dispersed along the rivers. While in 1915 a traveler could count 107 houses along the Atrato River from Yuto to Lloró, in 1923 these two towns combined had only sixty houses. Likewise, along the Andágueda River, in 1915 only forty of a total of 290 houses formed the town of Bagadó.[49]

As blacks came to be present throughout most of the lowlands, men who wrote about the places referred frequently to them, exposing prevailing understandings of race and nature. These men focused much less on the indigenous groups that often lived in secluded areas. Therefore the writings about the rainforests of the Pacific coast of Colombia differed from those of similar environments in Latin America, which dealt mostly with indigenous peoples. In the lowlands, as blacks came to enjoy freedom and endow it with meaning, environmental determinism and racial thinking reinforced each other in observers' minds who interpreted it as a wasted gift.

RACE AND NATURE

Members of the local elite, as well as travelers and clergymen, considered that blacks belonged to the hellish jungles. Such "moral topography," to borrow Michael Taussig's expression, which inscribed meaning to national territories based on hierarchical views of race, guided elite understandings of Colombian geography.[50] José María Samper, the distinguished nineteenth-century politician and intellectual, used in 1861 an often-cited expression to associate different races with the temperate Andean highlands and the hot lowlands: "each race and caste had to have . . . its own *inevitable and fated* geography: whites as well as lightly bronze-colored Indians, and mestizos born of their crossing, congregated on the mountainous slopes and high tablelands; conversely, blacks, red- and darkly bronze-colored Indians, and the mestizos originating from their mixture, had to inhabit the coasts and hot valleys."[51] A renowned physician, Jorge Bejarano, repeated almost the exact same words six decades later in the public debate over the quandaries of race in Colombia, attesting to the endurance of these ideas.[52] Similar associations between peoples and environments came to characterize other Latin Americans countries.[53] Various scholars have examined readings of specific Colombian regions, among them the Pacific coast. Eduardo Restrepo, for example, analyzed how, in the 1990s, blacks were recast as the stewards of biodiversity, a reading that reworked under a much more positive lens the old notion of the unbreakable bond between blacks and the humid jungle.[54]

The ways in which observers of the Pacific coast, in the second half of the nineteenth and early twentieth centuries, understood the relation between race and nature also draws from European and American visions of the Tropics developed in the context of imperial expansion. The Tropics, as David Arnold has explained, were a conceptual as much as a physical space, which were mostly seen as its humid and hot lowlands rather than a diverse area of the globe. With its extreme humidity and high temperatures, the Pacific coast could be considered the prototypical tropics. Despite frequent generalizations, there existed different emphasis within the ambivalent ideas of tropicality: "In part an alluring dream of opulence and extravagance . . . the tropics also signified an alien world of cruelty and disease, oppression and slavery."[55] As Gaugin beautifully exemplifies, the islands of the South Pacific were portrayed as lost Edens where travelers could escape from the burdens of industrialized societies. Nothing farther from the images of the Pacific coast, which rather fit within another major theme in imaginaries about the tropics: "the primordial character of tropical landscapes was most forcefully suggested by the vast and seemingly inexhaustible forests."[56] And not just forests but jungles—associated with danger and discomfort.[57]

Contemporaries' readings of the Pacific coast and its black people were thus anchored in both a national moral topography and a prevalent (colonial) construction of the tropics. Blacks, just as natives belonging to the "Malay race" in the Philippines, were seen, to cite just one example, as living in an uncultivated state, spoiled by an "overnurturing Mother Nature."[58] Literate men's cosmopolitan certainty of the inferiority of certain races, and their belief in the influential powers of the physical environment, blended in a reading that naturalized both the coastal landscape and its dwellers. Conceiving black lowlanders as part of nature ignored or minimized their role in settling and humanizing the forests. In a republican and postemancipation world, these ideas did not serve to justify colonial rule over native peoples, but they did reinforce racial inequalities. More importantly, equating the descendants of enslaved people with the lowland environment contributed to erase them from history and denied freedom its rich meaning. In the same vein, the idea that whites could not withstand the unhealthiness of the humid forests (or of tropical environments) posed a conundrum for both the writers examined here and colonial authorities in Asia and Africa. While faith in science—medicine, agricultural techniques, and forestry—uplifted the morale of colonial officials, education proved the lifeline to deal with blacks as a necessary evil in the lowlands' future. Optimism stemmed from a belief shared by many Latin American elites in elevating inferior races by improving their social conditions.[59]

Interpretations of blacks' relationship with the lowland environment give much weight to the ubiquitous presence of robust forests, seen as evidence of blacks' incapacity to create a welcoming, ordered, and productive landscape. To the American consular agent, writing in the 1910s, the "whole of Chocó [was] a mass of forests, which [would] have to be cleared off for the development of the region."[60] Following that same ideal, the members of the Corographic Commission who toured the country in the middle of the nineteenth century contrasted the Andean highlands with the Pacific lowlands: in their view,

Andean people had domesticated nature by planting grasses to produce meat, the most valued food; by contrast, lowlanders had barely humanized the inhospitable environment that remained best suited for beasts.[61] One could argue that the commission, which visited the region when the most intense wave of settlement was just beginning, did not fully appreciate the transformation of the lowland landscape. Yet subsequent decades of colonization apparently did not lead to a positive appreciation of the changes blacks introduced to the land. In the 1910s, a local official described the Chocó coast as "[a] few miserable huts, surrounded by stunted crops, and inhabited by wretched people who live far from God or the Law; lacking even the most elementary notions of morals and justice!"[62]

The lack of ordered agricultural fields held great significance to many liberals for whom small farmers represented ideal citizens.[63] A form of agriculture, learned from the Indians and which intermixed crops and blended with the forest, was hardly valued. The small-eared corn that grew in the lowlands gave the impression of stunted development when contrasted to the larger and more productive varieties of the Andes, while the slash-and-mulch method of cultivating it suggested to observers a lack of agricultural knowledge. Such practices led to calls for experts to come and teach local peasants how to properly till the land.[64] These observers failed to notice that by adopting agricultural practices adapted to the humid environment, blacks embodied many of the ideals they reserved for the highland peasantry. The huts and crops they looked down upon symbolized the astounding efforts of a people who had struggled for their freedom and gradually occupied the region.

Exceptionally, observers conceded that by constituting a human presence in those territories, blacks were the bearers of nation-building along this frontier. "It is true," a Barbacoano reporter accepted, "that we owe the African race for the existence of these settlements."[65] The 1903 secession of Panama, as well as the government's policy of granting national forests in concession, prompted an unusual recognition of black settlers' importance near the Darien border. When settlers in Urabá and the Pacific coast of Chocó saw their rights to freely collect vegetable ivory jeopardized by forest concessions, local officials reported in dismay that those lands risked becoming depopulated because local dwellers were leaving and threatening to leave for Panama, the dismembered part of the nation. Officials' alarm reflected the mentality of the Antioqueño authorities who, in 1927, wrote to Bogotá opposing the granting of a concession near Turbo and stated: "The government has the obligation to watch over the interests of the real sappers of progress and most effective defenders of national integrity in those far-away lands."[66]

The more general underappreciation of blacks' achievements was intertwined with the notion that they fared well under a harmful climate that decimated whites, an idea common to the tropics everywhere and associated with maladies such as malaria, yellow fever, and yaws, whose understanding and treatment was still uncertain.[67] Bureaucrats sent here from other parts of the country tried to return home promptly for they feared "leaving behind their bones in such a harmful climate."[68] Most of the lowlands receive over 4,000 mm of rain a year, an extremely high amount even for a tropical forest, and some portions receive twice as much or more.[69] Largely for its high precipitation and humidity, the region had an unhealthy and even lethal reputation.[70] The experts of the Corographic Commission were among the very few visitors who tried to explain how the elements translated into illness. Based on contemporary notions of miasmas, they wrote that mangrove trees along the southern coast emanated carbonic acid, while the putrid soils on which they grew produced harmful vapors, which together made the littoral a place prone to disease and infection.[71] Rather than venturing elaborate explanations for disease, observers complained about the endless rains and the accompanying humidity and high temperatures that they had to suffer. The American consular agent in Quibdó, for instance, upon arriving in the region, wrote back to Washington: "I will only briefly mention a few of the hardships and discomforts encountered by me, such as, tropical rains and drenchings . . . mosquito and gnat bites, of which I am covered from head to foot . . . suffocating temperatures, poor food, etc."[72] For missionaries, such hardships only added to their sacrifice. Yet Claretians tried to diminish their suffering by having a farm located in the more benign climate of the western Andean slopes, where they could restore their energies and fight malaria.[73]

Local whites thought that fears of sickness and death were exaggerated and worried that such a reputation would keep away investors and retard progress. Journalists in Quibdó mocked outsiders who believed that before coming to Chocó they needed to leave their affairs in order, write their testaments, and confess.[74] A booster from Barbacoas even turned the climate into an asset by explaining that daily rains made mining possible all year round.[75] Although local elites believed that whites could live without peril in the lowlands, they still agreed with outsiders that blacks (and Indians) naturally fit its environment. Privileged whites from Barbacoas and Chocó accepted the idea expounded by national intellectuals that the Spanish had appropriately introduced Africans to the lowland mines, since their color and robust physique made them particularly suited for what awaited them.[76] A local journalist explained that "neither the strong climate, nor the type of labor managed to destroy them, as happened with people of other races. The particular oily secretion of their skin under the heat . . . makes them resistant to the effects of the sun."[77] To local privileged whites, blacks seemed well adapted not only to the climate but also to the general conditions of the lowlands. A former governor to Chocó explained that "only men of color can penetrate [the uninhabited and unhealthy Munguidó River] for more than two weeks, surmount its rushing torrent, sleep under the foliage of the trees, and resist the insects' attack."[78]

These ideas made sense within a framework that divided the world between civilization and barbarism or savagery. Those who wrote about the lowlands conceived of themselves as educated, cultured, or civilized and saw the region as a savage place fit for primitive peoples.[79] A government commission reflected these notions of race when it wrote that the black peasants from Chocó lived in a state of backwardness—or savagery, even—with little more civilization than their ancestors had when they were taken out of the forests of Africa.[80] Whites considered the region's emerging cities as their own civilized spaces, in which blacks did not really fit. As a local journalist plainly put it, ". . . instead of representing justice and security, the uncultured and illiterate blacks [who form the Tumaco police] should be, with paddle in hand, carrying in their canoes plantains to the market . . . , because that is and should be their place. . . ."[81] No wonder, then, that when talking about blacks, observers did not privilege the bureaucrats and small merchants who lived in Tumaco and Quibdó but the rural dwellers who in their view expressed the quintessential nature of blacks.

And the dominant trait of that nature, according to these educated observers, was laziness.[82] The supposed relaxed work ethic of the lowland inhabitants always figured prominently in writings about the region. In 1855, the Italian geographer Agustín Codazzi referred to this "lazy and indolent race [who spent its time] doing nothing," while for the intendant of Chocó in 1913, blacks "completely lacked work habits."[83] A native white considered laziness a defect so serious as to be almost tantamount to disease: "Most of the inhabitants of this province are inferior men . . . without morality, without ambition or knowledge, befallen by syphilis and laziness and disseminated through the river banks in intimate contact with the mud of the beasts."[84] Blacks' scant needs and lack of a profit motive allegedly reinforced their innate laziness. Since they lived in miserable huts without basic amenities, barely covered themselves with clothes, and ate anything they had at hand commentators opined the region's inhabitants had no incentive to take work seriously.[85] In the words of a local journalist, "the people of this area . . . who have inherited the habits and frugality of slaves, do not aspire to better their moral condition; for this reason their needs are extremely limited, and limited too is their productive labor."[86] Furthermore, according to the reports of the Corographic Commission, the "lack of the noble incentive of enriching oneself to enjoy life" stifled their ambition, prevented them from working hard, and kept them in their abject condition.[87]

The notion of indolent blacks drew on stereotypes prevalent throughout Latin America, but it also owed much to the independent character of black labor in this region.[88] As explained in part I, manumission led to the formation of a class of independent workers rather than wage laborers. A relatively scarce population that could provide for much of its needs through agriculture, using forest products, fishing, and hunting, set conditions for working the mines and collecting rubber and vegetable ivory. The local elite resented this independence and bargaining power and thought that local people only "worked under the direction of a boss" and should work for them.[89] The report of the Corographic Commission illustrates these ideas:

> The individuals of the African race, who used to work the mines, today, improperly using their recently acquired freedom, have abandoned most of that work to live in complete independence along the river banks, cultivating a little plantains, corn, and sugarcane, which, in addition to the abundant fish in the rivers and the wild pigs, provide them with crude but certain food. Since they live almost naked, the men with a simple loincloth and the women with a piece of fabric around their waist, if they want to get an outfit to visit town, they go to the river beaches to wash the auriferous gravel, and in a few hours have what they need for their purchases.[90]

This quote also shows, once again, how race was correlated to nature: the men who wrote about the lowlands conceived of the environment as prolific and therefore as another excuse for blacks to remain idle. The Colombian traveler José María Cordovez Moure, who visited Tumaco in 1854, provides a telling example of the idea of nature's generosity:

> Those people [living north of the port], without aspirations . . . were really happy and independent; they led an animal life, free of envy and ambition, because

> the prodigal and fertile nature provided them with everything . . . not even the universal law of labor seemed to affect them or be necessary. We saw nets . . . full of shad, lobster, and other fish in such profusion that they threw back what they could not consume; after the tide receded they offered us [wonderful] oysters; if they did not feel like fishing, they gathered clams, winkles, crab, and other seafood that were left stranded on the beach . . . ; if they got tired of the sea pantry, it was easy to hunt a variety of aquatic birds that come by the thousands to search for the daily sustenance they find in those abandoned regions.[91]

The notion of a bountiful environment served both to explain the indolence of blacks and to blame them for the backwardness of the region. The natural wealth of the lowlands, many contended, contrasted with its poverty and the inexcusable attitude of the population.[92] An inspector to Guapi informed the central government that the area had "rich minerals, timber, rubber, balata, *sande*, *popa*, vanilla, and other valuable products. For agriculture it [had] fertile lands that [produced] food for these localities and even for export. Only the negligence of the inhabitants keeps them uncultivated."[93]

Every now and then, local elites tried unsuccessfully to argue against these hegemonic views of blacks' character, for they feared negative portrayals would prevent foreigners from visiting and fostering progress in the region. An article by Heliodoro González published in a Quibdó newspaper in 1890 is a case in point. González was responding to Medardo Rivas, a well-respected journalist, politician, and writer from Bogotá, who in the same journal followed a well-worn path by saying that, "due to the natural wealth of the area, [blacks] are immersed in an inactivity that inspires pity."[94] González's lukewarm defense ultimately maintained the negative stereotypes repeated ad nauseam:

> The black man of Chocó not only professes the religion of he who was crucified, but in his beliefs reaches the most demanding fanaticism.
>
> It is true that he is lazy, but not so much to conform himself to "live surrounded by a plantain grove that provides him with enough food." Although in small scale they are devoted to agriculture, and most of them extract the gold . . . exported from here. The amount of metal serves to appreciate the labor of those who extract it.[95]

González also argued against Rivas's belief in blacks' violent character; in doing so, he spoke against a strong trope elsewhere in Colombia, which never took hold in the lowlands, but ultimately portrayed his fellow countrymen as timorous children who believed in the same racial order he ultimately upheld.[96] "The Chocoano peasant . . . has a timid character and in the white man sees a superior being whom he fears. To the first news of war he seeks refuge in the deep forests and does not appear in town until he knows for sure that all danger has passed. Being a coward by nature, he cannot take his machete and prepare himself for defense, or run in search of danger. . . ."

Twenty-four years after this controversy, another reporter attempted to defend blacks, this time against the ideas expressed by the foreign intendant. That not much had been gained is evident in his central argument: "Let it be known that blacks also think!"[97]

Men who wrote about the lowlands between 1850 and 1930 combined in three fundamental ways the two tropes that dominate Western thought on tropical environments—that they are rich but hellish—with notions of race that depicted blacks as uncivilized. First, they emphasized the natural aspects of the landscape and, in this manner, overlooked the ways in which blacks had transformed it. Second, these men argued that blacks' semisavage nature relegated them to the unhealthy lowland jungles. And third, white men considered that the environment—now conceived as prolific and fecund—reinforced the corrupted character of blacks. These ideas underplayed any achievement related to the autonomy with which blacks exercised freedom and led to disheartening conclusions about the future of the place. Yet missionaries, visitors, and local merchants and bureaucrats retained a sense of optimism. As in other parts of Latin America, the state and the elites sought better prospects by calling for immigration and educating the people.

IMMIGRATION AND EDUCATION

A racialized problem called for a racialized solution. To overcome "the apathy and ignorance of blacks," observers dreamed of whitening the region through immigration. Such solution mirrored elite desires throughout Latin America; but Colombia as a whole attracted very few European immigrants, and the entrenched idea that whites' well-being was at risk in the lowlands ran against such prescription. Education, which as a broad civilizing project was also a form of whitening, proved more feasible. In the lowlands, establishing schools to teach children how to read and write, as designed by the founding fathers for the entire country, implied efforts by whites to uplift blacks by setting a good example and instilling work habits.

Some members of the local elite cringed when they thought about the lowlands being forever covered by lush forests and inhabited by blacks. "Is Chocó condemned," asked one of them, "to be a damned land, patrimony of the beasts of the forest or of the African races, the only ones resistant to malaria, beriberi, and tropical anemia? No! And a thousand times No!"[98] Some men hoped for a brighter future by bringing white people to the region, as expressed by the protagonist of the 1927 novel *Quibdó*. As he traveled upstream the Atrato River,

> [f]our naked black boys greeted with jubilant cries, from the river bank, the passage of the vessel.
>
> —It is not people like that—remarked Sergio Belarco, pointing at the four kids who jumped on the bank—who will help you transform this splendid area.
>
> —You are right—replied Hugo Atanasio Farbel.—We need to bring in Europeans to mix them with the natives. The result of such crossing is excellent.[99]

Yet calls for European immigration and hopes for whitening through miscegenation were exceptions rather than the norm. Since the late eighteenth century, Colombian elites, just as their Brazilian peers, had manifested their longing for a gradual whitening of the population through racial mixing. In this manner, they upheld a racial ideology based on white superiority, while simultaneously turning on its head the notion of miscegenation as a form of degeneration.[100] These biased readings were inspired by the undeniable fact of population mixing in many parts of Latin America. That such ideas did not take hold in writings about the Pacific coast is very likely related to the relatively low level of racial mixing in this region. A 1942 article on race in Chocó confirms the lack of support for miscegenation as a proposed solution to the purported racial problem of the lowlands. It identified the existence of a mixed Chocoano race—with Indian, Spanish, black, and Syrian blood—whose attributes seemed all too similar to those ascribed to blacks: instead of imposing itself over the environment, "it tended to assimilate itself to it . . . to passively resist its action. . . ."[101]

Men worried about the future of the lowlands more readily envisaged waves of white immigrants who themselves, rather than any mixed offspring, would transform the region.[102] Considering it impossible to bring in Europeans, they looked for options within Colombia. Antioqueños, a people portrayed as white and hardworking, who colonized a good portion of the western Andean region, including the upper parts of the mountains that run alongside Chocó, seemed to provide the best option.[103] The conclusions of the 1908 commission that visited Chocó to examine its economic potential expressed such sentiments:

> Immigration from Italy, Spain, and Germany, which has produced good results in the United States, Brazil, and Argentina, would not produce those same results here, and perhaps nowhere else in Colombia either—because Colombia is a tropical country, different from theirs. We do not know if Coolies, Chinese, and Japanese, as immigrants, have anywhere helped to enhance the countries that received them. In Chocó, given its conditions, any kind of immigration seems dangerous, except that of nationals. . . . Antioqueños can help effectively to the progress of Chocó by chopping down jungles, then scattering themselves through the numerous spurs and valleys of the tributaries of the western side of the Atrato, which have good climate.[104]

Given the entrenched perception of the region's deadly climate, in the 1850s the Corographic Commission fantasized about a way in which immigrants could help from a distance. It anticipated that a hardworking and intelligent race would settle the higher parts of the western slope of the Andes without descending into the malarial lowlands, and from there set an example for blacks to follow.[105] This idea did not gain much traction, just as decades later national legislation proved ineffective.

Law 82 of 1913, promoting development in the intendancy of Chocó, led to Decree 264 of 1914, which provided for the establishment of an agricultural colony in the northern Pacific coast. Although bureaucrats referred to the project for a few years, it never came to fruition.[106] The idea, however, survived. In 1928, Decree 1110 set aside an area of the Pacific coast of Chocó for a colonization scheme, and in 1935, Decree 925 called for the establishment of an agricultural colony in Bahía Solano, in which each settler would receive seventy-five hectares plus a lot in the planned town; a salary for ten months; and subsidies for housing, medications, seeds, and tools. The place already had a few settlers, but the landscape they created did not measure up to the large scale fields that the government envisaged. The first ten families came from Ulloa, an area settled by Antioqueños in northern Valle; but shortly after their arrival, most returned home. Although other settlers subsequently arrived, the difficulties in attracting people led the director to consider incorporating the families originally established in the area. By the early 1940s it was evident that the scheme had been a complete disaster. In the late 1970s, locals referred with tragic overtones to the great fiasco: "That was the biggest failure. . . . The 40 Antioqueño families . . . arrived and shortly afterwards died. Only four families survived, no more. We had to bury them until 6 p.m., and sometimes even until 7 or 8 p.m."[107]

Given the doubts about the convenience and likely success of white colonization, but persuaded that an abundant labor force was needed to achieve the region's potential, a few observers brought up the possibility of black immigration. In 1894, a local newspaper stated: "The problem of this province boils down to population immigration, but population that works and resists the climate; the African race adapts perfectly well and reproduces wonderfully in . . . precarious and abnormal [conditions] . . . it is therefore urgent that the American and French companies that have started mining works introduce at least five thousand blacks from the West Indies."[108] But only a trickle of Jamaicans came in the 1910s to work for the Chocó Pacífico Mining Company. In any case, the proposal of black immigration did not catch on, for it contradicted the idea of "improving the race," which lay at the core of social thinking at the time.

However, most observers realized that any progress in the lowlands had to include native blacks, and they believed that educating them was necessary to transform them from obstacles to contributors to the betterment of the region.[109] This faith in education followed the prescribed route for achieving the republican ideal of creating citizens. For this purpose, the 1821 Congress of Cúcuta called for the creation of schools in all sizeable Colombian towns. In the following two decades, the aspiration of having a literate citizenry with allegiance to the republic led to the establishment of several hundred primary schools across the country. The lowlands did not escape from this effort. However, the governors of Chocó constantly complained that lack of funds hindered the achievement of such goals: "The scant rents of the province devoted to schools have left them in a state of neglect, reinforced by the poverty of its inhabitants." In 1845, the existing schools in Chocó had 141 students; a couple of years later, only two schools remained (in Quibdó and Tadó) servicing 155 kids.[110] A new push for basic education came in 1870, under the radical liberal government, with the presidential decree that declared primary instruction free and mandatory. In the following four years, the total number of primary schools in the country increased by 39 percent.[111] This impulse also affected the lowlands. By 1880, the present-day coastal portion of the department of Nariño had nine schools that reflected the "program of public instruction promoted by liberalism since 1870."[112] Yet the lowlands still had to wait a few decades for a more decisive program of primary education.

Such a policy was conceived within a strongly racialized framework, as expressed, in 1913, by the newly appointed intendant to Chocó: "[T]hose who visit this . . . region, populated for the most part by the black race, convince themselves immediately of the imperious duty that those of us who rule and are part of the 'superior races' have of working incessantly to increase the intellectual level of these unfortunate illiterates . . . who live like pariahs . . . under the terrible weight of their crass ignorance and savage instincts."[113] White's moral burdens were not only deeply prejudiced but also had very practical and self-serving motivations, as they sought to guarantee a dependable workforce: "The innate indolence of blacks . . . and the ease with which they have, up to the present, procured their livelihood and even attended to their vices, have created in them, not bad working habits but an absolute lack thereof, for this reason we almost can say that they are unreliable as help for the great mining enterprises until they are adequately educated and forced to work at least ten hours a week."[114]

Particular readings of history and scientific ideas further reinforced the faith in education. Some, as did a member of Quibdó's merchant elite, weaved in the past in trying to explain a reality they found deplorable. They freed blacks from responsibility by identifying slavery as the culprit of their condition but also erased the command they had had over their lives by considering manumission an insufficient *gift*: "Today, more than half a century after [abolition], one can appreciate here [in Chocó] the vices that . . . have been transmitted to [blacks] as legacy of the opprobrious slavery. To form citizens worthy of a Christian republic, with full consciousness of their obligations and rights, it was necessary to do more than just freeing them."[115] And it was never too late to promote education. Optimism stemmed partly from an implicit acceptance among Latin American elites of a Lamarkian view of evolution, according to which acquired characteristics were passed from one generation to the next. Education and hygiene campaigns thus provided a way to ameliorate deficient populations within the prevailing eugenicist ideas, without threatening the racial hierarchy that placed whites above blacks (and everybody else).[116]

Expectations for the advancement of primary instruction finally began to be met with the resources that resulted from making Chocó an independent administrative unit in 1907, and from a tax on vegetable ivory in Tumaco in 1908. The five schools that in 1881 remained from the liberal education program in the coast of Nariño had increased to thirty-six by 1913.[117] The city council of Tumaco founded ten of these schools and paid all expenses: buildings, furniture, and teachers, something that constituted "a veritable exception," since primary education was the responsibility of departments not municipalities.[118] Ten years later, the municipality of Tumaco alone had twenty-five schools, most of them set up and financed by the city council.[119] Primary instruction also made its way north to the department of Cauca, where, in 1921, Father Merizalde reported the existence of fourteen schools.

After the creation of the short-lived department of Quibdó in 1907, local authorities moved fast to erect schools in Chocó, even where no settlements existed. As the governor explained, he "believed in carrying out the sacrifice of creating . . . schools in depopulated places because [he] saw the pitiful state of savagery and backwardness of the inhabitants of distant areas, and tried to bring to them some light relative to their obligations with God . . . and teach them the duties with the nation."[120] The town of Tanguí, located along the Atrato River not far from Quibdó, provides an example of a school successfully created where no settlement existed.[121] Despite his advocacy for founding schools, the governor advocated closing thirty-seven out of the eighty-four created by 1908. He explained that the teachers were pernicious, had poor habits, and could not be controlled by regional authorities because they lived in isolated areas.[122] By 1914, the number of schools in Chocó had decreased to fifty-nine.[123] Public instruction still remained a major concern, as indicated by the existence, in 1913 and 1914, of the *Revista de Instrucción Pública*, which informed Chocoanos about the creation and closure of schools, the appointment of teachers, and all other matters concerning the functioning of the intendancy's primary education program. And although the entire Pacific littoral of Chocó had no schools in 1913, by 1917 four had been established in Nuquí, El Valle, Juradó, and Cupica.[124]

Bureaucrats in charge of promoting primary education in the lowlands complained about the many obstacles they encountered. Insufficient funds led to low salaries, which added to the lack of qualified people and made it hard to find teachers, especially in faraway rural areas.[125] Besides, parents often preferred to send their kids to work in the fields rather than to school. An official sent to Acandí in 1913 wrote that the local school closed because only four or five children attended. He added that, "[a]long with the mayor, I toured the hamlet several times . . . explaining to parents the advisability of having their children educated . . . they replied that they were very poor and their children needed to go to the forests to gather vegetable ivory . . . and that . . . they very well knew that no law existed that forced them to send their kids to school."[126]

Regional authorities also created night schools to educate adults living in the small lowland cities. In 1879, one such establishment opened in Buenaventura to give the numerous workers of the port an opportunity to learn how to read and write. Tumaco opened similar schools in 1906 and then again in 1910, while Quibdó also had one such establishment. The number of students enrolled varied greatly and, with it, the success of these institutions.[127] With schools for children and adults, whites expected to fulfill their duties as superior peoples, not realizing how much their views were conditioned by the dominant ideology of the time.

This racial ideology produced a reading of the Pacific lowlands that denoted an unfortunate paradox. This was one of many Latin American frontiers, but a particular one: rainforests were extremely rainy and black free and independent people—instead of indigenous groups—formed the majority of the population. After fighting for their freedom, they became the bearers of national institutions throughout this region: wherever they went, they took Spanish and Catholicism with them and left their imprint on the landscape. Furthermore, they notarized their land acquisitions, officially bringing those forests into Colombian national territory. Yet local elite men, state officials, and even visitors followed contemporary prejudices to interpret the realities and potential of the lowlands. Convinced of blacks' inferiority, they denied lowlanders' role in achieving and exercising freedom, one of the pillars of republicanism. Their reading of the humid environment strengthened their biased views of blacks' defective character and lack of achievements: they reported that untouched forests provided rural dwellers with their scant needs, condemning them to indolence. Instead of recognizing that blacks were carrying out the national goal of settling the country, they considered that only education promoted by whites could save a wretched race and bring hope to the lowlands. Nation-building in the Pacific coast of Colombia happened along these fractured lines: a white elite blinded by widely accepted preconceptions, and a black population that, without recognition, fulfilled some of the most cherished republican ideals.

This chasm extended to cities, another type of racialized landscape, which materialized the profits of the extractive economy. White merchants—who made those profits—resided in the ports to conduct their import and export businesses. The trade in natural products gave them status and spurred in them the desire to transform those places to conform to their expectations of civilized life. Well aware of the negative reputation of the lowland jungles, and their association with blacks, they wanted to distance themselves from both. Cities constituted their attempt to build a refuge from the environment and the people from which they derived their position. Given the role these small, provincial elites assigned to urban landscapes and culture, they continuously lamented the limited scale of their accomplishments in this respect. The economy that spurred their urban dreams could only deliver third-rate cities inhabited mostly by the same black people who provided the manual labor in the extraction of natural resources. The tensions their presence, culture, and aspirations generated stemmed from the contradictions of blacks attaining freedom in a society in which racial prejudice and disparities kept alive the legacy of slavery.

6

URBAN DREAMS AND NIGHTMARES

THE RISE OF Tumaco and Quibdó gave birth, in the early twentieth century, to urban life in the lowlands and provided the physical and social space in which racial tensions reached their historical peak. Colonial administrative centers did not look like cities; these minuscule towns simply grouped a few regional authorities, a couple of merchants, and, especially in the case of Barbacoas, mine owners. Itinerant mining camps constituted the main—and almost exclusive—settlement unit of the slave-based economy. In the nineteenth century, as slavery waned, river and maritime ports acquired strategic importance thanks to the trade in gold, rubber, and vegetable ivory. A new white elite formed in the few ports that overshadowed the old administrative centers. In the south, Tumaco grew as Barbacoas declined, while in the north, Quibdó became the capital of Chocó and Nóvita sank into oblivion. Colonial hubs had been built inland, in the middle of the most productive mining districts; steep and muddy trails connected them to the Andean centers of power. Their successors lay on the Pacific coast and the banks of the Atrato River, where gold and vegetable ivory could be shipped to New York or Hamburg.

Urban life emerged here at a time when Latin American cities grew and modernized as a product of the export boom of the late nineteenth century. Lowland urban development was part of this general trend, but the limited scope of its extractive economy generated more aspirations than achievements: Tumaco and Quibdó were very small and lacked basic amenities. In the lowlands, the urban landscape—redeemed by handsome houses, public buildings, and monuments—could not be taken for granted. It was a product of hard efforts and the source of much frustration. With all their shortcomings, these ports provided opportunities for free blacks who shaped and infused life in these landscapes. Black men and women worked as laundresses, construction workers, and stevedores. A few fared better by engaging in artisanal trades, filling in some of the jobs opened for literate people in state offices, or by setting up stores. The imposing (by local standards), and at the same time wanting, urban landscape indicated both the nonpeasant routes that had opened for free blacks and their restricted scope.[1]

These port cities served as fertile ground for racial tensions to emerge. For the first time in the region's history a few thousand people lived together—as free citizens—in a relatively small space. Mirroring the racial divide of the region's economy, the white merchant elite presided over these cities' development, while blacks formed the majority of the population. The urban geography marked that divide: the prosperous center, where the commercial houses were located and everybody mingled, represented the power of the white elite, whereas the new streets that signaled the ports' growth were associated with black people. Furthermore, the elite conceived of the new urban spaces as oases in which they could distance themselves from the savage jungles. To their dismay, blacks' culture, which they related to the unforgiving environment they tried to escape, crept into the city. Nowhere was this invasion clearer than with marimba music in Tumaco: as blacks sang and danced, it traveled undeterred and settled in the atmosphere for long nights and even days at a time.

By partaking in marimba dances or writing against them, port dwellers negotiated the place of blacks (and whites) in a free society. The insecure Tumaco elite strove to replace marimba music with European rhythms; but just as the population was largely black, so too were the sounds that gave the city its character. This negotiation could have more dramatic manifestations, as it did in Quibdó, where a black man with a good social position, as indicated by the fact that he had served as a judge, tried unsuccessfully to burn down the city center. It took just a few days for the authorities to send the culprit to the scaffold. After decades of a republican doctrine that preached the equality of Colombians, wide racial disparities—that nonetheless allowed certain social mobility—generated contradictions that signaled life in the lowland ports. Freedom implied navigating the opportunities and limitations brought about by a rainforest economy in the context of persistent racial prejudice.

People familiar with the Pacific lowlands of Colombia might ask where the port of Buenaventura stands in this tale of emerging cities. At the turn of the nineteenth century, a unique dynamic brought this pacific port to life. Unlike Tumaco and Quibdó, Buenaventura did not primarily export regional products; it exported coffee from the Andes and imported merchandise for western Colombia via the city of Cali. This port was an enclave, a warehouse for commodities coming into and out of the interior of the country. Its merchants belonged more to Cali than to the port. For these reasons, Buenaventura did not have as much of a local elite as Tumaco and Quibdó, and prior to 1930 it lagged behind them. Soon after, however, Buenaventura became the center of the Pacific coast and the largest city in the lowlands.

THE GROWTH OF TUMACO AND QUIBDÓ

In the late nineteenth century, the commerce in natural products allowed the ports of Tumaco and Quibdó to assume city airs. They grew to house, in the early 1910s, close to five thousand people each. Tumaco used money from the vegetable ivory tax to erect remarkable public buildings, while Quibdó battled against water. They both inaugurated a main church, a proper central square, schools, a hospital, and a cemetery, establishing a clear difference with the villages that were emerging in the river levees and coasts. In both places, the well-to-do built two-story houses in the center of town and opened shops on the first floor, giving life to the ports and establishing the reputation of its owners.

In colonial times, these settlements did not have any urban pretensions whatsoever. Tumaco, a village on an island of the same name, was the more insignificant of the two. Far away from the mines and with commerce proscribed by the Spanish Crown, the port barely existed. The census data of 1778 and 1788 suggest that free blacks, along with a few whites and perhaps some Indians, inhabited the 200-hectare island.[2] These people lived off a scant trade in pita, tar, timber, and, in all likelihood, the introduction of contraband for the mining area of Barbacoas.[3] By the mid-nineteenth century, Tumaco's commercial role grew. It imported salt and various foreign goods for Barbacoas and even the southern Andes. The port had a commercial street parallel to the sea and a few other houses. In 1854, this little town burned to the ground, and many years after locals still remembered the disastrous effect of the fire.[4] But even before the tragedy, visitors did not retain a good impression of Tumaco. The members of the Corographic Commission described it as unhealthy and its houses as miserable. They nevertheless opined that the local merchants already formed a small genteel society.[5]

The transformation of Tumaco accelerated in the 1860s when commerce in vegetable ivory took off. The first steamship stopped in the port in 1860, and soon commercial houses began to form. Duty exemptions and other measures intended to encourage commerce, enacted between 1841 and 1890, must have also contributed to the port's growth.[6] By 1881, Tumaco had about 1,200 inhabitants; ten years later, a European traveler put its population at 1,500. He found the port charming, as the houses reminded him of Swiss chalets.[7] A more complete description comes from a Colombian who spent a few days in Tumaco in 1891. He described it as a

> beautiful settlement, relatively large, built all in timber and with zinc or thatched roofs. Its main street . . . runs straight for several blocks by the edge of the sea. [This street] is the center of commerce . . . of the port. There are many comfortable and elegant buildings, and the stores, which are many, are well stocked with all types of commodities, because Tumaco is the commercial metropolis of the south.
>
> The streets that depart towards the center of the city are straight . . . but in them there is little activity and the houses are not as good. The plaza is spacious and pretty, but deserted, and the church, which even on Sunday looks like the plaza, is an elegant building also made of timber.[8]

Quibdó followed a similar trajectory but enjoyed a slightly better start. Known as Citará, it was the capital of the province of the same name, a part of Chocó that encompassed the upper Atrato basin, as well as an Indian village.[9] In the late 1700s, the settlement housed the province's highest official, who apparently held all available public positions; he lived in the center of town with very few whites and some slaves and free blacks. Indians, who comprised the majority of the population, lived in the two ends of town. Merchants occasionally visited Quibdó on their way to the mines, where most of the Spanish and slave population lived. Even Indians spent much of their time away from town tending their fields or working as canoemen. In the late eighteenth century, the center of town had around fifty houses, surrounded by a larger number of Indian dwellings.[10]

By the mid-nineteenth century, Quibdó had acquired its current name and changed some. After 1804, when the governor of Chocó moved there from Nóvita, it gained administrative status.[11] In 1852, John Cresson Trautwine, the canal explorer, noted it was the largest settlement of the province with around 1,500 inhabitants, two-thirds of whom were black and most of the rest Indian. He also gave a very complete description of the town's architecture:

> The houses of Quibdó are, with very few exceptions, one story in height, and constructed chiefly on split palms and canes, with a small proportion of hewn timber. The floors of the poorer kind are of earth, while those of superior class are formed of split strips of the outer part of the palm, boards, or brick. Two or three, which were formerly occupied by persons of wealth, while the country was subject to Spanish dominion, have floors of tessellated Italian marble, which forms an odd contrast with the perishable materials on the walls. The roofs are generally thatched with palm leaves, but some are covered with earthen tiles made at the town. These tiles are merely laid on the woodwork of the roof, at a pretty steep angle, without any fastening, inasmuch as winds sufficiently strong to displace them are almost unknown in Quibdó.
>
> The . . . windows . . . are merely protected by cross-bars of wood or iron. The entire details of construction would be considered very rude with us; nevertheless, the buildings are comfortable and commodious, to one who can lay aside his predilections for finished workmanship, and become oblivious to the interstices in most of the partitions, which conflict shockingly with our ideas of privacy.[12]

Despite its growth, Quibdó remained a small and, in Trautwine's view, completely destitute of the picturesque. This traveler felt trapped in its center, which was paved with large rounded pebbles. He ventured the opinion that, because of the surrounding swamps, the wealthiest inhabitants had never walked for more than ten minutes. Even if virtually every house was a shop, the place lacked atmosphere and basic amenities.[13] A member of the Corographic Commission echoed this view when he lamented that Quibdó did not have "a factory, a public establishment, or a good building."[14] The commission's artist produced a discouraging vista of its central square that, rather than focusing on the built environment, offers social commentary: it portrays a white woman, whose status is indicated by the contrast that her size, shoes, and umbrella establish with a black woman and her daughter (see fig. 17).[15] Twenty years later, in 1871, Thomas Oliver Selfridge, another canal explorer, observed that Quibdó seemed perfectly dead.[16]

FIGURE 17 Quibdó's Plaza, 1853. Watercolor by Manuel María Paz, 1853. Láminas de la Comisión Corográfica, Biblioteca Nacional de Colombia.

By the 1890s, however, commerce had picked up. While Selfridge only mentioned rubber and gold among the products exported from Quibdó, Jorge Brisson, who visited the port in 1893, referred to deer and otter skins, vegetable ivory, rubber, the medicinal copaiba balsam and *lirio* milk, *corozo* oil to light lamps, different kinds of timber, palo de mora sold for its khaki dye, cacao, gold, and platinum. He praised the well-supplied stores that formed the animated main street running parallel to the river. He was referring to the Calle del Puerto, one of the four long streets extending north to south, intersected by at least six other streets forming about twenty blocks of different sizes. Brisson visited Quibdó a year and a half after a terrible fire consumed thirty-five houses, among them some of the best in town. Yet he does not mention the disaster: Quibdoseños had worked quickly to rebuild the lost residences. A newspaper description of these houses shows how new materials had been incorporated into the town's architecture. Only a handful of the houses that burned down had split-palm walls and thatched roofs, most had timber walls and about ten had iron roofs. Several also had two stories.[17] Despite the improvements, Quibdó still lacked comfort, making it unappealing to outsiders. The challenging paths and unreliable boats that connected it with the rest of the world made imports and life expensive. Nonetheless, Brisson foresaw a solid future for this place.[18]

The transformation the town underwent in the first three decades of the twentieth century probably surpassed this optimistic observer's expectations. Quibdó, and Tumaco as well, turned rapidly into small cities. The years 1907 and 1908 serve to symbolically mark their urban transformation. In 1907, the Reyes government separated Chocó from Cauca by granting it status as an intendancy, a territory directly administered by the national government.[19] The local elite strove to turn its capital—Quibdó—into a city deserving of its new position. A different sort of event signaled Tumaco's makeover. In 1908, the national government granted the usufruct of the public lands of the municipality of Tumaco to the city council. Since collecting vegetable ivory was the most productive activity carried out in public lands, the measure translated into a levy on these nuts. Charging merchants the equivalent of an export tax provided the easiest way to collect this money, which tripled the municipality's budget overnight.[20]

The city council invested much of these resources in giving Tumaco an urban appearance (see figs. 18 and 19). The elite understood well that cities are more than collections of houses and need to contain attractive public buildings. As in all Colombian towns, and since the late nineteenth century, a church properly located in the central plaza had given the port some respectability. In 1902, when the municipal theater opened, Tumaco began to build more exceptional public edifices. With the vegetable ivory income, the city council continued this urban development. It took care to adequately accommodate public offices in a handsome house in the plaza. The most impressive building was erected for the Pedagogical Institute, that is, the high school for boys. This elegant structure, painted all in white, occupied a whole block right by the plaza. Windows gracefully topped by arches lined its first floor. Similar but longer windows with balconies adorned the second floor, which ended in a cornice, while a recessed third story was reminiscent of French republican architecture.[21] The school for girls, located behind the church, followed the same general style but

FIGURE 18 Tumaco: Pedagogical Institute. Source: Francisco Benítez Acevedo. *Mosaico de una época*. N.p., Colombiana de Impresos, 1985.

was simpler. It lacked the balconies and had a plain tile roof. The new school for younger boys, located a few blocks away from the center of town, brought dynamism to another part of the island. With its ample exterior hallway, this charming one-story building drew inspiration from Caribbean architecture.[22] The municipality also bought and fixed, between 1912 and 1915, a house to serve as hospital. The inaugurations of these landmarks were celebrated with pompous speeches and music.

The city used its resources in other ways as well. In 1912, it developed the extensive Christopher Columbus plaza into a park with a kiosk and many walking paths. The tower of the church was adorned with a clock that served to teach Tumaco's residents the modern way of tracking time. The city council also built a slaughter house, three piers, and two bridges over the tidal channel that crossed the island on which Tumaco sat. The municipality paved several streets with stone and constructed sidewalks. It put iron railings around a few key places such as the school for girls, installed lamps on main streets, and added three public toilets. All these works effectively gave Tumaco a new face. They filled its inhabitants with pride and made this port into a charming little city.[23]

FIGURE 19 Tumaco: El Progreso Bridge. Source: Bernardo Merizalde del Carmen. *Estudio de la costa colombiana del Pacífico*. Bogotá: Imprenta del Estado Mayor General, 1921.

Tumaco residents and local authorities feared losing the income that had contributed so much to the making of their city. They sought to avoid a practice known as *maceo*—the cutting down palms to harvest unripe nuts—which they feared would destroy vegetable ivory groves and endanger the port's main source of revenue. Newspapers voiced many complaints and threatened to publish the names of the merchants who bought unripe vegetable ivory. In 1910, both Tumaco's mayor and the commissary of one of the collection areas where this problem prevailed summoned the merchants to discuss the matter. Soon after, the authorities established fines for those who collected and bought unripe nuts, and they hired a warden to weigh all the vegetable ivory that arrived in Tumaco and identify culprits. Local authorities did fine people but could not collect most of the money, so they tried closing access to the forests where gatherers cut down the palm trees. These measures might have deterred some from continuing this practice, but they failed to completely end it, since in 1924 the mayor was still conducting a battle against maceo.[24] In any case, maceo never posed a serious threat to Tumaco's budget, as did national legislation, which in 1912 shed doubt over the right of municipalities to benefit from the exploitation of national forests and left the matter in the hands of departmental authorities. Once again, local reporters wrote pieces fearing the disastrous outcome of such an eventuality. The uncertainty ended in 1914 when the department of Nariño ratified Tumaco's right to collect money off its public lands.[25]

The efforts of private citizens, largely financed by the vegetable ivory trade as well, further helped turn Tumaco into a city. The wealthy built attractive two-story houses, which usually had a shop and warehouses on the first floor and living quarters on the second. Balconies adorned the facades and zinc roofs stood as evidence of the new character of the place. The most important commercial houses were themselves landmarks, to the point that the author of a 1918 map of the city felt compelled to show the locations of five of them, as well as of the church and the schools (see fig. 20 and map 10). Residents helped in other ways to make Tumaco look like a city. A few had cement sidewalks in front of their houses. In 1908, the Ecuadorian colony donated a column for the Christopher Columbus Plaza to commemorate the first century of independence. Residents also collected funds to renovate the church and build a second one, inaugurated in 1918. The Augustinian priests directed the works of the church, as well as those of the cemetery, which included walkways, mausoleums, and an iron railing.[26]

Like Tumaco, Quibdó underwent a transformation in the first three decades of the twentieth century, which architect Luis Fernando González thoroughly

FIGURE 20 The Duclerq's family house on Calle del Comercio, Tumaco. Source: Francisco Benítez Acevedo. *Mosaico de una época*. N.p., Colombiana de Impresos, 1985.

FIGURE 21 Quibdó: vista. Source: Francisco Gutiérrez, editor. *Relación de algunas excursiones apostólicas en la misión del Chocó*. Bogotá, Imprenta Nacional, 1924.

studied (see fig. 21).[27] By the turn of the nineteenth century, Quibdó had little to show in terms of buildings and public works. By 1898, a local newspaper cheerfully announced that the fine appearance, comfort, and spaciousness of the church, which had previously been a neglected hut, finally allowed Quibdó to assert that, like every cultured city, it had a decent temple.[28] In 1907, the new status of Quibdó as capital of an intendancy gave a new impulse to the desire for urban renovation. The province of Chocó suddenly had boards of public works and ornament and hygiene, and even a Public Works Bulletin, all of which operated in Quibdó. These initiatives did not last long and were superseded by other similar efforts, such as the 1914 Society for Public Improvement and the 1919 Society for Public Promotion.[29] Local authorities set out first to renovate the government building and erect a public market by the river.[30] The arrival of the Claretians in 1909 revived the interest in the church. Its interior and exterior were duly renovated with the generous contributions of the inhabitants. The renovation included an expansion of the naves, new arches and benches, a frontispiece, an organ, and exterior altars.[31] The central plaza ultimate symbol of the city was turned into a park surrounded by an iron railing, and centered by a kiosk (see fig. 22).[32]

FIGURE 22 Quibdó: central square. Source: Francisco Gutiérrez, editor. *Relación de algunas excursiones apostólicas en la misión del Chocó*. Bogotá, Imprenta Nacional, 1924.

Unlike Tumaco, however, the drainage of swamps and muddy streets necessarily had priority over the erection of edifices.[33] After all, with over 10,000 mm of rain a year, Quibdó is one of the rainiest spots in one of the rainiest regions of the world.[34] The city owed its position to its strategic location, which allowed it to connect the upper Atrato mining district to Antioquia, the Caribbean, and the upper San Juan. But Quibdó suffered from the same limitations of every town along the middle Atrato: the swamp (*basín*) that stood behind the alluvial terrace and hindered construction. By the late 1860s, Quibdó already had three streets parallel to the river, the last of which bordered the basín.[35] To make matters worse, a stream curbed the growth of the city to the north. Becoming capital of an intendancy did not itself add the extraordinary resources needed to transform the city. Given these hydrological priorities, the authorities focused on opening drainage channels to reclaim terrain for the city, as well as fixing and extending streets and building bridges. Concern for streets did not simply mean making them passable, but making them worthy of a real city. Thus the state set off to embellish the Alameda Reyes, a boulevard planted with ceibas and eucalyptus named after the president who gave Chocó province its greater status.[36]

Quibdó had to battle against water in yet another way. For Chocó to be an integral part of Colombia, its capital needed a reliable trail to connect it to the Andean core of the country. Because the trail traversed a very rainy area, torrents of water made construction difficult and constant maintenance necessary. As early as 1868, national and regional authorities devised a project to build a trail from Quibdó to Bolívar in Antioquia (via El Carmen). However, this initiative began in earnest only after the creation of the intendancy, and even then work advanced slowly. In 1912, a local newspaper triumphantly announced that the first packtrain of mules from El Carmen had arrived. But the trail had not been finished. By 1914, after 37 km and three bridges had been built, 6 km still remained to be done. Three years later the trail desperately needed repair. By 1920, mules arrived more readily in Quibdó but during the whole decade maintenance proved a tough challenge. Besides the problems posed by the constant downpours and the terrain, the money available for these works varied with the whims of the national government and with the income and plans of the intendancy. By the end of the decade, work began to convert the trail into a road, which finally opened in 1944. It thus took almost forty years to fulfill the desire for a reliable land route connecting Quibdó and Medellín.[37] After 1907, Quibdoseños also strove for a trail and then a road to Istmina.[38]

Despite the diversion of funds and efforts to overcome the negative effects of rain on Quibdó's urban aspirations, the state and its residents did invest in public and private buildings. As González aptly explains, Quibdó's more drastic architectural changes occurred in the 1920s with the introduction of concrete. Between 1923 and 1927, the intendancy built three impressive landmarks that even today draw the attention of passersby. The most imposing was the penitentiary: a long one-story building with neoclassical features that enhanced the Alameda Reyes on the fringe of the city. The second building, which housed the school in a more central location, had a showy Greek portico and long elegant windows on both sides. The third structure, a hospital, ultimately solved a concern that had loomed large for civil and ecclesiastical authorities for more than a decade. Earlier hospitals did not satisfy the most basic standards and, in 1920, one that was under construction collapsed. With columns, a banister, and a vault adorning its entrance, the new hospital capped a small hill just outside the city. Thirty patients could be accommodated in its spacious interior.[39] Luis Llach, a Spanish engineer who resided in the city between 1907 and 1908 and again between 1920 and 1925, designed the penitentiary and the school. He also designed a concrete cemetery on a nearby hill that replaced an old one where graves became inundated before receiving the coffins.[40] This dynamic period also included the installation of monuments—one to Bolívar and two to renowned sons of Quibdó—in the main park and a new smaller square.[41]

Although the state developed the most outstanding structures, wealthy Quibdoseños—as with their peers in Tumaco—contributed to the building of an urban landscape by using the profits of the extractive economy to construct houses for themselves. The wooden houses that characterized Quibdó's early urban aspirations had two-stories and bordered the sidewalks. Tall doors on the first floor opened the family's store to the public. The living quarters upstairs looked onto the street through balconies that stood above each first-floor door (see fig. 23). Little by little these houses filled the main streets of Quibdó and Tumaco, and even prominent towns such as Istmina, and helped lowlanders believe that they too had a civilized space to live in. Another architectural style, expressed in concrete, began to develop in Quibdó in the late 1920s—especially after the 1926 fire consumed some of the best houses in town. A few entrepreneurs built unusual one-story villas (*quintas*) with porches, banisters, and front yards in the undeveloped northern part of the city. The municipality encouraged the occupation of this area by building an avenue that helped incorporate this former swamp.[42]

FIGURE 23 Quibdó: Calle Larga. Source: Francisco Gutiérrez, editor. *Relación de algunas excursiones apostólicas en la misión del Chocó*. Bogotá, Imprenta Nacional, 1924.

TABLE 10 Estimates of Tumaco's population

YEAR	POPULATION
1881	1,200 (a)
1891	1,500 (b)
1906	2,500 (c)
1912	5,000 (d)
1919	6,000 (e)
1921	15,000 (f)

Table based on data taken from (a) *Eco del Pacífico* No. 3, Tumaco, October 23, 1881; (b) Jorge Brisson, *Viajes por Colombia en los años de 1891 a 1897*. Bogotá: Imprenta Nacional, 1899, 12; (c) Miguel Triana, *Por el Sur de Colombia*. Bogotá: Biblioteca Popular de Cultura Colombiana, 1950, 71; (d) *El Litoral Pacífico* No. 112, Tumaco, December 28, 1912; (e) *El Anzuelo* No. 4, Tumaco, May 11, 1919; (f) Bernardo Merizalde del Carmen, *Estudio de la costa colombiana del Pacífico*. Bogotá: Imprenta del Estado Mayor General, 1921, 132.

A growing number of inhabitants made possible the urban transformation of Tumaco and Quibdó. Population data for these ports is inexact, for most figures are simple guesses by reporters and visitors. According to these estimates, Tumaco grew from about 2,000 inhabitants in 1900 to more than 15,000 in the 1920s (see table 10). Information for Quibdó is confusing. In the middle of the nineteenth century, a visitor calculated that the town had 1,500 inhabitants, the same number as Tumaco in 1890. Yet in 1913, the American consular agent estimated Quibdó's population at 3,500, and just a year later a local newspaper put it at slightly more than 4,000 people, a bit less than Tumaco at the time.[43] And, most puzzling of all, in 1929 the Claretian missionaries wrote that Quibdó had again just a little over 4,000 inhabitants.[44] Other sources place this port's population in the 1920s above 20,000 people.[45] The latter figure probably refer to the municipality rather than the city alone. In any case, Tumaco and Quibdó grew as people from the countryside settled in.

URBAN LIFE AND ITS LIMITATIONS

Tumaqueños and Quibdoseños not only built urban landscapes but strove to infuse them with an atmosphere that superseded village life. The urban feeling of these ports derived from the formation of various social classes and the amenities these groups demanded and began to offer, such as public concerts and movies, newspapers and clubs. Yet the changes remained limited, because the extractive economy that brought them about did not generate other productive activities and a strong market that could lead to a more robust transformation. So these were modest cities that additionally replicated the racial divide that separated manual labor in the forests from trading in the ports.

The establishment of a few manufacturing businesses was the most novel aspect of economic diversification and one of the sources of a working class. Quibdoseños bought boards and furniture made in their hometown, while Tumaqueños took pride in their shipyard and, by 1930, its button factory, owned by an Italian and known as *La Botonera*. Entrepreneurs in both places imported machines to freeze water and developed soda and pasta factories. In addition, Quibdó had locally manufactured candles, soap, and candy, while Tumaco could boast about its cigarette production.[46] Sawmills and workshops, as well as the construction of houses, public buildings, streets, bridges, and piers, provided work for men who migrated from the rural areas. Poorer male residents also labored as stevedores and even bootblacks.[47] Fishermen, especially in Tumaco, now had a larger market to supply. Lower-class women hired themselves as maids and nannies, worked as laundresses and ironing ladies, or prepared food for their kids to sell in the streets. Some, particularly in Tumaco, sold their favors to men.[48]

As towns turned into cities, opportunities also opened for the formation of a middling group. Various kinds of artisans offered their services to the growing population of the ports. Carpenters made furniture and coffins and repaired houses. Tinsmiths, blacksmiths, and painters helped, among other things, with making tools and signs. Urban dwellers sought hairdressers, jewelers, tailors, and shoe, watch, and hat repairers to maintain a proper attire and appearance. As did their peers, photographers announced their services in the local newspapers and competed for clientele.[49] Cities also needed a telegrapher, some typographers, nurses, and school teachers. The state offered jobs to qualified residents to serve as secretaries, councilmen, judges, and even mayors. The growing local market allowed for a few grocery stores and other kinds of shops, including one or two drugstores.[50] In 1911, for example, besides the commercial houses, Tumaco had twenty-three stores and thirty-four grocery stores.[51] The owners of the better establishments, including a handful of restaurants and hotels, joined the big merchants to form the region's elites. A small number of professionals mainly lawyers, a couple of doctors, and an occasional dentist, accountant, or engineer joined the ranks of the business class.[52]

Rich and poor, white and black, and even rural dwellers came together to share the main urban public spaces in religious celebrations, open-air concerts, and sports. Everyone participated in religious processions, especially those in honor of Saint Francis and the virgin of Las Mercedes, the patrons of these ports. Although these rituals had existed in the nineteenth century, they gained in prominence with the arrival of missionaries in both places.[53] The urban transformation of Quibdó and Tumaco also generated new forms of collective entertainment. As long as a band existed, the municipalities organized weekly evening concerts (*retretas*) in the kiosks of the parks, as recounted in the following section. Besides music, sports joined the amusement options of the urban population. In Tumaco, the cycling and athletic clubs organized bicycle races, while basketball games began to entertain both players and observers.[54] Quibdó, for its part, inaugurated a soccer field in 1926.[55] People from the countryside came for special occasions such as religious festivities, election days, and market days and sometimes partook in these activities.[56]

The city also began to offer a more varied array of indoor entertainment, particularly for men. Billiards remained, as they had been before the turn of the century, a favorite activity.[57] Lower-class games such as *bolo* and *chimba*, as well as cockfights, were popular in Tumaco. But elite men did not approve of them and instead created clubs where they could eat, drink, talk politics, and play billiards, cards, and chess.[58] In Tumaco, these men attended the Central and Santander clubs, while their peers in Quibdó shared their leisure time at the Atrato and Continental clubs or visited El Encloche, a renowned bar.[59] In the 1920s, black men and even black and mulatto women living in Quibdó created their own clubs.[60] Largely barred from these establishments, women could attend a few other places. Somewhere between a club and a grocery store, Tumaco's The White Rose, for example, must have served people of both sexes, just as the hall that in 1920 offered soft drinks and ice cream by the central plaza.[61]

Elite and middle-class whites, along with successful black officials, small traders, and artisans, enjoyed these new ways to spend their free time. Urban development came with clear marks of differentiation; access to performing arts and cinema was another one of them.[62] Since 1902, Tumaco had a decent theater, which artists traveling along the Pacific coast could use for their performances. Tumaqueños enjoyed plays and zarzuelas, and even violin concerts and magic shows.[63] Quibdó's location was not along artists' traveling routes, so locals developed their own performing groups. Starting in the late 1910s, various theatrical troupes appeared, some promoted by the Claretian priests, and performed throughout the 1920s in the city's three halls.[64] Cinema provided a more prevalent form of entertainment than the sporadic artistic presentations. Both ports inaugurated nickelodeons in 1914: their names—Kosmos Hall and Colombia Hall—attested to residents desires to partake in larger cosmopolitan and national communities.[65]

Hotels and restaurants added to the new urban atmosphere of the ports. Since at least 1905, visitors to Tumaco, on their way to Barbacoas or Pasto, could find a hotel along one of the two main streets of the port to spend the night.[66] Some of their owners also had restaurants, many with place-related names such as Tumaco, El Pacífico, and Colombia.[67] Quibdó also had a few hotels with imposing names such as El Republicano and El Metropolitano. These establishments offered various services for the local population, not only food but also games and even haircuts.[68]

Newspapers and educational institutions contributed to create a learned environment. The city government as well as a few residents purchased printing presses where they published, between 1900 and 1930, more than twenty newspapers in each of these two cities. *El Litoral Pacífico* (1909–15) and *El Fiscal* (1914–19) stand among the longer lasting papers in Tumaco. But with thirty-two years (1913–44) in print, Quibdó's *A.B.C.* surpassed all competitors.[69] These papers served as forums to discuss the region's news, problems, and politics, spread information about the rest of the world, and promote literature. Local intellectuals had occasional literary meetings, formed literary societies, and even organized literary competitions.[70] They also created public libraries with books donated primarily by themselves.[71] In the 1910s, high school students—the first the region ever had—benefitted and reinforced these developments.[72] The municipality of Tumaco hired, between 1911 and 1914, Max Seidel, a German pedagogue, as director of its new high school.[73] In Quibdó, the Colegio Carrasquilla, founded in 1915, produced a generation of men who presided over Chocó in the 1930s.[74] The city councils gave some scholarships and made extraordinary efforts to send students to Cali, Medellín, and Bogotá to complete the last grades, not available locally.[75]

Due to all the aforementioned changes, the author of the novel *Quibdó*, published in 1927, proclaimed triumphantly,

> The small city, a bit somnolent and carefree, was rapidly transforming itself into a cosmopolitan center, with a plethora of desires for progress and eager to occupy a place of honor among the great cities of Colombia and the Americas. . . . Its renovation was evident everywhere. Cement and brick buildings of attractive style. . . .

> New streets and avenues emerged constantly in places where thickets and mud seemed to have established themselves forever. Well maintained plazas populated by plants in bloom surfaced in places that . . . used to shelter pigs, donkeys, and goats. Modest "cabarets" gave their corrupting, exotic, and noisy touch in some suburbs.[76]

However, the transformation of Quibdó and Tumaco rested on an economy that could more readily generate urban dreams than a solid and self-reinforcing urban network. The diversification of trades paradoxically showed the limits, as much as the extent, of the urban achievements of these rainforest towns. The soda factories, the photo studios, and other businesses that sprang up before 1930 departed from the logic that governed the extractive sector—selling the region's natural resources in external markets—but did not constitute real economic alternatives. This moderate economy based on the extraction of natural resources could not create urban and rural markets large enough to generate further initiatives that would compete with extraction itself. For these reasons, it produced urban facades more than full-fledged urban landscapes.

The shortfalls of the urban landscapes and the life that sprang from them were everywhere to be seen. They expressed more than the inherent contrasts and contradictions of urban life: they showed the limited extent of the transformations of these two places. The frustration of the author of a 1920 article in a Tumaco newspaper serves to illustrate the point:

> Even though the . . . place is attractive . . . because most of the houses have two stories, it leaves a lot to be desired. . . . [W]e have huts, small and big houses . . . almost all lacking spacious rooms and good floors; the walls are badly painted and the rooms badly connected; the ceilings are too low and, what is still worse, the rooms are not well ventilated. . . . There are wide streets, but there are others—the so-called *dark alleys*—that are very narrow. . . . The *Calle del Comercio* is tortuous like the island. In the Christopher Columbus plaza one still sees old and rustic houses and it needs a gardener and an iron railing. . . . [The church's] decoration is terrible and the building lacks a tower. . . .[77]

The church was not the only public building with problems. Even the more cherished achievements could eventually generate more shame than pride. In 1914, an irritated observer referred to the municipal palace as the municipal pigsty, while five years later another viewer expressed with contempt that the city had a thatched hut for a theater.[78] Just two years after its creation, Quibdó's central park closed temporarily due to lack of maintenance.[79] The construction of public buildings proceeded slowly and never realized many of the fundamental aspirations of the city's better-off residents. Quibdó, for instance, never built its much-desired theater, while Tumaco lacked a proper jail.[80]

Other public works did not live up to basic expectations. Even the principal streets remained dirty, muddy, full of puddles, and overgrown by weeds. In consequence, local people had a hard time getting around the city without making a mess of themselves, especially when it rained.[81] A reporter from Tumaco decided to take it with humor and wrote: "Ocean inlet, swamp, pond, lake, or what should we call the mistakenly denominated Calle de Popayán?"[82] Observers complained about the pathetic condition of public toilets and of bridges' state of near collapse; and they equated plazas with jungles.[83] Dogs, cows, goats, and cats roamed the streets. When local authorities ordered cows out of Quibdó, their owners responded by halting milk delivery. A reporter wondered whether he would still be able to purchase eggs if the authorities took similar steps to free the town of roving hens.[84] Public lighting malfunctioned and did not encompass the entire cities.[85] To complete this grim picture, the telegraph often did not work and the mail took weeks to arrive.[86] Who could believe in the refinement and cosmopolitanism of these ports when the people remained cut off from the rest of the world, their streets resembled neglected trails, and their plazas looked like farms?

The history of the works carried out to guard Tumaco against the destructive force of the sea is emblematic of the restricted urban achievements of these ports. The ocean hit the island hard and eroded away a whole section known as La Punta. High tides could inundate major parts of the town, including the central plaza.[87] Since at least 1890, Tumaqueños had intended to build a retaining wall. Between 1903 and 1905 the municipality destined part of the customs income for the defense of the island, but the money served primarily to protect the houses of a few individuals. In the 1910s, the city council finally built an embankment made partly with mangrove wood. In 1919, however, a high tide destroyed the wall, leaving Tumaco as unprotected as it had ever been.[88]

Cultural accomplishments could also be seen as failures. Tumaco's "high school" for boys initially could not find students—so it had to function as a primary school—and after just three years it closed, while the famous Colegio Carrasquilla lacked the last two grades.[89] The performances that gave cultured airs to the cities were rare events, and the ostentation with which certain people dressed to go to the movies provoked laughs among the few who considered themselves free of such provincial attitudes.[90] Music bands often fell apart leaving residents longing for open-air concerts, and without funds to run them public libraries often remained closed. Some of the cities' few "professionals" had never obtained degrees.[91] These places clearly lacked many amenities that urban residents elsewhere took for granted.

The lowland economy not only spurred urban dreams that it could barely fulfill but also opened roads for social mobility that nonetheless had blatant racial limits. Paradoxically, as whites and blacks interacted more than ever before and in more equal terms, racial tensions reached their historic peak. Never before in lowland history had so many people lived together. As in the mining camps, almost everyone was black and a few of them were better off, before as captains of the slave gangs, now as small merchants or public servants. Some mulattoes joined the ranks of these well-to-do blacks. Whites continued to comprise a very small minority and among them and only among them were the owners of the commercial houses, the ultimate source of prestige. Their power, as well as their discriminatory practices and ideology, were all too evident in the constrained urban landscape.

Most blacks formed the cities' working classes, which literate men often disdained, as shown by Tumaco newspapers. One reporter complained that people needed to learn how to walk, instead of gallop, on the sidewalks. Others cringed when men swore and urinated in the streets and criticized Tumaqueños who showed up at the plaza for the evening concerts without shoes. Similarly, they felt ashamed that some women did the dishes in a central well destined to supply the city with water when it did not rain. One observer even dismayed at the impossibility of separating the "despicable whores" from the ladies in the port's public spaces.[92] Complaints of these sort happened in every Latin American city and everywhere they had racial overtones; but these were probably stronger in Tumaco than elsewhere.

Black people comprised not only the poorer sectors of the population but also most of the middling groups. Miguel Triana, a traveler from Bogotá who visited Tumaco in 1906, provides a rare and very positive glimpse of the status achieved by some black people:

> We passed every day in front of a public office where employees of color worked with such seriousness and dedication that made us believe we were in a black republic. Black families send their children to school, with great benefit to their

> race: almost all the laborers who unload merchandise for the customs office know how to write and carry their notes in hand bags. . . .
>
> In church, in the theater, in the main streets, the young black ladies, despite the eclectic and exaggerated taste of their dresses, show that there has been a real selection of the African race, given their elegant grace and the modesty of their manners and movements. The white families, forgetting their aristocratic preoccupations, know how to appreciate such distinction and to open space for blacks who, due to their talents and application, have started to become notable people.[93]

Despite this openness, there were limits to the positions blacks could achieve. A black man could open a store with the money made in mining and build a house for his family that mimicked those of the white elite.[94] He could share an office with white men and discuss political strategies in party meetings. His wife could chat with her white neighbor and they could sit next to each other in the movies. But no single black person owned a commercial house, that is, enjoyed firsthand the profits of the lowland economy. Besides, whites established barriers to their interaction with people with dark skins, as expressed in a 1920 newspaper article: "We have been notified that after some young women of the so-called humble race requested admission in the Sacred Heart of Jesus School, they were informed by the reverend mother superior that if they were admitted . . . they would be subject to the daily vexation of the students of the white race, whom she would not be able to punish in order to avoid displeasing their parents."[95] The racial divide, all too obvious in the Sacred Heart of Jesus School of Tumaco, had its equivalent in Quibdó at La Presentación. High society parties to which blacks were not invited also revealed that elite whites believed blacks had no place in advanced social spheres.[96]

The geographies of these expanding cities further stood as powerful reminders of the racial hierarchy of these societies (see maps 10 and 11). Tumaco extended to the west and to the north across the inlet of the sea that cuts the island in two, while by 1930 Quibdó counted eight neighborhoods.[97] As the cities grew, the centers of town acquired more symbolic value as the areas that tied the places together and—with its public landmarks and the houses of the rich—best represented their urban characters. In this part of town, commercial houses displayed imported merchandise. In Tumaco, most of them were found near the conjunction of the two main streets: the Calle del Comercio, which ran along the waterfront, and the Calle Márquez, named after the owner of one of the city's commercial houses. In Quibdó, these establishments stood along the

MAP 10 Tumaco, 1918. Source: Bernardo Merizalde del Carmen. *Estudio de la costa colombiana del Pacífico*. Bogotá: Imprenta del Estado Mayor General, 1921.

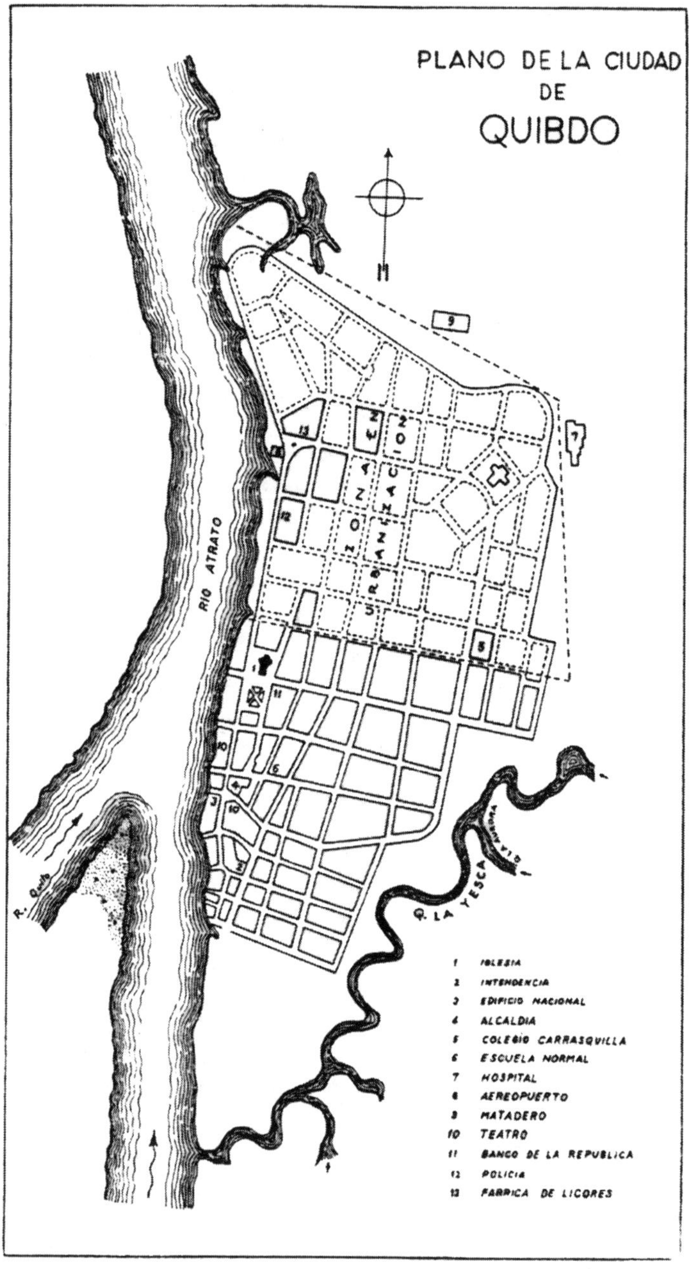

MAP 11 Quibdó, 1920s. Source: Contraloría General de la República. *Geografía Económica de Colombia, Tomo VI: Chocó*. Bogotá: Litografía Colombia, 1943.

Calle del Puerto and the Calle del Comercio. Commercial houses, but more generally the core of the city, represented both the modern face of the lowlands and the power of its white elite.

Unprecedented social mobility and aspirations met racial discrimination in the few blocks that comprised the region's two major cities. Thus during the first three crucial decades of the twentieth century, racial tensions increased as lowlanders built cities. Opposing music traditions and a historical arson attempt illustrate the racial contradictions that defined Quibdó and Tumaco's urban dreams.

MARIMBA MUSIC

In Tumaco, one of the key ways in which racial tensions were manifested was through clashes over music. Along the rivers of the southern half of the Pacific coast, from Buenaventura to Esmeraldas, blacks danced to the beat of drums and marimbas. Local white elites stationed mainly in Tumaco, and to a lesser extent in Buenaventura and Barbacoas, preferred bambucos and waltzes and other rhythms of European origin. As part of their efforts to conform to a cultured way of life, the coastal powerful followed the musical tastes of "decent" people in central Colombia and elsewhere. And they frowned on the intrusion of black music into their city. The lyrics, dancing styles, and everything related to parties organized by blacks repulsed local commentators and led them to openly reject the marimba culture. Imbued by a sense of superiority, civic and ecclesiastic authorities strove to put an end to such entertainment, while they promoted the formation of bands that would provide open-air concerts on Sundays and brighten up special occasions. Although Tumaco's ruling group managed to establish its musical preferences in the city's public space, it did not succeed in curtailing the *bailes de marimba*.[98]

These parties, also called *currulaos*, occurred throughout the rural areas, both in towns and in isolated rural dwellings, for every hamlet and every important family had a marimba.[99] Like today, artisans found in the forests hard palm-wood with which to make the keys, as well as bamboo for the resonators. Two men played these large xylophones using sticks with rubber heads. Marimba ensembles also had *bombos*, large double-headed drums, and *cununos*, single-head tubular drums. Men played them, beating bombos with cloth-covered sticks and cununos with their palms. Several women sang as they shook bamboo rattles called *guasás*. Marimbas and drums have obvious African roots, but the early development of this music remains a mystery. In the 1960s, anthropologist Norman Whitten studied the coastal communities of Ecuador and southern Colombia and provided a unique look into musical gatherings that earlier commentators criticized but failed to describe.[100] At the time, parties took place on Saturday nights and on festivals and religious holidays. The owners of the house with the marimba requested permission with the local police officer when they wanted to hold a party and paid a fee for a permit. Neighbors began to gather as the *marimberos* warmed up with a few songs. At around 9 p.m., when *bomberos*, *cununeros*, *cantadoras*, and a male singer joined, the dance began in earnest. It continued until dawn, when exhausted musicians and singers who had lost their voices returned home for a good rest. Sometimes, however, their energies lasted two or three days. The group played a variety of rhythms, most of them still practiced, such as *bambuco*, *agua larga*, *caderona*, and *andariele*. Whitten describes the *bambuco* movements in ways similar to what has now become a folkloric performance:

> A man who wishes to dance signals by standing quietly, and erect, with handkerchief in right hand hanging gently over his right shoulder. The woman holds her skirt slightly out to one side and in a distinct dance step . . . approaches the man; he moves toward her, moving his handkerchief, and as they nearly meet she turns, and he moves toward her, but she turns toward him, and he rapidly retreats. This pattern is repeated again and again. The woman steadily advances, pivots, retreats, while the man becomes more and more excited, leaps into the air, stamps his feet in time with the bombo, shouts and waves his handkerchief or hat.[101]

At the turn of the nineteenth century, literate men in the southern lowlands complained bitterly about these dance parties. Their criticisms constitute the most frequent way in which they referred to city blacks. Everything about these merrymakings ran against local reporters' notions of civilized urban life. From the 1870s through the 1920s, upset city dwellers considered the music monotonous and tiresome and the lyrics immoral.[102] But what most disgusted them was the dancing, as the words, in 1879, of a pundit from Buenaventura illustrate: "With the same disorder and frenzy with which they play it, they dance it . . . without any rule of courtesy, attention, or gallantry towards the beautiful . . . sex."[103] Four decades later, Father Merizalde offered more detail about the dancing: "In the beginning, dances are performed with certain order, but as blacks drink alcohol, the movements turn into outrageous jumps, the chants into strident screams, the music into rough and dissonant sounds. Not infrequently dances end in punches, garroting, and stabbings. Coastal dances remind one of those practiced in Africa: in both you see all sorts of pirouettes and jumps."[104]

Father Merizalde was not alone in portraying these parties as out-of-control and degenerate affairs. Heavy drinking and fights figure prominently in other references too. A Tumaco observer noted with disgust that "in those bacchanalias . . . the drunkenness that dominates generates brawls, wounds, and atrocious scandals."[105] Someone else even associated drunkards on binges with "public women given over to the vice of sensuality."[106] The volume, frequency, and duration of blacks' parties further bothered literate men.

Complaints about these gatherings rested on the dichotomies with which elites made sense of their world. They considered themselves civilized Colombians in contrast to lowland blacks, whose music, they believed, exposed their backward—and even savage—nature and ways of life. For them, as for people of their time, race was as much about appearance as about character and habits.[107] A Tumaco journalist reflected this general sentiment when he said, "Culture is precious, and no one can deny that it is related to race."[108] For these reasons, their criticisms were widespread and also applied to dances that apparently did not have marimbas, and even to the vigils held for saints and deceased people.[109] Until today, black people from the coast spend long nights singing to honor a saint or someone from the community who died. These rituals are called *novenas*, or *gualís* or *chigualos* when the deceased is an angel, that is, an infant. Black music, whether religious or pagan, accompanied by dancing or not, provoked white observers' disapproval.

In the eyes of an insecure provincial elite, such traditions prompted allegations of savagery—and savagery had its place and time. In very telling fashion, a newspaper compared blacks' savage rhythms to the chants of monkeys in the jungle.[110] Marimbas did not belong in cities; in fact, they corrupted them. Their sound represented the incursion of the unruliness of the forests into the humanized urban environment. As a Tumaco journalist expressed, this music belonged to the past, understood both as the colonial dark ages and the remote origins of the lowland population in faraway Africa. "It is time," he wrote in 1913, "that Tumaco, a town that is acquiring tints of civilization and progress, forsakes those old colonial habits. The marimba, instrument of savage peoples, makes us think we are in some town in Africa."[111] Appalled local elites thought blacks acted as if they had never left the savage continent. A Tumaco resident asked, "Are we in Kaffirland? We believe that only there people can tolerate that a group of idle men and women get together in a house . . . around a gallon of *aguardiante*, the monotonous beat of a bombo, with the pretext of adoring a ridiculous figure compared to a saint, to deprive a whole neighborhood of sleep."[112] And just as, for these men, Africa symbolized savagery in the world at large, so did the forests in the Pacific coast and the black neighborhood of Pueblo Nuevo in Tumaco, renowned for its "wild parties."[113]

The association of marimba music with Africa represented one way to set apart lowland black culture from what elites considered Colombian. Observers also made this point by contrasting music from the southern lowlands with bambuco, the rhythm that in the late nineteenth century came to be associated with the nation. Bambuco emerged in the Andean interior and was already popular in Bogotá in the middle of the nineteenth century. As music became one of the constituents of Colombian national identity, bambuco surfaced as the quintessential Colombian rhythm.[114] If endorsing it meant embracing things Colombian, then, commentators reasoned, adhering to marimba music indicated a reluctance to conform to national lore.[115]

Cultural manifestations that ran counter to national ideals and notions of propriety, local elites believed, as did their peers in other Latin American cities with a population of African descent, deserved to be abolished. In the Colombian Pacific coast it was not *camdomblé* and *capoeira*, as in northern Brazil, but bailes de marimba.[116] Besides contrasting the parties and vigils unfavorably to civilized ideals, elite men argued that such dances impinged on neighbors' right to sleep.[117] For this reason, one person went so far as to consider currulaos unconstitutional.[118] Others worried about the lack of respect for the dead, for Pueblo Nuevo neighbored the cemetery.[119] In consequence, according to a local journalist, "The city council should impose a heavy fee on them, or the mayor should suppress them altogether, as Father Hilario Sánchez managed to do for some time."[120] At least in Tumaco, marimba dances required licenses, and local authorities sometimes denied them.[121] Religious authorities, it seems, attacked currulaos more eagerly. Another priest, Father Manuel María Mera, also made himself known, around 1910, for his "campaign against the savage dances of coastal blacks."[122] No wonder that people say that, in the old days, when a marimba floated down a stream, it indicated the presence of a furious priest.

For their own entertainment, whites preferred what they considered more refined instruments. During their literary evenings, filled with readings and speeches, a local lady would perhaps play the piano—an expensive instrument that exemplified the sophistication the elite aspired to.[123] In 1913, a snobbish journalist wrote with pride that "the use of pianos, as well as violins, is increasing in the littoral and [replacing] the guitar."[124] Whites also danced, sometimes until dawn, but to other rhythms.[125] In a contemporary novel that depicted life in Quibdó, for instance, the protagonists enjoyed a foxtrot at one of their parties.[126] At the turn of the nineteenth century, elites throughout Colombia enjoyed waltzes, contredances, polkas, and mazurkas. Like their peers from larger cities, privileged people from the coast looked to Europe for inspiration.[127]

Besides listening to the music they treasured, the regional elite repeatedly tried to make it public and official by sustaining municipal bands that would bring "cultured" entertainment to the urban population. For this purpose they created music schools, attended mostly by artisans. But schools and bands had erratic existences. In the first few months of 1879, for instance, Barbacoas had a music school that closed due to irregular attendance and a lack of a permanent space. The town opened another school in 1892, which lasted only a few years.[128] In 1908, the band from Barbacoas played in the inauguration ceremony of the extremely short-lived department of Tumaco.[129] The port could not again suffer the humiliation of having the band of decrepit Barbacoas come play on important occasions. So a year later, Tumaco created its own school and band. Yet in 1910, 1912, 1915, and 1920, new schools or bands formed, proof of the short life of their predecessors.[130] Tumaco's municipal band performed marches, boleros, pasillos, and mazurkas on Sunday nights, and sometimes on Thursdays, at Parque Colón.[131] It also performed at special occasions such as holidays and inaugurations of public buildings. Local journalists referred to these concerts with great pleasure and called for them whenever they ceased to happen.[132]

Different musical traditions stood in stark contrast to one another only in the minds of those who yearned to strengthen Tumaco's civilized credentials. After all, the same black men who grew up listening to marimba music took their place in bands with a trumpet or a clarinet in hand. Probably, more than once, they performed after having partied all night in Pueblo Nuevo to the melodious sound of a marimba. The director of Tumaco's municipal band between 1912 and 1914 was a man of African descent, as indicated by his last name, Biafara. Here, as in other Latin American cities, being a musician brought no prestige among the higher ranks of society.[133] Judith Ferrer, who was born in Quibdó in 1904 to one of the most prestigious local families, remembered that black men made up the city's band, which was no place for a member of her family or a man of her color.[134] Blacks performed in city bands and played European instruments not simply because they were forced to by an arrogant elite; they most likely welcomed and supported these bands, as suggested by the independent formation of some of them in certain towns. A missionary provided unusual evidence when he recalled that rural inhabitants received priests "with a band composed of several drums, some flutes and *chirimías* [wooden clarinets], and even . . . a violin with *pita* strings. The band plays at night, at dawn, at noon, and during processions. To those instruments one must add, in solemn festivities, an accordion."[135]

Similarly, while journalists opposed marimba music to the Andean bambuco, one of the rhythms most played by lowland blacks was also called bambuco. Curiously enough, both kinds of bambucos are courtship dances in which men use handkerchiefs and the couples move describing figures of eight with their feet.[136] Perhaps for this reason a journalist from Buenaventura referred to the currulao as a bastard degeneration of "our national bambuco."[137] A traveler from Bogotá simply dismissed the "maddening notes of the African bambuco."[138]

The scorn for marimba music in Tumaco at the turn of the nineteenth century exemplifies everyday racial tensions in the emerging urban settings of the Pacific lowlands. Visitors in general proved more tolerant, and even interested, in this musical manifestation and in this manner anticipated developments of the 1950s, when modernized versions of marimba rhythms made their way into the national music scene. Paradoxically, the instrument that epitomized this kind of music was left behind as its notes came to represent the southern lowlands in the national mosaic.[139] Since the 1990s, a search for the black roots and components of national culture led to the rescue of the marimba as a symbol of the Pacific coast and to the reinvigoration of its music.[140] In the twentieth century, then, marimba music passed from being outside of accepted notions of nationhood to represent the essence of a black region in the nation. As a symbol of both blackness and the southern lowlands it resembles the role that the figure of Manuel Saturio Valencia—an educated black man who was executed in 1907—played in the second half of the twentieth century for the northern part of the region. His execution and the arson attempt that lead to it provide a unique opportunity to explore how Chocoano identity was constructed around the memory of urban racism at the beginning of the century. More important for our understanding of the building of a postemancipation society up to 1930, it allows us a rare glimpse into the racial tensions of those years.

ARSON AND DEATH

At 1 a.m. in the morning of May 1, 1907, while Quibdó's residents slept, Manuel Saturio Valencia allegedly lit a rag soaked in kerosene and threw it on the thatched roof of one of the houses located in the heart of the city. Alarmed, neighbors reacted quickly and stopped the fire. Authorities promptly found the culprit, who by 7 p.m. supposedly confessed. The following day, General Enrique Palacios, the intendant, wrote to President Reyes and the Ministry of War informing them about the crime and the confession. He suggested that martial law be declared in the District of Quibdó and that the military should judge the crime. The president, a general himself, responded on May 5 by qualifying the offense as atrocious, approving the creation of a court-martial, appointing Palacios as civil and military chief of Chocó, and declaring martial law in the area. Imbued with his new authority, General Palacios issued two decrees: one created the court-martial, while the other determined that arson offenses would be tried by the military and in very serious cases would carry the death penalty. On May 6 the court sentenced Saturio to death, and the following day, after the Ministry of War approved of this decision, the offender was publicly executed at 4 p.m. by a firing squad.[141] The expeditious reaction of local authorities and the extreme punishment imposed can be largely explained by the gravity of the offense, which stemmed from an entrenched fear that the town could be reduced to ashes, or, perhaps even worse, that the social order could be turned on its head.

Any person who lived in the lowland towns and cities until the 1970s had memories of some remote or recent conflagration and understood all too well the fear provoked by the cry of "Fire."[142] A liberal-party newspaper from Barbacoas illustrates the point by the way it recounted, in 1880, one such incident: "Fire. It has been several months since we last heard that terrifying word, even more alarming than that of regeneration [the conservative party motto]; but on the night of the 3rd we had a big fright with the one that tried to develop in the house of Mr. Rafael Rodríguez."[143] Short pieces on averted fires, such as this one, abound in the region's newspapers.[144] In some cases, though, fires raged out of control causing great ruin. All major settlements in the lowlands were at some point partially burnt down. Before that grim night in 1907, Barbacoas had been partly devoured by flames in 1788, 1853, and 1902; Tumaco had similar disasters in 1855 and yet again sometime before 1874; Buenaventura burned in 1881; and half of Quibdó itself suffered from fires not too long before, in 1882 and 1891.[145]

While everyone panicked over fire, the better-off particularly worried that the craving some had for their possessions and merchandise would lead them to arson. In 1918, a newspaper announced that in Barbacoas, "after the criminal arson attempt that readers already know about, there have been others of lesser importance . . . always in the commercial neighborhood, in all probability with the intention of stealing."[146] In Quibdó, in 1868, local authorities attempted to create a civil defense group in part due to fears of arson.[147] Quibdoseños suspected that both the 1882 and 1891 fires had been premeditated. In the second case, the fire razed twenty-five of the principal houses, causing great losses (partly through robbery) among the city merchants and more prosperous residents.[148]

The gravity attributed to arson is clear throughout the case's record. The intendant cited previous fires as a reason to have arson tried by a court-martial, while the sentence considered that "[t]the impunity allowed to all perpetrators of the previous fires that have afflicted Quibdó and Chocó in general and the need to establish a precedent as an exemplary lesson for the future, demand in this case a severe . . . punishment to avoid similar attempts in the future."[149] Saturio himself apparently acknowledged that he was paying for his deed and that of his predecessors. In the speech he allegedly read before his death, he said: "Today I have to pay the debt left by a few jackals, who having committed the same offense I did, are today free. . . ."[150] Saturio was not the first person to attempt such an atrocious crime, nor was he—I imagine—the first whose condition of being black worsened his deed in the eyes of the authorities.

Just as in colonial times white administrators in the mining camps knew the limits of their power, so too the owners of the commercial houses and their peers shared a sense of vulnerability. The intendant let his uneasiness of being part of a very small white minority show, as he played on contemporary stereotypes by suggesting that violent blacks were behind one such incident. In a telegram he sent to Bogotá the day after the attack, Palacios wrote that during the fire "a bunch of *blacks*, armed with sticks and machetes, had been seen in the vicinity on the watch of the outbreak, but when they saw the . . . force I displayed . . . they disappeared." And immediately afterwards he added, "[The offender] is *black*." Although Saturio allegedly confessed that "the only culprit of the . . . fire that took place last night . . . is me," the authorities requested that martial law be declared in order to give them the authority to arrest the whole gang.[151] Palacios was shifting the guilt from a stray individual to a group that could become a mob—a mob of blacks in a town where a few whites held the upper hand in politics and the economy.

The transgression against which the intendant reacted went beyond the perceived threat of a horde of blacks hoping to achieve material gain through arson. At least some of Quibdó's privileged wanted an exemplary punishment for Saturio, a former black judge who had questioned the foundations of the social order, dared to find the powerful guilty, and taken justice into his own hands. The intendant hinted at the accused's motivations when he emphasized Saturio's socialist and anarchist inclinations. A local newspaper addressed the issue in a piece titled "Anarchism," which speculated on the apparent motives of the crime. The article showed complete certainty of Saturio's guilt (including an image of him, see fig. 24) and responded at least partially to Saturio's alleged confession, which appears in the telegram the intendant sent to Bogotá after

FIGURE 24 Manuel Saturio Valencia. Source: *Ecos del Chocó* No. 6, May 19, 1907.

the execution and was partially quoted during the sentencing and in the newspaper itself.[152] In it, Saturio not only admitted committing the hideous crime and expressed no remorse but presented himself as a man defeated by alcohol, a pariah: "I did it due to mental confusion [*extralimitación*] when I saw that all my aspirations and hopes had been frustrated, and I also wanted those who live well to feel the weight of suffering. Unfortunately my plan failed and I could not achieve what I wanted. Since I was a child I have sought to acquire money and a good social position but the vice of alcohol prevented me from doing so."[153]

Saturio's thinking was flawed, opined the journalist who, given the size of Quibdó, must have known him, because it stemmed from foreign ideas he misinterpreted, not from the reality in which he lived: "Fond of readings of all kinds, which he could not fully understand, [Saturio] ended up intellectually corrupting himself to the extreme of aspiring to Nero's celebrity. It also appears that he wanted to imitate Salvat, the character portrayed by Zola in his *Paris*." According to this view, Saturio, intellectually avid but somehow impaired, dreamed of burning Quibdó as Nero allegedly had Rome burnt. More telling, he followed the ideology of Salvat, a Parisian anarchist who planted a bomb outside the house of a rich baron. But why?

The wrongs Saturio apparently reacted against combined class and racial inequalities, as can be inferred from the journalist's rebuke. Providing a watered-down version of the myth of racial harmony, he asserted that to be an anarchist in Quibdó was unjustified because "whites and blacks, poor and rich, have their homes intermingled . . . blacks and whites, rich and poor reciprocally need each other, because we are few." While Saturio himself never mentioned race explicitly, commentators did, tacitly implying that racial barriers ultimately motivated the offender. In a context of racial imbalances in which Saturio's putative views could be shared by others, reporters strengthen their argument by pointing out that "the torch of the incendiary in a city built with timber burns everybody equally, it does not distinguish between positions, fortunes, ages, sexes, or races."[154] Thus if anyone happened to agree with Saturio's thinking, no one should approve of his act, for it also harmed those it intended to avenge.

The case against Saturio rested largely on his confession. We will probably never know if the authorities forced him into a false confession, as Quibdoseños maintained decades later, or if they fabricated it altogether.[155] His alleged words served all too well to justify an unusually severe penalty. Yet it would have been odd to read to the appointed lawyers, who requested with reasonable arguments a more lenient punishment and were part of Quibdó's privileged few, a sentence that included words falsely attributed to the defendant. Also, in a speech supposedly pronounced minutes before his death, Saturio publicly accepted his guilt. That same day of the execution, the official newspaper of the intendancy published this speech, as did another local newspaper three days later.[156] Since the whole town witnessed the execution, it is unlikely that these newspapers fabricated this second confession. Saturio's alleged words could be read as those of a drunkard who attempted a pathetic act of personal vengeance. But his background as an educated black man and former judge suggests that the arson attempt could also be read as a message to others like him of his own disgrace, and thus as an attempt at social justice.

Manuel Saturio Valencia had been for various years municipal judge and at the time of his death, apparently at the age of forty, worked as secretary of a high official in the intendancy.[157] Given that he held these jobs, he must have been, at least by local standards, a fairly educated man and enjoyed a good reputation. Collective memory attributes his education to priests, who first taught him in Quibdó and then sent him to Popayán where he befriended young white students.[158] This literate man exemplifies the group of successful blacks and mulattos, referred to earlier in this chapter, who acquired a position through mining, by setting up stores, or by working in the state bureaucracy. It seems paradoxical that one of these fortunate men would want to set his hometown on fire.

Republican ideals of equality must have had a strong impact on a black man acting as judge in a place ruled largely by whites. James Sanders and Jason McGraw have artfully shown how, in the second half of the nineteenth century, people of African ancestry in Cauca and Caribbean Colombia debated ideas of citizenship and claimed a place in the political community that was forming.[159] That those ideas had been discussed among blacks in the lowlands is evident in an anecdote from one of the most remote corners of Chocó. In 1852, the canal explorer John Cresson Trautwine stayed in the small town located at the mouth of the Pepé River in the isolated Baudó Mountains. One night, as he talked with his French host, Antoine Posso, the local priest, and a doctor who traveled with him,

> [a] strapping, naked black fellow very unceremoniously entered the room, and without as much as a "by your leave," lay down on a table a few feet from us, to take a snooze. . . . Señor Posso very properly deemed it but a courteous concession to the clerical position of the Cura, and a manifestation of respect to the Doctor and myself as strangers, not to let it pass without a reprimand. He accordingly read a

> brute sharp lecture on the impropriety of his conduct; but received for a reply, that the intruder considered himself a *true citizen*, and *thoroughgoing "Democratico,"* and as such, did not choose to inconvenience himself by any squeamish respect to the Cura, the strangers, or any one else.[160]

Just a year after the abolition of slavery, this black man asserted to four prominent white men that as a citizen he did not need to pay respect to them. Ideas of equal citizenship, present deep in the Baudó Mountains in the 1850s, must have provoked agitated discussions in Quibdó, as apparently they did in Tumaco: "Unfortunately, on Independence Day 1911, we attended the inauguration of the Pedagogical School. The tribune was open and we heard the worst demagogical speeches, among them those of a black fellow, Klinger, who with an exaggerated notion of democracy and in the name of Liberty, Equality, and Fraternity, talked in an florid language and with the most preposterous metaphors and vulgar sayings—a wonderful strategy for those ignorant in history and for the notabilities of the hood. The people cheered with frenzy."[161]

This piece is unusual for it refers to Klinger as black. Direct references to race and racial differences are conspicuously absent in the historical record. Another rare instance in which race is mentioned touches on racial discrimination. In a case regarding some lands in Istmina, the plaintiffs referred to themselves as "settlers of the black race" and argued that "[b]ecause Mr. Millán is white and influential, the procurator, the mayor, and even the police chief, deny us protection."[162] Interestingly enough, Jaime Castillo, another former judge, wrote the letter, for the settlers were not literate.[163] The implicit desire to avoid these thorny issues, as well as the gray zone that social mobility itself exemplifies, partially explain at least the silences. Well-to-do blacks and mulattos interacted on a daily basis with members of the most prestigious white families. They run into each other in the streets, when buying or selling various sorts of merchandise, in government offices, and even in their own houses. A member of one of the most distinguished families of the time acknowledged (as her parents, who lived in Saturio's time, must have told her) that as a friend of the family Saturio visited her house, but she clarified that no blacks attended her family's parties.[164] Saturio might have looked up to an elite to which—as a black man—he could not fully belong. Whether he was guilty, a drunkard or not, these racial limits were evident and for that reason colored this landmark case.

However, had it not been for a particular conjuncture in which the military could attain extraordinary powers, the events of May 1, 1907, in which nothing much ultimately happened, and its protagonist would not have warranted historical notice. After President Reyes dissolved congress in 1905 and a national assembly granted him extraordinary powers, he presided over Colombia in a quasi-dictatorial manner. Additionally, both he and the intendant were generals. These circumstances permitted the creation of the court martial that had Saturio executed in just a few days. In the trial, the defendants asked that Saturio be given the punishment contemplated in the Penal Code; only arson that produced deaths carried the death penalty. Saturio's defendants also requested clemency from the president, who had the power to overturn death sentences. But they achieved nothing. A few years before or after, Saturio would have had an ordinary trial, which would have lasted longer; his sentence would have probably been more lenient, and he would have been able to appeal. Furthermore, in 1910, just three years after Saturio's execution, congress abolished the death penalty.[165]

Saturio's death earned him status as a regional symbol, as attested by the attention his life and death have received from leading Colombian black thinkers. Two of the most important Chocoano intellectuals wrote books about Saturio. The ethnologist Rogerio Velásquez (1908–65) published in 1953 *Memorias del Odio* (Memories of Hate), an autobiography supposedly written by Saturio in jail before being executed, and Miguel Angel Caicedo (1919–95), renowned poet and writer, published in 1992 *Manuel Saturio (El hombre)*, an inquiry into the truth of the events of May 1907. Even one of Colombia's leading black literati, Manuel Zapata Olivella, from the Caribbean, wrote a novel, *El Fusilamiento del Diablo* (The Devil's Execution, 1986), loosely based on Saturio's story. The lengthiest book on this historical character, however, is Teresa Martínez de Varela's 1983 novelized biography entitled *Mi cristo negro* (My Black Christ).[166]

As its name suggests, this book portrays Saturio as a martyr, an innocent victim of the white elite. Martínez de Varela depicts a charming black man, who worked hard to succeed and defend the people of his race against white oppression. His death resulted from a carefully planned vengeance. Saturio's real "crimes" consisted in being a leader of the black population and getting pregnant Deyanira Castro, a beautiful white woman. His affair destroyed the lady's honor, at the same time that he found out that the black woman he wanted to marry was his sister. Devastated, he started drinking. After being framed, Saturio paid the price of transgressing racial barriers. In this melodrama, Saturio's life and death acquire meaning against a background of strong racial disparities and discrimination. Caicedo, the poet, follows Martínez de Varela in presenting an innocent man who fought for the rights of black people in the context of a divided society and was framed by his enemies. But in a conciliatory (and contradictory) tone he interprets Saturio's death as the result of ill feelings between men (related to the beautiful Deyanira), in which race had no place. At the close of the century and the end of his successful life as a teacher, Caicedo wanted to leave behind the racial hatred that emanated from Saturio's memory and that so strongly inspired Velásquez forty years before. In his book, the ethnographer presents a corrupt society that produced a revulsive man, who nonetheless fought for the betterment of other blacks. Although Velásquez's Saturio did try to burn the city, this author places the ultimate blame on Quibdó's racist society.

As we can see, Saturio became a regional hero, as his image was cleaned, while the racist background of early twentieth-century Quibdó remained. His image served as a cornerstone in the development of a black Chocoano identity because of his association with a place and time remembered for its racism and the overwhelming power of the white elite. The oral tradition that inspired these books, and the books themselves, elevated Saturio to a prime place in the pantheon of Chocoano great men. A 1994 book intended to teach primary school children about Chocó, for instance, includes Saturio as the first Chocoano figure it depicts. This book says that he was a self-taught teacher, as well as the first black musician, poet, and captain. His concern for others and for justice led him to teach crafts to local kids and instruct them about their obligations and rights. Furthermore, as the first black prosecutor and judge he instructed Chocoanos about "human rights." The authors explain that all of this bore him the ill-will of the "aristocracy," and they repeat the erroneous belief that Saturio was the last person to be executed in Colombia.[167]

Saturio's execution elevated him into a regional symbol but also left his purported works undone. According to communal memory, however, others continued Saturio's quest for racial justice. For example, Diego Luis Córdoba (1907–64), born precisely the year of Saturio's death, is remembered as having continued Saturio's fight and became the most influential Chocoano politician of his time. He is recognized for achieving, in 1947, the elevation of Chocó from intendancy to department.[168] He studied in the Colegio Carrasquilla in Quibdó and later in Medellín and Bogotá, where he obtained a degree in law. Since his days as student activist, Córdoba and his peers, many of whom were white, used the figure of Saturio in their emerging regionalism. In 1926, Chocoanos studying in Medellín formed the Liga Pro-Chocó, which Córdoba headed. In 1930, they sent a letter to the government in Bogotá arguing, among other things, against having nonnatives governing Chocó. "History," they wrote, "demonstrates that all those foreign rulers have been a failure for the area: ever since that one under whose regime the intelligent Chocoano young-man Manuel Saturio Valencia died in the scaffold . . . for a culpability defectively proven."[169] Córdoba returned to Quibdó in 1932, where he again used Saturio's image, this time to gain the support of the black Chocoano majorities.[170] His campaigning included, and his own figure represented, a vindication of blackness in the face of white historical privilege.

Córdoba died still young, representing Colombia as ambassador to Mexico. Just two years after, a fire razed Carrera Primera, the section of the city that for decades represented white supremacy. While visiting Quibdó I learned that the fire ruined the white elite and drove it out of Chocó. By 1966, however, most members of these families had already left town. The fire did what Saturio could not: burn downtown Quibdó, yet the days of the prosperous commercial houses were long gone. The fire destroyed the symbol of white power, which stemmed from the period when Quibdó became a city presided by a commercial elite, not white power itself. Without white exporters and their establishments and with the rise of black politicians, Chocó remained in black hands, and being Chocoano became proudly equated with being black.

The birth of cities in the Pacific lowlands of Colombia came with limitations and contradictions proper to this region. Tumaco and Quibdó acquired an urban appearance in the early twentieth century and its population accompanied that physical change with novel amenities and an animated atmosphere. But the commerce in vegetable ivory, gold, and platinum that sustained the urban dream also imposed restrictions. These cities were too small for their aspirations, lacked basic services, and could not even produce high school graduates. More troubling still were the racial contradictions inherent to the cities' ascents. Free black labor in the forests ultimately sustained the building of urban landscapes, which acquired life with the sweat, laughs, and ingenuity of its inhabitants, most of whom were black. Yet just as a few whites controlled the region's economy, so too they stood at the apex of the emerging urban space, which they conceived in opposition to both the people and the environment that made it possible. Freedom exercised in the lowland forests allowed the creation of urban landscapes where freedom found other opportunities, and where it also clashed with the racist ideologies and practices that gave lowland cities their initial character.

CONCLUSION

A People and an Environment with History

THIS BOOK HAS DELVED into the history of black people in the rainforests of the Pacific coast of Colombia to reveal an unusual postemancipation trajectory characterized by high levels of autonomy. The story I recount adds a missing piece to the historical mosaic of the transition from slavery to freedom in the Americas; but it does more than that: it suggests that examining black people's access to and uses of various environments is necessary to fully assess how freedom was experienced and understood. The two main concepts that have guided this environmental approach to social history—extractive economy and racialized landscapes—provide ways to include both nature and disenfranchised people in history, particularly that of modern Latin America.

In a continent that had, in the early nineteenth century, more than two-thirds of its territory covered by forests, and whose colonial economy was to an important extent based on the enslavement of black people, the intertwined history of jungles and freedom—one of the pillars of republicanism—is particularly relevant.[1] For black people, the legal condition of freedom acquired concrete meaning through the increase in their possibilities to determine what to do with their bodies and time, and where. In the forested Pacific coast of Colombia, they had substantial leeway. Free blacks enjoyed freedom of movement, not just of using the paths that cross the forests or of paddling canoes along its rivers, but of choosing the place where they wanted to live. The region is large and sparsely populated, so even if some of the most desired spots were claimed, there were still unoccupied corners even in settled riverbanks and shores. While most people remained in the mining areas, some moved downstream to settle the lower parts of the river basins or the coast. Black people also regulated their work schedules and decided how they would collaborate to extract gold from the subsoil or tap rubber trees, or they simply went by themselves to work on a canoe or procure meat for their tables. Thus, unlike the plantation workers examined frequently in the literature, these peasants did not have to obey a boss or overseer or compete with a plantation for land on which to build their houses or cultivate a plantain grove. It is in this sense—of rural people who relied on family labor and had access to the means of production—that I have referred to black lowlanders as peasants. This concept allows us to understand who they were in relationship to other such rural people, black or not, in Latin America and elsewhere. In this manner, their singularity can be spelled out without considering them an isolated oddity.

This singularity centered on what in the lowlands counted as a means of production, which goes well beyond land, the natural resource most commonly singled out in agrarian studies and in plantation economies. These *rainforest peasants* used the various niches of the lowland environment to produce most of the resources they consumed, in addition to those they turned into commodities by selling them to white merchants who lived in town. Rivers, mangroves, wetlands, and the ocean provided them with fish and mollusks to obtain protein. Since the times of slavery, they also hunted for a wide variety of game in the forests, including various rodents and birds. They sweetened their palates and guaranteed they had enough energy by growing sugar cane, plantains, and other crops. To cultivate these foodstuffs they preferred small areas along the river levees where the most fertile soils are found. The surrounding forest had many uses besides providing game, the most important of which was as a source of timber to build houses, canoes, and tools, such as *bateas* for gold panning. Palms supplied thatch for making roofs, while lianas, resins, wild fruits, and a myriad other natural products helped provide the means to make a living in the jungle. Black labor and ingenuity went a long way not just to guarantee survival but also to make a home in the lowlands by getting to know and appropriate all of its niches. Since black people could not produce all they needed, they turned elements of nature into commodities—such as gold and vegetable ivory—by separating them from the soils and ecosystems where they were found and trading them for clothes, salt, and essential goods such as machetes.

Access to a wide and diverse territory explains the high levels of autonomy attained in the lowlands and points to the importance of examining access to different environments elsewhere in order to better understand the transition from slavery to freedom throughout the Americas. This transition happened in a continent dominated by forests, deserts, and wetlands that provided many useful resources. Native ecosystems expanded following the demise of the indigenous population in the sixteenth century, while the overall regional population grew only at a slow pace, concentrated in relatively few spaces. This population was mostly rural and thus tended to live close to rivers and woodlands. Since cities tended to be small, even there people could occasionally hunt or grow gardens. In this context, it is very likely that blacks had access to natural resources—communal or privatized—that increased their autonomy and shaped their lives in the aftermath of slavery. While most places did not have extensive rainforests, like those of the Pacific lowlands, the presence of a single mango tree could make a difference in times of want. A couple of less extreme examples from Brazil illustrate the broader point: many free blacks lived near the coast and close to productive mangroves where they could procure food, while some of those inhabiting Rio de Janeiro used the forests of their city's surroundings to produce charcoal for sale.[2] Fishing and hunting, pervasive before widespread deforestation and pollution, often supplemented families' protein intake and incomes. By earning some cash or providing food for the family's table through their independent labor, free blacks secured part of their survival and diminished their need to work for others. Nature often subsidized the transition to freedom, in societies that left black people to fare by themselves without compensation for their enslavement, and enhanced the meaning of this legal condition. In urban and plantation settings, and in virtually all rural economies, access (or the lack thereof) to natural resources had an impact on blacks' lives and thus on their experience of freedom.

Free blacks' access to natural resources tended to increase in contexts of economic marginality because of restricted competition. In the Pacific coast, which never boasted a powerful economy, competition for vegetable ivory and mineral deposits did limit access and hinder autonomy, but only partially. While those small entrepreneurs who wanted to secure exclusive access to vegetable ivory groves failed, the New Timbiquí Gold Mines Ltd. and the Chocó Pacífico Mining Company succeeded in appropriating vast mining deposits. In those places, they restrained people's mining options. But given that these companies worked with technologies that functioned only in certain spaces—shafts in high terraces and dredges in riverbeds and levees—local people could still mine elsewhere using their traditional methods. Furthermore, they could hunt, cultivate, and use forest resources to satisfy their needs. Had competition been fiercer and more widespread, spaces of autonomy would have shrunk. As explained in the introduction, profitable plantation economies in the Caribbean and Brazil established control over land, or at least over the best lands, leaving free blacks scant possibilities to become peasants and forcing them to continue toiling as plantation workers. In prosperous rural economies, monopolies over the means of production tended to obstruct access to key resources for former slaves and their descendants. Furthermore, plantations turned forests into fields, thus diminishing the supply of firewood, thatching material, and many other useful natural products.

These strong plantation economies produced large cities such as Havana and Rio, which allowed for a different form of autonomy based on skills rather than access to means of production. Black middle classes formed in these cities, given the opportunities opened in small-scale commerce and trades, such as blacksmiths, or through formal education. However, the majority of black people remained in the lower echelons of society. Given that Tumaco and Quibdó were small incipient cities that lacked the diversification of more complex urban centers, only a few prosperous blacks opened up a shop or found a job in government; most earned an income as laundresses, stevedores, and the like. The trading ports of the lowland marginal economy did not generate much social mobility and thus alternative ways of building autonomous lives.

This book has stressed autonomy—and its association with marginality—as fundamental for the understanding of the experience of freedom. Furthermore, it has grounded its explanation of the relationship between the postemancipation society of the Colombian Pacific coast and the forested environment in two concepts. The first is *extractive economy*, which signals the extraction and commodification of parts of nature as the basis of an economy. This concept stresses a relationship that a wide variety of societies have with forests, or with other environments such as oceans with their fisheries or mineral-rich subsoils, mediated by a dependence on the procurement of an assortment of resources that are primarily a product of nature's independent processes. Extraction can be thus distinguished from agriculture and industry, which have a more mediated dependence on nature. In the Pacific lowlands, gold mining started a long-lasting dependence on the natural supply of resources for the functioning of a market economy. While initially based on slavery, the regional extractive economy later served as the foundation for blacks' lives in freedom. It also diversified, as extraction for sale came to include platinum as well as forest resources, mainly black rubber and the seeds of vegetable ivory palms. Therefore, two very different political economies of extraction—one characterized by labor coercion, the other by autonomy—came to define the lowlands before and after the mid-nineteenth century. But an important caveat needs to be introduced here: before abolition, the extraction of a means of exchange through placering helps explain how many enslaved people purchased their freedom—relatively more than anywhere else in Afro-America—creating a growing population of free men and women.

This understanding of extractive economy offers an alternative way to think about extraction from the idea of extractivism that has become common in recent years. Extractivism tends to be used in two main and related ways: to refer to (mostly) mining industries, which have recently become the leading sectors of various Latin American economies, and to criticize economic models characterized by resource depletion and profit accumulation by a few. Such uses often include activities that are not in a strict sense extraction of resources produced primarily by nature with little human intervention, and leave out uses such as that exemplified by the "extractive reserves" that have been created in the Brazilian Amazon to protect the lifestyles of rubber tappers and small extractors of other resources. Extractivism then often ceases to be a term that signals a particular way of relating to the environment and obscures the existence of communities—such as rainforest peasants and fishermen—who live off the marketing of natural resources.[3]

The second concept is *racialized landscapes*, which calls attention to the physical transformation of the region and the way in which race—a lens that determined literate men's understanding of social differences—negatively affected the perception of this place and of blacks' accomplishments. In this manner, and by explaining the inception of an urban landscape and its contradictions, it stresses the racial tensions inherent in a society built on a racial division of labor. The notion of racialized landscapes can have wide use beyond the Pacific lowlands, for it draws attention to the connections between humanized environments and racialized social groups past and present. Although more important in the nineteenth century and first half of the twentieth, before the horrors of Nazism discredited it, race and racial categories (which vary across time and space) continue to mark social hierarchies and to guide understandings of places and their very concrete materialities. The primacy of racial thinking in the decades that followed emancipation in Colombia prompted prejudiced readings of the landscapes that were being shaped in the Pacific lowlands. Migration from the mining areas to the lower parts of the river basins and the coasts made this the predominantly black region we know today. Along rivers and shores, black people's houses and crops created the landscape that came to characterize the place in decades to come. Blacks also constituted the majority of the population in the small ports that served as trading centers of natural commodities. However, contemporary literate men, who overlooked blacks' role in their liberation, considered that blacks fit awkwardly in urban landscapes and failed to regard their shaping of a forested landscape and their lives in freedom as achievements of any sort.

This kind of oversight extends to recent historical accounts. This book, and the growing literature on postemancipation societies, should help to enrich broader historical narratives, such as national ones, and in this way contribute to lessen the sense of partial exclusion to our imagined communities that black people have.[4] For instance, although the transition from slavery to freedom is a building block of our present societies, of the three general histories of Colombia only Frank Safford and Marco Palacios's *Colombia, Fragmented Land, Divided Society*, published in 2002, addresses the issue and suggests its complexity.[5] The book acknowledges the importance of self-purchase in mining areas and even argues that the most significant social change, at the base of the society, brought about by the wars of independence "was the movement of uncounted numbers of Afro-Colombians from slavery to freedom." Even then, the book reproduces the general tendency to dismiss black people's agency: "Both royalists and patriots, as a matter of wartime necessity, filled out their military ranks by recruiting slaves, to many of whom they promised freedom."[6] The accent here is placed on the royalist and patriot leaders, when it could highlight those who risked their lives in order to free themselves from slavery. Similarly, blacks, who are included as slaves, disappear as free people.

Safford and Palacios's also miss an opportunity to help readers recognize that the Pacific coast and its black people are integral parts of the country. Their keen interest in geography leads them to treat the settling of public lands as a major topic in Colombian history. They focus on three currents of migration (which originated in the Andean highlands of Santander, Boyacá, Cundinamarca, and Antioquia) and conclude that "[t]he movement of these people from the cool highlands toward the warmer zones of the mountain slopes was the most important social phenomenon of the century from 1850 to 1950."[7] As this book has shown, especially from the mid-nineteenth century on, some free blacks moved from the mining areas to the rest of the region, bringing these spaces into the national territory. Furthermore, by notarizing their informal land purchases, they gave a place to these forests in state institutions. Excluding the entire Pacific coast, whose migration originated within the lowlands instead of the highlands, does not seem to have, in the authors' view, any bearing on their generalizing aspirations. I would like this book to sharpen the very blurred view that the Pacific coast and black people's history have in the mental map, not just of the best historians of Colombia, but of Colombians in general.

Similarly, this book seeks to call attention to the place that rainforests and other environments have in the social history of Colombia and elsewhere. Historians such as Safford and Palacios acknowledge that the country's broken terrain made transportation development harder, while a few nod at the astonishing diversity derived from having two coasts, extensive natural savannas, the Andes, and a wide variety of forests. However, these very concrete natural differences disappear in a mostly abstract regional geography when dealing, for example, with violence, a favorite national topic. If they receive a mention at all, it tends not to be as part of the toolkit used for analysis. The question of environmental change, for example, how armed struggles have affected environments, is notoriously absent in historical studies.[8] Because of jungles' powerful presence and the fact that they have always been there, they tend to be considered the quintessential "nature" and as such devoid of history.[9] However, as this book shows, they have for long been entangled with our social past in both symbolic and material ways. The jungles of the Colombian Pacific coast were the cradle for a particular experience of freedom, have a place in the symbolic geography of the country and of tropical lands, and supported an economy that slowly depleted mineral deposits but did not destroy the vegetation. Such developments are part, along with deforestation and forestry, of the world's forest past.

Landscapes of Freedom thus gives a place in forest history to what are perhaps the most humid rainforests in the world, illuminates postemancipation worlds by emphasizing their relationship to environments, and strives to make the Colombian national community more inclusive by reconstructing an important part of black people's past. But it does not explain an important paradox: while marginality initially allowed for an autonomous experience of freedom, in the long run it has reduced people's choices and opportunities—that is, their capacity to decide how to live their lives. This contradiction stems from the low levels of education and income associated with marginality, clearly shown by recent economic and social indicators for the lowlands. Between 1990 and 2004, Chocó (the northern part of the lowlands) had 1 percent of the Colombian population but only 0.4 percent of its GDP. Such figures have their parallels in education and well-being: in 2005, the percentage of people who could not read and write in Chocó more than doubled the national average, while most schools fared badly in national scholastic tests.[10] The very particular postemancipation trajectory of the Pacific lowlands, therefore, has a bittersweet flavor: while it enhanced freedom's meaning, it also had onerous costs, which are seen more clearly from a long-term perspective.

This book ends around 1930, after first providing an overview of slavery and freedom before abolition in 1851 and then explaining how lowlanders developed a postemancipation society. Looking beyond the period examined in this book would reveal how the gap separating the lowlands from the rest of the country widened. Colombia was among the poorest countries in Latin America until the coffee economy expanded in the 1920s.[11] Since then, regional differences increased, as some places fared better than others and, because they were deemed strategic for growth, received the best that the state had to offer. In the 1930s and 1940s, for instance, the recently created Agrarian Bank privileged servicing peasants in coffee areas, while the Department and then Ministry of Hygiene followed suit with yellow fever vaccination. The country also became more integrated through roads, a network of state institutions, and even the strengthening of nationalist sentiments, which made regional comparisons more pervasive. A study of the decades spanning the time of the Great Depression to at least the 1990s is still to be written and is crucial to understand the paradox brought about by persistent marginality: an increasingly limited autonomy, coupled with a strong feeling of having been left behind (a paradox shared by the very autonomous maroons of Suriname).

Marginality allowed black people the freedom to occupy, control, and give meaning to the rich coastal jungles, all of which has left an important cultural legacy, underappreciated and even scorned until its official acknowledgment by the 1991 constitution. Based on black people's occupation of the region, and their control and management of the environment, Law 70 of 1993 recognized their right to communal land titles, which were issued in the following years. A radical change in perception, therefore, laid the foundation for the most important act of social justice in the region's history and reinforced a positive understanding of black people's autonomous lives and cultures. But we must not forget that the loss of a child is often an avoidable tragedy and that studying in some of the worst schools in the country constitutes a serious handicap. While the recognition of black communities' practices and worldviews has been a necessary development, it should not overshadow its connections to some of the difficulties with which many black people have to cope.[12]

NOTES

VOYAGES INTO THE RAINFOREST

1. By way of comparison, in Brazil there are 111 officially recognized *quilombos* (black communities) with more than eleven thousand families covering almost one million hectares. In the Pacific lowlands of Colombia, which cover more than eight million hectares, more than five million of them have been titled to more than sixty thousand families. The Suriname maroons have the second-largest territory inhabited by black people. See "Terras Quilombolas of the Comissão Pró-Indio de São Paulo," accessed November 16, 2012, http://www.cpisp.org.br/terras/asp/terras_tabela.aspx.
2. Timothy Farnhamn, *Saving Nature's Legacy: Origins of the Idea of Biological Diversity* (New Haven: Yale University Press, 2007); and Edward O. Wilson and Frances M. Peter, eds., *Biodiversity* (Washington, D.C.: National Academy Press, 1988).
3. Robert West, *The Pacific Lowlands of Colombia* (Baton Rouge: Louisiana State University Press, 1957), 27; John Kricher, *A Neotropical Companion: An Introduction to the Animals, Plants, and Ecosystems of the New World Tropics* (Princeton: Princeton University Press, 1999), 5.
4. Alwyn Gentry, "Phytogeographic Patterns as Evidence for Chocó Refuge," in *Biological Diversification in the Tropics*, ed. Ghillean T. Prance (New York: Columbia University Press, 1982); Alwyn Gentry, "Species Richness and Floristic Composition of the Choco Region Plant Communities," *Caldasia* 15 (1986); Enrique Forero and Alwyn Gentry, *Lista anotada de las plantas del departamento del Chocó* (Bogotá: Universidad Nacional, 1989); Alwyn Gentry, "Sabemos más de la luna que del Chocó," *Eco-Lógica* 15–16 (1993).
5. Claudia Leal, "Conservation Memories. Vicissitudes of a Biodiversity Conservation Project in the Rainforests of Colombia, 1992–1998," *Environmental History* 20,

no. 3 (2015): 368–95; Peter R. Wilshusen, "Territory, Nature, and Culture. Negotiating the Boundaries of Biodiversity Conservation in Colombia's Pacific Costal Region," in *Contested Nature: Promoting International Biodiversity Conservation with Social justice in the Twenty-first Century*, ed. Steven R. Brechin, Crystal L. Fortwangler, Peter R. Wilshusen, and Patrick C. West (Albany: State University of New York Press, 2003).

6. On that experience see Claudia Leal, *A la Buena de Dios, Colonización en La Macarena, ríos Duda y Guayabero* (Bogotá: CEREC-FESCOL, 1995).
7. On this general Latin American trend see Donna Lee Van Cott, *The Friendly Liquidation of the Past: The Politics of Diversity in Latin America* (Pittsburgh: University of Pittsburgh Press, 2000).
8. DANE, *Colombia, una nación multicultural: Su diversidad étnica* (Bogotá, 2007), 20, 23.
9. Transitory Article 55, Colombian Constitution, 1991.
10. Law 70, 1993, article 2.
11. See Astrid Ulloa, *The Ecological native: Indigenous Peoples Movements and Eco-Governmentality in Colombia* (New York: Routledge, 2005).
12. Instituto Colombiano de Antropología and Proyecto de Zonificación Ecológica del Pacífico Colombiano, Instituto Geográfico Agustín Codazzi, which were financed by the World Bank.
13. See Arturo Escobar, *Territories of Difference: Place, Movements, Life, Redes* (Durham: Duke University Press, 2008); Eduardo Restrepo, *Etnización de la negridad: la invención de las 'comunidades negras' como grupo étnico en Colombia* (Popayán: Editorial de la Universiad del Cauca, 2013); and "Ethnicization of Blackness in Colombia: Toward De-racializing Theoretical and Political Imagination," *Cultural Studies* 18, no. 4 (2004); Kiran Asher, *Black and Green, Afro-Colombians, Development, and Nature in the Pacific Lowlands* (Durham: Duke University Press, 2009); Ulrich Oslender, *Comunidades negras y espacio en el Pacífico colombiano: hacia un giro geográfico en el estudio de los movimientos sociales* (Bogotá: Instituto Colombiano de Antropología e Historia, 2008); Odile Hoffmann, *Comunidades negras en el Pacífico colombiano: Innovaciones y dinámicas étnicas* (Quito: Instituto Francés de Estudios Andinos, Institut de Recherche pour le Dévelopment, Ediciones Abya-Yala, Centro de Investigaciones y Estudios Superiores en Antropología Social, Centro de Estudios Mexicanos y Centroamericanos, 2007).
14. Constanza Millán Echavarría (Coordinadora de la investigación). *Buenaventura: un puerto sin comunidad* (Bogotá: Centro de Memoria Histórica, 2015).
15. Researchers who have studied rainforest extractive economies tend to ask why they did not lead to sustained growth, and in some cases this question has led them to conflate the definition of extractive economies with their perceived outcomes. Camilo Domínguez and Augusto Gómez define extractive economy as a productive process that generates surplus value from a commodity whose exchange and accumulation happens extra-regionally, while Stephen G. Bunker says that this type of economies produce social and environmental disruption in the extraction

peripheries, while creating value in the regions of consumption or transformation. In this view, the relationship that extractive economies establish with environments (which I believe defines them) ends up backstage. Camilo Domínguez and Augusto Gómez, *La economía extractiva en la Amazonía colombiana* (Bogotá: Tropenbos-Araracuara, 1990), 9; Stephen G. Bunker, *Underdeveloping the Amazon: Extraction, Unequal Exchange, and the Failure of the Modern State* (Chicago: University of Chicago Press, 1985) and "Modes of Extraction, Unequal Exchange, and Progressive Underdevelopment on an Extreme Periphery: The Brazilian Amazon, 1600–1980," *American Journal of Sociology* 89, no. 5 (1984).

16. For a general overview of the modern history of Latin American rainforests from an environmental perspective see Claudia Leal, "From Threatening to Threatened Jungles," in *A Living Past, Environmental Histories of Modern Latin America*, ed. John Soluri, Claudia Leal, and José Augusto Pádua (New York: Berghahn Books, forthcoming). On the Amazon rubber boom see Barbara Weinstein, *The Amazon Rubber Boom, 1850–1920* (Stanford: Stanford University Press, 1983); Domínguez and Gómez, *La economía extractiva*, and Bradford L. Barham and Oliver Coomes, *Prosperity's Promise: The Amazon Rubber Boom and Distorted Economic Development* (Boulder: Westview Press, 1996). On the Amazonian colonial extractive economy see David Cleary, "Towards an Environmental History of the Amazon: From Prehistory to the Nineteenth Century," *Latin American Research Review* 36, no. 2 (2001). For Petén, Mosquitia, and Yucatán see Norman B. Schwartz, *Forest Society: A Social History of Petén, Guatemala* (Philadelphia: University of Pennsylvania Press, 1990); Karl H. Offen, "The Geographical Imagination, Resource Economies and Nicaraguan Incorporation of the Mosquitia, 1838–1909," in *Territories, Commodities, and Knowledges: Latin American Environmental History in the Nineteenth and Twentieth Century*, ed. Christian Brannstrom (London: Institute of Latin American Studies, 2004); and Herman W. Konrad, "Capitalism in the Tropical Forest Frontier, Quintana Roo, 1880–1930," in *Land, Labor, and Capital in Modern Yucatán*, ed. Jeffery T. Brannon and Gilbert M. Joseph (Tuscaloosa: University of Alabama Press, 1991). Schwartz examines the environmental aspects of natural resource trade, while Konrad's work exemplifies how the study of such an economy can be done while completely ignoring environmental aspects. Although not a historical study, Norman Whitten, *Black Frontiersmen, A South American Case* (New York: Schenkman Publishing Company, 1974), interprets the culture of the southern Pacific lowlands as a product of the adaptation to the environment and the boom and bust cycles of natural resource exploitation.

17. Alexander V. Chayanov and Eric Wolf emphasize access to land and family labor (a family farm equipped with means of production, according to the former, or rural cultivators who run households rather than businesses, according to the latter), as well as production for the family's consumption and the market, as characteristic traits of peasantries. Alexander V. Chayanov, *The Theory of Peasant Economy*, ed. Daniel Thorner, Basile Kerblay, and R. E. F. Smith (Homewood, Ill: Irwin, Inc., 1966 [1925]); Eric Wolf, *Peasants* (New York: Prentice Hall, 1966). While discussing

black peasantries, Sidney Mintz defined peasants as "Landholders who produce much or most for their own consumption, while also producing items for sale," in "The Origins of Reconstituted Peasantries," in *Caribbean Freedom: Economy and Society from Emancipation to the Present*, ed. Hilary Beckles and Verene Shepher (Princeton: Markus Wiener Publishers, 1996), 95.

18. See Woodville K. Marshall, "Peasant Development in the West Indies since 1838," in *Caribbean Freedom: Economy and Society from Emancipation to the Present*, ed. Hilary Beckles and Verene Shepher (Princeton: Markus Wiener Publishers, 1996) and Hebe Maria Mattos de Castro and Ana Lugão Rios, "O pós-aboliçao como problema histórico: balanços e perspectivas," *Topoi* 5, no. 8 (2004), and "Para além das senzalas: campesinato, política e trabalho rural no Rio de Janeiro pós-Abolição," in *Quase-Cidadão: histórias e antropologias da pós-emancipação no Brasil*, ed. Flávio dos Santos Gomes and Olívia Gomes da Cunha (Rio de Janeiro: FGV, 2007).

19. Marshall, "Peasant Development in the West Indies," 100.

20. Ralph-Michel Trouillot, *Haiti: State against Nation. The Origins and Legacy of Duvalierism* (New York, Monthly Review Press, 1990), 39–40. Sydney Mintz has stressed the importance of these "proto-peasantries" in the emergence of peasantries in *Caribbean Transformations* (Chicago: Aldine Publishing Company, 1974), chapter 5; "Slavery and the Rise of Peasantries," in *Roots and Branches: Current Directions in Slave Studies*, ed. Michel Craton (Toronto: Pergamon, 1979), 213–53; and "The Origins of Reconstituted Peasantries." See also Jean Besson, "Freedom and Community: The British West Indies," in *The Meaning of Freedom: Economics, Politics, and Culture after Slavery*, ed. Frank McGlynn and Seymour Drescher (Pittsburgh: University of Pittsburgh Press, 1992), 189–91.

21. Louis A. Pérez, "Politics, Peasants, and People of Color: The 1912 'Race War' in Cuba Reconsidered," *The Hispanic American Historical Review* 66, no. 3 (1986); Sidney Mintz, "The Origins of Reconstituted Peasantries," 94–95; Luis A. Figueroa, *Sugar, Slavery and Freedom in Nineteenth-Century Puerto Rico* (Chapel Hill: University of North Carolina Press, 2005); Sônia Maria de Souza, *Terra Família e Solidariedade: estratégias de convivência camponesa no período de transição—Juiz de Fora (1870–1920)* (Bauru: Edusc, 2007), 69, shows peasant units producing food for plantations while recognizing that "access to land was extremely restricted."

22. For Cauca see Mateo Mina, *Esclavitud y libertad en el valle del río Cauca* (Bogotá: Fundación Rosca de Investigación y Acción Social, 1975); Claudia María Correa González, "Integración socio-económica del manumiso caucano, 1850–1900" (BA thesis, Universidad de los Andes, 1987), Eduardo Mejía, *Origen del Campesino Vallecaucano, siglos XVIII y XIX* (Cali: Universidad del Valle, 1993), and *Campesinos, poblamiento y conflicto: Valle del Cauca 1800–1848* (Cali: Universidad del Valle, 2002). For the Caribbean see Orlando Fals Borda, *Historia doble de la Costa, Tomo 3: Resistencia en el San Jorge* (Bogotá: Carlos Valencia Editores, 1986), and *Historia doble de la Costa, Tomo 4: Retorno a la tierra* (Bogotá: Carlos Valencia Editores, 1986).

23. Catherine LeGrand, *Frontier Expansion and Peasant Protest in Colombia, 1850–1936* (Albuquerque: University of New Mexico Press, 1986).
24. Sydney Mintz, "Slavery and the Rise of Peasantries"; Marshall, "Peasant Development in the West Indies"; Rebecca Scott and Michael Zeuske, "Property in Writing, Property on the Ground: Pigs, Horses, Land, and Citizenship in the Aftermath of Slavery, Cuba, 1880–1909," *Comparative Studies in Society and History* 44, no. 4 (2002). On the importance of land for building community see Jean Besson, "Freedom and Community."
25. Elione Guimarães, *Terra de preto, usos e ocupação da terra por escravos e libertos (Vale do Paraíba meneiro, 1850–1920)* (Niterói: Editora da UFF, 2009), 54, referring to Maria Helena Toledo Machado's *O plãno e o pánico: Os movimentos sócias na década da abolição* (Rio de Janeiro: Editora UFRJ, 1994).
26. Hebe Mattos, "Beyond Masters and Slaves: Subsistence Agriculture as a Survival Strategy in Brazil during the Second Half of the Nineteenth Century," *Hispanic American Historical Review* 68, no. 3 (1988); and *Ao Sul da História: Lavradores pobres na crise do trabalho escravos* (Rio de Janeiro: Universidade Federal Fluminense, 2009 [1987]).
27. Rebecca Scott, "Defining the Boundaries of Freedom in the World of Cane: Cuba, Brazil and Louisiana after Emancipation," *American Historical Review* 99 (1994): 92–98.
28. Louis A. Pérez, "Politics, Peasants, and People of Color," and *Lords of the Mountain: Social Banditry and Peasant Protestin Cuba, 1878–1918* (Pittsburgh: University of Pittsburgh Press, 1989).
29. Marshall, "Peasant Development in the West Indies," 101. See also Douglas Hall, *Free Jamaica, 1838–1865* (New Haven: Yale University Press, 1959).
30. Trouillot, *Haiti: State against Nation*, 73, see also 59–62, 72; and Robert K. LaCerte, "The Evolution of Land and Labour in the Haitian Revolution, 1791–1820," in *Caribbean Freedom: Economy and Society from Emancipation to the Present*, ed. Hilary Beckles and Verene Shepher (Princeton: Markus Wiener Publishers, 1996).
31. Rebecca Scott and Michael Zeuske, "Property in Writing, Property on the Ground: Pigs, Horses, Land, and Citizenship in the Aftermath of Slavery, Cuba, 1880–1909," *Comparative Studies in Society and History* 44, no. 4 (2002), 672, 683–84. See also Rebecca Scott, "Defining the Boundaries of Freedom," 86.
32. Philippe I. Bourgeois, *Ethnicity at Work: Divided Labor on a Central American Banana Plantation* (Baltimore: John Hopkins University Press, 1989), 67.
33. Scott E. Giltner, *Hunting and Fishing in the New South: Black Labor and White Leisure after the Civil War* (Baltimore: John Hopkins University Press, 2008), 7. Walter da Silva Fraga, *Crossroads of Freedom: Slaves and Freed People in Bahia, Brazil, 1870–1910* (Durham: Duke University Press, 2016), x, suggests that in Bahia access to mangroves made a difference to free blacks.
34. Flávio Gomes dos Santos, "A 'Safe Haven': Runaways Slaves, Mocambos, and Borders in Colonial Amazônia, Brazil," *The Hispanic American Historical Review* 82, no. 3 (2002); and "Fronteiras e mocambos: o protesto negro na Guiana brasileira,"

in *Nas terras do Cabo Norte. Fronteiras, colonização e escravidão na Guiana brasileira, séculos XVIII/XIX*, org. Flávio Gomes dos Santos (Belém: Editora Universitária UFPA, 1999).

35. Eurípides A. Funes, "'Nasci nas matas, nunca tive senhor'—história e memoria dos mocambos do baixo Amazonas" (PhD diss., Universidade de São Paulo, 1995); Eliane Cantarino O'Dwyer and José Paulo Freire de Carvalho, "Jamary dos Pretos, municipio de Turiaçu (MA)," and Eliane Cantarino O'Dwyer, "Os quilombos do Trombetas e do Erepecuru-Cuminá," in *Quilombos, identidade étnica e territorialidade*, org. Eliane Cantarino O'Dwyer (Rio de Janeiro: Editora FGV, 2001); and Rosa Acevedo Marin and Edna Ramos de Castro, *No caminho de pedras de Abacatal: experiência social de grupos negros no Pará* (Belém: Universidade Federal do Pará, 2004).

36. Richard Price, *The Guayana Maroons: A Historical and Bibliographical Introduction* (Baltimore: John Hopkins University Press, 1976), 2. Emphasis added.

37. Weak ties to the market, or greater isolation, have casted doubts of their status as peasants. Mintz, "The Origins of Reconstituted Peasantries," 97. Studies of the maroons have concentrated on their history of maroonage or their culture rather than their systems of production. See Silvia W. De Groot, *From Isolation towards Integration: The Surinam Maroons and their Colonial Rulers, 1845–1863* (La Haya: Nijhoff, 1977 [1963]) and Richard Price, *First-Time: The Historical Vision of an Afro-American People* (Baltimore: John Hopkins University Press, 1983).

38. O. Nigel Bolland, *Colonialism and Resistance in Belize: Essays in Historical Sociology* (Benque Viejo del Carmen: Cubola Productions, 2003 [1988]). For the entire description of the system see his essay "Labour Control and Resistance in Belize in the Century after 1838" in the cited collection.

39. For overviews of the field see Tom Perreault, Gavin Bridge, and James McCarthy, eds., *The Handbook of Political Ecology* (London: Routledge, 2015); Paul Robbins, *Political Ecology: An Introduction*, 2nd edition (Oxford: Wiley-Blackwell, 2011); and Roderick Neumann, *Making Political Ecology* (New York: Routledge, 2005). Some relevant studies of struggles over natural resources different from land are Susanna Hecht and Alexander Cockburn, *The Fate of the Forest: Developers, Destroyers and Defenders of the Amazon* (New York: Verso, 1989); Nancy Peluso, *Rich Forests, Poor People: Resource Control and Resistance in Java* (Berkeley: University of California Press, 1992), Richard Peet and Michael Watts, eds., *Liberation Ecologies: Environment, Development, Social Movements* (London and New York: Routledge, 1996) and Nancy Peluso and Michael Watts, eds., *Violent Environments* (Ithaca: Cornell University Press, 2001). The journal *Ecología Política* has been the main reference for the field in the Spanish-speaking world.

40. For a history of racial thinking see John P. Jackson Jr. and Nadine Weidman, *Race, Racism, and Science, Social Impact and Interaction* (New Brunswick: Rutgers University Press, 2006) and Michael Banton, *Racial Theories* (Cambridge: Cambridge University Press, 1988 [1974]). For Latin America see George Reid Andrews, *Afro-Latin America, 1800–2000* (New York: Oxford University Press, 2004), chapter 4 and Thomas Skidmore, *Black into White, Race and Nationality in Brazilian Thought*

(Durham: Duke University Press, 1998). On the history of the concept of race in Colombia see Claudia Leal, "Usos del concepto raza en Colombia," in *Debates sobre ciudadanía y políticas raciales en las Américas negras*, ed. Claudia Mosquera Rosero-Labbé and Agustín Laó-Montes y César Rodríguez (Bogotá: Universidad Nacional de Colombia, sede Bogotá, CES, IDCARAN, sede Medellín, Universidad de los Andes, 2010).

41. For discussions about the meaning and uses of landscape in geography, see Marvin Mikesell and Philip Wagner, "The Themes of Cultural Geography," in *Readings in Cultural Geography*, ed. Marvin Mikesell and Philip Wagner (Chicago: University of Chicago Press, 1962); Denis Cosgrove, "New Directions in Cultural Geography," *Area* 19, no. 2 (1987); James Duncan and Nancy Duncan, "(Re)reading the Landscape," *Environment and Planning D: Society and Space* 6 (1988); Marie Price and Martin Lewis, "The Reinvention of Cultural Geography," *Annals of the American Association of American Geographers* 83, no. 1 (1993); Paul Groth, "Frameworks of Cultural Landscape Study," in *Understanding Ordinary Landscapes*, ed. Paul Groth and Todd W. Bressi (New Haven: Yale University Press, 1997); Don Mitchell, "Landscape," in *Cultural Geography: A Critical Dictionary of Key Concepts*, ed. David Atkinson, Peter Jackson, David Sibley, and Neil Washbourne (New York: Palgrave Macmillan, 2005). Within the framework of the influential Berkeley School of Geography, that is, using Carl Sauer's concept cultural landscape, Robert C. West published in 1957 the best study of this region to this day: *The Pacific Lowlands of Colombia* (Baton Rouge: Louisiana State University Press).

42. Warren Dean, *With Broadax and Firebrand: The Destruction of the Brazilian Atlantic Forest* (Berkeley: University of California Press, 1997); Reinaldo Funes Monzote, *From Rainforest to Cane Field in Cuba: An Environmental History since 1492* (Chapel Hill: University of North California Press, 2008 [2004]); and John Soluri, *Banana Cultures: Agriculture, Consumption, and Environmental Change in Honduras and the United States* (Austin: University of Texas Press, 2005). Shawn Van Ausdal, "Pasture, Profit, and Power: An Environmental History of Cattle Ranching in Colombia, 1850–1950," *Geoforum* 40, no. 5 (2009), also focuses on deforestation, but caused by ranching, an economic activity almost entirely geared toward the internal market. José Augusto Pádua's *Um sopro de destruição: pensamento político e crítica ambiental no Brasil escravista, 1786–1888* (Rio de Janeiro: Jorge Zahar, 2002) studies environmental thinking inspired by deforestation.

43. José María Samper, *Ensayo sobre las revoluciones políticas y la condición social de las repúblicas colombianas (hispanoamericanas)* (Bogotá: Universidad Nacional de Colombia, 1969 [1861]), chapter 4.

44. On black citizenship see Andrews, *Afro-Latin America*; Flávio dos Santos Gomes and Olívia Gomes da Cunha, eds., *Quase-Cidadão: histórias e antropologias da pós-emancipação no Brasil* (Rio de Janeiro: Fundação Getulio Vargas, 2007).

45. Martin Melosi, "Mainstreaming Environmental History," *RCC Perspectives* 3 (2011): 33; John R. McNeill, "The State of the Field of Environmental History," *Annual Review of Environment and Resources* 35 (2010): 345–74.

46. Overviews of Latin American environmental history do not explicitly mention its contribution to social history, suggesting that at least until recently its principal merits and contributions lay elsewhere. See Mark Carey, "Latin American Environmental History: Current Trends, Interdisciplinary Insights, and Future Directions," *Environmental History* 14 (2009); Christian Brannstrom and Stefania Gallini, "An Introduction to Latin American Environmental History," in *Territories, Commodities, and Knowledges: Latin American Environmental History in the Nineteenth and Twentieth Century*, ed. Christian Brannstrom (London: Institute of Latin American Studies, 2004), and Stefania Gallini, "Historia, ambiente y política: el camino de la historia ambiental en América Latina," *Nómadas* 30 (2009). In "Un balance de la historia ambiental latinoamericana," *Revista de Historia* 59–60 (2009), Patricia Clare does mention its relation to social history as one of its strengths but does not develop the point.
47. Karl Zimmerer, *Changing Fortunes, Biodiversity and Peasant Livelihood in the Peruvian Andes* (Berkeley: University of California Press, 1996); Angus Wright, *The Death of Ramon González: The Modern Agricultural Dilemma* (Austin: University of Texas Press, 2005 [1990]); Myrna Santiago, *The Ecology of Oil: Environment, Labor, and the Mexican Revolution 1900–1938* (Cambridge: Cambridge University Press, 2006); and "Extraction Stories: Workers, Nature, and Communities in the Mining and Oil Industries," in *A Living Past, Environmental Histories of Modern Latin America*, ed. John Soluri, Claudia Leal, and José Augusto Pádua (forthcoming); Alejandro Tortolero, "Water and Revolution in Morelos, 1850–1915," in *A Land Between Waters. Environmental Histories of Modern Mexico*, ed. Christopher R. Boyer (Tucson: University of Arizona Press, 2012). For the impact of environmental conditions of workers' health see also Nicholas A. Robbins, *Mercury, Mining, and Empire: The Human and Ecological Cost of Colonial Silver Mining in the Andes* (Bloomington: Indiana University Press, 2011). For labor unrest see also Thomas Rogers, *The Deepest Wounds: A Labor and Environmental History of Sugar in Northeast Brazil* (Chapel Hill: University of North Carolina Press, 2010). That environmental hardship causes political mobilization is not always easy to prove, as John Soluri has pointed out in "Labor Rematerialized: Putting Environments to Work in the Americas," *International Labor and Working Class History* 85 (2013). Other works on environmental history that involve labor are Soluri, *Banana Cultures*; and Sterling Evans, *Bound in Twine: The History and Ecology of the Henequen-Wheat Complex for Mexico and the American and Canadian Plains, 1880–1950* (College Station: Texas A&M University Press, 2007).
48. Christopher Boyer, *Political Landscapes: Forests, Community, and Conservation in Mexico* (Durham: Duke University Press, 2015); Thomas Miller Klubock, *La Frontera: Forests and Ecological Conflict in Chile's Frontier Territory* (Durham: Duke University Press, 2014). For an overview of African and South Asian environmental history see Paul Sutter, "What Can US Environmental Historians Learn from Non-US Environmental Historiography?," *Environmental History* 8, no. 1 (2003). Scholarship on India has explored many facets of struggles over forests, especially

in the context of colonial relations, for example Ramachandra Guha's classic *The Unquiet Woods: Ecological Change and Peasant Resistance in the Himalaya, Expanded Edition* (Berkeley: University of California Press, 2000 [1989]).

49. See María Camila Nieto Villamizar and María Riaño, *Esclavos, negros libres y bogas en la literatura del siglo XIX* (Bogotá: Ediciones Uniandes, 2011).

50. Germán Mejía Pavony, *Los años del cambio: historia urbana de Bogotá, 1820–1910* (Bogotá: CEJA, 1999), 117.

51. Frank Safford and Marco Palacios, *Colombia: Fragmented Land, Divided Society* (New York: Oxford University Press, 2002), 260.

52. José Antonio Ocampo, *Colombia y la economía mundial, 1830–1910* (Bogotá: Siglo XXI, 1984).

53. Andrew Archer, "Exploration in the Choco Intendancy of Colombia," *Scientific Monthly* 44, no. 5 (1937): 418; Jorge Brisson, *Exploración del alto Chocó* (Bogotá: Imprenta Nacional, 1895), 129.

54. Leo E. Miller, *In the Wilds of South America* (New York: Charles Scribner's Sons, 1919), 64; Jorge Álvarez Lleras, *El Chocó, Apuntamientos de viaje referentes a esta interesante región del país* (Bogotá: Minerva, 1923), 63–64, 72.

55. Santiago Pérez, *Selección de escritos y discursos de Santiago Pérez*, dir. Eduardo Rodríguez Piñeres (Bogotá: Academia Colombiana de Historia, 1950), 37.

56. Charles Stuart Cochrane, *Viajes por Colombia, 1823 y 1824: diario de mi residencia en Colombia* (Bogotá: Banco de la República, 1994), 274.

57. Álvarez Lleras, *El Chocó*, 9.

58. Agustín Codazzi, *Memorias de Agustín Codazzi* (Bogotá: Banco de la República, 1973), 355.

59. Nathaniel Michler, "Lieutenant Michler's Report of His Survey for an Interoceanic Ship Canal near the Isthmus of Darien," *Senate Executive Documents*, no 9, vol. 7, 36th Congress, 2nd Session, 1861; Oliver Selfridge, *Reports of Explorations and Surveys to Ascertain the Practicability of a Ship-canal between the Atlantic and the Pacific Oceans by the Way of the Isthmus of Darien by Thos. Oliver Selfridge, Commander US Navy* (Washington, D.C.: Government Printing Office 1874).

60. Jorge Brisson, *Viajes por Colombia en los años de 1891 a 1897* (Bogotá: Imprenta Nacional, 1899).

61. Codazzi, *Memorias de Agustín Codazzi*; Trautwine, John Cresson, *Rough Notes on the Exploration of an Interoceanic Canal by Way of the Rivers Atrato and San Juan in New Grenada, South America* (Philadelphia: Barnard & Jones, 1854).

62. Robert West, *The Pacific Lowlands of Colombia* (Baton Rouge: Louisiana State University Press, 1957), 193–94.

63. Brisson, *Exploración del alto Chocó*, 113. Francisco García, "Relación de una excursión al alto Atrato y al río Andágueda, por el reverendo padre Francisco García," in *Relación de algunas excursiones apostólicas en la misión del Chocó*, ed. Francisco Gutiérrez (Bogotá: Imprenta Nacional, 1924), 12.

64. Some do mention them, noting that they inhabited the upper Bebará, the upper Capá and Andágueda Rivers, as well as the Napipí and Truandó headwaters.

Brisson, *Viajes por Colombia en los años de 1891 a 1897*, 104; Brisson, *Exploración del alto Chocó*; Charles Friend, "Notes of an Excursion from the Banks of the Atrato to the Bay of Cupica, on the Coast of the Pacific, in the Year 1827," *Journal of the Royal Geographical Society* 23 (1853); Selfridge, *Reports of Explorations and Surveys.*

65. Gutiérrez, "Relación de una excursión al alto Atrato y al río Andágueda," 10–11.
66. Francisco Gutiérrez, *Informe que el Prefecto Apostólico rinde al ilustrísimo y Reverendísimo Arzobispo de Colombia, como presidente de la Junta Arquidiocesana de Misiones, 1919–1923*, (Bogotá: Imprenta Nacional, 1924), 35–36.
67. Gaspard-Théodore Mollien, *Viaje por la República de Colombia en 1823* (Bogotá: Colcultura, 1992), 316.
68. Rufino Gutiérrez, *Datos sobre la historia del ferrocarril del Pacífico* (Bogotá: Arboleda y Valencia, 1919); Juan Evangelista Cruz, *Visita al Chocó en noviembre de 1920* (Cali: Tipografía Moderna, 1921), 1–2. Caldas is today known as Dagua, and Juntas as Cisneros. For a trip in 1911 see Miller, *In the Wilds of South America*, 5–10.
69. Pérez, *Selección de escritos y discursos de Santiago Pérez*, 83.
70. Rufino Gutiérrez, "Noticias sobre Pasto y las demás provincias del sur," in *Monografías*, Tomo 1 (Bogotá: Imprenta Nacional, 1921), 150–51, 187–96; Pérez, *Selección de escritos y discursos de Santiago Pérez*, 81–83; Miguel Triana, *Por el Sur de Colombia* (Bogotá: Biblioteca Popular de Cultura Colombiana, 1950), 69–78; José María Cordovez Moure, *Reminiscencias de Santafé y Bogotá* (Madrid: Aguilar, 1957).
71. Minaudier, "Une région minière de la colonie à l'indépendance," 82; Triana, *Por el Sur de Colombia*, 43–49. In 1894, it took small canoes three to four days to reach Tumaco from Barbacoas via Chimbuza, while large ones had to follow the Patía River and took seven to eight days. Gutiérrez, "Noticias sobre Pasto y las demás provincias del sur," 137–39.
72. Miller, *In the Wilds of South America*, 3; Triana, *Por el Sur de Colombia*, 9.

CHAPTER 1

1. Kris Lane, "Mining the Margins: Precious Metals Extraction and Forced Labor Regimes in the Audiencia of Quito, 1534–1821" (PhD diss., University of Minnesota, 1996), 256.
2. Eric Werner Cantor, *Ni aniquilados ni vencidos. Los Emberá y la gente negra del Atrato bajo el dominio español. Siglo XVIII* (Bogotá: Instituto Colombiano de Antropología e Historia, 2000), 83–86, refers to the lower Atrato, and Orián Jiménez, *El Chocó: Un paraíso del demonio. Nóvita, Citará y el Baudó, siglo XVIII* (Medellín: Universidad Nacional de Colombia, 2004), 51–55, to the Baudó.
3. William Sharp, *Slavery on the Spanish Frontier: The Colombian Chocó 1680–1810* (Norman: University of Oklahoma Press, 1976), 39–40, 65; Cantor, *Ni aniquilados ni vencidos*, 73.
4. Jiménez, *El Chocó: Un paraíso del demonio*, 1–7.
5. Germán Colmenares, *Historia económica y social de Colombia, Tomo II: Popayán, una sociedad esclavista, 1680–1800* (Medellín: La Carreta, 1979), 21; Charles Stuart

Cochrane, *Viajes por Colombia, 1823 y 1824: diario de mi residencia en Colombia* (Bogotá: Banco de la República, 1994), 285. Another description cited by Caroline A. Williams, *Between Resistance and Adaptation: Indigenous Peoples and the Colonisation of the Chocó, 1510–1753* (Liverpool: Liverpool University Press, 2005), 227, gives the impression that circa 1753 only six white men (and their families) resided there: "Nóvita contains a public jail, a church, and 65 dwellings—including the residence of the governor and the *teniente*. The remaining dwellings are used by the merchants who come to the province to sell their wares. With the exception of four miners, there are no other residents."

6. Fray Juan de Santa Gertrudis, *Maravillas de la naturaleza*, Tomo III (Bogotá: Biblioteca Banco Popular, 1970), 153; Jean-Pierre Minaudier, "Une région minière de la colonie à l'indépendance: Barbacoas 1750–1830 (Economie, société, vie politique locale)," *Bulletin de l'Institut Français d'Etudes Andines* 17, no. 2 (1988): 85, 89.
7. Lane, "Mining the Margins," 67, and Kris Lane, "The Transition from Encomienda to Slavery in Seventeenth-Century Barbacoas (Colombia)," *Slavery & Abolition* 21, no. 1 (2000): 82.
8. Williams, *Between Resistance and Adaptation*, chapter 1. For early and failed efforts to conquer Chocó see also Juan David Montoya Guzmán, "Las más remotas tierras del mundo: historia de la frontera del Pacífico, 1573–1687" (PhD diss., Universidad Pablo de Olavide, 2014), 199–260.
9. Lane, "Mining the Margins," 71. For a detailed reconstruction and analysis of these wars see Marta Herrera, *El conquistador conquistado. Awás, Quayquer y Sindaguas en el Pacífico colombiano, siglos XVI-XVIII* (Bogotá: Ediciones Uniandes, 2016). See also Zamira Díaz, *Oro, sociedad y economía. El sistema colonial en la gobernación de Popayán: 1533–1733* (Bogotá: Banco de la República, 1994), 231; Sherwin Bryant, *Rivers of Gold, Lives of Bondage: Governing through Slavery in Colonial Quito* (Chapel Hill: University of North Carolina Press, 2014), 41–45.
10. Exact numbers are elusive. According to Lane, after the wars close to two thousand Indians survived, and by the end of the century only 168 tribute-paying males remained, many of who were illegally resettled highlanders. "The Transition from Encomienda to Slavery," especially page 83. Herrera found a larger number of survivors, but including part of the highlands, see *El conquistador conquistado*, 271–78.
11. Lane, "Mining the Margins," 69.
12. Mario Diego Romero, *Poblamiento y sociedad en el Pacífico colombiano siglos XVI al XVIII* (Cali: Universidad del Valle, 1995), 35–36.
13. Herrera, *El conquistador conquistado*, 224–25, 227, 272. See also Díaz, *Oro, sociedad y economía*, 233; Romero, *Poblamiento y sociedad en el Pacífico colombiano*, 26.
14. Romero, *Poblamiento y sociedad en el Pacífico colombiano*, 45.
15. Lane, "Mining the Margins," 70.
16. Williams, *Between Resistance and Adaptation*, chapters 2 and 3; Montoya Guzmán, *Las más remotas tierras*, chapter 11.
17. Kathleen Romoli, "El Alto Chocó en el siglo XVI. Parte 2: las gentes," *Revista Colombiana de Antropología* 20 (1976): 37–48, cited by Caroline A. Williams, "Resistance

and Rebellion on the Spanish Frontier: Native Responses to Colonization in the Colombian Chocó," *Hispanic American Historical Review* 79, no. 3 (1999): 403.

18. Williams, "Resistance and Rebellion on the Spanish Frontier"; Williams, *Between Resistance and Adaptation*, chapters 4 and 5, and Montoya Guzmán, *Las más remotas tierras*, chapter 12.
19. Colmenares, *Popayán, una sociedad esclavista*, 146.
20. Lane, "Mining the Margins," 74.
21. Germán Colmenares, "La economía y la sociedad coloniales, 1550–1800," in *Nueva Historia de Colombia*, Tomo 1 (Bogotá: Planeta, 1989), 123–24.
22. It is very likely that a part of the gold registered in Popayán also came from the lowlands.
23. Sharp, *Slavery on the Spanish Frontier*, 71.
24. Sharp, *Slavery on the Spanish Frontier*, 201; Jorge Orlando Melo, "Producción minera y crecimiento económico en la Nueva Granada durante el siglo XVIII," *Revista Universidad del Valle* 3–4 (1979), 34. Retrieved from http://www.jorgeorlandomelo.com/historia.htm as "Producción de oro y desarrollo económico en el siglo XVIII."
25. Lane, "Mining the Margins," 179.
26. Part of that increase is accounted for by the inclusion in the latter figure of gold from Raposo, which probably ended up in Popayán in former years, Lane, "Mining the Margins," 193. Díaz, *Oro, sociedad y economía*, 233, reports that taxes paid in Barbacoas for the period 1658–63 included payments from Timbiquí. See also Guido Barona, *La maldición de Midas en una región del mundo colonial, Popayán 1730–1830* (Cali: Universidad del Valle, 1995), 147, and Colmenares, *Popayán, una sociedad esclavista*, 167.
27. Colmenares, *Popayán, una sociedad esclavista*, 145.
28. Colmenares, *Cali: Terratenientes, mineros y comerciantes, siglo XVIII* (Cali: Universidad del Valle, 1975), 97, 99–100.
29. Mario Mejía, "La Agricultura alternativa," in *Colombia Pacífico*, Tomo II, ed. Pablo Leyva (Bogotá: Proyecto Biopacífico-FEN, 1993), 269. See also Robert West, *The Pacific Lowlands of Colombia* (Baton Rouge: Louisiana State University Press, 1957), 126–29.
30. Germán Colmenares, *Cali: Terratenientes, mineros y comerciantes*, chapter 4.
31. Colmenares, *Cali: Terratenientes, mineros y comerciantes*, 40, 60–61; Colmenares, *Popayán, una sociedad esclavista*, 87–88, 90; Germán Colmenares, "La formación de la economía colonial, 1500–1740," in *Historia económica de Colombia*, ed. José Antonio Ocampo (Bogotá: Siglo XXI, 1987), 13; Colmenares, "La economía y la sociedad coloniales," 136; Sharp, *Slavery on the Spanish Frontier*, 133.
32. Minaudier, "Une région minière de la colonie à l'indépendance," 88, 90.
33. Sharp, *Slavery on the Spanish Frontier*, 23.
34. Colmenares, *Popayán, una sociedad esclavista*, 73–74; Lane, "The Transition from Encomienda to Slavery," 87.
35. Hermes Tovar et al., *Convocatoria al poder del número. Censos y estadísticas de la Nueva Granada (1750–1830)* (Bogotá: Archivo General de la Nación, 1994), 321–23, 355–56.

36. Between 73 percent and 82 percent of the total population in the south, and 60 percent in Chocó. The difference between the two is accounted for mainly by Chocó's sizeable Indian population. Tovar et al., *Convocatoria al poder del número*, 88–89.
37. Colmenares, *Popayán, una sociedad esclavista*, 73; Lane, "The Transition from Encomienda to Slavery," 87; Herrera, *El conquistador conquistado*, 278–79. While Lane explains that at the time "a typical gold camp [in the south] consisted of a jumbled labor force made up of encomienda Amerindians, native and free black or mulatto wage workers, rented and personally owned slaves"; Herrera shows that in 1717 89 percent of the laborers were slaves.
38. Sharp, *Slavery on the Spanish Frontier*, 112–13; Bryant, *Rivers of Gold*, 53–63.
39. Robert West, *Colonial Placer Mining in Colombia* (Baton Rouge: Louisiana State University Press, 1952), 86.
40. Sharp, *Slavery on the Spanish Frontier*, 115–16, emphasis added. Mines in plural could perhaps mean that the cuadrilla moved from one mine to another. However, Colmenares, *Popayán, una sociedad esclavista*, 82, mentions a cuadrilla in Nóvita which in 1753 had 312 slaves and was split in two mines plus fields for growing plantains and corn, and raising pigs. He writes about another cuadrilla of 137 slaves working in mines in two different rivers. To confuse matters, West, *Colonial Placer Mining*, 103, says that not infrequently more than one cuadrilla made a single camp.
41. Colmenares, "La formación de la economía colonial," 37.
42. George Reid Andrews, *Afro-Latin America, 1800–2000* (New York: Oxford University Press, 2004), 24.
43. Colmenares, *Popayán, una sociedad esclavista*, 73; Sharp, *Slavery on the Spanish Frontier*, 115.
44. Williams, *Between Resistance and Adaptation*, 228–32.
45. Report by governor Carlos Ciaurriz of his visit between 1804 and 1807, Jiménez, *El Chocó: Un paraíso del demonio*, 74–76. These calculations do not include the mines in which free blacks labored with two or three slaves, mentioned elsewhere in the same report, Cantor, *Ni aniquilados ni vencidos*, 176.
46. Minaudier, "Une région minière de la colonie à l'indépendance," 86.
47. Besides purchases in 1788 and 1789 there is no evidence that in the late eighteenth century slave owners imported many slaves, Sharp, *Slavery on the Spanish Frontier*, 114, 123; Colmenares, *Popayán, una sociedad esclavista*, 73, 78, 84.
48. Williams, *Between Resistance and Adaptation*, 114, 124, 228–32; Sharp, *Slavery on the Spanish Frontier*, 203, 124; Jiménez, *El Chocó: Un paraíso del demonio*, 174–76; Colmenares, *Popayán, una sociedad esclavista*, 84.
49. Romero, *Poblamiento y sociedad en el Pacífico colombiano*, 71–73. In 1782, almost one-third of all slaves in Chocó were married, Sharp, *Slavery on the Spanish Frontier*, 124; Cantor, *Ni aniquilados ni vencidos*, 164–70.
50. Herrera, *El conquistador conquistado*, 279–80.
51. Bernardo Leal, "Pido se me ampare en mi libertad: Esclavizados, manumisos y rebeldes en el Chocó (1710–1810) bajo la lente colonial contemporánea" (MA thesis, Universidad Nacional de Colombia, 2006), 91.

52. Leal, "Pido se me ampare en mi libertad," 96; Romero, *Poblamiento y sociedad en el Pacífico colombiano*, 75–76.
53. West, *Colonial Placer Mining*, 103, emphasis added.
54. Colmenares, *Popayán, una sociedad esclavista*, 134.
55. West, *Colonial Placer Mining*, 102–3; Cantor, *Ni aniquilados ni vencidos*, 41–45; Jiménez, *El Chocó: Un paraíso del demonio*, 62–63. For various aspects of life in a real de minas in Chocó in the eighteenth century see Jiménez, *El Chocó: Un paraíso del demonio*, chapter 2.
56. Santa Gertrudis, *Maravillas de la naturaleza*, 153.
57. West, *Colonial Placer Mining*, 55–58; West, *The Pacific Lowlands of Colombia*, 176–77; Lane, "Mining the Margins," 104; Jiménez, *El Chocó: Un paraíso del demonio*, 57–62.
58. Colmenares, *Popayán, una sociedad esclavista*, 133–34; Lane, "Mining the Margins," 110–11; Cantor, *Ni aniquilados ni vencidos*, 99–100; Santa Gertrudis, *Maravillas de la naturaleza*, 144–45.
59. West, *Colonial Placer Mining*, 58–62; West, *The Pacific Lowlands of Colombia*, 174–76, 178. For an overview of works that describe current methods see Eduardo Restrepo, "Economía y simbolismo en el 'Pacífico negro'" (BA thesis, Universidad de Antioquia, 1996).
60. West, *Colonial Placer Mining*, 104–5.
61. Tovar et al., *Convocatoria al poder del número*, 310, 364. This number does not include Tumaco's 1,029 Indians in 1788, and about half that amount nine years later, because I suspect that most of them lived in Esmeraldas. See also Williams, *Between Resistance and Adaptation*, 227–28. Romero, *Poblamiento y sociedad en el Pacífico colombiano*, 55–60, informs that in the mid-eighteenth century one of the most prominent families in Popayán brought an Indian family from Nóvita to Raposo, and also "received" another family that moved to Naya. At the time there were around 250 Indians in the Raposo district, and they paid tribute.
62. Cited by Caroline A. Williams, "Adaptation and Appropriation on the Colonial Frontier: Indigenous Leadership in the Colombian Chocó, 1670–1808," *Bulletin of Latin American Research* 26, no. 2 (2007): 188.
63. Sven-Erik Isacsson, "Emberá: Territorio y regimen agrario de una tribu selvática bajo la dominación española," in *Tierra, tradición y poder en Colombia. Enfoques antropológicos*, ed. Nina S. Friedemann (Bogotá: Colcultura, 1976), 30–31. For the early impact of Spanish colonization on the indigenous peoples of Chocó, see Patricia Vargas, *Los Emberá y los Cuna: impacto y reacción ante la ocupación española Siglo XVI y XVII* (Bogotá: Instituto Colombiano de Antropología, 1993).
64. And Pavarandó, which had a short-lived existence from 1773 to 1806, Williams, *Between Resistance and Adaptation*, chapter 4 and 195–202. Nóvita also had six towns: Tadó, Noanamá, Los Brazos, Las Juntas, Sipí (and Baudó). Some Indians managed to live away from Spanish control and were referred to as cimarrones by the Spanish, Cantor, *Ni aniquilados ni vencidos*, 129–38; Sven-Erik Isacsson, "Indios cimarrones del Chocó (Colombia): Tradiciones y documentación histórica de los

emberá desde la Colonia," *Göteborgs Etnografiska Museum*, Arstryck 1973; Isacsson, "Emberá: Territorio y régimen," 27.

65. Cantor, *Ni aniquilados ni vencidos*, 153, 34–40, 109–15.
66. Williams, "Adaptation and Appropriation on the Colonial Frontier"; Cantor, *Ni aniquilados ni vencidos*, 60–67, 70–73, 116–26; Sven-Erik Isaacsson, "The Egalitarian Society in Retrospect: Emberá Leadership and Conflict Management under the Spanish, 1660–1810," in *Natives and Neighbors in South America: Anthropological Essays*, ed. H. O. Skar and F. Salomon (Gothenburg: Götenborgs Etnografiska Museum, 1987); Jiménez, *El Chocó: Un paraíso del demonio*, 12–14, 90–95; Sharp, *Slavery on the Spanish Frontier*, chapter 6. As Isaacson informs, the Indian leadership did not survive into the twentieth century.
67. Herbert Klein and Francisco Vidal Luna, *Slavery in Brazil* (New York: Cambridge University Press, 2010), chapter 3, and Herbert Klein and Ben Vinson III, *African Slavery in Latin America and the Caribbean* (New York: Oxford University Press, 2007), 66–68. For slavery in Mineiro cities see Mariana Dantas, *Black Townsmen: Urban Slavery and Freedom in the Eighteenth-Century Americas* (New York: Palgrave Macmillan, 2008), and Kathleen J. Higgins, *'Licentious Liberty' in a Brazilian Gold-Mining Region: Slavery, Gender, and Social Control in Eighteenth-Century Sabará, Minas Gerais* (University Park: Penn State University Press, 1999).
68. Rafael Antonio Díaz, *Esclavitud, región y ciudad. El sistema esclavista urbano-regional en Santafé de Bogotá, 1700–1750* (Bogotá: CEJA-2001), 164.
69. These are some authors who refer to the region as a frontier: Sharp, *Slavery on the Spanish Frontier*, 4; Cantor, *Ni aniquilados ni vencidos*, 13; Oscar Almario, "Territorio, etnicidad y poder en el Pacífico sur colombiano, 1780–1930" (PhD diss., Universidad de Sevilla, 2007), 2.
70. For maroons in Suriname see Silvia W. De Groot, *From Isolation towards Integration: The Surinam Maroons and Their Colonial Rulers, 1845–1863* (La Haya: Nijhoff, 1977) and Richard Price, *First-Time: The Historical Vision of an Afro-American People* (Baltimore: Johns Hopkins University Press, 1983). For maroons in Jamaica see Barbara Kopytoff, "Early Political Development of Jamaican Maroon Societies," *William & Mary Quarterly* 35, no. 2 (1978). For quilombos in Brazil see Joao Reis and Flavio dos Santos Gomes, eds., *Liberdade por um fio: Historia dos quilombos no Brasil* (Sao Paulo: Companhia das Letras, 1996).
71. Francisco U. Zuluaga, *Guerrilla y sociedad en el Patía* (Cali: Universidad del Valle, 1993), 34–43; Francisco U. Zuluaga, "Cimarronismo en el suroccidente del antiguo virreinato de Santafé de Bogotá," in *Colombia Pacífico*, Tomo II, ed. Pablo Leyva (Bogotá: Proyecto Biopacífico, 1993), 426; Colmenares, *Popayán, una sociedad esclavista*, 104–5; Kris Lane personal communication, September 2011. Zuluaga found the information from 1732 in the archives in Popayán, while Lane consulted the archives of Quito.
72. Sharp, *Slavery on the Spanish Frontier*, 155–56.
73. Jiménez, *El Chocó: Un paraíso del demonio*, 51–55.
74. Klein and Vinson III, *African Slavery*, 184.

75. Minaudier, "Une région minière de la colonie à l'indépendance," 95.
76. Tovar et al., *Convocatoria al poder del número*, 353.
77. Bernardo Leal, "'Matar a los blancos bueno es, luego el Chocó acabará.' Cimarronaje de esclavos jamaiquinos en el Chocó," *Fronteras de la Historia* 2 (1998); Sharp, *Slavery on the Spanish Frontier*; Colmenares, *Popayán, una sociedad esclavista*, 100–10; Bernardo Leal personal communication, May 2012. In "'Matar a los blancos bueno es,'" 154, Leal informs of another rebellion in the mid-eighteenth century, in Cértegui, in which slaves requested protection from the authorities and a change in the mine administrator.
78. Leal, "Pido se me ampare en mi libertad," 124–26.
79. Colmenares, *Popayán, una sociedad esclavista*, 101.
80. See Leal, "Pido se me ampare en mi libertad," 173–79, 187–88, 191, 332–33; Cantor, *Ni aniquilados ni vencidos*, 155; Germán De Granda, "Onomástica y procedencia africana de esclavos negros en las minas del sur de la gobernación de Popayán, siglo XVIII," *Revista Española de Antropología Americana* 6 (1971), 408–9; Romero, *Poblamiento y sociedad en el Pacífico colombiano*, 81; Sharp, *Slavery on the Spanish Frontier*, 157; Santa Gertrudis, *Maravillas de la naturaleza*, 211.
81. On the destruction of local archives see Sharp, *Slavery on the Spanish Frontier*, 142, 227, and Leal, "Pido se me ampare en mi libertad," 199–200. Colmenares, *Popayán, una sociedad esclavista*, 98, believes that manumissions were too important not to be registered in Popayán, whose records he examined. But he does not try to explain the existence of a large free black population in the lowlands.
82. For Latin America and the Caribbean see Klein and Vinson III, *African Slavery*, 202–6. Jaime Jaramillo, "La controversia jurídica y filosófica librada en la Nueva Granada en torno a la liberación de los esclavos y la importancia económica y social de la esclavitud en el siglo XIX," in *Ensayos de historia social*, Tomo I: La sociedad neogranadina (Bogotá: Tercer Mundo-Uniandes, 1989); Anthony McFarlane, *Colombia Before Independence: Economy, Society, and Politics under Bourbon Rule* (New York: Cambridge University Press, 1993), and David Bushnell, *The Making of Modern Colombia: A Nation in Spite of Itself* (Berkeley: University of California Press, 1993) do not even mention self-purchase. Frank Safford and Marco Palacios, *Colombia: Fragmented Land, Divided Society* (New York: Oxford University Press, 2002), 51, 183, do mention self-purchase, but fail to acknowledge its relevance, as they stress maroonage.
83. Jaime Jaramillo Uribe, "Mestizaje y diferenciación social en el Nuevo Reino de Granada en la segunda mitad del siglo XVIII," *Anuario Colombiano de Historia Social y de la Cultura* 3 (1965): 125–26. On free men of all colors, see Margarita Garrido, "'Free Men of All Colors' in New Granada: Identity and Obedience before Independence," in *Political Cultures in the Andes (1750–1950)*, ed. Nils Jacobsen and Cristóbal Aljovín de Losada (Durham: Duke University Press, 2005).
84. See Jorge Andrés Tovar and Hermes Tovar, *El oscuro camino de la libertad. Los esclavos en Colombia, 1821–1851* (Bogotá: Universidad de Los Andes, 2009), 1, 53, 81, and 130 for examples of the interchangeable use of black and slave.

85. Alfonso Múnera, *Fronteras imaginadas. La construcción de las razas y de la geografía en el siglo XIX colombiano* (Bogotá: Planeta, 2005), 140–41.
86. Jiménez, *El Chocó: Un paraíso del demonio*, 17–20 refers to "*amores zambos*" to argue that the segregation established by the Spanish authorities had its limits, but acknowledges that evidence is extremely limited. Barbacoas must have been the place where the largest mixed population existed, due to early encomiendas and mixture, as well as a slightly larger white population. Minaudier, "Une région minière de la colonie à l'indépendance," 86, says that 44 percent of slaves in Barbacoas were mulattoes (a term that included zambos), but does not give a date.
87. Tovar et al., *Convocatoria al poder del número*, 321–22, 360.
88. This change could happen if they ceased paying tribute, since in the censuses *Indian* was a tax-related category. In other parts of the colony Indians who left their communities and lived intermixed with the rest of the population were counted as libres. But there is no evidence that such a thing happened in the Pacific lowlands. Neither do the historical works on the Indian population mention any cause, such as an epidemic, that could explain their decrease in numbers.
89. Cantor, *Ni aniquilados ni vencidos*, 174, 175, 178.
90. Minaudier, "Une région minière de la colonie à l'indépendance," 94.
91. Stuart B. Schwartz, "The Manumission of Slaves in Colonial Brazil: Bahia, 1684–1745," *Hispanic American Historical Review* 54, no. 4 (1974): 619–22.
92. Sharp, *Slavery on the Spanish Frontier*, 137.
93. Leal, "Pido se me ampare en mi libertad," 198–99.
94. Colmenares, *Popayán, una sociedad esclavista*, 98.
95. Leal, "Pido se me ampare en mi libertad," 204, 332–33.
96. Klein and Vinson III, *African Slavery*, 202–3. They give examples that go from 12 to 41 percent.
97. Klein and Vidal Luna, *Slavery in Brazil*, chapter 7, the one case above half is Salvador de Bahia between 1684 and 1745 with 57.9 percent. Schwartz, "The Manumission of Slaves in Colonial Brazil," informs that in this same place from the 1680s through the 1720s 48 percent of manumissions were bought.
98. Klein and Vinson III, *African Slavery*, 205, and Klein and Vidal Luna, *Slavery in Brazil*, chapter 7.
99. Cited by Jiménez, *El Chocó: Un paraíso del demonio*, 66.
100. Dantas, *Black Townsmen*, 98.
101. Donald Ramos, "O quilombo e o sistema escravista en Minas Gerais de século XVIII," in *Liberdade por um fio: Historia dos quilombos no Brasil*, ed. Joao Reis and Flavio dos Santos Gomes (Sao Paulo: Companhia das Letras, 1996).
102. Sharp, *Slavery on the Spanish Frontier*, chapter 10, and William Sharp, "The Profitability of Slavery in the Colombian Chocó, 1610–1810," *Hispanic American Historical Review* 55, no. 3 (1975). This might also be the case of Cantor's claim (*Ni aniquilados ni vencidos*, 171–72) that some mineros abandoned their mines due to debts, so slaves worked them to pay for their freedom. But he cites only one case.
103. Cited by Romero, *Poblamiento y sociedad en el Pacífico colombiano*, 77.

104. Sharp, *Slavery on the Spanish Frontier*, 49–50, 134–36; Jiménez, *El Chocó: Un paraíso del demonio*, 70; Minaudier, "Une région minière de la colonie à l'indépendance," 88; Leal, "Pido se me ampare en mi libertad," 108–9, 228; Barona, *La maldición de Midas*, 74–77; Almario, "Territorio, etnicidad y poder," 204. Fray Juan de Santa Gertrudis visited the mines in Barbacoas in the 1760s and received alms from slaves in virtually all of them, which proves that they had access to cash, *Maravillas de la naturaleza*, 174–210. No author mentions theft as a problem that masters and overseers complained about. This could be because gold was separated from the black mixture that remained in bateas only every several days or weeks, making the control of these operations easier.
105. Santa Gertrudis, *Maravillas de la naturaleza*, 184–85.
106. Minaudier, "Une région minière de la colonie à l'indépendance," 88. For another interesting and rather exceptional case see Bernardo Leal, "Paulina Montaño demanda su libertad. Aproximación a una etnografía performativa de un pleito judicial, Chocó, 1838," *Revista Colombiana de Antropología* 46, no. 2 (2010).
107. Sergio Mosquera, "Los procesos de manumisión en las provincias del Chocó," in *Afrodescendientes en las Américas. Trayectorias sociales e identitarias a 150 años de la abolición de la esclavitud en Colombia*, ed. Claudia Mosquera et al. (Bogotá: UN-ICANH-IRD-ILSA, 2002), 113–18.
108. The remaining cases were purchased by "others" or have no information, Leal, "Pido se me ampare en mi libertad," 204, 335; Bernardo Leal personal communication, July 2012.
109. Leal, "Pido se me ampare en mi libertad," 199.
110. Rebecca Scott, *Slave Emancipation in Cuba. The Transition to Free Labor, 1860–1899* (Pittsburgh: Pittsburgh University Press, 2000), 13–14, 67, 74–77; Klein and Vidal Luna, *Slavery in Brazil*, chapter 7.
111. Sharp, *Slavery on the Spanish Frontier*, 143–44.
112. Sharp, *Slavery on the Spanish Frontier*, 144–46; Leal, "Pido se me ampare en mi libertad," 212–28. Similarly, Marcela Echeverri has argued that through six infanticides committed in Barbacoas, slaves sought access to the courts, denounced the extreme conditions of their captivity, and requested protection under the law, "'Enraged to the Limit of Despair': Infanticide and Slave Judicial Strategies in Barbacoas, 1789–1798," *Slavery & Abolition* 30, no. 3 (2009); and *Indian and Slave Royalists in the Age of Revolution: Reform, Revolution, and Royalism in the Northern Andes, 1780–1825* (New Haven: Yale University Press, 2016), chapter 3. Marta Herrera, "En un rincón de ese imperio en que no se ocultaba el sol: Colonialismo, oro y terror en Barbacoas, siglo XVIII," *Anuario Colombiano de Historia Social y de la Cultura* 32 (2005); and Romero, *Poblamiento y sociedad en el Pacífico colombiano*, 108–14, have also examined these infanticides.
113. Andrews, *Afro-Latin America*, chapter 2.
114. Juan Ignacio Arboleda, "Entre la libertad y la sumisión. Estrategias de liberación de los esclavos en la gobernación de Popayán durante la Independencia, 1808–1830," Documento CESO No. 10 (2006); Almario, "Territorio, etnicidad y poder,"

chapter 2; Marcela Echeverri, "Popular Royalists, Empire, and Politics in Southwestern New Granada, 1809–1819," *Hispanic American Historical Review* 91, no. 2 (2011); Echeverri, *Indian and Slave Royalists*, chapter 5.

115. Offering slaves freedom in exchange for joining the armies became a widely used recruitment strategy throughout Latin America. Peter Blanchard, "The Slave Soldiers of Spanish South America: From Independence to Abolition," in *Arming Slaves: From Classical Times to the Modern Age*, ed. Christopher Leslie Brown and Philip D. Morgan (New Haven: Yale University Press, 2006).
116. Echeverri, *Indian and Slave Royalists*, 169–71.
117. Echeverri, *Indian and Slave Royalists*, 159.
118. Alfonso Zawadsky, *Las ciudades confederadas del Valle del Cauca en 1811* (Cali: Imprenta Bolivariana, 1943), 129, emphasis added, see also 109, 128, 134–35.
119. Arboleda, "Entre la libertad y la sumisión," 25; Echeverri, *Indian and Slave Royalists*, 162, 173–74.
120. Arboleda, "Entre la libertad y la sumisión," 28.
121. Almario, "Territorio, etnicidad y poder," 257–60.
122. Echeverri, *Indian and Slave Royalists*, 164.
123. Echeverri, *Indian and Slave Royalists*, 180.
124. Minaudier, "Une région minière de la colonie à l'indépendance," 102; Echeverri, *Indian and Slave Royalists in the Age of Revolution*, 206 footnote 29.
125. As Echeverri, *Indian and Slave Royalists*, 1, 160–61, 186, suggests.
126. Arboleda, "Entre la libertad y la sumisión," 32.
127. Arboleda, "Entre la libertad y la sumisión," 27, see also 26; Echeverri, *Indian and Slave Royalists*, 184, see also 175–86; Almario, "Territorio, etnicidad y poder," 261–64.
128. Echeverri, *Indian and Slave Royalists*, 184; Arboleda, "Entre la libertad y la sumisión," 28; Almario, "Territorio, etnicidad y poder," 264.
129. Arboleda, "Entre la libertad y la sumisión," 35.
130. Sergio Mosquera, *Don Melchor de Barona y Betancourt y la esclavización en el Chocó* (Quibdó: Universidad Tecnológica del Chocó, 2004), 164, 260–61.
131. Minaudier, "Une région minière de la colonie à l'indépendance," 102.
132. Almario, "Territorio, etnicidad y poder," 359–66.
133. Williams, *Between Resistance and Adaptation*, 228–32; Tovar and Tovar, *El oscuro camino de la libertad*, 142–43. (On page 137 Tovar and Tovar invert their numbers: 73 percent of the owners freed 53 percent of the slaves, but the former figure is correct as it is backed with the actual number of slave owners.) Mosquera, "Los procesos de manumisión," 102, found the wills of several slave owners living in the Atrato River in Chocó during the Independence period (1808–26); thirteen out of twenty had less than nineteen slaves, five had between thirty-five and sixty-five, and one owned 134.
134. The three largest slave owners from Popayán at midcentury, with 184, 162, and 143 slaves, respectively (two of whom belonged to the Arboleda and Mosquera families), had slaves in either Chocó or Barbacoas. Tovar and Tovar, *El oscuro camino de la libertad*, 163–69.
135. Tovar and Tovar, *El oscuro camino de la libertad*.

136. James E. Sanders, *Contentious Republicans: Popular Politics, Race, and Class in Nineteenth-Century Colombia* (Durham: Duke University Press, 2004), 68; see also Jason McGraw, *The Work of Recognition: Caribbean Colombia and the Postemancipation Struggle for Citizenship* (Chapel Hill: University of North Carolina Press, 2014), 29–33; Tovar and Tovar, *El oscuro camino de la libertad*, 133, 135, and 145; Margarita Pacheco, *La fiesta liberal en Cali* (Cali: Universidad del Valle, 1992), 108–9; Dolcey Romero, "Manumisión, ritualidad y fiesta liberal en la provincia de Cartagena durante el siglo XIX," *Historia Crítica* 29 (2005).
137. Tovar and Tovar, *El oscuro camino de la libertad*, 35, 142.
138. Tovar and Tovar, *El oscuro camino de la libertad*, 84.
139. He found 404 manumission letters for the period 1808–48. I multiplied that number by three to account for Nóvita that had about two-thirds of the slave population. Mosquera, "Los procesos de manumisión," 115.
140. Mosquera, *Don Melchor de Barona y Betancourt*, 190–92.
141. Tovar et al., *Convocatoria al poder del número*, 88, 355.
142. It is difficult to estimate accurately how many slaves lived in the Pacific coast, for the data is aggregated by regions that include areas that lie both in the littoral and in the Andean region. I calculated this number by first adding the slave population of the two places that lay entirely there, Chocó (1,725) and Barbacoas (2,550); then added slaves from Cauca (2,949), assuming that Popayán (2,161) accounted for the Andean portion of Cauca. Lastly, I added one-third of the population of Buenaventura (1,132), which was the equivalent of the present department of Valle del Cauca.

CHAPTER 2

1. Despite the use of the word *libre*, until recently, many people in the lowlands were unaware of its origin in slavery, see Eduardo Restrepo, "Ethnicization of Blackness in Colombia: Toward De-racializing Theoretical and Political Imagination," *Cultural Studies* 18, no. 4 (2004): 701, 703, and Anne-Marie Losonczy "'Sentirse negro' Empreintes du passé et mémoire collective au Chocó," *Annales. Histoire, Sciences Sociales* 3 (2004): 598. According to Robert West, *The Pacific Lowlands of Colombia* (Baton Rouge: Louisiana State University Press, 1957), 103, only in the more isolated localities of the lowlands did people still use the term. Angela Castillo, who during the last years has worked in the San Juan basin, told me (January 28, 2013) that it was mostly people older than forty who used the term, especially when distinguishing blacks from indigenous peoples or *cholos*, and whites or *paisas*. Various works confirm the latter use of the term: Eduardo Restrepo, "Los tuqueros negros del Pacífico surcolombiano," in *Renacientes del Guandal: "Grupos negros" de los ríos Satinga y Sanquianga* (Bogotá: Proyecto Biopacífico-Universidad Nacional de Colombia, 1996), 338–42; Sandra Patricia Martínez, "La construcción cotidiana del estado: el proceso de titulación colectiva a las comunidades negras del pacífico colombiano" (PhD diss., Universidad Iberoamericana de México, 2010), 10; and

José Fernando Serrano, "Cuando canta el guaco: La muerte y el morir en poblaciones afrocolombianas del río Baudó, Chocó" (BA thesis, Universidad Nacional de Colombia, 1994), 33. Terms like *moreno* have been more frequently used in recent times.

2. José Antonio Ocampo, *Colombia y la economía mundial* (Bogotá: Siglo XXI-Fedesarrollo, 1984), 100–1.
3. Eric Werner Cantor, *Ni aniquilados ni vencidos. Los Emberá y la gente negra del Atrato bajo el dominio español. Siglo XVIII* (Bogotá: Instituto Colombiano de Antropología e Historia, 2000), 172–73, 180; Mario Diego Romero, *Poblamiento y sociedad en el Pacífico colombiano siglos XVI al XVIII* (Cali: Universidad del Valle, 1995), 78.
4. Cited by Orián Jiménez, *El Chocó: Un paraíso del demonio. Nóvita, Citará y el Baudó, siglo XVIII* (Medellín: Universidad Nacional de Colombia, 2004), 26–27.
5. Guido Barona et al., *Geografía Física y Política de la Confederación Granadina. Vol. 1: Estado del Cauca. Tomo II: Provincias de Chocó, Buenaventura, Cauca y Popayán. Obra dirigida por el General Agustín Codazzi* (Popayán: Universidad del Cauca, 2002), 105.
6. On ex-slaves and libres as slave owners see also Fray Juan de Santa Gertrudis, *Maravillas de la naturaleza*, Tomo III (Bogotá: Biblioteca Banco Popular, 1970), 185; Sergio Mosquera, *De esclavizadores y esclavizados en Citará* (Quibdó: Promotora Editorial de Autores Chocoanos, 1997), 16, 21, 23; and William Sharp, *Slavery on the Spanish Frontier: The Colombian Chocó 1680–1810* (Norman: University of Oklahoma Press, 1976), 151.
7. Romero, *Poblamiento y sociedad en el Pacífico colombiano*, 87–99; Oscar Almario, "Territorio, etnicidad y poder en el Pacífico sur colombiano, 1780–1930" (PhD diss., Universidad de Sevilla, 2007), 211–18; Jean-Pierre Minaudier, "Une région minière de la colonie à l'indépendance: Barbacoas 1750–1830 (Economie, société, vie politique locale)," *Bulletin de l'Institut Français d'Etudes Andines* 17, no. 2 (1988), 94.
8. Cited by Almario, "Territorio, etnicidad y poder en el Pacífico sur colombiano," 212.
9. AGN, República, *Ministerio de Gobierno*, Sección 4ª, t. 51, ff. 404–8.
10. Agustín Codazzi, "Informe sobre los baldíos del Chocó, 1853," in Barona et al., *Geografía Física y Política de la Confederación Granadina*, 105.
11. Because of abandonment, mine prospectors in the late nineteenth century had a hard time finding old mines, as happened both in the Bebará and Micay Rivers. See Jorge Brisson, *Viajes por Colombia en los años de 1891 a 1897* (Bogotá: Imprenta Nacional, 1899), 101–29, and E. L. Ragonnet, "Journal of Voyage" (Paris: n.p., 1895, in manuscript). For additional evidence of abandoned placers see Cantor, *Ni aniquilados ni vencidos*, 175, 179.
12. Commenting on his 1823 trip to Nóvita, a British traveler wrote: "the best mines of Chocó . . . cannot defray the hire of free negroes, who demand six rials, or three shillings and three-pence, per day," Charles Stuart Cochrane, *Viajes por Colombia, 1823 y 1824: diario de mi residencia en Colombia* (Bogotá: Banco de la República, 1994), 420.
13. Codazzi, "Informe sobre los baldíos del Chocó."

14. Anthropological studies carried out in the 1970s and 1980s attest to the ways in which miners organized themselves independently. See Nina S. de Friedemann, "Güelmambí: Formas económicas y organización social," *Revista Colombiana de Antropología* 14 (1969); Aquiles Escalante, *La minería del hambre: Condoto y la Chocó Pacífico* (Medellín: Universidad de Medellín, s.f.); Víctor Jiménez, "Guaitadó: Una comunidad minera del río Atrato" (BA thesis, Universidad de Los Andes, 1982); Jorge Abad Vélez et al., "Una economía familiar de reproducción simple: el caso de la pequeña minería chocoana" (BA thesis, Universidad de Antioquia, 1982); Hernando Bravo Pazmiño, "Mineros negros de La Aurora: la creatividad y la supervivencia. Caserío La Aurora, municipio Payán, Nariño" (BA thesis, Universidad Nacional de Colombia, 1991).
15. Cited by Vicente Restrepo, *Estudio sobre las minas de oro y plata de Colombia* (Bogotá: Silvestre y Compañía, 1888 [1882]), 59.
16. Beatriz Patiño Millán, "La provincia en el siglo XVIII," in *Historia de Antioquia*, ed. Jorge Orlando Melo (Medellín: Editorial Presencia, 1991), 83.
17. Perry Belden, Chargé d'Affaires, to Secretary of State, December 1, 1917, NARA, M1294, Roll 26 821.6343/12, RG59, and letter from the *personero* of San Pablo, AGN, República, *Ministerio de Gobierno*, Sección 4ª, t. 3, f. 450.
18. Almario, "Territorio, etnicidad y poder en el Pacífico sur colombiano," 376–77.
19. Report prepared by Vice Consul Thomas McEnelly, Buenaventura, from notes by A. H. Noyes, March 14, 1923, NARA, RG59, 821.63/16, M1294, Roll 26, RG59; Agustín Codazzi, "Carta al gobernador de la provincia de Barbacoas sobre la provincia y el camino, 24 de junio de 1853," in Barona et al., *Geografía Física y Política de la Confederación Granadina*, 451; Restrepo, *Estudio sobre las minas de oro y plata de Colombia*, 65; Oscar Almario, "Territorio, etnicidad y poder en el Pacífico sur colombiano," 364–66, and by the same author, *Los renacientes y su territorio. Ensayos sobre la etnicidad negra en el Pacífico sur colombiano* (Medellín: Universidad Pontificia Bolivariana, 2003), 173.
20. *Registro Municipal*, Barbacoas, No. 9, March 20, 1894.
21. Codazzi, "Informe sobre los baldíos del Chocó."
22. Mario Diego Romero, *Historia y etnohistoria de las comunidades afrocolombianas del río Naya* (Cali: Gobernación del Valle, 1997), chapter 4.
23. Codazzi, "Carta al gobernador," 451.
24. Jorge Orlando Melo, "La evolución económica de Colombia, 1830–1900," in *Nueva Historia de Colombia*, Tomo 1. (Bogotá: Editorial Planeta, 1989), 92, 95; Ocampo, *Colombia y la economía mundial*, 347; Roger Brew, *El desarrollo económico de Antioquia desde la Independencia hasta 1920* (Medellín: Universidad de Antioquia, 2000 [1977]), 102.
25. Cited by Restrepo, *Estudio sobre las minas de oro y plata de Colombia*, 62.
26. Restrepo, *Estudio sobre las minas de oro y plata de Colombia*, 25.
27. María Mercedes Botero, *La ruta del oro. Una economía primaria exportadora, Antioquia, 1850–1890*, (Medellín: Fondo Editorial Universidad Eafit, 2007), 70. See also pp. 67, 74, 173, as well as Brew, *El desarrollo económico de Antioquia*, 17–27.
28. Melo, "La evolución económica de Colombia," 92–93. Emphasis added.

29. José Antonio Ocampo, *Colombia y la economía mundial*, 350.
30. Ann Twinam, *Miners, Merchants, and Farmers in Colonial Colombia* (Austin: University of Texas Press, 1982), 34–35; Germán Colmenares, "¿Si será verdad tanta igualdad?," *Boletín Cultural y Bibliográfico* 22, no. 4 (1985).
31. Patiño Millán, "La provincia en el siglo XVIII," 82–83.
32. Minaudier, "Une région minière de la colonie à l'indépendance," 93; Romero, *Poblamiento y sociedad en el Pacífico colombiano*, 78, 89, 100, 103, 105.
33. Cantor, *Ni aniquilados ni vencidos*; 182, Romero, *Poblamiento y sociedad en el Pacífico colombiano*, 102; Hermes Tovar et al., *Convocatoria al poder del número. Censos y estadísticas de la Nueva Granada (1750–1830)* (Bogotá: Archivo General de la Nación, 1994), 329–32.
34. Cochrane, *Viajes por Colombia*, 423–24. This author also reports that the rubber tree was used locally to prepare ink, while four decades later Michler observed that the Chocó Indians made a kind of cloth out of it that they used for sleeping. Patiño reports that in Ecuador rubber was also employed to make torches. Nathaniel Michler, "Lieutenant Michler's Report of His Survey for an Interoceanic Ship Canal near the Isthmus of Darien," *Senate Excecutive Documents*, No. 9, Vol. 7, 36th Congress, 2nd Session, 1861, 66; Víctor Manuel Patiño, *Plantas cultivadas y animales domésticos en América equinoccial. Tomo III: Fibras, medicinas, misceláneas* (Cali: Imprenta Departamental, 1967), 351–59.
35. The vine is *Landolphia owariensis* and the tree *Funtumia elastica*. For information on the African rubber trade see Robert Harms, "The End of Red Rubber: A Reassessment," *Journal of African History* 16, no. 1 (1975); Raymond Dumett, "The Rubber Trade of the Gold Coast and Asante in the Nineteenth Century: African Innovation and Market Responsiveness," *Journal of African History* 12, no. 1 (1971); J. F. Munro, "Monopolists and Speculators: British Investment in West African Rubber, 1905–1914," *Journal of African History* 22, no. 2 (1981); Catherine Coquery-Vidrovitch, *Le Congo au temps des grandes compagnies concessionnaires, 1898–1930* (Paris: Mouton & Co., 1972); and Martin Ewans, *European Atrocity, African Catastrophe: Leopold II, the Congo Free State and Its Aftermath* (London: Routledge Curzon, 2002), 157–232.
36. Camilo Domínguez and Augusto Gómez, *La economía extractiva en la Amazonía colombiana* (Bogotá: Tropenbos-Araracuara, 1990), 82. This genus probably accounts for the extraction of "white rubber" in the Pacific coastal region of Colombia. According to the collections of several herbariums in Bogotá and Medellín, *S. caudatum*, *S. cuatrecasani* and *S. laurifolium* are present in the region. Historical evidence of the extraction of white rubber comes from Jorge Brisson, *Exploración del alto Chocó* (Bogotá: Imprenta Nacional, 1895), 58–59, 128–29. Likewise, an 1891 list of prices in Quibdó, Chocó, mentioned both black and white rubber; *Los Avisos*, Quibdó, No. 12, June 10, 1891. A more recent text, Contraloría General de la República, *Geografía Económica de Colombia, Tomo VI: Chocó* (Bogotá: Litografía Colombia, 1943), 463, states that there are two types of rubber in Chocó: black rubber and white rubber or *cauchillo*.
37. Cervantes first described the genus in Mexico in 1794 and named it Castilla, probably in honor of Juan de Castillo, a Spanish botanist who died in 1793 while engaged

in the preparation of a flora of Mexico. Charles Marie de La Condamine had described it earlier from samples from the Amazon and named it differently. In 1805 a translation of the 1794 description was published in English, which changed the name to Castilloa. For a long time the latter name was used. O. F. Cook, *The Culture of the Central American Rubber Tree*, Bureau of Plant Industry, Bulletin No. 49 (Washington, D.C.: Government Printing Office, 1903), 19. The most comprehensive studies of Castilla are C. C. Berg, "Olmedieae, Brosimeae (Moraceae)," *Flora Neotropica* 7 (1972); Cook, *The Culture of the Central American Rubber Tree*; and Henry Pittier, "A Preliminary Treatment of the Genus Castilla," *Contributions from the US National Herbarium* 13 (1910).

38. Barbara Weinstein, *The Amazon Rubber Boom, 1850–1920* (Stanford: Stanford University Press, 1983), 10.
39. Weinstein, *The Amazon Rubber Boom*, 53, 218.
40. Weinstein, *The Amazon Rubber Boom*, 218. See also W. J. Baulkwill, "A History of Natural Rubber Production," in *Rubber*, ed. C. C. Webster and W. J. Baulkwill (Essex: Longman Scientific & Technical, 1989), 6–11.
41. John Cresson Trautwine, *Rough Notes on the Exploration of an Interoceanic Canal by Way of the Rivers Atrato and San Juan in New Grenada, South America* (Philadelphia: Barnard & Jones, 1854), 8.
42. Barona et al., *Geografía Física y Política de la Confederación Granadina*, 75–76.
43. Michler, "Lieutenant Michler's Report of His Survey," 27–28.
44. Armando Reclus, *Exploraciones a los istmos de Panamá y Darién en 1876, 1877 y 1878* (Panamá: Publicaciones de la Revista Lotería, 1958 [1881]), 78.
45. Oliver Selfridge, *Reports of Explorations and Surveys to Ascertain the Practicability of a Ship-Canal between the Atlantic and the Pacific Oceans by the Way of the Isthmus of Darien by Thos. Oliver Selfridge, Commander US Navy* (Washington, D.C.: Government Printing Office 1874), 81.
46. Jorge Alberto Restrepo and Manuel Rodríguez, "La actividad comercial y el grupo de comerciantes de Cartagena a finales del siglo XIX," *Estudios Sociales*, no. 1 (September 1986), 56.
47. *Anuario Estadístico de Colombia, 1875*, 150.
48. Ocampo, *Colombia y la economía mundial*, 382.
49. "Método para beneficiar el hule o el caucho," in *La Epoca*, Barbacoas, No. 5, December 1, 1867.
50. Michael Edward Stanfield, *Red Rubber, Bleeding Trees* (Albuquerque: University of New Mexico Press, 1998), 25.
51. Evidence for Panama, Chocó, and Tumaco can be found in Henry C. Pearson, *What I Saw in the Tropics* (New York: India Rubber Publishing Co., 1906), 221–22, 256; Reclus, *Exploraciones a los istmos de Panamá y Darién*, 78, 84, 172, 269; Rodolfo Castro Baldrich, ingeniero de la Intendencia, "Informe del jefe de la Comisión Especial á las regiones de Salaquí y Cacarica, y limítrofe con Panamá, ordenada por el Ministerio de Guerra", Quibdó, 31 de octubre de 1911, AGN, República, *Ministerio de Gobierno*, Sección 1ª, t. 659, ff. 260–68; and "Costumbre perniciosa,"

in *El Fiscal*, Tumaco, No. 114, August 13, 1918. For Mexico and Central America see Daniel Morris, *Plantes produisant le caoutchouc du commerce*, conférences publiées par la Sociéte por l'encouragement du commerce, des arts et manufactures de Londres (n.d.), 193. Domínguez and Gómez, *La economía extractiva en la Amazonía colombiana*, 84–90, document well the felling of *Castilla ulei* in the Colombian Amazon. Barham and Coomes, *Prosperity's Promise*, 37–38 also refer to this practice.

52. Pearson, *What I Saw in the Tropics*, 256.
53. Brisson, *Exploración del alto Chocó*, 14, 58–59; Reclus, *Exploraciones a los istmos de Panamá y Darién*, 86.
54. Pearson, *What I Saw in the Tropics*, 221–22.
55. Rodolfo Castro Baldrich, ingeniero de la Intendencia, "Informe del jefe de la Comisión Especial á las regiones de Salaquí y Cacarica, y limítrofe con Panamá, ordenada por el Ministerio de Guerra", Quibdó, 31 de octubre de 1911, AGN, República, *Ministerio de Gobierno*, Sección 1ª, t. 659, ff. 260–68.
56. "Geografía física y política de la Provincia del Chocó," in Barona et al., *Geografía Física y Política de la Confederación Granadina*, 75; Santiago Pérez, *Selección de escritos y discursos de Santiago Pérez* (Bogotá: Biblioteca de Historia Nacional, 1950), 67; Michler, "Lieutenant Michler's Report of His Survey," 48; Brisson, *Viajes por Colombia en los años de 1891 a 1897*, 104.
57. Brisson, *Exploración del alto Chocó*, 58.
58. On partnerships in timber extraction see Claudia Leal and Eduardo Restrepo, *Unos bosques sembrados de aserríos* (Medellín: Universidad de Antioquia, 2003), 103–6; Eduardo Restrepo, "Los tuqueros negros del Pacífico surcolombiano," in *Renacientes del Guandal: "Grupos negros" de los ríos Satinga y Sanquianga* (Bogotá: Proyecto Biopacífico-Universidad Nacional de Colombia, 1996).
59. Brisson, *Exploración del alto Chocó*, 14.
60. Reclus, *Exploraciones a los istmos de Panamá y Darién*, 78; *El Correo de la Costa*, Buenaventura, No. 6, March 9; No. 10, April 13; No. 12, May 1; No. 13, May 22, 1879; Brisson, *Viajes por Colombia en los años de 1891 a 1897*, 18; Brisson, *Exploración del alto Chocó*, 128–29; Pearson, *What I Saw in the Tropics*, 256.
61. Even if Cartagena's exports came from both Chocó and the Sinú valley, the relative importance of Cartagena's exports suggests that Chocó produced more rubber than did the southern part of the region. Ocampo, *Colombia y la economía mundial*, 382.
62. Ciceron Angel, Carlos Ferrer, Gonzalo Zúñiga, and Ernesto Zúñiga, Letter to the Minister of Public Works, November 3, 1905, AGN, República, *Baldíos*, t. 31, f. 10.
63. Informe de Miguel Triana al Ministro de Obras Públicas (1906), cited in *Revista Nacional de Colombia* 22, Bogotá, December 7, 1912.
64. AGN, República, *Baldíos*, t. 42, f. 507.
65. Louis G. Dreyfus, "Conditions and Possibilities in the Chocó," NARA, RG 84, Records of Foreign Service Posts. Consular Posts. Quibdó, Colombia, Vol. 4, 1914. The Baudó Mountains and the Pacific coast had 454,942 trees, the majority of them (365,982) in Pié de Pató. "Informe del comisario especial de Juradó," March 1914, AGN, *Ministerio de Gobierno*, Sección 1ª, t. 730, f. 485. Despite the scope of

rubber cultivation in the region, it is only mentioned by Jorge Gamboa, "La política de baldíos en el Chocó durante la segunda mitad del siglo XIX," in *Construcción territorial en el Chocó, Vol. 1: Historias regionales*, ed. Patricia Vargas (Bogotá: ICAN-PNR-Obapo, 1999), and Luis Fernando González, "Sirio-libaneses en el Chocó, cien años de presencia económica y cultural," *Boletín Cultural y Bibliográfico* 34, no. 44 (1997), 82.

66. Pearson, *What I Saw in the Tropics*, 257, see also 258–59.

67. "Cartagena, junio 8 de 1908. Informe de la comisión nombrada por el gobierno Reyes para explorar las posibilidades económicas del Chocó," AGN, República, *Baldíos*, t. 30, ff. 144–55, 188–89, 500; t. 35, ff. 297–98, 604–7; "Tercer informe del comisario especial de Juradó, de 10 de mayo de 1913," *Ministerio de Gobierno*, Sección 1ª, t. 718, ff. 153–60; t. 730, f. 418; Notaría Primera de Quibdó, 1903, No. 87, f. 304; 1905, No. 12, f. 28; 1911, No. 140, f. 734; No. 145, f. 757; No. 146, f. 765; No. 156, f. 819; 1916, No. 16, f. 63; No. 20, f. 84; No. 21, f. 85; No. 29, f. 122; 1921, No. 25, f. 103.

68. AMP, Gobernación, *Correspondencia*, Caja 1: "Informe sobre navegación fluvial en los ríos Patía y Telembí"; Notaría de Timbiquí, 1911, No. 16, f. 54; 1916, No. 4, f. 9; 1917, No. 12, f. 45; No. 14, f. 50; 1918, No. 15, f. 50; No. 23, f. 107; Notaría de Guapi, 1915, No. 6, f. 19; No. 26, f. 41.

69. Pearson, *What I Saw in the Tropics*, 258–59. Ofelia Rentería's grandfather and José de la Cruz Murillo had small plantations in the Baudó River of three thousand and two thousand trees, respectively. Interview with Ofelia Rentería and Notaría Primera de Quibdó, 1916, No. 23, f. 92.

70. Along with these, there was at least one other small plantation in that area, in the Arquía River, which had four thousand trees. Notaría Primera de Quibdó, 1911, No. 105, f. 568. Thomas Reynolds, a Briton, developed the only one outside of Chocó, along the Mira River. *El Fiscal*, Tumaco, No. 96, April 27, 1916.

71. "Tercer informe del comisario especial de Juradó." Zúñiga himself estimated his plantation as having one thousand trees in 1912 and 150,000 in 1914, AGN, República, *Ministerio de Gobierno*, Sección 1ª, t. 605, ff. 421–23.

72. These plantations were located in the upper Magdalena valley, the lower Cauca valley, and the Sinú. "El caucho y el café," *Gaceta Agrícola* 1, 1879, 5; Pearson, *What I Saw in the Tropics*; Ocampo, *Colombia y la economía mundial*, 388; AGN, República, *Baldíos*, t. 29, ff. 583, 596.

73. Pearson, *What I Saw in the Tropics*; Morris, *Plantes produisant le caoutchouc du commerce*.

74. Equivalent to about 12 percent of the area cultivated in Asia. *India Rubber World* Vol. 46, No. 2, May 1, 1912, 393.

75. *India Rubber World* Vol. 44, No. 2, May 1, 1911, 280–81. More information on Mexican plantations in: *India Rubber World* Vol. 43, No. 4, January 1, 1911, 123; Vol. 44, No. 4, July 1, 1911, 361; Vol. 44, No. 5, August 1, 1911, 411–13; Vol. 45, No. 3, December 1, 1911, 115; Pearson, *What I Saw in the Tropics*. In the Amazon, by the early 1920s there were about two million planted rubber trees, but they were rarely

tapped. The South America Leaf disease attacked *Heveas* planted in their native habitat, so plantations did not prosper. Warren Dean, *Brazil and the Struggle for Rubber* (Cambridge: Cambridge University Press, 1987). Europeans also experimented with rubber cultivation in East and West Africa. Munro, "Monopolists and Speculators," and "British Rubber Companies in East Africa before the First World War," *Journal of African History* 24, no. 3 (1983).

76. Law 15 of 1884 and articles 36 and 37 of Decree 1113 of 1905. AGN, República, *Baldíos*, t. 31, ff. 9–10; t. 33, ff. 292–93.
77. *Registro de Bolívar*, Cartagena, August 29, 1905; Pearson, *What I Saw in the Tropics*; and interview with Luis Palacios. Plantation owners and peasants cultivated *Castilla elastica*, with two exceptions. The plantation at Acandí, used *Manihot* spp seeds brought from a ranch in the upper Magdalena River that got its seeds from Ceylon. And in 1911, Thomas Reynolds tried *Hevea* in his Castilla plantation. *El Fiscal*, Tumaco, No. 96, April 27, 1916. On Castilla cultivation methods see Cook, *The Culture of the Central American Rubber Tree*, 56, 59, 64.
78. Pearson, *What I Saw in the Tropics*, 256.
79. This kind was, I believe, the same Mexican scrap rubber that appears in the rubber price citations of the *India Rubber World*. In places where Castilla latex flowed well, collectors could also gather it in receptacles or holes in the ground. According to Ofelia Rentería, an old woman from the Baudó who I interviewed, the product of this method is called *andullo*. Yet, according to a 1943 publication, andullo was the method used by Indians to collect rubber: they used condensed milk purified with water to make thin strips that they later wrapped to form a ball that weighted a kilo. Contraloría, *Geografía Económica de Colombia*, 464. See also Cook, *The Culture of the Central American Rubber Tree*, 63, 73; *India Rubber World* Vol. 44, No. 2, May 1, 1911, 281.
80. *Registro de Bolívar*, Cartagena, August 29, 1905.
81. Mexican plantations were not only hit by the fall in prices but also by the revolution. *India Rubber World* Vol. 46, No. 2, May 1, 1912, 336.
82. AGN, República, *Baldíos*, t. 30, ff. 144–55.
83. By 1916, the Atrato and the San Juan together were exporting even less: 17,586 kilos. AGN, República, *Ministerio de Gobierno*, Sección 1ª, t. 603, f. 143; t. 796, f. 248; NARA, RG 84, Records of Foreign Service Posts. Consular Posts. Quibdó, Colombia, Vol. 4.
84. *El Litoral Pacífico*, Tumaco, No. 146, March 14, 1914.
85. *Unión Obrera*, Tumaco, No. 6, May 10, 1919.
86. This gum is produced by the species *Manilkara bidentata* from the Sapotaceae family. *India Rubber World* 43, no. 2 (1910): 49; 57, no. 2 (1917).
87. *Anuario de Comercio Exterior*, years 1916, 1918, 1919, 1922–29.
88. *El Litoral Pacífico*, Tumaco, No. 217, October 16, 1915. At least between 1916 and 1919, merchants advertised that they purchased balata in Tumaco's newspapers. *El Eco del Pacífico*, Tumaco, No. 10, October 14, 1916; *El Fiscal*, Tumaco, No. 104, August 13, 1918; No. 113, October 22, 1918; No. 125, January 15, 1919.

89. AGN, República, *Ministerio de Gobierno*, Sección 1ª, t. 77, f. 87, "Informe del Intendente Vaca (mayo, 1918) que se refiere a su periodo, que comenzó el 12 de agosto de 1917," t. 796, ff. 248–79; *Baldíos*, t. 41, f. 414; t. 43, f. 80; t. 7, f. 20; *El Fiscal* No. 114, Tumaco, October 29, 1918. The fall in price also contributed to the end of this trade, Francisco Gutiérrez, ed., *Relación de algunas excursiones apostólicas en la misión del Chocó* (Bogotá, Imprenta Nacional, 1924).

90. This gum was also referred to locally as cauchillo. *Anuario de Comercio Exterior* years 1918, 1919, 1922–24. See also *El Fiscal* No. 113, No. 114, and No. 125, cited in the two previous notes.

91. Charles Saffray, *Viaje a Nueva Granada* (Bogotá: Biblioteca Popular de Cultura Colombiana, 1948), 68–69; AGN, República, *Baldíos*, t. 31, f. 363; t. 37, ff. 100–2; Bell, *Colombia, A Commercial Handbook*, 90; *Anuario Estadístico de Colombia, 1875*.

92. Vegetable ivory palms form a subfamily (Phytelephantoidae) within the palm family (Araceae) composed of three genera (Ammandra, Aphandra, and Phytelephas) and seven species. Three species inhabit the Upper Amazon basin and the Magdalena Valley in Colombia, of which only *Phytelephas macrocarpa* produced marketable nuts. A fourth species, *Aphandra decasperma*, known as *cabecita* and *tagua de monte*, is distributed mostly around Buenaventura and produces small seeds that were not marketable. The genus was first described in 1798 but only studied in the early twentieth century by O. F. Cook, of the U.S. Bureau of Plant Industry. In the 1940s, M. Acosta Solís, director of the Ecuadorian Institute of Natural Sciences, published a few seminal works on Ecuadorian *tagua*. O. F. Cook, "The Relationships of Ivory Palms," *Contributions from the US National Herbarium* 13, no. 5 (1910); and "Ivory Palms in Panamá," *Journal of the Washington Academy of Sciences* 3, no. 5 (1913); Misael Acosta Solís, *Tagua* (Quito: Editorial Ecuador, 1944), 5. The information that follows comes from Anders S. Barfod, "A Monographic Study of the Subfamily Phytelephantoideae (Araceae)," *Opera Botanica* 105 (1991), unless otherwise noted.

93. Rodrigo Bernal, "The Growth of *Phytelephas seemannii*—a potentially immortal solitary palm," *Principes* 42, no. 1 (1998).

94. Henrik Borgtoft Pedersen, "Ivory Nuts, Fruits and Thatch: Use and Management of *Phytelephas aequatorialis* (palmae) in Ecuador" (Unpublished: n.d.).

95. Berthold Seemann, *Narrative of the Voyage of the H.M.S. Herald During the Years 1845–51, Under the Command of Captain Henry Kellett, R.N., C.B.; Being a Circumnavigation of the Globe, and Three Cruizes to the Arctic Regions in Search of Sir John Franklin*, Vol. 1 (London: Reeve and Co., 1853), 222, 224.

96. Ocampo, *Colombia y la economía mundial*, 418–20; *El Litoral Pacífico*, Tumaco, No. 17, March 23, 1910; P. L. Bell, *Colombia, A Commercial Handbook*, Department of Commerce, Special Series No. 206. (Washington, D.C.: Government Printing Office, 1921), 90; *El Correo de la Costa*, Buenaventura, No. 4, February 23; No. 6, March 9; No. 8, March 23, No. 10, April 13, No. 12, May 1.

97. Factories were located in Rochester (New York), Brooklyn (New York), Springfield (Massachusetts), and Newark (New Jersey). By 1921, the Button Manufacturers Corporation of Newark had established a factory in Panama City. William A.

Reid, "A Brief Talk about Tagua . . . ," *Commodities and Commerce Series* 21 (Pan American Union: Washington, D.C., 1936); Acosta Solís, *Tagua*; United States Department of Labor, "The Button and Buckle Manufacturing Industry" (1942), and Bell, *Colombia, A Commercial Handbook*, 90–91. Before plastic, vegetable ivory had one main substitute: another seed known as dum produced by the palm *Hyphaene thebaica*, native of the Sahel in Africa, which is smaller than and not as hard as vegetable ivory, and was cheaper. F. P. Farhar, "From Tagua to Buttons" (1928?); Misael Acosta Solís, "Tagua or Vegetable Ivory—A Forest Product of Ecuador," *Economic Botany* 2, no. 1 (1948).

98. Justiniano Jaramillo, *En el Darién. Informe de una expedición ordenada por el Ministerio de Guerra* (Bogotá: Imprenta Eléctrica, 1910), 10–15; Ernesto Restrepo Tirado, "Un viaje al Darién (apuntes de cartera)," *Repertorio Colombiano* No. 11 and No. 12, November–December (1887), 356.
99. Dreyfus, "Conditions and Possibilities in the Chocó."
100. AGN, República, *Baldíos*, t. 44, f. 350; t. 63, ff.195–202, 229.
101. "Informe del comisario especial de Juradó, Fabricio Ochoa, abril 1912," AGN, República, *Ministerio de Gobierno*, Sección 1ª, t. 677, ff. 65–72; Selfridge, *Reports of Explorations and Surveys*, 54.
102. Buenaventura exported eighty tons per year. Dreyfus, "Conditions and Possibilities in the Chocó," Op. cit.
103. *El Litoral Pacífico*, Tumaco, No. 87, May 18, 1912.
104. *El Concejal*, Tumaco, No. 119, September 30, 1911.
105. AGN, República, *Baldíos*, t. 2, ff. 291–92.
106. *Anuario Estadístico* 1875; *El Vapor* No. 9, Tumaco, February 10, 1878.
107. *El Fiscal*, Tumaco, various numbers, 1909–15.
108. *Anuario de Comercio Exterior, 1917*.
109. Paulo Emilio Escobar, *Bahías de Málaga y Buenaventura, la costa colombiana del Pacífico, 1918–1920* (Bogotá: Imprenta Nacional, 1921), 86; Bernal "The Growth of *Phytelephas seemannii*"; J. W. Dalling et al. "Natural History and Uses of Tagua (Phytelephas seemannii) in Panama," *Principes* 40, no. 1 (1996); F. Claès, "Quelques données utiles sur le Phytelephas macrocarpa Ruiz et Pav," *L'Agronomie Coloniale* 13 (1925); Fundación Inguedé, "Memorias del taller sobre planes de desarrollo de la cuenca del Pacífico y el proyecto Productos del Bosque, El Valle, octubre de 1991," unpublished (1991); *El Concejal* No. 119, Tumaco, September 30, 1911; *El Litoral Pacífico,* Tumaco, No. 175, October 3, 1914, No. 181, November 14, 1914; *El Fiscal*, Tumaco, No. 20, July 8, 1914; AGN, República, *Ministerio de Gobierno*, Sección 1ª, t. 628, ff. 6–10; Dreyfus, "Conditions and Possibilities in the Chocó"; "Tercer informe del comisario especial de Juradó." According to West, *The Pacific Lowlands*, 27, and Jesús Eslava, "Climatología," in *Colombia Pacífico*, Tomo I (Bogotá: Proyecto Biopacífico, Fondo FEN, 1993), 142, unlike all other vegetable ivory gathering areas, average annual rainfall in the Valle River exceeds 5,000 mm per year.
110. Seeds procured this way had a light coffee or blond color and were known in the Ecuadorian market as *tagua rubia* (blond) or *colorada* (red). These commanded

higher prices, but their export was prohibited because their harvest caused the destruction of the forests. Acosta Solís, "Tagua or Vegetable Ivory"; Farhar, "From Tagua to Buttons"; Reid, "A Brief Talk about Tagua. . . ." For more information on the collection of unripe vegetable ivory see chapter 7.

111. Seemann, *Narrative of the Voyage of the H.M.S. Herald*, 224; Reid, "A Brief Talk about Tagua . . ."; and Acosta Solís, "Tagua or Vegetable Ivory" report this use for Ecuador, and Dalling et al., "Natural History and Uses of Tagua," for the Embera and Wounaan Indians in Panama. In the 1990s I saw vegetable ivory fruits being sold for their water in Tumaco.
112. Seemann, *Narrative of the Voyage of the H.M.S. Herald*, 224; and O. F. Cook, "New Genera-Species of Ivory Palms from Colombia, Ecuador and Peru," *Journal of the Washington Academy of Sciences* 17 (1927).
113. Acosta Solís, "Tagua or Vegetable Ivory"; Anders S. Barfod, "Usos pasados, presentes y futuros de las palmas Phytelephantoidées (Araceae)," in *Las plantas y el hombre, Memorias del Primer Simposio Ecuatoriano de Etnobotánica y Botánica Económica*, ed. Monserrat Ríos and Henrik Borgtoft (Quito: Ediciones ABYA-YALA, 1991), 23–46; Borgtoft, "Ivory Nuts, Fruits and Thatch"; Dalling et al., "Natural History and Uses of Tagua."
114. Cook, "New Genera-Species of Ivory Palms"; Barfod, "Usos pasados, presentes y futuros de las palmas"; Acosta Solís, "Tagua or Vegetable Ivory"; and Borgtoft, "Ivory Nuts, Fruits and Thatch."
115. Bell, *Colombia, A Commercial Handbook*, 90; "Canal de Atrato," in *Revista de Colombia*, Volumen Centenario No. 5, June 30, 1910, Bogotá, 139.
116. AGN, República, *Ministerio de Gobierno*, Sección 1ª, t. 628, ff. 6–10.
117. Juan C. Olier, a local entrepreneur, was interested in solving the problem by building a trail but realized that this project would only be profitable if he was given a concession, which most likely did not happen. "Informe de la comisión nombrada por el gobierno Reyes," t. 34, ff. 272–73.
118. Acosta Solís, "Tagua or Vegetable Ivory."
119. Notaría de Quibdó, 1911, No. 4, f. 9; 1916, No. 53, f. 229.
120. Bernal, "The Growth of *Phytelephas seemannii*."
121. *El Litoral Pacífico*, Tumaco, No. 88, May 25, 1912; No. 146, March 14, 1914; *El Fiscal*, Tumaco, No. 61, May 26, 1915; No. 93, April 10, 1916; *El Eco del Pacífico*, Tumaco, No. 13, November 4, 1916.
122. AGN, República, *Baldíos*, t. 68, f. 267. There is a chance that a small percentage was planted. An inhabitant of the Mira River told Eduardo Restrepo in 1997 that vegetable ivory had been planted there. Eduardo Restrepo, "Hacia la periodización de la historia de Tumaco," in *Tumaco: haciendo ciudad*, ed. Michel Agier, Manuela Alvarez, Odile Hoffman, and Eduardo Restrepo (n.p.: Instituto Colombiano de Antropología, IRD, Universidad del Valle, 1999), 61.
123. Bell, *Colombia, A Commercial Handbook*, 91; Dreyfus, "Conditions and Possibilities in the Chocó."
124. See Leal and Restrepo, *Unos bosques sembrados de aserríos*.

125. Jorge Mercado, for instance, sold timber in his store in Tumaco. *El Micrófago*, Tumaco, No. 16, December 6, 1913, *El Fiscal*, Tumaco, No. 1, March 12, 1914.
126. For example, Juan Bautista Mainero y Trucco shipped timber to Cartagena from the Atrato in the 1850s, Luis Fernando Molina Londoño, "'El viejo Mainero': Actividad empresarial de Juan Bautista Mainero y Trucco en Bolívar, Chocó, Antioquia y Cundinamarca, 1860–1918," *Boletín Cultural y Bibliográfico* 25, no. 16 (1988), 4–5, 21. See also *El Correo de la Costa* No. 8, Buenaventura, March 23, 1876; *El Vapor*, Tumaco, No. 9, February 10, 1878; Leal and Restrepo, *Unos bosques sembrados de aserríos*, 48. Local newspapers and archival sources corroborate the existence of timber exports from Tumaco in the 1910s and 1920s; AGN, República, *Baldíos*, t. 58, f. 398; "Informe del Prefecto de la Provincia de Nuñez, año 1923,"Archivo Municipal de Pasto (AMP), Gobernación, *Correspondencia*, Caja 9; Evidence of timber exports from Quibdó in 1908, 1914, and 1927: AGN, República, *Ministerio de Gobierno*, Sección 1ª, t. 603, f. 143; *A.B.C.*, Quibdó, No. 17, April 24, 1914; No. 1349, February 12, 1927.
127. In 1890, for instance, Juan C. Olier shipped 1,500 cedar logs from the mouth of the Atrato River, and in around 1908, sailboats from Peru used to stop in the mouth of the Tapaje River, north of Tumaco, to exchange salt and foodstuffs for timber. *Los Avisos*, Quibdó, No. 4, September 30, 1890; AGN, República, *Ministerio de Gobierno*, Sección 4ª, t. 41, f. 487; Bernardo Merizalde del Carmen, *Estudio de la costa colombiana del Pacífico* (Bogotá: Imprenta del Estado Mayor General, 1921), 108.
128. Leal and Restrepo, *Unos bosques sembrados de aserríos*, 46; *El Revisor*, Tumaco, No. 2, February 10, 1909; *El Litoral Pacífico*, Tumaco, No. 103, September 7, 1912; No. 143, February 21, 1914; *El Camarada*, Tumaco, No. 30, Abril 22, 1916; *El Eco del Pacífico*, Tumaco, No. 13, November 4, 1916.
129. Leal and Restrepo, *Unos bosques sembrados de aserríos*, 47–48; interview with Teodoro Vanín; AGN, República, *Baldíos*, t. 48, f. 505; *El Fiscal* No. 2, Tumaco, March 18, 1914.
130. Dreyfus, "Conditions and Possibilities in the Chocó"; AGN, República, *Ministerio de Gobierno*, Sección 1ª, t. 638, ff. 220-ss.; *Ministerio de Gobierno*, Sección 4ª, t. 90, ff. 128–47; Joaquín Paredes Cruz, *Monografía de Buenaventura* (Cali: Imprenta Márquez, 1949), 122.
131. Dreyfus, "Conditions and Possibilities in the Chocó"; Jaramillo, *En el Darién*, 23–26.
132. "Informe de la comisión nombrada por el gobierno Reyes"; Leal and Restrepo, *Unos bosques sembrados de aserríos*, 46–47; *Albores*, Barbacoas, No. 1, February 1, 1906. *Por el Sur de Colombia*, Barbacoas, March 20, No. 8, 1909; *El Istmo*, Istmina, No. 2, August 10, 1912; Merizalde, *Estudio de la costa colombiana del Pacífico*, 90.
133. See for example "Carta de Antonio Asprilla," NARA, RG 84, Records of Foreign Service Posts. Consular Posts. Quibdó, Colombia, Vol. 4.
134. The species are red mangrove (*Rhizophora mangle*) and a palm known locally as *naidí* in the lowlands and as açai in the Brazilian Amazon (*Euterpe oleracea*). See Claudia Leal, "Manglares y economía extractiva," in *Geografía humana de Colombia,*

Tomo VI: Los Afrocolombianos (Bogotá: Instituto Colombiano de Cultura Hispánica, 1998), 397–429; and Martha Isabel Vallejo, Natalia Valderrama, Rodrigo Bernal, Gloria Galeano, Gerardo Arteaga, and Claudia Leal, "Producción de palmito de *Euterpe oleracea* Mart. (Araceae) en la costa pacífica colombiana: estado actual y perspectivas," *Colombia Forestal* 14, no. 2 (2011): 191–212.

CHAPTER 3

1. *El Litoral Pacífico* No. 17, Tumaco, March 23, 1910. Ecuadorian exporters led the way, albeit late, in sorting the nuts into three categories by size, which gave their product a good reputation. Acosta Solís, "Tagua or Vegetable Ivory"; Bell, *Colombia, A Commercial Handbook*, 91; Farhar, "From Tagua to Buttons."
2. Minaudier, "Une région minière de la colonie à l'indépendance," 92.
3. Fundación Inguedé, "Memorias del taller sobre planes de desarrollo."
4. AGN, República, *Ministerio de Gobierno*, Sección 1ª, t. 728, f. 447.
5. *El Litoral Pacífico*, Tumaco, No. 2, October 10, 1909; No. 36, October 9, 1910.
6. *El Fiscal*, Tumaco, No. 1, March 12, 1914.
7. *El Montaraz*, Barbacoas, No. 1, May 1, 1878; No. 5, July 20, 1878; *El Elector*, Tumaco, No. 5, November 20, 1878.
8. Some of the merchants who did not survive for long were Juan N. Gómez, Grindale & Co, Nicolás Arias, J. Lowenthal, Benedetto Solari, Felipe S. Arias, Rafael Valdez, Margarita Vivanco, Elías D. Morcillo, Manuel M. Cortés, Manuel L. Velasco, José Lorenzo Benítez, Garcés & Suarez, Francisco y Sanhing & Co., and Acevedo Hnos. *El Tumaqueño*, Tumaco, No. 3, August 12, 1878; *El Litoral Pacífico*, Tumaco, No. 42, November 19, 1910; No. 86, Mayo 11, 1912; No. 122, June 14, 1913; No. 148, March 28, 1914; *Gaceta Departamental*, Tumaco, No. 14, February 29, 1909; *El Fiscal*, Tumaco, No. 63, June 9, 1915; No. 113, October 22, 1918.
9. Brisson, *Viajes por Colombia en los años de 1891 a 1897*, 15.
10. "Informe de la comisión nombrada por el gobierno Reyes"; *El Litoral Pacífico*, Tumaco, No. 155, May 16, 1914.
11. AGN, República, *Baldíos*, t. 50, f. 516; Gutiérrez, *Relación de algunas excursiones apostólicas*, 101. See also Teodoro Maetzu, "Prefectura Apostólica de Tumaco. Bellezas de la costa del Pacífico," *Revista de Misiones*, Año 4, No. 24, March (1928), 67–77; Claudia Steiner, *Imaginación y poder: El encuentro del interior con la costa en Urabá, 1900–1960*, (Medellín: Universidad de Antioquia, 2000), 36.
12. *El Litoral Pacífico*, Tumaco, No. 2, October 10, 1909; No. 36, October 9, 1910.
13. Both father and son were called Marcos A. del Castillo. *El Litoral Pacífico*, Tumaco, No. 27, July 16, 1910.
14. On Escrucería Hnos. see AGN, República, *Baldíos*, t. 50, f. 516; t. 69, f. 387. In 1919, Jorge Mercado died and his firm continued under the name Pugliese, Frigeiro & Mayolo. (This business was an anomaly because it was a branch of a commercial house from Buenaventura.) William Jarvis kept the house Gaminara & Leeder after it dissolved. *El Fiscal*, No. 125, Tumaco, January 15, 1919; *El Eco del Pacífico*,

Tumaco, No. 93, November 20, 1919; *Unión Obrera*, Tumaco, No. 2, April 12, 1919; *La Juventud*, Tumaco, No. 1, September 4, 1920.

15. See for example *El Litoral Pacífico*, Tumaco, No. 18, April 2, 1910; No. 166, August 1, 1914.
16. Toward the late nineteenth century, Federico Archer, Nicolás Martán, and Fidel D'Cross settled as merchants in El Charco, followed later by Adolfo Cuevas. Meanwhile Baudilo Revelo traded in Iscuandé and the Martán's, and Agustín Olaya in Guapi. Additionally, in 1870, there were two merchants in both the Timbiquí and Micay basins. *Albores*, Tumaco, No. 12, February 25, 1907; *El Litoral Pacífico*, Tumaco, No. 202, April 10, 1905; No. 128, August 2, 1913.
17. Agustín Codazzi, *Memorias de Agustín Codazzi* (Bogotá: Banco de la República, 1973), 362–63.
18. Mosquera, *De esclavizadores y esclavizados en Citará*, 45, referred to six Englishmen who settled in Chocó in the 1820s. But Cochrane, *Viajes por Colombia, 1823 y 1824*, 291, who visited Quibdó in 1823, wrote that there was only one British merchant in town and mentioned his partner, a Jamaican named Coutin. According to Sergio Mosquera, *Diccionario genealógico de la Provincia de Citará, siglos XIX y XX* (Quibdó: Fondo Mixto para la Promoción de la Cultura y las Artes, 1997), 39, Coutin was French. Trautwine, *Rough Notes on the Exploration of an Interoceanic Canal*, who visited Quibdó in 1852, mentioned a physician, Dr. Key, who had lived in town since at least Cochrane's visit, and had become a merchant.
19. Michler, "Lieutenant Michler's report of his survey," 27–28, 42.
20. A channel—the *canal del Dique*—that linked Cartagena with the Magdalena River was plugged until the 1880s, forcing Cartageneros to seek economic alternatives in the west. Restrepo and Rodríguez, "La actividad comercial y el grupo de comerciantes de Cartagena," 51, 55–58.
21. Steiner, *Imaginación y poder*, 93. In 1876 the main merchant in Turbo was Mr. Burgos, who was from Cartagena. Reclus, *Exploraciones a los istmos de Panamá y Darién*, 172.
22. Mosquera, *Diccionario genealógico de la Provincia de Citará*, 26, 32, 48, 65, mentions Juan Botín y Capurro, Antonio Botto, Juan Capela Jobet, José Di Marchi, and Lázaro Geovo.
23. The Bonolli family also owned land in the Atrato. Notaría de Quibdó, 1891, No. 5; 1892, No. 85. Restrepo, *Estudio sobre las minas de oro y plata de Colombia*, 76–77, mentions that Mr. Bonolli, an Italian who made money in Cartagena, sold much platinum in Europe before 1850. Mosquera, *De esclavizadores y esclavizados en Citará*, 26, mentions a Nicolás Bognoli buying slaves around 1823.
24. Molina, "El viejo Mainero," 4–5. In 1855, a Quibdó newspaper had an advertisement of the merchandise offered by Mainero, *Unión Chocoana*, Quibdó, No. 18, April 28, 1855.
25. An unclassified document in the Fondo Provincias (AHC) referred to a man from Cartagena who in 1904 went to the Atrato to sell merchandise. It is likely that he was following a tradition started several decades earlier.

26. Mainero y Trucco, for instance, left and sold the properties he had acquired. In 1897, Pedro Salge Piagzo, a man from Corsica who lived in Quibdó, sold a lot that Mainero bought in 1856 and was in charge of selling the rest of his possessions. Notaría Primera de Quibdó, 1897, No. 42.
27. Germán De Granda, *Estudios sobre un área dialectal hispanoamericana de población negra, las tierras bajas occidentales de Colombia* (Bogotá: Instituto Caro y Cuervo, 1977), 191. According to Mosquera, *De esclavizadores y esclavizados en Citará*, 45, in 1803, the Ferrer family formed a commercial house with branches in Havana, Cartagena and Quibdó, which closed in 1813, when the partners settled in Quibdó.
28. Luis Fernando González, *Quibdó, Contexto histórico, desarrollo urbano y patrimonio arquitectónico* (Medellín: Instituto de Investigaciones Ambientales del Pacífico, 2003), 87.
29. González, *Quibdó, Contexto histórico*, 82.
30. Such was the case of Hortensio and Enrique Ferrer, who created a commercial house in 1884. Notaría de Quibdó, 1884, No. 32, f. 85. A decade later, this family stood out among local merchants with two commercial houses and one individual business. Brisson, *Exploración del alto Chocó*, 128.
31. Notaría de Quibdó, 1891, No. 4, f. 18; *Los Avisos*, Quibdó, No. 13, June 18, 1891.
32. Juan Carlos Vélez Rendón, *Los pueblos allende el río Cauca: La formación del Suroeste y la cohesión del espacio en Antioquia, 1830–1877* (Medellín: Universidad Nacional de Colombia, sede Medellín, Universidad de Antioquia, 2002), 102–7.
33. Notaría de Quibdó, 1870, No. 39, f. 95; 1880, No. 1, f. 1.
34. On Syrio-Lebanese immigration to Colombia see Louise Fawcett de Posada and Eduardo Posada Carbó, "En tierra de oportunidades: los sirio-libaneses en Colombia," *Boletín Cultural y Bibliográfico* 29, no. 29 (1992).
35. Notaría Primera de Quibdó, 1895, No. 31; No. 60; 1897, No. 24; No. 46; 1898, No. 26, f. 132; No. 32, f. 249; No. 38, f. 279; No. 45, f. 400; No. 61.
36. Besides Miguel, the initial partners of Abuchar Hermanos were Rafael, César, Alejandro, Salomón, and Carlos; the latter left the partnership in 1900. AHC, Notaría de Cartagena, 1900, No. 101, ff. 328–331. With respect to A & T Meluk see Archivo Histórico de Cartagena (AHC), Notaría de Cartagena, 1908, No. 48.
37. Mosquera, *Diccionario genealógico de la Provincia de Citará*, 96; interview with Emilio Meluk; Notaría de Quibdó, 1911, No. 152, f. 790.
38. Antonio, Camilo, and Luis; the latter two settled in Quibdó. In 1909, Camilo left the house, and in 1920 Antonio died. Notaría Primera de Quibdó, 1903, No. 23, f. 70; AHC, Notaría de Cartagena, 1909: No. 460; Luis Fernando González, "Sirio-libaneses en el Chocó, cien años de presencia económica y cultural," *Boletín Cultural y Bibliográfico* 34, no. 44 (1997).
39. Elías, Miguel, and Carlos Rumié created Rumié Hermanos in 1909. Five years later, Alejandro, Abraham, and José joined. The Dualiby brothers were called Salomón and Carlos; the Chamat, Elías, Alberto, and Alfredo; and the Cudsi, Abraham and Antonio. Notaría Primera de Quibdó, 1909, No. 22, f. 83; No. 75, f. 305; No. 83, f. 338; 1910, No. 129, f. 448; AHC, Notaría de Cartagena, 1914, No. 773.

40. *Ecos del Chocó*, Quibdó, No. 3, February 27, 1907; interview with Emilio Meluk; González, "Sirio-libaneses en el Chocó."
41. A few newcomers joined in the 1920s, such as Manasseh & Mabardi and Zaher Hermanos, González, "Sirio-libaneses en el Chocó."
42. Enrique Ferrer & Hijo, Ferrer Hermanos, and Ferrer & Andrade. Notaría Primera de Quibdó, 1905: No. 3, f. 5; 1906: No. 87, f. 342; 1908, No. 11, f. 39.
43. Notaría Primera de Quibdó, 1880, No. 13, f. 45; 1893, No. 88, f. 425; 1899, No. 75, f. 387; 1910, No. 83, f. 356; 1905, No. 72, f. 302; 1908, No. 15.
44. *Los Hércules*, Quibdó, No. 2, March 12, 1908; Dreyfus, "Conditions and Possibilities in the Chocó"; Notaría Primera de Quibdó, 1908, No. 35, f. 170; 1913, No. 37, f. 193; 1916, No. 132, f. 752; 1921, No. 6, f. 28.
45. Enrique Ferrer and Gonzalo Zúñiga died in 1914. *A.B.C.*, Quibdó, No. 14, March 29, 1914; No. 30, July 26, 1914; Dreyfus, "Conditions and Possibilities in the Chocó"; González, *Quibdó, Contexto histórico*, 168–69.
46. Notaría Primera de Quibdó, 1918, No. 49; 1921, No. 12, f. 49; AHC, Notaría de Cartagena, 1909: No. 773.
47. Notaría Primera de Quibdó, 1916, No. 89, f. 580.
48. Notaría Primera de Quibdó, 1905, No. 27, f. 66; No. 45, f. 130; 1906: No. 127, f. 467; 1909, No. 102, f. 414; No. 152, f. 790; 1916, No. 43, f. 200; No. 96, f. 611; No. 129, f. 744; No. 132, f. 752; 1921, No. 8, f. 36; No. 13, f. 52.
49. Notaría Primera de Quibdó, 1905, No. 161, f. 631; AHC, Notaría de Cartagena, 1909, No. 460.
50. González, "Sirio-libaneses en el Chocó."
51. AGN, República, *Ministerio de Gobierno*, Sección 4ª, t. 56, ff. 484–500.
52. *El Litoral Pacífico*, Tumaco, No. 154, May 9, 1914; *El Fiscal*, Tumaco, No. 18, June 24, 1914.
53. González, "Sirio-libaneses en el Chocó," 78–79.
54. Notaría Primera de Quibdó, 1907, No. 143, f. 727; Interview with Ofelia Rentería; AHC, Notaría de Cartagena, 1899, No. 351, f. 1636; 1900, No. 236; Notaría Primera de Quibdó, 1905, No. 90, f. 389; Pearson, *What I Saw in the Tropics*, 258–59; Dreyfus, "Conditions and Possibilities in the Chocó"; Edgar Toro Sánchez, ed., *Memorias de Julián Uribe Uribe* (Bogotá: Banco de la República, 1994), 377; "Tercer informe del comisario especial de Juradó"; AGN, República, *Ministerio de Gobierno*, Sección 1ª, t. 605, ff. 421–23.
55. Michler, "Lieutenant Michler's Report of His Survey," 43; *Anuario Estadístico* 1875, 149; Brisson, *Exploración del alto Chocó*, 129; Brisson, *Viajes por Colombia en los años de 1891 a 1897*, 18.
56. Cacao (*Theobroma cacao*) originated in the Amazon basin. Ecuador exported cacao since colonial times from plants that were either wild or introduced by indigenous groups in pre-Columbian times, Stuart McCook, "Las epidemias liberales: Agricultura, ambiente y glocalización en Ecuador (1790–1930)," in *Estudios sobre historia y ambiente en América Latina II: Norteamérica, Sudamérica y el Pacífico*, ed. Bernardo García Martínez and María del Rosario Prieto (México: El Colegio de México, Instituto Panamericano de Geografía e Historia, 2002), 227–28.

57. Posada Carbó, Eduardo, *El Caribe colombiano, una historia regional (1870–1950)* (Bogotá: Banco de la República-El Áncora Editores, 1998), 100–3; AHC, Notaría de Cartagena, 1900, No. 239; and Notaría Primera de Quibdó, 1905, No. 90, f. 389. Other evidence of cacao in the lower Atrato: Notaría Primera de Quibdó, 1899, No. 31.
58. AGN, República, *Ministerio de Gobierno*, Sección 1ª, t. 730, f. 485. Dreyfus, "Conditions and Possibilities in the Chocó." For more evidence of cacao in Baudó, see AGN, República, *Ministerio de Gobierno*, Sección 1ª, t. 718, f. 153; Notaría Primera de Quibdó, 1903, No. 6 f. 18; No. 92, f. 327; No. 132, f. 536; 1907, No. 143; 1911, No. 44, f. 221; No. 132, f. 705; No. 138, f. 729; No. 140, f. 734; No. 146, f. 765; No. 156, f. 819; 1916, No. 21, f. 85; No. 23, f. 92; No. 29, f. 122; No. 53, f. 229; No. 54, f. 233; 1921, No. 25, f. 103.
59. Gutiérrez, Rufino, "Noticias sobre Pasto y las demás provincias del sur," in *Monografías*, Tomo 1 (Bogotá: Imprenta Nacional, 1921), 149, 205 visited the area in 1893 and noted cacao planted in the Patía, he mentioned that in colonial times there were large cacao plantations there, which were abandoned since the Independence Wars. Tumaco newspapers have ample evidence of cacao plantings from 1906 to 1917. See for example *El Litoral Pacífico*, Tumaco, No. 30, August 19, 1910. When Miguel Triana, *Por el Sur de Colombia* (Bogotá: Biblioteca Popular de Cultura Colombiana, 1950), 39, visited Tumaco 1907, he noted that cacao was one of the products that had given life to the port. It seems that peasants beyond the Chocó and the Tumaco area also planted cacao, see Notaría de Timbiquí, 1912, No. 1, f. 1; 1918, No. 23, f. 107.
60. *El Fiscal*, Tumaco, various numbers. Merchants advertised that they purchased cacao in Tumaco newspapers from at least 1910 through 1919. See for example *El Litoral Pacífico*, Tumaco, No. 10, January 22, 1910.
61. *El Litoral Pacífico*, Tumaco, No. 146, March 14, 1914; AGN, República, *Baldíos*, t. 50, f. 516.
62. Manuel Chiriboga, *Jornaleros y gran propietarios en 135 años de exportación cacaotera (1790–1925)* (Quito: edición auspiciada por el Consejo Provincial de Pichincha, 1980), chapter 13.
63. McCook, "Las epidemias liberales," 231–43. Cacao disease caused concern in Tumaco since at least 1912. *El Litoral Pacífico* Tumaco, No. 110, December 14, 1912; AGN, República, *Baldíos*, t. 69, f. 387; *Unión Obrera*, Tumaco, No. 6, May 10, 1919. On Chocó see AGN, República, *Baldíos*, t. 30, ff. 144–55.
64. AGN, República, *Baldíos*, t. 29, ff. 409-ss; AGN, República, *Baldíos*, t. 30, ff. 144–55.
65. Posada, *El Caribe colombiano*, 103–4.
66. Louis G. Dreyfus, "Turbo, Puerto Cesar and La Patria," NARA, RG 84, Records of Foreign Service Posts. Consular Posts. Quibdó, Colombia, Vol. 4 (1914).
67. Steiner, *Imaginación y poder*, 46–60; Rodrigo García Estrada, "El Consorcio Albingia en los inicios de la explotación bananera en Urabá 1909–1915," *Revista Augura* Año 18, Edición 1 (1995).
68. Marcelo Bucheli, *Bananas and Business: The United Fruit Company in Colombia, 1899–2000* (New York: New York University Press, 2005).

69. In the 1960s, commercial agriculture of African palm developed near Tumaco where precipitation also decreases below 3,000 mm per year. Absalón Machado, "La agricultura del litoral Pacífico," in *Colombia Pacífico* (Bogotá: Proyecto Biopacífico, Fondo FEN, 1993).
70. Interview with Eliseo Mena.
71. Notaría Primera de Quibdó, 1899, No. 31; No. 39.
72. AHC, Notaría de Cartagena, 1900, No. 236.
73. Notaría Primera de Quibdó, 1905, No. 90, f. 389.
74. The request for a title got halted with Law 19 of 1904 that forbade the adjudication of public lands in Chocó to foreigners. However, the Ministry of Public Works agreed to grant the title because it had been requested before the expedition of the law. AGN, República, *Baldíos*, t. 23, ff. 1–3. It seems that the title was finally granted in 1909: AGN, República, *Baldíos*, t. 31, f. 301.
75. Notaría Primera de Quibdó, 1905, No. 90, f. 389.
76. AHC, Notaría de Cartagena, 1919, No. 510; Oscar Gerardo Ramos, "La caña de azúcar en la cultura colombiana," unpublished (1996); Alcides Fernández, *Carabelas y alcatraces* (Medellín: Especial Editores, 1991); L. M. Guerrero, "Un gran establecimiento industrial en el Chocó," *Mundo al Día* (no exact date, 1924), 19; AGN, República, *Ministerio de Gobierno*, Sección 1ª, t. 836, ff. 108–50.
77. Guerrero "Un gran establecimiento industrial en el Chocó," Contraloría, *Geografía Económica de Colombia*, 442–47.
78. AGN, República, *Ministerio de Gobierno*, Sección 1ª, t. 920, ff. 228–92.
79. Fernández, *Carabelas y alcatraces*, 68.
80. AGN, República, *Ministerio de Gobierno*, Sección 1ª, t. 988, f. 862.
81. Posada, *El Caribe colombiano*, 97–99.
82. Contraloría, *Geografía Económica de Colombia*, 444; González, *Quibdó, Contexto histórico*, 187.
83. *El Tumaqueño*, Tumaco, No. 2, July 20, 1878.
84. *El Litoral Pacífico*, Tumaco, No. 10, January 22, 1910; *El Fiscal*, Tumaco, No. 20, July 8, 1914; "Informe sobre la navegación fluvial en los ríos Telembí y Patía," AMP, Correspondencia, Caja 1.
85. Evidence exists of state subsidies along the Atrato from the 1870s, but it is hard to assess their importance. González, *Quibdó, Contexto histórico*, 72–73; *Ecos del Chocó*, Quibdó, No. 2, August 5, 1890. For the Telembí there is only evidence of subsidies offered in 1887 for five years to whoever established steam navigation. Merizalde, *Estudio de la costa colombiana del Pacífico*, 115–16.
86. *Anuario Estadístico de 1875*, 149; González, *Quibdó, Contexto histórico*, 71–74; Molina, "El viejo Mainero," 4–5; *Ecos del Chocó*, Quibdó, No. 2, August 5, 1890. Earlier, in the 1850s, the first steamboats had ventured up the Atrato, González, *Quibdó, Contexto histórico*, 71.
87. González, *Quibdó, Contexto histórico*, 72; Notaría Primera de Quibdó, 1880 and 1881, No. 1, f. 1.
88. *El Atratense*, Quibdó, No. 3, October 19, 1880.

89. *La Situación*, Quibdó, No. 4, January 4, 1895; Dreyfus, "Conditions and Possibilities in the Chocó."
90. González, *Quibdó, Contexto histórico*, 145. According to Restrepo and Rodríguez, "La actividad comercial y el grupo de comerciantes de Cartagena," 94, in 1888 the company López, Navarro y Jaspe, from Cartagena, imported a steamship to navigate the Sinú and Atrato rivers.
91. González, *Quibdó, Contexto histórico*, 146; *El Istmo*, Istmina, No. 12, August 31, 1913.
92. Fawcett and Posada, "En tierra de oportunidades"; Notaría Primera de Quibdó, 1921, No. 2, f. 2. According to Louise Fawcett de Posada, *Libaneses, palestinos y sirios en Colombia*, Documentos CERES No.9 (Barranquilla: Centro de Estudios Regionales, Universidad del Norte, 1991), 20, Rumié Brothers operated two steamships between Cartagena and Quibdó, and Chagüí Brothers had vessels traveling in the Sinú and Atrato rivers. Rumié named its boats Bolívar and Cartagena, and Chagüí had the Sinú and the Bogotá. González, "Sirio-libaneses en el Chocó."
93. AGN, República, *Ministerio de Gobierno*, Sección 1ª, t. 965, f. 446. According to Eliseo Mena and Alberto Abouchaar (interviews), Sautatá owned the Cucharo and the Oscar. See also González, "Sirio-libaneses en el Chocó," 81.
94. *El Montaraz*, Barbacoas, No. 3, March 1, 1893; Merizalde, *Estudio de la costa colombiana del Pacífico*, 116.
95. At least in 1893 there was another steamboat (Elisa) in operation. *El Tumaqueño*, Tumaco, No. 4, August 31, 1878; Gutiérrez, "Noticias sobre Pasto y las demás provincias del sur"; *La Empresa*, Barbacoas, No. 3, March 1, 1893; *El Telégrafo* Barbacoas, No. 6, October 4, 1897.
96. *Gil Blas*, Tumaco, No. 23, October 13, 1912.
97. AGN, República, *Ministerio de Gobierno*, Parte Antigua, t. 528, f. 458; *El Litoral Pacífico*, Tumaco, No. 10, January 22, 1910, No. 17, March 23, 1910, No. 86, May 11, 1912, No. 95, July 13, 1912; *La Estrella*, Tumaco, No. 1, March 11, 1906; *Albores* No. 1, Tumaco, February 25, 1907.
98. When he died in 1919, Pugliese, Frigeiro y Mayolo carried on his business. *Albores*, Barbacoas, No. 1, February 1, 1906; *El Litoral Pacífico*, Tumaco, No. 11, January 29, 1910; No. 17, March 23, 1910; No. 95, July 13, 1912; No. 113, January 4, 1913; No. 141, February 7, 1914; *El Eco del Pacífico*, Tumaco, No. 93, November 20, 1919; *La Voz* Tumaco, No. 6, February 15, 1920.
99. The steamship Buenaventura began covering the San Juan route around 1913. It ran every ten days from Buenaventura to Negría on the San Juan River in a one- to two-day journey. It took two hours in canoe from Negría to Istmina, Dreyfus, "Conditions and Possibilities in the Chocó"; *El Faro*, Buenaventura, No. 64, March 29, 1913; *El Litoral Pacífico*, Tumaco, No. 110, December 14, 1912.
100. *El Istmo*, Istmina, No. 12, August 31, 1913; No. 64, March 23, 1918; Louis G. Dreyfus, "Mining in the Chocó District" NARA, RG 84, Records of Foreign Service Posts. Consular Posts. Quibdó, Colombia, Vol. 4 (1914); AGN, República, *Ministerio de Gobierno*, Sección 1ª, t. 796, f. 230.

101. *El San Juan*, Istmina, No. 8, March 5, 1913; *Ecos del Chocó*, Quibdó, No. 1, July 2, 1890; No. 2, August 5, 1890.
102. Dreyfus, "Conditions and Possibilities in the Chocó"; AGN, República, *Ministerio de Gobierno*, Sección 1ª, t. 936, f. 104; *A.B.C.*, Quibdó, No. 12, February 22, 1914.
103. *El Sur de Colombia*, Barbacoas, No. 1, October 25, 1908; *El Litoral Pacífico*, Tumaco, No. 115, January 18, 1913; *La Idea*, Tumaco, No. 2, October 21, 1916.
104. "Informe sobre la navegación fluvial en los ríos Telembí y Patía," AMP, Gobernación, *Correspondencia*, Caja 1; *El Litoral Pacífico*, Tumaco, No. 104, September 14, 1912; No. 169, August 22, 1914. Boats also risked running aground in the Atrato River mouth: AGN, República, *Ministerio de Gobierno*, Sección 1ª, t. 836, ff. 189–91.
105. Steamships used from the 1880s through the 1910s had cargo capacities that varied from 25 to 106 tons, with 61 tons on average, and could carry between 6 and 356 passengers. Brisson, *Viajes por Colombia en los años de 1891 a 1897*, 102; Dreyfus, "Conditions and Possibilities in the Chocó"; "Informe sobre la navegación fluvial en los ríos Telembí y Patía," AMP, Gobernación, *Correspondencia*, Caja 1.
106. On the poor condition of boats see *El Montaraz*, Barbacoas, No. 2, February 15, 1876; *La Situación*, Quibdó, No. 4, January 4, 1895; *La Antorcha*, Quibdó, No. 4, October 14, 1890. On shipwrecks see *Por el Sur de Colombia*, Tumaco, No. 22, September 23, 1915; AGN, República, *Ministerio de Gobierno*, Sección 1ª, t. 754, f. 471; t. 965, f. 446; *A.B.C.* n. 7, Quibdó, January 18, 1914.
107. The expression comes from Rebecca Scott, *Degrees of Freedom: Louisiana and Cuba after Slavery* (Cambridge: Harvard University Press, 2005).
108. Claudia Leal and Eduardo Restrepo, *Unos bosques sembrados de aserríos* (Medellín: Universidad de Antioquia, 2003).
109. See evidence provided by Luis Fernando González, "Ocupación, poblamiento y transformación ambiental del Darién, una revisión histórica," in *Evaluación integral del Darién colombiano* (CD-ROM, Fundación Natura, Universidad Nacional de Colombia, Universidad de Antioquia). See also Restrepo, "Un viaje al Darién," 358, and Reclus, *Exploraciones a los istmos de Panamá y Darién*, 90.
110. Dreyfus, "Conditions and Possibilities in the Chocó." For evidence of indebtedness in 1907 and 1908 in this area see AGN, República, *Baldíos*, t. 30, ff. 144–55; t. 28, f. 63.
111. Jaramillo, *En el Darién*, 10. See also, Steiner, *Imaginación y poder*, 93.
112. Cited by Steiner, *Imaginación y poder*, 37.
113. AGN, República, *Baldíos*, t. 27, f. 314.
114. Selfridge, *Reports of Explorations and Surveys*, 81.
115. AGN, República, *Ministerio de Gobierno*, Sección 1ª, t. 608, ff. 25–30.
116. AGN, República, *Ministerio de Gobierno*, Sección 1ª, t. 628, ff. 6–10.
117. *El Litoral Pacífico*, Tumaco, No. 175, October 3, 1914.
118. Jaramillo, *En el Darién*, 10–15.
119. Miguel Triana, *Por el Sur de Colombia* (Bogotá: Biblioteca Popular de Cultura Colombiana, 1950), 48.

120. Arnold J. Bauer, "Rural Workers in Spanish America: Problems of Peonage and Oppression," *Hispanic American Historical Review* 59, no. 1 (1979); Alan Knight, "Mexican Peonage: What Was It and Why Was It?," *Journal of Latin American Studies* 18, no. 1 (1986); Alan Knight, *Interpreting the Mexican Revolution* (Austin: University of Texas Press, 1988); Sarah Washbrook, *Producing Modernity in Mexico. Labour, Race, and the State in Chiapas, 1876–1914* (Oxford: Oxford University Press, 2012).
121. Cited in Gloria Isabel Ocampo, "Haciendas y campesinos en el Sinú: Formas de vida y formas de trabajo en 'Marta Magdalena' (1912–1954)," in *Boletín Museo del Oro* 20 (1988), 121–22, 126.
122. O. Nigel Bolland, *Colonialism and Resistance in Belize: Essays in Historical Sociology* (Benque Viejo del Carmen: Cubola Productions, 2003 [1988]), 160. For the entire description of the system see his essay "Labour Control and Resistance in Belize in the Century after 1838" in the cited collection.
123. Weinstein, *The Amazon Rubber Boom*, 22, 25, and chapter 1; see also Barham and Coomes, *Prosperity's Promise*, chapter 4.
124. Knight "Mexican Peonage," 46, and Knight, *Interpreting the Mexican Revolution*, 109.
125. Almario, "Territorio, etnicidad y poder en el Pacífico sur colombiano," 742.
126. Frank Safford and Marco Palacios, *Colombia: Fragmented Land, Divided Society* (New York: Oxford University Press, 2002), 236–96; David Bushnell, *The Making of Modern Colombia: A Nation in Spite of Itself* (Berkeley: University of California Press, 1993), 140–80.
127. *El Litoral Pacífico*, August 1913–April 1915; *El Micrófago*, December 1913–November 1914; *El Ariete*, July 1915; *El Camarada*, July–November 1915; *El Eco del Pacífico*, October 1916.
128. An order to confiscate a warehouse suggests that city dwellers were among the debtors. *El Litoral Pacífico* Tumaco, No. 159, June 13, 1914.
129. Weinstein, *The Amazon Rubber Boom*, 23.
130. Knight, *Interpreting the Mexican Revolution*, 109.

CHAPTER 4

1. Catherine LeGrand, *Frontier Expansion and Peasant Protest in Colombia, 1850–1936* (Albuquerque: University of New Mexico Press, 1986), 78–79.
2. Letter from José María Reinel and Manuel Velasco to the President of the Nation, October 28, 1878. AGN, República, *Baldíos*, t. 2, ff. 291–92.
3. Law 61 of 1874 and Law 48 of 1882. LeGrand, *Frontier Expansion and Peasant Protest in Colombia*, 14–16, 56–57.
4. Letter to the Secretary of Treasury and Development, March 12, 1879, AGN, República, *Baldíos*, t. 2, ff. 190–92. This document refers to the area in dispute as "Iscuandecito" and does not mention the Caunapí River. However, given the coincidence in times, arguments, and protagonists, I assume that it refers to the same case.

5. Telegram from the Secretary of Treasury of the Department of Cauca to the Minister of Treasury with reference to some supposed abuses of farmers in Cajapí, November 30, 1889, AGN, República, *Baldíos*, t. 10, ff. 134–35; Telegram to the Minister of Treasury regarding the lands of Cajapí, Tumaco, October 25, 1889, AGN, República, *Baldíos*, t. 10, f. 300; Telegram regarding the lands of Cajapí from the municipal ombudsman from Bocagrande in Cabo Manglares, Buenaventura, November, 1889, AGN, República, *Baldíos*, t. 11, f. 106; Letter from Francisco Otero, municipal ombudsman from Bocagrande, to the Minister of Treasury regarding the forests of Cajapí, November 1, 1889, AGN, República, *Baldíos*, t. 11, ff. 107–9; Letter from Francisco Otero to the Minister of Treasury, November 15, 1889, AGN, República, *Baldíos*, t. 11, f. 110; Letter from various residents of Cajapí to the Minister of Treasury, Tumaco, June 28, 1889, AGN, República, *Baldíos*, t. 11, ff. 210–42, citation from f. 213.
6. *Diario Oficial*, Bogotá, No. 7.864, August 28, 1889, and *Diario Oficial*, Bogotá, No. 8.005, March 13, 1890.
7. Petition to the Attorney General from the residents of the district of Tumaco regarding the problems of the vegetable ivory groves of Chilví, March 1, 1897, AGN, República, *Baldíos*, t. 17, ff. 376–77.
8. Letter from Francisco Otero, municipal ombudsman from Bocagrande, to the Minister of Treasury regarding the forests of Cajapí, November 1, 1889, AGN, República, *Baldíos*, t. 11, ff. 107–8.
9. Letter from various residents of Cajapí to the Minister of Treasury, June 28, 1889, AGN, República, *Baldíos*, t. 11, f. 210.
10. In 1893 and 1897, gatherers from Chilví complained about the efforts of some (perhaps including one of their peers) to restrict access to vegetable ivory groves and different public instances declared in both cases free access to the forests. AGN, República, *Baldíos*, t. 14, f. 85; Petition to the Attorney General from the residents of the district of Tumaco regarding the problems of the vegetable ivory groves of Chilví, March 1, 1897, AGN, República, *Baldíos*, t. 17, ff. 376–77.
11. AGN, República, *Baldíos*, t. 163, ff. 196–202.
12. AGN, República, *Baldíos*, t. 163, ff. 195–202. In a less notorious case, people from Jiguamiandó complained in 1919 that certain individuals tried to restrict access to the forest based on property claims registered in Quibdó since 1867. AGN, República, *Baldíos*, t. 44, f. 350.
13. Decree 552 of 1905, Law 30 of 1907; Decree 976 of 1907 and Decree 625 bis of 1910. These regulations can be looked up in Juan José Botero Villa, *Adjudicación, explotación y comercialización de baldíos y bosques nacionales. Evolución histórico-legislativa, 1830–1930* (Bogotá: Banco de la República, 1994); and in Ministerio de Industrias, *Memoria del Ministerio de Industrias al Congreso Nacional en las sesiones ordinarias* (Bogotá: Imprenta Nacional, 1931).
14. Since early on, national policy makers attempted, without much success, to regulate access to forests within the public domain by subscribing rental contracts or giving licenses for the extraction of specific resources. However, in 1870 the government declared free access to national forests, with which it endorsed the de

facto situation in areas containing vegetable ivory. In 1884 and 1892, new regulations established that whoever wanted to exploit national forests should obtain a license and made explicit that such requirement applied to vegetable ivory collectors. However, there are no indications that these regulations had practical effect.

15. AGN, República, *Baldíos*, t. 29, ff. 768–71; t. 30, ff. 571–77.
16. AGN, República, *Baldíos*, t. 29, f. 327.
17. *El Fiscal*, Tumaco, No. 45, February 3, 1915.
18. AGN, República, *Ministerio de Gobierno*, Sección 1ª, t. 677, ff. 1, 65–72.
19. AGN, República, *Ministerio de Gobierno*, Sección 1ª, t. 677, ff. 65–72, 76; t. 26, ff. 262–63.
20. AGN, República, *Baldíos*, t. 26, ff. 719–22.
21. AGN, República, *Baldíos*, t. 33, f. 212; t. 34, ff. 261–62; *Ministerio de Gobierno*, Sección 1ª, t. 659, ff. 260–68.
22. AGN, República, *Ministerio de Gobierno*, Sección 1ª, t. 677, ff. 65–72. See also AGN, República, *Baldíos*, t. 26, f. 610; t. 35, ff. 1, 43–44, 328, 564; t. 34, ff. 261–62.
23. AGN, República, *Ministerio de Gobierno*, Sección 1ª, t. 718, ff. 153–60.
24. Eduardo Restrepo, "Los tuqueros negros del Pacífico sur colombiano," in *Renacientes del guandal: "grupos negros" de los ríos Satinga y Sanquianga Pacífico sur colombiano*, ed. Jorge Ignacio del Valle y Eduardo Restrepo (Bogotá: Biopacífico, Universidad Nacional, 1996), 294–98; Nelly Yulissa Rivas, "Prácticas espaciales y construcción territorial en el Pacífico nariñense: el río Mejicano, municipio de Tumaco," *Cuadernos de trabajo CIDSE* 41 (Cali: Centro de Investigaciones y de Documentación Socioeconómica, 1999), 21–47; Odile Hoffmann, *Comunidades negras en el Pacífico colombiano: Innovaciones y dinámicas étnicas* (Quito: Instituto Francés de Estudios Andinos, Institut de Recherche pour le Dévelopment, Ediciones Abya-Yala, Centro de Investigaciones y Estudios Superiores en Antropología Social, Centro de Estudios Mexicanos y Centroamericanos, 2007), 86–93.
25. Letter from various residents of Cajapí to the Minister of Treasury, June 28, 1889. AGN, República, *Baldíos*, t. 11, ff. 210–14r.
26. Frank Safford and Marco Palacios, *Colombia: Fragmented Land, Divided Society* (New York: Oxford University Press, 2002), 184–86, 224.
27. AGN, República, *Baldíos*, t. 30, f. 256; t. 28, ff. 451–56.
28. AGN, República, *Baldíos*, t. 28, ff. 63–69.
29. Carlos R. Muñoz, *Problemas de Urabá: informe rendido al señor gobernador del departamento por el visitador fiscal Carlos Muñoz* (Medellín: Imprenta Oficial, 1931), cited by Claudia Steiner, *Imaginación y poder: El encuentro del interior con la costa en Urabá, 1900–1960* (Medellín: Universidad de Antioquia, 2000), 41; LeGrand, *Frontier Expansion and Peasant Protest in Colombia, 1850–1936*, 187.
30. Muñoz, *Problemas de Urabá*; AGN, República, *Baldíos*, t. 63, f. 125.
31. AGN, República, *Baldíos*, t. 64, f. 30; t. 21, ff. 282, 388; t. 65, f. 46; t. 67, f. 59.
32. Comisión Corográfica bajo la dirección de Agustín Codazzi, *Geografía física i política de las provincias de la Nueva Granada, Segunda parte: informes* (Bogotá: Banco de la República, 1959), 335.

33. On world gold production in the second half of the nineteenth century see María Mercedes Botero, *La ruta del oro: una economía primaria exportadora, Antioquia 1850–1890* (Medellín: Universidad EAFIT, 2007), chapter 1.

34. Andrew Meyer, "In the Chocó, Colombia," *Engineering and Mining Journal* 142 (1941): 35–36. For more evidence of rosy reports see *Los Avisos*, No. 1, Quibdó, August 14, 1890; Jorge Brisson, *Exploración del alto Chocó* (Bogotá: Imprenta Nacional, 1895), 70; Henry Granger and Edward B. Trewille, "Mining Districts of Colombia," *Transactions of the American Institute of Mining Engineers* 39 (1899), 76.

35. Granger and Trewille, "Mining Districts of Colombia," 77. Similarly, in 1887, a Panama merchant wrote encouragingly that his father had "made a fortune washing gold in small wooden vessels [in Chocó]." "Letter to E. Manning, Boston, from M. E. Recuing (Panama, Aug. 16th 1887)," Flat Letters File, Vol. 9, Chocó Hydraulic Mining Company Collection, Harvard Business School Baker Library.

36. *La Epoca*, Barbacoas, No. 5, December 1, 1867; *El Montaraz*, Barbacoas, No. 63, February 18, 1882; *El Telembí*, Barbacoas, No. 2, October 20, 1897; *El Montañes*, Barbacoas, No. 8, May 15, 1876.

37. Rufino Gutiérrez, "Noticias sobre Pasto y las demás provincias del sur," in *Monografías*, Tomo I (Bogotá: Imprenta Nacional, 1921), 217. E. L. Ragonnet, "Journal of Voyage" (Paris: n.p., 1895, in manuscript), refers to "un aventurier Californien" who arrived in Buenaventura in 1895 planning to pan for gold in the San Juan River. See also Meyer, "In the Choco, Colombia," 35–39.

38. Granger and Trewille, "Mining Districts of Colombia," 77.

39. I would like to thank Ann Farnsworth who without even knowing me lent me the notes she took in the Harvard Business School Baker Library, which constitute my main source on B. S. Pray.

40. "Charles Perkins to B. S. Pray, March 4, 1887," Flat Letters File, Vol. 9, Chocó Hydraulic Mining Company Collection, Harvard Business School Baker Library.

41. Untitled typewritten manuscript, in Folder "Mines—Colombia." Atrato Mining and Development Company Collection, Harvard Business School Baker Library.

42. "Letter from John Sweetwer, treasurer and assistant secretary of the Atrato Mining and Developing Company," in folder "Mines—Colombia," "Colombia, Its geographical situation and present political aspect," and untitled document, in folder "Mines—Colombia." Atrato Mining and Development Company Collection, Harvard Business School Baker Library.

43. Granger and Trewille, "Mining Districts of Colombia," 83; Louis G. Dreyfus "Mining in the Chocó District," RG 84, Records of Foreign Service Posts, Consular Posts, Quibdó, Colombia, Vol. 4, NARA; "Book of Minutes," in folder "Mines—Colombia." Atrato Mining and Development Company Collection, Harvard Business School Baker Library.

44. Dreyfus, "Mining in the Chocó District"; Henry Granger, "Gold-Dredging on the Choco Rivers, Republic of Colombia, South America," *Transactions of the American Institute of Mining Engineers* 39 (1908): 415.

45. *Ecos Republicanos*, Quibdó, No. 25, February 7, 1911; Brisson, *Exploración del alto Chocó*, 274; Dreyfus, "Mining in the Chocó District."
46. T. C. Earl, *Gold Dredging* (London: E & F. N. Spon, 1913), v, vii; J. H. W. McGeorge, *Dredging for Gold: The History of Two Successful but Contrasting Enterprises* (Melbourne: N.R. 1964), 8–9; Genevieve M. Haynor, "The History of Gold Dredging in California, 1848–1940" (MA thesis, University of California, Berkeley, 1941), 11–12, 16, 21–25, 27–28, 34, 36–38.
47. Many notarial deeds (1884–1908) from the Notaría Primera de Quibdó, for example: 1884, No. 22, f. 52; No. 46, f. 126; "President's Report to Stockholders of the Chocó Hydraulic Mining Company, Portland." Folder "Minutes–Notices of Meetings," v. 6, Chocó Hydraulic and Mining Company, Harvard Business School Baker Library.
48. Granger and Trewille, "Mining Districts of Colombia," 78.
49. "Charles J. Perkins to Bowman F. Wilder, March 18, 1889," Flat Letters file, Vol. 9, Chocó Hydraulic and Mining Company, Harvard Business School Baker Library. For a description of the remains of the mine three years later see Brisson, *Exploración del alto Chocó*, 273–74.
50. In 1899, a local firm also tried to use hydraulic mining in the Andágueda River and failed, see *La Situación*, Quibdó, No. 1, November 23, 1894; No. 4, January 4, 1895; Notaría Primera de Quibdó, 1894, No. 50; 1897, No. 29; 1905 (illegible); and Granger and Trewille, "Mining Districts of Colombia," 79. Miners also used monitors in Barbacoas, but to a very limited extent. See *El Montaraz* No. 62, Barbacoas, February 4, 1882; Vicente Restrepo, *Estudio sobre las minas de oro y plata de Colombia* (Bogotá: Silvestre y Compañía, 1888 [1882]), 85; Gutiérrez, "Noticias sobre Pasto y las demás provincias del sur," 217. After the failures in the Andágueda River, another tributary of the Atrato—the Bebará—caught miners' fancies, but again nothing came out of haphazard prospecting and forming of ephemeral mining companies. See *Los Avisos*, Quibdó, No. 4, September 30, 1890; No. 9, Quibdó, February 10, 1891; Jorge Brisson, *Viajes por Colombia en los años de 1891 a 1897* (Bogotá: Imprenta Nacional, 1899), 101–29.
51. Brisson, *Viajes por Colombia en los años de 1891 a 1897*, 105.
52. Prior to 1886, when Colombia changed from a federal to a central form of government, each state used to have its own mining code. In 1887, Antioquia's code was nationally adopted since that was the leading mining territory of the country.
53. Law 59 of 1909 forbade mine adjudication in rivers navigable by steamboat.
54. Granger and Trewille, "Mining Districts of Colombia," 85; Antonio Olano, *La propiedad minera, Su estado legal y modos de adquirirla en la intentencia del Chocó y departamentos que formaron el Antiguo Estado del Cauca* (Bogotá: Talleres Tipográficos de Régulo Domínguez, 1913); P. L. Bell, *Colombia: A Commercial Handbook*, Department of Commerce, Special Series No. 206. (Washington, D.C.: Government Printing Office, 1921), 100–1, 118–19.
55. AGN, República, *Ministerio de Minas*, t. 10, t. 12; *Baldíos*, t. 31, ff. 309–11.

56. Henry C. Pearson, *What I Saw in the Tropics* (New York: India Rubber Publishing Co., 1906), 258–59; "Miscellaneous Items," RG 84, Records of Foreign Service Posts, Consular Posts, Quibdó, Colombia, Vol. 1, NARA; Granger and Trewille, "Mining Districts of Colombia," and Granger, "Gold-Dredging on the Choco Rivers, Republic of Colombia, South America"; Bell, *Colombia: A Commercial Handbook*, 100.
57. AGN, República, *Baldíos*, t. 22, f. 145; "List of American citizens in the district," RG 84, Records of Foreign Service Posts, Consular Posts, Quibdó, Colombia, Vol. 1, NARA.
58. AGN, República, *Baldíos*, t. 24, f. 252; t. 25, f. 299; *Ministerio de Minas*, t. 12, In the listing complied by the Ministry of Mines, it appears that Granger himself was granted three mines in 1906.
59. AGN, *Ministerio de Gobierno*, Sección 1ª, t. 965, ff. 1, 502–63.
60. *Ecos Republicanos*, Quibdó, No. 27, April 2, 1911.
61. On Angel's deals see AGN, República, *Ministerio de Gobierno*, Sección 1ª, t. 602, ff. 471-ss; t. 603, ff. 121, 142; Notaría Primera de Quibdó, 1908, No. 87, f. 436; 1909, No. 60, f. 238; No. 175, f. 711; No. 184; 1910, No. 6, f. 22; No. 15, f. 48; No. 17, f. 54; No. 115, f. 386; No. 96, f. 314; No. 141, f. 501; 1911, No. 1, f. 1; No. 5, f. 31; No. 147, f. 768; No. 10, f. 68; No. 82, f. 452; No. 112, f. 598; 1914, No. 64; 1916, No. 47, f. 246. He also rented a number of mines in the Andágueda in 1911 and made deals with an American miner. Notaría Primera de Quibdó, 1911, No. 86, f. 465; 1913, No. 5, f. 20. On the Malluk's mining businesses see Notaría Primera de Quibdó, 1903, No. 23, f. 70; No. 26, f. 79; No. 49, f. 160; 1905, No. 49, f. 140; 1908, No. 37, f. 180; 1909, No. 119, f. 492; 1913, No. 72, f. 33; No. 153, f. 831; 1914, No. 17, f. 82; No. 24; No. 25; No. 78; No. 113, f. 527; No. 132, f. 616; No. 140; 1916, No. 51, f. 223; No. 63, f. 269; AHC, Notaría de Cartagena, 1910, No. 286, f. 1168; AGN, República, *Ministerio de Gobierno*, Sección 1ª, t. 796, ff. 300–15. They even hired an American to prospect for them in the Neguá River. "List of American citizens in the district," RG 84, Records of Foreign Service Posts, Consular Posts, Quibdó, Colombia, Vol. 1, NARA. Other Syrian-Lebanese merchants also speculated intensively. For the Abuchar see Notaría Primera de Quibdó, 1895, No. 31; 1903, No. 1, f. 1; No. 2, f. 5; 1906, No. 80, f. 309; No. 81, f. 314; No. 83, f. 327; No. 84, f. 331; No. 85, f. 309; No. 103, f. 400; No. 104, f. 405; AHC, Notaría de Cartagena, 1899, No. 351, f. 1636. For Rumié see Notaría Primera de Quibdó, 1911, No. 154, f. 800; 1914: No. 83, f. 389. For Chamat see Notaría Primera de Quibdó, 1911, No. 155, f. 818.
62. On Meluk's mining concerns see Notaría Primera de Quibdó, 1899, No. 34; No. 62, f. 328; No. 72, f. 371; 1903, No. 20, f. 62; No. 25, f. 76; No. 27, f. 82; No. 34, f. 104; No. 45, f. 141; No. 48, f. 150; 1907, No. 32, f. 145; No. 59, f. 252; No. 60, f. 263; No. 62, f. 272; No. 63, f. 277; No. 64, f. 282; No. 65, f. 287; No. 66, f. 292; No. 82, f. 348; No. 83, f. 355; No. 90, f. 390; No. 91, f. 396. 1921, No. 46, f. 216; AHC, Notaría de Cartagena, 1904, No. 593, f. 2706; 1906, No. 426, f. 1799; No. 429, f. 1810; No. 430, f. 1815; No. 431, f. 1820; No. 432, f. 1825; No. 434, f. 1831; No. 436, f. 1837; No. 437,

f. 1842; 1910, No. 111, f. 379; AGN, República, *Ministerio de Gobierno*, Sección 4ª, t. 141, f. 305; AGN, República, *Baldíos*, t. 33, f. 552.

63. In 1909, for instance, a partner of the firm Salazar Hermanos of Anserma was head of a mining company in Condoto. Several paisas from Medellín were co-owners of La Argelia mine in Bagadó in 1911. Five years later, seven men from Urrao helped create a mining company interested in the Bebará and Bebaramá rivers. Even as late as 1921 two women from Medellín joined the company El Progreso Minero del Chocó. See Notaría Primera de Quibdó, 1903, No. 51, f. 160; No. 27, f. 82; No. 40, f. 124; No. 84, f. 296; No. 102, f. 388; No. 130, f. 528; 1916, No. 63, f. 269; 1921, No. 46, f. 210. *Ecos Repúblicanos*, Quibdó, No. 6, November 4, 1909.

64. At the time of his death in 1919, he also owned a fifth of the sales commission of the mine Alto Opogodó and eight hundred shares of the British Platinum and Gold Corporation Limited. Jacques Aprile, *Habitats y sociedades del Pacífico Vol. 2: Génesis de Buenaventura* (Buenaventura: Universidad del Pacífico, 2002), 339–402.

65. Aprile, *Habitats y sociedades del Pacífico*, 413–16; AGN, República, *Baldíos*, t. 34, f. 171–74.

66. Notaría de Timbiquí, 1912, No. 2, f. 3; Aprile, *Habitats y sociedades del Pacífico*, 419. These men had a few other mining interests. Notaría de Timbiquí, 1917, No. 9, f. 35; 1918, No. 11, f. 34. Vanín came from Panama to work for the French company New Timbiquí Gold Mines Ltd., Interview with Teodoro Vanín.

67. AGC, Títulos de Minas, 1914–34.

68. AGN, República, *Baldíos*, t. 35, f. 6.

69. Archivo de la Gobernación del Cauca (AGC), Títulos de Minas, 1896–98. This finding coincides with an observation by anthropologist Nina S. de Friedemann, who wrote that at the end of the nineteenth century black miners in the Güelmambí River acquired titles to their mines, although she only provides one example. Nina S. de Friedemann, "Minería de Oro y Descendencia: Güelmambí, Nariño," *Revista Colombiana de Antropología* 16 (1974), 15, 18, 33.

70. *El Fiscal*, Tumaco, No. 67, June 23, 1915. A few years later an engineer working nearby remembered that long ago in Barbacoas the wealthy claimed as many gold mines as they could, even in nonmining areas, and forced "proletarians" to work the mines of the company or pay rents for growing crops. AGN, República, *Baldíos*, t. 50, f. 136.

71. AGN, República, *Baldíos*, t. 36, f. 330.

72. AGN, República, *Ministerio de Gobierno*, Sección 1ª, t. 836, ff. 108–50.

73. AGN, República, *Ministerio de Gobierno*, Sección 1ª, t. 685, ff. 147–148; *Baldíos*, t. 31, f. 289. Notaría de Timbiquí, 1911, No. 3, f. 10; No. 7, f. 20; No. 8, f. 22.

74. See for example how Pray and Curtis carefully defended their properties, *Los Avisos*, Quibdó, No. 12, June 10, 1891; Notaría Primera de Quibdó, 1899, No. 77, f. 394.

75. AGN, República, *Ministerio de Gobierno*, Sección 4ª, t. 64, unnumbered folios, between 199 and 200; t. 65, ff. 238–43, 387, 384–86; Notaría Primera de Quibdó, 1910, No. 96, f. 314; 1914, No. 60, f. 288; No. 64.

76. AGN, República, *Ministerio de Gobierno*, Sección 4ª, t. 64, ff. 333–335; *Baldíos*, t. 35, ff. 199–200.
77. AGN, República, *Baldíos*, t. 26, ff. 625–26.
78. AGN, República, *Baldíos*, t. 34, ff. 169, 171–74, 337; t. 33, ff. 215–16. Other inhabitants of the Saija River also opposed Davidson, Notaría de Timbiquí, 1911, No. 13, f. 41.
79. AGN, República, *Ministerio de Gobierno*, Sección 4ª, t. 63, f. 398. See also: t. 64, ff. 207–11. Also, in 1912 the editor of a newspaper from Istmina argued that mining titles served as passports for well-off people to get into poor peasants' properties and turn them into tenants. *El Istmo*, Istmina, No. 2, August 10, 1912. Even the intendant wrote that year to the central government asking for guidelines for solving this problem. AGN, República, *Baldíos*, t. 35, f. 322.
80. AGN, República, *Baldíos*, t. 35, ff. 604–7. Also, in 1911 a Quibdó newspaper doubted that many of the so-called mines contained gold. *Ecos Republicanos*, Quibdó, No. 27, April 2, 1911.
81. AGN, República, *Baldíos*, t. 35, ff. 297–98.
82. *El Litoral Pacífico*, Tumaco, No. 168, March 13, 1915; *El Fiscal*, No. 49, Tumaco, March 3, 1915; No. 50, March 10, 1915, No. 56, April 21, 1915; No. 64, June 12, 1915; *El Ariete*, No. 14, Tumaco, August 21, 1915.
83. Gutiérrez, "Noticias sobre Pasto y las demás provincias del sur," 217; *El Montaraz*, Barbacoas, No. 62, February 4, 1882. Other well-known mine owners from Barbacoas traveled to San Francisco to sell a mine, but it is unclear whether or not they succeeded. *El Montaraz*, Barbacoas, No. 45, June 11, 1881.
84. Ragonnet, "Journal of Voyage."
85. As late as 1868 there was an administrator living in Santa María de Timbiquí. Notaría de Timbiquí, 1917, No. 7, f. 26. The same was true for the San José mine up to 1911. Notaría de Timbiquí, 1912, No. 8, f. 28.
86. Aprile, *Habitats y sociedades del Pacífico*, 411–12; Notaría de Timbiquí, 1911, No. 23, f. 81.
87. Aprile, *Habitats y sociedades del Pacífico*, 412; Notaría de Timbiquí, 1911, No. 23, f. 81.
88. E-mail from Alan Longbottom regarding South American Mines 1908 Pt 4 L-P posted at http://archiver.rootsweb.com/th/read/SOUTH-AM-EMI/2000-09/0969297140 (on file with author); Álvaro Tirado Mejía, "El caso de las minas de Timbiquí," *Cuadernos Colombianos* 1, no. 1 (1974), 51, 56. The history of the property transfers is not altogether clear. Vogt later sold the property to the NTGM, probably eliminating all previous transfers. Notaría de Timbiquí, 1911, No. 23, f. 81. For information on the company's capital, address, members, etc., see AGN, República, *Ministerio de Gobierno*, Sección 4ª, t. 5, ff. 55–62.
89. Notaría de Timbiquí, 1912, No. 15, f. 51; see also 1912, No. 4, f. 18.
90. Santa Bárbara, the river's main settlement, located in the lower part, and Coteje, San José, and Santa María in the upper mining area. In 1870, the drainage had 1,247 inhabitants. AGN, Archivo Anexo II, *Censos*, Serie Censos de poblaciones, Cauca, Caja 20, Carpeta 1.

91. Robert West, *The Pacific Lowlands of Colombia* (Baton Rouge: Louisiana State University, 1957), 178.
92. Phanor J. Eder, *Colombia* (London: 1913), cited by Bell, *Colombia: A Commercial Handbook,* 99.
93. E-mail from Alan Longbottom cited above. Teodoro Vanín (interview), son of one of the company's French employees told me that the company suspended works in 1928. Yacup says that the company closed down "at the beginning of the European war" and that in 1929 it had declined. Sofonías Yacup, *Litoral Recóndito* (Buenaventura: Asociación para la Defensa de los Recursos Naturales y Patrimonio Cultural del Pacífico Colombiano, 1976 [1934]), 149.
94. The first one sunk in the Telembí River around 1903, before starting to work. Then, in 1908, the Patia Sindicate introduced a dredge, but no evidence exists that it actually operated. Five years later another dredge sunk in the Patía River mouth on its way to the Telembí. Gustavo Arbeláez, *Monografías mineras, Aluviones en zonas auríferas del Telembí y el San Juan* (Bogotá: Editorial de la Litografía Colombia, 1940), 13.
95. *El Litoral Pacífico*, Tumaco, No. 116, January 26, 1913; Earl, *Gold Dredging*, 170; W. T. Dinneen, "Report on the Dredging Area: Sindicato Minero de Guajui, Guajui river, Colombia, S.A.," in Folder 15, Charles Janin Papers, Huntington Library; AGN, República, Baldíos, t. 29, f. 623; Arbeláez, *Monografías mineras*, 13–14, reports that a dredge brought by the del Castillo family sunk in the Patía river mouth. That could have been the same 1913 dredge referred to here, which according to El Litoral Pacífico was brought by Thomas Brown.
96. After the Anglo Colombian Development Company imported the first one in 1915, the Chocó Pacífico purchased two more in 1920 and 1923. Until 1930, the first two dredged the Condoto River, although one of them had several interruptions occasioned by legal disputes. The third dredged parts of the San Juan and then reworked some of the Condoto's gravel. AGN, República, *Ministerio de Minas*, t. 16.
97. David Bushnell, *The Making of Modern Colombia* (Berkeley: University of California Press, 1993), 155–61; Humberto Vélez Ramírez, "Rafael Reyes: Quinquenio, régimen político y capitalismo (1904–1909)," in *Nueva Historia de Colombia,* Tomo I (Bogotá: Planeta, 1989), 187.
98. The most famous concessions were granted in 1905 to extract oil to Virgilio Barco and Roberto de Mares, see Jorge A. Villegas, *Petróleo, oligarquía e imperio* (Bogotá: ediciones E.S.E., 1969). For Antioqueño mining development, see Roger Brew, *El desarrollo económico de Antioquia desde la independencia hasta 1920* (Medellín: Editorial Universidad de Antioquia, 2000), especially page 122.
99. Except perhaps the Patía and Telembí concession. It is unclear if the Patia Syndictate obtained the concession from the government or by transfer from a Colombian. AGN, República, *Baldíos*, t. 25, f. 484; t. 36, ff. 23, 24, 332.
100. AGN, República, *Baldíos*, t. 30, ff. 144–55.
101. The titles had been issued to Benjamin S. Pray, Willian T. Curtis, Cornelio W. Brooks, and Charles I. Perkins. W. T. Curtis had secured the property over the

Quito River by paying the equivalent of twenty years in taxes, which exempted the titleholders from having to pay any further taxes. AGN, República, *Baldíos*, t. 29, ff. 406–7.

102. Kris Lane, "Gone Platinum: Contraband and Chemistry in Eighteenth-Century Colombia," *Colonial Latin American Review* 20, no. 1 (2011): 61–79.
103. Roberto Wokittel, "Apuntes sobre el platino," *Minería* 28 (1934): 1876–78; David T. Day, "Platinum," *Mining Resources of the U. S.* (1906): 551–59.
104. Unless otherwise noted, the information used for reconstructing the history of the Castillo Concession and the creation of the Chocó Pacífico Mining Company was taken from AGN, República, *Ministerio de Minas*, t. 12. Castillo formed the Sindicato Minero de Condoto to manage the concession without ever making a formal transfer. According to Condoto's mayor, Castillo began works in June 1908. The following year Guillermo O. Hurtado, then governor of the ephemeral department of Quibdó, suspended these works, which were being carried out under the direction of the American G. H. Nisbet, arguing that they were located outside the concession in a mine belonging to the heirs of Julio Arboleda. AGN, República, *Baldíos*, t. 31, ff. 347, 413; t. 32, ff. 462, 407; *Ministerio de Gobierno*, Sección 1ª, t. 606, f. 3.
105. AGN, República, *Baldíos*, t. 36, f. 375.
106. Juan Evangelista Cruz, *Visita al Chocó en noviembre de 1920* (Cali: Tipografía Moderna, 1920), 15; Dreyfus, "Mining in the Chocó District."
107. It is likely that Granger and Lewisohn had been considering a deal for a couple years given that the GDC had brought engineers in 1914. Dreyfus, "Mining in the Chocó District."
108. Its capital amounted to $10,000, its partners were Newton C. Marshall, Cicerón Angel, Carlos A. Fellencer, Maria Cervera de Granger, Henry Granger, and A. H. Case, and its president was E. H. Westlake of New York.
109. Information on this conflict was taken from AGN, República, *Ministerio de Minas*, t. 13 and 14; and Santiago Ospina, *Mina de 'El Salto,' Resolución ministerial y documentos relacionados con este asunto* (Bogotá: Imprenta Nacional, 1925).
110. The mine was titled to Alejandro Frigerio (from Buenaventura) and José M. Lozano in 1892. In 1911, Lozano sold his share to Guillermo O. Hurtado, and that same year Hurtado sold it to Mayolo.
111. Asprilla bought the island from a family who owned it since 1888 and claimed it as a mine in 1922, 1923, and again in 1925. The 1922 claim was not approved because the intendant considered El Salto to be part of the Condoto River concession and the Ministry of Public Works considered it violated Article 5 of Law 72 of 1910 (related to claims in navigable rivers, because the island was very small and by dredging it the mine would become part of the riverbed). In May 1924, the Council of State nullified the Ministry of Public Works' 1923 resolution, which rejected the claim, so the intendancy granted Asprilla a title in 1925.
112. AGN, República, *Ministerio de Gobierno*, Sección 1ª, t. 965, ff. 502–63; Wokittel, "Apuntes sobre el platino," 1878–83.

113. Unless otherwise noted, information on the NTGM was taken from Tirado, "El caso de las minas de Timbiquí."
114. Yacup, *Litoral Recóndito*, 147.
115. AGN, República, *Baldíos*, t. 37, ff.27, 152, 239; *Ministerio de Minas*, t. 16, ff. 111–12.
116. Yacup, *Litoral Recóndito*, 148–49.
117. Tirado, "El caso de las minas de Timbiquí"; Bernardo Merizalde, *Estudio de la costa colombiana del Pacífico* (Bogotá: Imprenta del Estado Mayor General, 1891), 91, also mentions the tension between "the Frenchmen and the inhabitants of Santa Bárbara . . . caused by the former's monopoly of trade in Santa María."
118. Yacup, *Litoral Recóndito*, 145–46; Tirado, "El caso de las minas de Timbiquí," 52.
119. Interviews with Saturia Martínez and Leticia Grueso, daughters of Clímaco Martínez. The records of the Notaría de Timbiquí attest to Martínez's success. See also Yacup, *Litoral Recóndito*, 150.
120. See for example Notaría de Timbiquí, 1911, No. 1, f. 1; No. 4, f. 11; No. 11, f. 33; No. 16, f. 54; No. 17, f. 57; No. 19, f. 64; No. 21, f. 73; No. 22, f. 77; No. 25, f. 95.
121. Cruz, *Visita al Chocó en noviembre de 1920*, 10, italics in the original. Gabriel García Márquez wrote an article for *El Espectador* about Andagoya in October 1954 titled "La riqueza inútil del platino colombiano." For a later and much more detailed description see Adiela Valencia, "Poblamiento negro en la hoya del río San Juan, Chocó, 1851–1974," (MA thesis, Universidad del Valle, 1997), 190–216.
122. Cruz, *Visita al Chocó en noviembre de 1920*, 11.
123. Cruz, *Visita al Chocó en noviembre de 1920*, 11; Valencia, "Poblamiento negro en la hoya del río San Juan," 217–18.
124. Jorge Álvarez Lleras, *El Chocó, Apuntamientos de viaje referentes a esta interesante región del país* (Bogotá: Minerva, 1923), 35, 38.
125. Valencia, "Poblamiento negro en la hoya del río San Juan," 207.
126. AGN, República, *Ministerio de Minas*, t. 16.
127. Henrique White Uribe, "Apuntamientos sobre la Intendencia Nacional del Chocó y sobre el municipio de Urrao, Antioquia," *Boletín de Minas y Petróleos* 21–22 (1930), 224; Cruz, *Visita al Chocó en noviembre de 1920*, 15.
128. AGN, República, *Ministerio de Minas*, t. 16, f. 212.
129. *El Istmo*, Istmina, No. 65, April 18, 1918; AGN, República, *Baldíos*, t. 31, f. 251; t. 32, f. 406; t. 33, f. 241; t. 35, f. 303; Escalante, *La minería del hambre*, 100.
130. Aquiles Escalante, *La minería del hambre, Condoto y la Chocó Pacífico* (Barranquilla: Tipografía Dovel, 1971), 100–2; Cruz, *Visita al Chocó en noviembre de 1920*, 15, 39–40; William Villa, personal communication; AGN, República, *Ministerio de Gobierno*, Sección 1ª, t. 977, ff. 142–44.
131. *El Istmo*, Istmina, No. 1, July 11, 1912; AGN, República, *Ministerio de Gobierno*, Sección 1ª, t. 920, f. 324; t. 977, f. 141–44.
132. *El Istmo*, Istmina, No. 12, August 31, 1913; AGN, República, *Ministerio de Gobierno*, Sección 4ª, t. 139, f. 23; *Ministerio de Minas*, t. 16.
133. AGN, República, *Ministerio de Gobierno*, Sección 1ª, t. 936, ff. 155–293.

134. *El Istmo* No. 12, Istmina, August 31, 1913; AGN, República, *Ministerio de Gobierno*, Sección 4ª, t. 139, f. 23; *Ministerio de Minas*, t. 16.
135. AGN, República, *Ministerio de Minas*, t. 16; White Uribe, "Apuntamientos sobre la Intendencia Nacional del Chocó y sobre el municipio de Urrao, Antioquia," 12–13.
136. NARA M1294 Roll 26 dec #821.6343/5 and /11; AGN, República, *Ministerio de Gobierno*, Sección 1ª, t. 907, f. 276. When prices began to rise, the government tried to establish a monopoly over platinum (1907–10), but this scheme failed, probably because the state lacked enforcement capacity and locals protested against the measure. Antonio Olano, *La propiedad minera, Su estado legal y modos de adquirirla en la intendencia del Chocó y departamentos que formaron el Antiguo Estado del Cauca* (Bogotá: Talleres Tipográficos de Régulo Domínguez, 1913); AGN, República, *Baldíos*, t. 42, ff. 204, 223. See Claudia Leal, "La Compañía Minera Chocó Pacífico y el auge del platino en Colombia, 1897–1930," special issue, *Historia Crítica* (November 2009).
137. AGN, República, *Ministerio de Gobierno*, Sección 1ª, t. 920, ff. 228–92; Lisandro Mosquera, "Monografía general del Chocó," *Dyna* 9 (1934), 290.
138. Mosquera, "Monografía general del Chocó," 289.
139. Tirado, "El caso de las minas de Timbiquí," 53; Merizalde, *Estudio de la costa colombiana del Pacífico*, 91, says that the company had an average of two hundred workers in the mines.
140. Álvarez Lleras, *El Chocó*, 34.
141. Francisco Gutiérrez, *Informe que el Prefecto Apostólico del Chocó rinde al Ilustrísimo y Reverendísimo Arzobispo de Colombia, como presidente de la Junta Arquidiocesana de Misiones, 1919–1923* (Bogotá: Imprenta Nacional, 1924), 97.

CHAPTER 5

1. Louis A. Pérez, "Politics, Peasants, and People of Color: The 1912 'Race War' in Cuba Reconsidered," *Hispanic American Historical Review* 66, no. 3 (1986): 511. See also Rebecca Scott and Michael Zeuske, "Property in Writing, Property on the Ground: Pigs, Horses, Land, and Citizenship in the Aftermath of Slavery, Cuba, 1880–1909," *Comparative Studies in Society and History* 44, no. 4 (2002): 683–84.
2. The most important work is Catherine LeGrand's *Frontier Expansion and Peasant Protest in Colombia, 1850–1936* (Albuquerque: University of New Mexico Press, 1986). The most extensive literature deals with Antioqueño colonization starting with James Parsons's *Antioqueño Colonization in Western Colombia* (Berkeley: University of California Press, 1968 [1948]) and including, among others, Keith Christie, "Antioqueño colonization in Western Colombia: A Reappraisal," *Hispanic American Historical Review* 58, no. 2 (1978): 260–83; Albeiro Valencia Llano, *Vida cotidiana y desarrollo regional en la colonización antioqueña* (Manizalez: Universidad de Caldas, 1990); Claudia Steiner, *Imaginación y poder, el encuentro del interior con la costa en Urabá, 1900–1960* (Medellín: Editorial Universidad de Antioquia, 2000);

and Nancy P. Appelbaum, *Muddied Waters: Race, Region, and Local History in Colombia, 1846–1948* (Durham: Duke University Press, 2003). Rainforests, especially those located on the fringes of the Amazon, have also received some attention, but since their occupation has been more recent, this literature deals mostly with the second half of the twentieth century. See for example Corporación Araracuara, *Colonización del bosque húmedo tropical* (Bogotá: Corporación Araracuara, 1991) and Alfredo Molano, *Siguiendo el corte: relatos de guerras y tierras* (Bogotá: Alfaguara, 2006 [1989]).

3. Eunice Nodari and João Klug, eds., *História Ambiental e Migrações* (São Leopoldo: Oikos Editora, 2012).

4. In the process indigenous areas shrank, but are still important, as shown by the legal recognition they have had since the 1970s. For Chocó see Jesús Alfonso Flórez López, *Autonomía indígena en Chocó* (Quibdó: Centro de Estudios Etnicos, 2007).

5. Guido Barona et al., *Geografía Física y Política de la Confederación Granadina. Vol.1: Estado del Cauca. Tomo II: Provincias de Chocó, Buenaventura, Cauca y Popayán. Obra dirigida por el General Agustín Codazzi* (Popayán: Universidad del Cauca, 2002), 75; Oliver Selfridge, *Reports of Explorations and Surveys to ascertain the practicability of a ship-canal between the Atlantic and the Pacific Oceans by the way of the Isthmus of Darien by Thos. Oliver Selfridge, Commander US Navy* (Washington, D.C.: Government Printing Office, 1874), 36, 54; AGN, *Baldíos*, t. 30, ff. 188–89; t. 39, f. 574; *Ministerio de Gobierno*, Parte Antigua, t. 528, ff. 264–79; Bernardo Merizalde del Carmen, *Estudio de la costa colombiana del Pacífico* (Bogotá: Imprenta del Estado Mayor General, 1921), 116, 146–47.

6. On the vigía's location see Eric Werner Cantor, *Ni aniquilados ni vencidos. Los Emberá y la gente negra del Atrato bajo el dominio español. Siglo XVIII* (Bogotá: Instituto Colombiano de Antropología e Historia, 2000), 73. On habitation along the river see Agustín Codazzi, *Memorias de Agustín Codazzi* (Bogotá: Banco de la República, 1973), 362, and Charles Stuart Cochrane, *Viajes por Colombia, 1823 y 1824: diario de mi residencia en Colombia* (Bogotá: Banco de la República, 1994), 446–55. The 1783 Chocó census mentioned the area of Riosucio for the first time, with a population that included 172 libres and 140 slaves. Hermes Tovar et al., *Convocatoria al poder del número. Censos y estadísticas de la Nueva Granada (1750–1830)* (Bogotá: Archivo General de la Nación, 1994).

7. John Cresson Trautwine, *Rough Notes on the Exploration of an Interoceanic Canal by Way of the Rivers Atrato and San Juan in New Grenada, South America* (Philadelphia: Barnard & Jones, 1854), 7–20; Barona et al., *Geografía Física y Política*, 77; Lt. N. Michler, "Lieutenant Michler's report of his survey for an interoceanic ship canal near the Isthmus of Darien," Senate Excecutive Documents, No. 9, vol. 7, 36th Congress, 2nd Session (1861), 25, 27–28, 42–43; Nimio Pérez Meza, *Monografía del municipio de Riosucio* (Medellín: Editorial Lealón, 1988), 22.

8. The Cuna Indians destroyed the settlement three times, Justiniano Jaramillo, *En el Darién. Informe de una expedición ordenada por el Ministerio de Guerra* (Bogotá: Imprenta Eléctrica, 1910).

9. Jacques Aprile-Gniset, *Poblamiento y hábitats del Pacífico* (Cali: Universidad del Valle, 1993), 58; Prefectura Apostólica del Chocó, *Informe de la Prefectura Apostólica del Chocó durante la administración de los misioneros hijos del inmaculado Corazón de María, 1909–1929* (Quibdó: Imprenta Claret, 1929), 26.
10. On the Munguidó see Cantor, *Ni aniquilados, ni vencidos*, 35; and Francisco Gutiérrez, *Relación de algunas excursiones apostólicas en la misión del Chocó* (Bogotá: Imprenta Nacional, 1924), 48, 81. For other rivers see Barona et al., *Geografía Física y Política*, 75; Anne-Marie Losonczy, *La Trama interétnica. Ritual, sociedad y figuras de intercambio entre los grupos negros y Emberá del Chocó* (Bogotá: Enstituto Colombiano de Antropología e Historia, Instituto Francés de Estudios Andinos, 2006), 64–65, 68.
11. Codazzi, *Memorias de Agustín Codazzi*, 367; Gutiérrez, *Relación de algunas excursiones apostólicas*, 141–42, 155–203; Francisco Gutiérrez, *Informe que el Prefecto Apostólico del Chocó rinde al Ilustrísimo y Reverendísimo Arzobispo de Colombia, como presidente de la Junta Arquidiocesana de Misiones, 1916–1918* (Bogotá: Imprenta Nacional, 1919), 26; Orián Jiménez, *El Chocó: Un paraíso del demonio. Nóvita, Citará y el Baudó, siglo XVIII* (Medellín: Universidad Nacional de Colombia, 2004), 51–55.
12. AGN, *Baldíos*, t. 18, f. 335; t. 44, f. 450; t. 47, f. 9.
13. AGN, *Baldíos*, t. 63, f. 62.
14. AGN, *Baldíos*, t. 43, f. 257; t. 47, f. 24. Although in 1918 the intendant "created" four contiguous resguardos in the upper Andágueda, by 1920 no resguardos existed in the area. AGN, *Ministerio de Gobierno*, Sección 4ª, t. 90, ff. 128–47; *Ministerio de Gobierno*, Sección 1ª, t. 836, ff. 108–50. For information on Law 89 and Decree 74 issued by the governor of Cauca in 1898 see Nancy Appelbaum, *Muddied Waters, Race, Region, and Local History in Colombia, 1846–1948* (Durham: Duke University Press, 2003), 110–14.
15. When in 1848 the naturalist Berthold Seemann visited the Pacific coast of Chocó he saw mostly Indians, and the mayors from both Juradó and Cupica were Indians. When Selfridge, the canal explorer, visited Cupica thirteen years later, the mayor was a black man. According to a booklet put together by the Church around 1981, the first black inhabitants of Juradó arrived from Timbiquí in the 1830s, and the Indians died shortly after from smallpox. Berthold Seemann, *Narrative of the Voyage of the H.M.S. Herald During the Years 1845–51, Under the Command of Captain Henry Kellett, R.N., C.B.; Being a Circumnavigation of the Globe, and Three Cruizes to the Arctic Regions in Search of Sir John Franklin, Vol. 1* (London: Reeve and Co., 1853), 220–27; Selfridge, *Reports of Explorations and Surveys*, 54; Father Jairo González, *Juradó* (n.d.), 4.
16. José Benjamín Arteaga, "Del Urabá. Diario de un misionero," *Revista de Misiones* Year 3, No. 27 (1927): 83. In 1914, Cunas in Urabá formed six communities (Tolo, Tanela, Cutí, Cuqué, Tigre, and Arquía) with 215 people, which grew to 289 in 1929. On the western side of the Gulf there was only one community (Caiman Nuevo), but it was the largest (97 people in 1914).
17. AGN, *Baldíos*, t. 45, f. 587; t. 47, ff. 8, 19; t. 50, f. 61; *Ministerio de Gobierno*, Sección 1ª, t. 965, ff. 502–63; t. 977, f. 156; t. 988, ff. 798–853; Arteaga, "Del Urabá," 87.

18. Some indigenous families inhabited the Naya basin, while those who occupied twenty huts in the Rosario River left in the first decade of the twentieth century. Merizalde, *Estudio de la costa colombiana*, 75–76, 79–81, 83, 85; Edgard Aubert de la Rue and Edmond Bruet, "La hoya del río Naya," *Revista de la Universidad del Cauca* no.1 (1943), 146; Juan Antonio Juaristi, Manuscript with information taken in 1963 and 1964 on the formation of several towns located close to Tumaco, transcribed by Father José Miguel Garrido (n.d.). Archivo Vicariato de Tumaco.
19. AGN, *Baldíos*, t. 2, ff. 291-ss; t. 11, ff. 210–42; Archivo Anexo II, *Censos*, Serie Documental Censos de Poblaciones, Cauca, Caja 20, Carpeta 1. Life expectancy in the lowlands probably did not differ much from that of the rest of the country, which was 30.5 years in 1910 and 34 years in 1930, David Bushnell, *The Making of Modern Colombia* (Berkeley: University of California Press, 1993), 167.
20. Rufino Gutiérrez, "Noticias sobre Pasto y las demás provincias del sur," in *Monografías, Tomo 1*, (Bogotá: Imprenta Nacional, 1921), 133; Barona et al., *Geografía Física y Política*, 84, 405; Santiago Pérez, *Selección de escritos y discursos de Santiago Pérez* (Bogotá: Biblioteca de Historia Nacional, 1950), 41–42; Trautwine, *Rough Notes on the Exploration*, 29; E. L. Ragonnet, "Journal of Voyage" (Paris, 1895); Michler, "Lieutenant Michler's report," 43.
21. For descriptions by contemporaries see Barona et al., *Geografía Física y Política*, 83, 9, 410–11; Pérez, *Selección de escritos y discursos*, 47; Jorge Brisson, *Exploración del alto Chocó* (Bogotá: Imprenta Nacional, 1895), 77; Gutiérrez, "Noticias sobre Pasto y las demás provincias del sur," 149; Trautwine, *Rough Notes on the Exploration*. On lowland agriculture see Robert West, *The Pacific Lowlands of Colombia* (Baton Rouge: Louisiana State University Press, 1957), 126–46; Proyecto Biopacífico, *Informe Final General, Tomo IV: Los sistemas productivos tradicionales. Una opción propia de desarrollo sostenible* (Bogotá: Ministerio del Medio Ambiente, 1998); Víctor Manuel Patiño, *Plantas cultivadas y animales domésticos en América Equinoccial, Tomo IV: Plantas introducidas* (Cali: Imprenta Departamental, 1969), 173–77, 210–14; Víctor Manuel Patiño, "El maíz chococito," *América Indígena* 16, no. 4 (1956); Carlos Tapia, Rocío Polanco, and Claudia Leal, *Los sistemas productivos de la comunidad negra de la cuenca del río Valle, Bahía Solano, Chocó* (Bogotá: Proyecto Biopacífico, Fundación Natura, 1997).
22. AGN, *Baldíos*, t. 49, f. 50; t. 47, ff. 11, 15; t. 65, f. 50.
23. For Naya see Mario Diego Romero, *Historia y etnohistoria de las comunidades afrocolombianas del río Naya* (Cali: Gobernación del Valle, 1997); for Timbiquí see chapter 4; for Jiguamiandó see AGN, *Baldíos*, t. 44, f. 350; for Murindó see AGN, *Baldíos*, t. 63, ff. 195–202; for Cértegui see "Informe de la Comisión Minera del Chocó. Urrao, octubre 19 de 1929," AGN, *Baldíos*, t. 70, ff. 14–39; for Dagua see AGN, *Baldíos*, t. 54, f. 563; t. 55, ff. 171, 441, 444.
24. Sergio Mosquera, *De esclavizadores y esclavizados en Citará* (Quibdó: Promotora Editorial de Autores Chocoanos, 1997), 73–74.
25. Mario Diego Romero, *Sociedades Negras en la Costa Pacífica del Valle del Cauca durante los siglos XIX y XX* (Cali: Gobernación del Valle-Colección de Autores Vallecaucanos, 2003), 94–95.

26. Anchicayá River. AGN, Archivo Anexo II, *Censos*, Serie Documental Censos de Poblaciones, Cauca, Caja 20, Carpeta 1, ff. 61–75.
27. Juaristi, Manuscript.
28. Óscar Almario, *Los renacientes y su territorio. Ensayos sobre etnicidad negra en el Pacífico sur colombiano* (Medellín: Universidad Pontificia Bolivariana y Consejo de Medellín, 2003), 212–13.
29. AGN, *Ministerio de Gobierno*, Sección 4ª, t. 90, ff. 128–47.
30. Trautwine, *Rough Notes on the Exploration*; Gutiérrez, *Relación de algunas excursiones apostólicas,* 81.
31. Brisson, *Exploración del alto Chocó*, 77.
32. Romero, *Sociedades Negras en la Costa Pacífica*, 199.
33. Merizalde, *Estudio de la costa colombiana*, 73.
34. Merizalde, *Estudio de la costa colombiana*, 229.
35. Jane M. Rausch, *The Llanos Frontier in Colombian History, 1830–1930* (Albuquerque: University of New Mexico Press, 1993), 149; Merizalde, *Estudio de la costa colombiana,* 97, 172.
36. Prefectura Apostólica del Chocó, *Informe de la Prefectura Apostólica del Chocó*. By 1922, the Prefecture of Urabá had been created, it included Riosucio and Acandí.
37. Gutiérrez, *Relación de algunas excursiones apostólicas*, 77.
38. Gutiérrez, *Relación de algunas excursiones apostólicas*, 47–48.
39. Francisco Gutiérrez, *Informe que el Prefecto Apostólico del Chocó rinde al Ilustrísimo y Reverendísimo Arzobispo de Colombia, como presidente de la Junta Arquidiocesana de Misiones, 1919–1923* (Bogotá: Imprenta Nacional, 1924), 40.
40. Juaristi, Manuscript.
41. Jacques Aprile-Gniset and Gilma Mosquera, *Habitats y sociedades del Pacífico Vol. 1: La Bahía de Solano* (Cali: Universidad del Valle, 2001), 82.
42. AGN, *Baldíos*, t. 41, ff. 178–79; *Ministerio de Gobierno*, Sección 1ª, t. 796, ff. 248–79; Gutiérrez, *Informe que el Prefecto Apostólico . . . 1916–1918*, 21–22.
43. Gutiérrez, *Informe que el Prefecto Apostólico . . . 1916–1918*, 22–23 and Gutiérrez, *Relación de algunas excursiones apostólicas,* 195–96.
44. AGN, *Ministerio de Gobierno*, Sección 1ª, t. 694, ff. 350–60.
45. Aprile-Gniset, *Poblamiento y hábitats del Pacífico*; Juaristi, Manuscript.
46. Playas de Mulatos, Vigía, Amarales, Boquerones and San Juan de la Costa. For an early reference to these settlers see Barona et al., *Geografía Física y Política*, 403. For a study of these people, know as *culimochos* or people without behinds, see Stella Rodríguez, "Libres y culimochos: ritmo y convivencia en el Pacífico sur colombiano," in *Afrodescendientes de las Américas, trayectorias sociales e identitarias,* ed. Claudia Mosquera, Mauricio Pardo, and Odile Hoffman (Bogotá: Universidad Nacional de Colombia, Instituto Colombiano de Antropología e Historia, Institut de la Recherche pour le Dévelopment, Instituto Latinoamericano de Servicios Legales Alternativos, 2002).
47. Aprile-Gniset, *Poblamiento y hábitats del Pacífico*; Gutiérrez, *Relación de algunas excursiones apostólicas,* 108–9, 116, 143; Paulo Emilio Escobar, *Bahías de Málaga y Buenaventura, la costa colombiana del Pacífico, 1918–1920* (Bogotá: Imprenta Nacional,

1921), 240; Juaristi, Manuscript; *El Tumaqueño*, Tumaco, No. 1, June 28, 1878; *Celajes*, Barbacoas, No. 1, February 22, 1906.

48. Aprile-Gniset, *Poblamiento y hábitats del Pacífico*, 98–102; Gilma Mosquera, "Los hábitats aldeanos del Chocó: mejoramiento de vivienda y equipamientos comunitarios," *Revista de la Universidad del Valle* 5 (1993).

49. Gutiérrez, *Informe que el Prefecto Apostólico . . . 1919–1923*, 94–100; Gutiérrez, *Relación de algunas excursiones apostólicas*, 9, 12.

50. Michael Taussig, *Shamanism, Colonialism, and the Wild Man: A Study in Terror and Healing* (Chicago: University of Chicago Press, 1987), 287–335.

51. José María Samper, *Ensayo sobre las revoluciones políticas y la condición social de las repúblicas colombianas (hispanoamericanas)*, (Bogotá: Universidad Nacional de Colombia, 1969[1861]), 69.

52. Cited by Eduardo Restrepo, "Imágenes del 'negro' y nociones de raza en Colombia a principios del siglo XX," in *Historias sobre raza y nación en América Latina*, ed. Claudia Leal and Carl Langebaek (Bogotá: Ediciones Uniandes, 2010), 284.

53. Benjamin S. Orlove, "Putting Race in Its Place: Order in Colonial and Postcolonial Peruvian Geography," *Social Research* 60, no. 2 (1993).

54. Eduardo Restrepo, "El giro a la biodiversidad en la imaginación del Pacífico colombiano," *Revista de Estudios del Pacífico Colombiano* 1 (2013); Peter Wade, *Blackness and Racial Mixture: The Dynamics of Racial Identity in Colombia* (Baltimore: John Hopkins University Press, 1993), chapters 3 and 6; Appelbaum, *Muddied Waters*; Claudia Steiner, *Imaginación y poder*.

55. David Arnold, *The Problem of Nature: Environment, Culture, and European Expansion* (Cambridge: Blackwell, 1996), 142.

56. David Arnold, "'Illusory Riches': Representations of the Tropical World, 1840–1950," *Singapore Journal of Tropical Geography* 21, no. 1 (2000): 10.

57. Stephen Frenkel, "Jungle Stories: North American Representations of Tropical Panama," *Geographical Review* 86, no. 3: 317–33.

58. Warwick Anderson, "The Natures of Culture: Environment and Race in the Colonial Tropics," in *Nature in the Global South: Environmental Projects in South and Southeast Asia*, ed. Paul Greenough and Anna Lowenhaupt Tsing (Durham: Duke University Press, 2003), 34.

59. Nancy Leys Stepan, *"The Hour of Eugenics": Race, Gender, and Nation in Latin America* (Ithaca: Cornell University Press, 1991); Julyan G. Peard, *Race, Place, and Medicine: The Idea of the Tropics in Nineteenth-Century Brazilian Medicine* (Durham: Duke University Press, 1999).

60. Louis G. Dreyfus, "Letter to timber company," NARA, RG 84, Records of Foreign Service Posts. Consular Posts. Quibdó, Colombia, Vol. 4, 1914.

61. Barona et al., *Geografía Física y Política*, 140.

62. AGN, *Ministerio de Gobierno*, Sección 1ª, t. 659, ff. 252–59.

63. AGN, *Ministerio de Gobierno*, Sección 1ª, t. 755, ff. 296–308.

64. *El Montaraz*, Barbacoas, No. 16, June 14, 1879; AGN, *Baldíos*, t. 988, ff. 798–853; *Ministerio de Gobierno*, Sección 1ª, t. 988, ff. 798–853; *La Voz*, Tumaco, No. 1, December 1, 1919.

65. *El Montaraz*, Barbacoas, No. 15, May 24, 1879. See also *El Litoral Pacífico*, Tumaco, No. 94, July 6, 1912.
66. AGN, *Baldíos*, t. 68, f. 382.
67. West, *The Pacific Lowlands of Colombia*, 83–87.
68. AGN, *Ministerio de Gobierno*, Sección 1ª, t. 912, f. 146.
69. West, *The Pacific Lowlands of Colombia*, 27; Jesús Eslava, "Climatología," in *Colombia Pacífico, Tomo I* (Bogotá: Proyecto Biopacífico-Fondo FEN, 1993), 138–42.
70. *El Indígena Chocoano*, Quibdó, No. 29, December 10, 1834; AGN, *Baldíos*, t. 33, ff. 323–32; *Ministerio de Gobierno*, Sección 1ª, t. 912, f. 146.
71. Barona et al., *Geografía Física y Política*, 404–5.
72. Louis G. Dreyfus, "Turbo, Puerto Cesar and La Patria," NARA, RG 84, Records of Foreign Service Posts, Consular Posts, Quibdó, Colombia, Vol. 4.
73. AGN, *Baldíos*, t. 36, ff. 293–94.
74. *A.B.C.*, Quibdó, No. 27, June 5, 1914.
75. *El Montaraz*, Barbacoas, No. 62, February 4, 1882.
76. Numerous examples of this position exist, see Trautwine, *Rough Notes on the Exploration*, 28, and Escobar, *Bahías de Málaga y Buenaventura*, 220. For more general explanations of the country's formation see José María Samper, *Ensayo sobre las revoluciones políticas*, chapter 4; Sergio Arboleda, *La República en la América Española* (Bogotá: Biblioteca Banco Popular, 1973[1867]).
77. *El Montaraz*, Barbacoas, No. 15, May 24, 1879.
78. The Munguidó River referred to here is the one in the San Juan Basin, not the Atrato Basin. AGN, *Ministerio de Minas*, t. 9, f. 215.
79. For a portrayal of Chocó as a savage place see AGN, *Ministerio de Gobierno*, Sección 4ª, t. 64, ff. 203–6. It was also frequent to refer to people as savage or semisavage, see *El Litoral Pacífico*, Tumaco, No. 142, February 14, 1914.
80. AGN, *Baldíos*, t.30, ff. 144–55.
81. *El Fiscal*, Tumaco, No. 12, May 13, 1914.
82. See for instance AGN, *Baldíos*, t. 43, ff. 509–15; Juan Evangelista Cruz, *Visita al Chocó en noviembre de* 1920 (Cali: Tipografía Moderna, 1921), 8; Cochrane, *Viajes por Colombia*, 420.
83. Barona et al., *Geografía Física y Política*, 25 and AGN, *Ministerio de Gobierno*, Sección 1ª, t. 713, ff. 355–66.
84. AGN, *Ministerio de Gobierno*, Sección 4ª, t. 90, ff. 128–47.
85. AGN, *Ministerio de Gobierno*, Sección 1ª, t. 713, ff. 396–405. On similar ideas regarding Indians see Frank Safford, "Race, Integration, and Progress: Elite Attitudes and the Indian in Colombia, 1750–1870," *Hispanic American Historical Review* 71, no. 1 (1991), 23–24.
86. *La Situación*, Quibdó, No. 1, November 23, 1894.
87. Comisión Corográfica bajo la dirección de Agustín Codazzi, *Geografía física i política de las provincias de la Nueva Granada, Segunda parte: informes* (Bogotá: Banco de la República, 1959), 325.
88. Eduardo Restrepo, "Imágenes del 'negro' y nociones de raza en Colombia a principios del siglo XX," *Revista de Estudios Sociales* 27 (2007).

89. *El Montaraz*, Barbacoas, No. 62, February 4, 1882. See also Michler, "Lieutenant Michler's report," 47.
90. Comisión Corográfica, *Geografía física i política*, 333.
91. José María Cordovez Moure, *Reminiscencias de Santafé y Bogotá* (Madrid: Aguilar, 1962), 522.
92. AGN, *Ministerio de Gobierno*, Sección 1ª, t. 988, ff. 798–853.
93. Sande and popa are trees that give useful milks. AGN, *Baldíos*, t. 48, f. 503.
94. *Los Avisos*, Quibdó, No. 5, October 22, 1890.
95. *Los Avisos*, Quibdó, No. 4, September 30, 1890.
96. Safford, "Race, Integration, and Progress," 30.
97. *A.B.C.*, Quibdó, No. 50, September 30, 1914.
98. *A.B.C.*, Quibdó, No. 27, June 5, 1914.
99. Pedro Sonderéguer, *Quibdó* (Buenos Aires: Hermanos Maucci, 1927), 8–9. See also Merizalde, *Estudio de la costa colombiana*, 208.
100. On ideas of whitening through miscegenation in Colombia see Alfonso Múnera "En busca del mestizaje" in his collection of essays *Fronteras imaginadas. La construcción de las razas y de la geografía en el siglo XIX colombiano* (Bogota: Planeta, 2005) and Safford, "Race, Integration, and Progress," 27–29. For a telling example of this kind of idea in nineteenth-century Colombia see Samper, *Ensayo sobre las revoluciones políticas.* For an analysis of similar ideas in Brazil see Thomas Skidmore, *Black into White: Race and Nationality in Brazilian Thought* (Durham: Duke University Press, 1998[1993]).
101. José María Echeverry Lozano, "Consideraciones raciales acerca del Chocó," *Estudios de derecho* Vol. II, (1942).
102. Nancy Appelbaum, Anne S. Macpherson, and Karin Alejandra Rosemblat, eds., *Race and Nation in Modern Latin America* (Chapel Hill: University of North Carolina Press, 2003), 6.
103. Brisson, *Exploración del alto Chocó*, 126; AGN, *Ministerio de Gobierno,* Sección 1ª, t. 755, ff. 396–405; t. 836, ff. 108–50; José Vallejo, *Por el Atrato* (Jericó: Imprenta de La Merced, 1910), prologue; *A.B.C.*, Quibdó, No. 27, June 5, 1914; *La Situación*, Quibdó, No. 2, December 6, 1894. On Caucano desire of Antioqueño immigrants see Nancy Appelbaum "Whitening the Region: Caucano Mediation and 'Antioqueño Colonization' in Nineteenth-Century Colombia," *Hispanic American Historical Review* 79, no. 4 (1999), and Appelbaum, *Muddied Waters*. Antioqueños already occupied El Carmen de Atrato, on the upper Atrato, and Pueblo Rico, in the upper San Juan. For information on Antioqueño colonization into these basins see Hans Bloch, "La colonización del Chocó desde el Valle del Cauca," *Boletín de la Sociedad Geográfica de Colombia* 8, no. 1 (1948), and West, *The Pacific Lowlands of Colombia*, 110–12.
104. AGN, *Baldíos*, t. 30, ff. 144–55.
105. Barona et al., *Geografía Física y Política*, 85–86.
106. AGN, *Baldíos*, t. 41, f. 238; t. 43, ff. 509–15; Luis Fernando González "Cartografía histórica del Chocó," *Boletín Cultural y Bibliográfico* 33, no. 43 (1996), 112–13.

107. Aprile-Gniset and Mosquera, *Habitats y sociedades del Pacífico*, 82. On previous settling in the area see Escobar, *Bahías de Málaga y Buenaventura*, 264; Aprile-Gniset and Mosquera, *Habitats y sociedades del Pacífico*, 25–86; and Eduardo García Vega and Jaime Echavarría, *Mutis y Bahía Solano, 50 años* (Quibdó: Universidad Tecnológica del Chocó, 1984). Decrees 1110 of 1928 and 925 of 1935 were based on Law 114 of 1922, which authorized the government to create agricultural colonies. Decree 925 and a 1936 report of the colony's director are reproduced in Aprile-Gniset and Mosquera, *Habitats y sociedades del Pacífico*, 90–106. On the colony's situation in the early 1940s see Contraloría General de la República, *Geografía Económica de Colombia, Tomo VI: Chocó* (Bogotá: Litografía Colombia, 1943), 461–62.
108. *La Situación*, Quibdó, No. 1, November 23, 1894.
109. AGN, *Ministerio de Gobierno*, Sección 1ª, t. 713, ff. 396–405; Appelbaum, Macpherson, and Rosemblat, *Race and Nation*, 4.
110. Report by the governor of Chocó, year 1845, AGN, *Gobernaciones Varias*, Legajo 105, f. 311. See also reports from 1844 and 1847, Legajo 95, ff. 929–61, and Legajo 149, ff. 1–12.
111. Frank Safford and Marco Palacios, *Colombia, Fragmented Land, Divided Society* (New York: Oxford University Press, 2002), 109, 186–87, 237; Bushnell, *The Making of Modern Colombia*, 128–29.
112. *El Montaraz*, Barbacoas, No. 24, March 6, 1880; No. 50, August 20, 1881; No. 51, September 3, 1881.
113. AGN, *Ministerio de Gobierno*, Sección 1ª, t. 713, ff. 355–66.
114. AGN, *Baldíos*, t. 30, ff. 144–55.
115. AGN, *Ministerio de Gobierno*, Sección 4ª, t. 90, ff. 128–47.
116. For eugenics in Latin America see Nancy Leys Stepan, *"The Hour of Eugenics": Race, Gender, and Nation in Latin America* (Ithaca: Cornell University Press, 1991); for a study on how ideas of race influenced education in Brazil see Jerry Dávila, *Diploma of Whiteness, Race and Social Policy in Brazil, 1917–1945* (Durham: Duke University Press, 2003). Appelbaum, Macpherson, and Rosemblat, *Race and Nation*, 6.
117. *El Montaraz*, Barbacoas, No. 50, August 20, 1881; No. 51, September 3, 1881.
118. "Informe del director de Instrucción Pública Idelfonso Díaz del Castillo, año 1912–1913," AMP, Fondo Gobernación, Serie Correspondencia, Caja 3.
119. "Informe del prefecto de la Provincia de Nuñez, J. M. Márquez, año 1923," AMP, Fondo Gobernación, Serie Correspondencia, Caja 9; *El Anzuelo* No. 4, Tumaco, May 11, 1919.
120. AGN, *Ministerio de Gobierno*, Sección 1ª, t. 603, ff. 1–78.
121. Oral testimonies collected in Tanguí in 1994.
122. AGN, *Ministerio de Gobierno*, Sección 1ª, t. 603, ff. 1–78.
123. "Letter from the Visitaduría de instrucción pública to Louis Dreyfus," NARA, RG 84, Records of Foreign Service Posts, Consular Posts, Quibdó, Colombia, Vol.4.
124. AGN, *Ministerio de Gobierno*, Sección 1ª, t. 718, ff. 153–60; t. 791, f. 154.

125. AGN, *Ministerio de Gobierno*, Sección 1ª, t. 730, ff. 418-ss; *A.B.C.* No. 19, May 10, 1914.
126. AGN, *Ministerio de Gobierno*, Sección 1ª, t. 718, ff. 243–49. See also the 1920 report by the intendant: AGN, *Ministerio de Gobierno*, Sección 1ª, t. 836, ff. 108–50.
127. *El Correo de la Costa*, Buenaventura, No. 7, March 16, 1879; *La Estrella*, Tumaco, No. 2, April 5, 1906; *El Litoral Pacífico*, Tumaco, No. 11, January 29, 1910; No. 18, April 2, 1910; *El Concejal*, Tumaco, No. 109, May 31, 1911; *El Fiscal*, Tumaco, No. 3, March 25, 1914; AGN, *Ministerio de Gobierno*, Sección 1ª, t 791, ff. 154-ss.

CHAPTER 6

1. Several authors have studied how cities provided opportunities for free blacks: see Kim D. Butler, *Freedoms Given, Freedoms Won. Afro-Brazilians in Post-Abolition Sao Paulo and Salvador* (New Brunswick: Rutgers University Press, 2000); Luz Mena, "Stretching the Limits of Gendered Spaces: Black and Mulatto Women in 1830s Havana," *Cuban Studies* 36 (2005): 87–104; Mariana Dantas, *Black Townsmen: Urban Slavery and Freedom in the Eighteenth-Century Americas* (New York: Palgrave Macmillan, 2008); Fernando Urrea, "La conformación paulatina de clases medias negras en Cali y Bogotá a lo largo del siglo XX y la primera década del XXI," *Revista de Estudios Sociales* 39 (2011): 24–41.
2. Hermes Tovar Pinzón et al., *Convocatoria al poder del número, Censos y estadísticas de la Nueva Granada, 1750–1830* (Bogotá: Archivo General de la Nación, 1994).
3. Bernardo Merizalde del Carmen, *Estudio de la costa colombiana del Pacífico* (Bogotá: Imprenta del Estado Mayor General, 1921), 128.
4. José María Cordovez Moure, *Reminiscencias de Santafé y Bogotá* (Madrid: Aguilar, 1962), 525; *El Eco del Pacífico*, Tumaco, No. 10, October 14, 1916.
5. Santiago Pérez, *Selección de escritos y discursos de Santiago Pérez* (Bogotá: Biblioteca de Historia Nacional, 1950), 81; Guido Barona et al., *Geografía Física y Política de la Confederación Granadina. Vol. 1: Estado del Cauca. Tomo II: Provincias del Chocó, Buenaventura, Cauca y Popayán* (Popayán: Universidad del Cauca, 2002), 404, 430.
6. Merizalde, *Estudio de la costa colombiana*, 129–30.
7. *Eco del Pacífico*, Tumaco, No. 3, October 23, 1881; Jorge Brisson, *Viajes por Colombia en los años de 1891 a 1897* (Bogotá: Imprenta Nacional, 1899), 12.
8. Rufino Gutiérrez, "Noticias sobre Pasto y las demás provincias del sur," in *Monografías, Tomo 1* (Bogotá, Imprenta Nacional, 1921), 141.
9. Eric Werner Cantor, *Ni aniquilados, ni vencidos. Los Emberá y la gente negra del Atrato bajo el dominio español. Siglo XVIII* (Bogotá: Instituto Colombiano de Antropología e Historia, 2000), 33.
10. Luis Fernando González, *Quibdó, Contexto histórico, desarrollo urbano y patrimonio arquitectónico* (Medellín: Instituto de Investigaciones ambientales del Pacífico, 2003), 46, 48, 51.
11. Quibdó remained the capital of Chocó ever since, except for a nine-year return to Nóvita in the 1840s. González, *Quibdó, Contexto histórico*, 66.

12. John Cresson Trautwine, *Rough Notes on the Exploration of an Interoceanic Canal by Way of the Rivers Atrato and San Juan in New Grenada, South America* (Philadelphia: Barnard & Jones, 1854), 36–37. For earlier more timid descriptions see Agustín Codazzi, *Memorias de Agustín Codazzi* (Bogotá: Banco de la República, 1973), 362–63, 365, and *Constitucional del Chocó*, Quibdó, No. 1, September 3, 1835. According to González, *Quibdó, Contexto histórico*, 96, in 1851, twelve houses had tiles, three of them belonging to foreigners.
13. Trautwine, *Rough Notes on the Exploration* 34, 37.
14. Pérez, *Selección de escritos y discursos*, 58.
15. For an analysis of the Commission's work and watercolors see Nancy Appelbaum, *Mapping the Country of Regions: The Corographic Commission of Nineteenth-Century Colombia* (Chapel Hill: University of North Carolina Press, 2016), chapter 4.
16. Oliver Selfridge, *Reports of Explorations and Surveys to Ascertain the Practicability of a Ship-Canal between the Atlantic and the Pacific Oceans by the Way of the Isthmus of Darien by Thos. Oliver Selfridge, Commander US Navy* (Washington, D.C.: Government Printing Office, 1874), 81.
17. *Los Avisos*, Quibdó, No. 21, September 14, 1891, 83. See also González, *Quibdó, Contexto histórico*, 97.
18. Jorge Brisson, *Exploración del alto Chocó* (Bogotá: Imprenta Nacional, 1895), 129.
19. For a year and a half, between 1908 and 1910, Chocó became the Department of Quibdó. This higher status did not last because the area lacked population and income requirements. Chocó remained an intendancy until 1947 when it became a department.
20. *Gil Blas*, Tumaco, No. 20, September 19, 1912; *El Concejal*, Tumaco, No. 101, March 10, 1911; *El Eco del Pacífico*, Tumaco, No. 10, October 14, 1916; *La Idea*, Tumaco, No. 2, October 21, 1916.
21. *El Litoral Pacífico*, Tumaco, No. 113, January 4, 1913.
22. *Revista de Colombia*, Volumen Centenario, Bogotá, No. 12, December 15, 1910, 365.
23. *El Litoral Pacífico*, Tumaco, No. 86, May 11, 1912; No. 88, May 25, 1912; No. 108, October 12, 1912; No. 114, January 4, 1913; No. 123, June 21, 1913; No. 143, February 21, 1914; No. 212, September 11, 1915; *Gil Blas*, Tumaco, No. 12, July 26, 1912; No. 20, September 19, 1912; *El Revisor*, Tumaco, No. 2, February 10, 1909; *El Fiscal*, No. 66, Tumaco, November 10, 1917; *Revista Nacional de Colombia*, Bogotá, No. 22, December 7, 1912.
24. *Albores*, Tumaco, No. 12, February 25, 1907; *El Litoral Pacífico*, Tumaco, No. 10, January 22, 1910; No. 15, March 1, 1910; No. 18, April 2, 1910; No. 27, July 16, 1910; No. 28, August 6, 1910; No. 34, September 23, 1910; No. 37, October 15, 1910; No. 40, November 15, 1910; No. 90, June 8, 1912; No. 93, June 28, 1912; No. 96, July 20, 1912; No. 101, August 24, 1912; No. 141, February 7, 1913; *El Concejal*, Tumaco, No. 108, May 20, 1911; No. 119, September 30, 1911; *Gil Blas*, Tumaco, No. 18, September 5, 1912; No. 23, October 13, 1912; No. 27, November 9, 1912; *El Micrófago*, Tumaco, No. 49, November 21, 1914; No. 50, November 28, 1914; AGN, Fondo Baldíos, Tomo 33, f. 38–47; Tomo 57, f. 44; Tomo 58, f. 61.

25. *El Litoral Pacífico*, Tumaco, No. 122, June 14, 1913; No. 139, January 24, 1914; No. 142, February 14, 1914; *El Micrófago*, Tumaco, No. 1, July 12, 1913.
26. *El Litoral Pacífico*, Tumaco, No. 90, June 8, 1912; No. 1, October 2, 1909; No. 8, January 8, 1910; No. 30, August 19, 1910; No. 139, January 24, 1914; Merizalde, *Estudio de la costa colombiana*, 192, 198.
27. González, *Quibdó, Contexto histórico*.
28. *El Ensayo*, Quibdó, No. 2, October 31, 1898. See also *El Zancudo*, Quibdó, No. 2, March 7, 1876; *Los Avisos*, Quibdó, No. 14, June 25, 1891.
29. Sociedad de Mejoras Públicas, *A.B.C.*, Quibdó, No. 39, August 30, 1914; and Sociedad de Fomento Público, *Boletín de la Sociedad de Fomento Público de Quibdó*, Quibdó, No. 1, September 7, 1919.
30. AGN, *Ministerio de Gobierno*, Sección 1ª, t. 603, ff. 1–78; *Los Hércules* No. 2, Quibdó, March 12, 1908; *Boletín de Obras Públicas*, Quibdó, No. 5, July 1, 1908; *Revista de Colombia*, Volumen Centenario, Bogotá, No. 5, June 30, 1910, 137.
31. *Ecos del Chocó*, Quibdó, No. 7, July 20, 1907; *Ecos Republicanos*, Quibdó, alcance al No. 5, October 12, 1909; No. 6, November 4, 1909; No. 16, June 16, 1910; No. 25, February 7, 1911; *Prosa y Versos*, Quibdó, No. 4, December 24, 1911; No. 12, September 27, 1912.
32. *Boletín de Obras Públicas*, Quibdó, No. 5, July 1, 1908; *Ecos Republicanos*, alcance al No. 5, Quibdó, October 12, 1909; *Revista de Colombia*, Volumen Centenario, Bogotá, No. 5, June 30, 1910, 135; González, *Quibdó, Contexto histórico*, 213–15.
33. *Ecos del Chocó*, Quibdó, No. 2, August 5, 1890.
34. Robert West, *The Pacific Lowlands of Colombia* (Baton Rouge: Louisiana State University, 1957), 27.
35. González, *Quibdó, Contexto histórico*, 97, 199; Notaría de Quibdó: 1868: No. 2, f. 4.
36. AGN, *Ministerio de Gobierno*, Sección 1ª, t. 603, ff. 1–78; t. 796, ff. 248–79; *Boletín de Obras Públicas*, Quibdó, No. 3, February 13, 1908; No. 5, July 1, 1908; *Ecos del Chocó*, No. 3, February 27, 1907; González, *Quibdó, Contexto histórico*, 121.
37. AGN, Baldíos, t. 10, f. 145; Ministerio de Gobierno, Sección 1ª, t. 602, ff. 1–78; t. 920, ff. 228–92; 336–63; t. 954, f. 219; t. 796, ff. 248–79; t. 836, f.f 108–50; *Ecos del Chocó*, Quibdó, No. 3, February 27, 1907; *Boletín de Obras Públicas* No. 4, Quibdó, April 15, 1908; No. 7, September 3, 1908; Quibdó, *Gaceta Departamental*, Quibdó, No. 5, January 7, 1909; *Ecos Republicanos*, Quibdó, No. 30, April 29, 1911; *Prosa y Versos*, Quibdó, No. 5 and 6, January 17, 1912; *A.B.C.*, Quibdó, No. 69, November 18, 1914; González, *Quibdó, Contexto histórico*, 187.
38. AGN, *Ministerio de Gobierno*, Sección 1ª, t. 603, ff. 1–78; t. 605, f. 392; t. 796, ff. 248–79; t. 836, ff. 108–50.
39. González, *Quibdó, Contexto histórico*, 263–83; *Prosa y Versos*, Quibdó, No. 1, October 3, 1911; No. 10, June 13, 1912; *El Citará*, Quibdó, No. 17, May 11, 1920; AGN, *Ministerio de Gobierno*, Sección 1ª, t. 796, ff. 248–79; t. 836, ff. 108–50.
40. González, *Quibdó, Contexto histórico*, 224–33, 245–48, 263–83; AGN, *Ministerio de Gobierno*, Sección 1ª, t. 965, ff. 502–63.
41. AGN, *Ministerio de Gobierno*, Sección 1ª, t. 920, ff. 228–92; t. 954, ff. 164–77; González, *Quibdó, Contexto histórico*, 216.

42. González, *Quibdó, Contexto histórico*, 205–9, 236–423, 313–40; AGN, *Ministerio de Gobierno*, Sección 1ª, t. 920, ff. 228–92.
43. Louis G. Dreyfus, "Construction Work in Quibdó, Colombia," NARA, RG 84, Records of Foreign Service Posts, Consular Posts, Quibdó, Colombia, Vol. 4 (1913); *A.B.C.*, Quibdó, No. 32, August 6, 1914.
44. Prefectura Apostólica del Chocó, *Informe de la Prefectura Apostólica del Chocó durante la administración de los misioneros hijos del inmaculado Corazón de María, 1909–1929* (Quibdó: Imprenta Claret, 1929), 32.
45. González, *Quibdó, Contexto histórico*, 120, 194.
46. González, *Quibdó, Contexto histórico*, 141–42, 169; interview with Judith Ferrer; Louis G. Dreyfus, "Conditions and Possibilities in the Chocó," NARA, RG 84, Records of Foreign Service Posts. Consular Posts. Quibdó, Colombia, Vol.4 (1914); Notaría Primera de Quibdó, 1911, No. 94, f. 518; *El Litoral Pacífico*, Tumaco, No. 11, January 29, 1910; No. 22, May 21, 1910; No. 24, June 19, 1910; No. 141, February 7, 1914; No. 190, January 16, 1915; *El Fiscal*, Tumaco, No. 19, July 1, 1914; No. 110, October 1, 1918; No. 116, November 12, 1918; *Unión Obrera*, Tumaco, No. 4, April 26, 1919; *El Anzuelo*, Tumaco, No. 5, May 18, 1919; Interview with Teófila Sinisterra.
47. *El Litoral Pacífico*, Tumaco, No. 160, June 20, 1914.
48. *Gil Blas*, Tumaco, No. 10, July 11, 1912; No. 15, August 17, 1912; No. 20, September 19, 1912; *El Litoral Pacífico*, Tumaco, No. 133, September 6, 1913; No. 175, October 3, 1914; *El Fiscal*, Tumaco, No. 2, March 18, 1914; *Unión Obrera*, Tumaco, No. 3, April 19, 1919.
49. For some examples, see *El Litoral Pacífico*, Tumaco, No. 101, August 24, 1912; No. 145, March 7, 1914; No. 175, October 3, 1914; *Gil Blas*, Tumaco, No. 3, May 11, 1912; No. 27, November 9, 1912; *Virutas* No. 3, Tumaco, June 22, 1913; *El Micrófago*, Tumaco, No. 20, January 3, 1914; No. 42, October 3, 1914; No. 47, November 7, 1914; *El Fiscal*, Tumaco, No. 21, July 15, 1914; No. 67, June 23, 1915; *El Ariete*, Tumaco, No. 12, August 7, 1915; *El Eco del Pacífico*, Tumaco, No. 18, December 9, 1916; No. 93, November 20, 1919; No. 94, November 30, 1919; *Unión Obrera*, Tumaco, No. 3, April 19, 1919; No. 4, April 26, 1919; *El Chocoano*, Quibdó, No. 6, March 15, 1899; *Los Hércules*, Quibdó, No. 1, March 5, 1908; No. 2, March 12, 1908; *Ecos Republicanos*, Quibdó, No. 18, September 18, 1910; *El Citará*, Quibdó, No. 25, July 6, 1920; *A.B.C.*, Quibdó, No. 18, May 3, 1914; No. 20, May 17, 1914.
50. For some examples, see *La Palabra*, Tumaco, No. 2, November 17, 1910; *El Litoral Pacífico*, Tumaco, No. 103, September 7, 1912; No. 115, January 18, 1913; *El Ariete*, Tumaco, No. 14, August 21, 1915; *El Anzuelo*, Tumaco, No. 3, May 4, 1919; *La Antorcha*, Quibdó, No. 4, October 14, 1890; *A.B.C.*, Quibdó, No. 29, July 19, 1914.
51. *El Concejal*, Tumaco, Nos. 96, 97, and 98, January 31, 1911.
52. *El Litoral Pacífico*, Tumaco, No. 43, November 26, 1910; No. 89, June 1, 1912; No. 139, January 24, 1914; *El Micrófago*, Tumaco, No. 24, January 31, 1914; No. 33, July 4, 1914; *El Fiscal*, Tumaco, No. 65, June 16, 1915; *El Eco del Pacífico*, Tumaco, No. 67, November 24, 1917; No. 93, November 20, 1919; *La Voz*, Tumaco, No. 2, December 18, 1919; *El Anzuelo*, Tumaco, No. 6, May 25, 1919; *Ecos del Choco*, Quibdó, No. 2, February 2, 1907; *Prosa y Versos*, Nos. 5 and 6, Quibdó, January 17, 1912.

53. *El Litoral Pacífico*, Tumaco, No. 136, September 27, 1913; No. 150, April 12, 1914; *El Fiscal*, Tumaco, No. 18, June 24, 1914; *Ecos del Chocó*, Quibdó, No. 3, August 30, 1890; *Ecos del Chocó*, Quibdó, No. 8, July 20, 1907; *El Ensayo*, Quibdó, No. 4, April 25, 1908; *Ecos Republicanos*, Quibdó, alcance al No. 5, October 12, 1909; *A.B.C.*, Quibdó, No. 51, October 2, 1914.
54. *El Litoral Pacífico*, Tumaco, No. 15, March 1, 1910; No. 123, June 21, 1913; *La Juventud*, Tumaco, No. 1, September 4, 1920.
55. *El Citará*, Quibdó, No. 16, May 4, 1920; González, *Quibdó, Contexto histórico*, 162, 173.
56. *La Voz Liberal*, Barbacoas, No. 3, 15, 1898; *El Litoral Pacífico*, Tumaco, No. 150, April 12, 1914; No. 206, May 8, 1915; *Unión Obrera*, Tumaco, No. 8, May 24, 1919.
57. *El Litoral Pacífico*, Tumaco, No. 11, January 29, 1910; *El Chocoano*, Quibdó, No. 2, January 10, 1899; Notaría de Quibdó: 1868, No. 1, f. 1; No. 56, f.131; No. 57, f. 134; 1880–1881, f. 135; 1886–1887, No. 51, f. 135; No. 63, f. 180; 1921, No. 23, f. 95; Miguel Triana, *Por el Sur de Colombia* (Bogotá, Biblioteca Popular de Cultura Colombiana, 1950), 39.
58. *El Litoral Pacífico*, Tumaco, No. 24, June 19, 1910; No. 110, December 14, 1912; *El Fiscal*, Tumaco, No. 7, April 18, 1914; No. 17, June 17, 1914; No. 125, January 15, 1919; *El Micrófago*, Tumaco, No. 35, July 18, 1914.
59. *El Litoral Pacífico*, Tumaco, No. 40, November 5, 1910; No. 44, December 3, 1910; *El Micrófago*, Tumaco, No. 5, August 9, 1913; No. 12, November 8, 1913; *La Juventu*, Tumaco, No. 1, September 4, 1920; *Ecos del Chocó* Quibdó, No. 9, November 30, 1907; *Boletín de la Sociedad de Fomento Público de Quibdó*, Quibdó, No. 2, October 23, 1919.
60. González, *Quibdó, Contexto histórico*, 161.
61. *El Litoral Pacífico*, Quibdó, No. 95, July 13, 1912; *La Juventud*, Tumaco, No. 1, September 4, 1920.
62. *A.B.C.*, Quibdó, No. 86, December 30, 1914.
63. *El Litoral Pacífico*, Tumaco, No. 10, January 22, 1910; No. 18, April 2, 1910; No. 113, January 4, 1913; No. 114, January 11, 1913; No. 178, October 24, 1914; *El Micrófago*, Tumaco, No. 33, July 4, 1914; No. 45, October 24, 1914; *El Fiscal*, Tumaco, No. 14, June 3, 1914; No. 68, June 26, 1915.
64. González, *Quibdó, Contexto histórico*, 162, 172–73.
65. *El Litoral Pacífico*, Tumaco, No. 141, February 7, 1914; No. 209, August 21, 1915; *A.B.C.*, Quibdó, No. 62, November 1, 1914; No. 72, November 25, 1914; *El Citará*, Quibdó, No. 15, January 7, 1920.
66. *El Litoral Pacífico*, Tumaco, No. 26, July 9, 1910; *El Micrófago*, Tumaco, No. 26, March 7, 1914; *El Fiscal*, Tumaco, No. 1, March 12, 1914.
67. *El Litoral Pacífico*, Tumaco, No. 35, October 2, 1910; No. 125, July 5, 1913; No. 179, October 31, 1914; No. 188, January 2, 1915; *Gil Blas*, Tumaco, No. 17, August 29, 1912; No. 24, October 19, 1912; *El Micrófago*, Tumaco, No. 2, July 19, 1913; *El Fiscal*, Tumaco, No. 39, December 9, 1914; *Unión Obrera*, Tumaco, No. 4, April 26, 1918; *La Voz*, Tumaco, No. 2, December 18, 1919.

68. *Ecos Republicanos*, Quibdó, No. 25, February 7, 1911; *El Citará*, Quibdó, No. 8, November 5, 1919.
69. González, *Quibdó, Contexto histórico*, 151; Daniel Valois Arce, *Departamento del Chocó* (Medellín: Tipografía Industria, 1945), 99–109.
70. *El Litoral Pacífico*, Tumaco, No. 6, November 26, 1909; *Ecos del Chocó*, Tumaco, No. 7, June 11, 1907, *Ecos Republicanos*, Quibdó, No. 14, [illegible date], 1910; *A.B.C.*, Quibdó, No. 45, September 17, 1914.
71. *El Litoral Pacífico*, Tumaco, No. 1, October 2, 1909; No. 162, July 4, 1914; *El Fiscal*, Tumaco, No. 65, June 16, 1915; *Ecos Republicanos*, Quibdó, No. 16, June 16, 1910.
72. *Ecos del Chocó*, Quibdó, No. 1, January 25, 1907; *Ecos Republicanos*, Quibdó, No. 25, February 7, 1911, *Prosa y Versos*, Quibdó, Nos. 7 and 8, February 23, 1912.
73. *El Litoral Pacífico*, Tumaco, No. 99, August 10, 1912; No. 113, January 14, 1913; No. 122, June 14, 1913; No. 168, August 15, 1914; No. 187, December 26, 1914.
74. *A.B.C.*, Quibdó, No. 276, February 7, 1916; Ramón Mosquera Rivas, *Recuerdos de un hijo de mineros* (Medellín: Editorial Difusión, 1985), 23–33.
75. *El Litoral Pacífico*, Tumaco, No. 11 January 29, 1910; *El Concejal*, Tumaco, No. 83 September 15, 1910; *La Idea*, Tumaco, No. 2, October 21, 1916; Mosquera Rivas, *Recuerdos de un hijo de mineros*, 23–33, 56–71.
76. Pedro Sonderéguer, *Quibdó* (Buenos Aires: Hermanos Maucci, 1927), 102–3.
77. *El Eco del Pacífico*, Tumaco, No. 101, January 22, 1920.
78. *El Litoral Pacífico*, Tumaco, No. 184, December 5, 1914; *Eco del Pacífico*, Tumaco, No. 95, December 8, 1919.
79. *Ecos Republicanos*, Quibdó, No. 23, January, 1911; No. 26, March 17, 1911.
80. *Ecos del Chocó*, Quibdó, No. 9, November 30, 1907.
81. *Ecos Republicanos*, Quibdó, No. 28, April 6, 1911; No. 38, September 19, 1911; *A.B.C.* No. 3, Quibdó, December 1, 1913; No. 16, April 19, 1914; No. 23, June 7, 1914; No. 35, August 16, 1914; No. 51, October 2, 1914; No. 62, November 1, 1914; *El Litoral Pacífico*, Tumaco, No. 37, October 15, 1910; No. 131, August 23, 1913; *Gil Blas*, Tumaco, No. 10, July 11, 1912; *Virutas*, Tumaco, No. 2, June 17, 1913; *El Micrófago*, Tumaco, No. 37, August 1, 1914.
82. *El Fiscal*, Tumaco, No. 11, May 9, 1914.
83. *Ecos Republicanos*, Quibdó, No. 33, June 25, 1911; *Prosa y Versos*, Quibdó, Nos. 7 and 8, February 23, 1912; *El Tipógrafo*, Quibdó, No. 1, May 11, 1913; *El Litoral Pacífico*, Tumaco, No. 110, December 14, 1912; No. 152, April 25, 1914; No. 191, January 23, 1915; *El Fiscal*, Tumaco, No. 19, July 1, 1914; No. 110, October 1, 1918.
84. *El Litoral Pacífico*, Tumaco, No. 8, January 8, 1910; No. 166, August 1, 1914; *El Micrófago*, Tumaco, No. 28, March 28, 1914; *El Eco del Pacífico*, Tumaco, No. 94, November 30, 1919, *Ecos del Chocó*, Quibdó, No. 1, July 20, 1890; No. 4, September 12, 1890; *Boletín de la Sociedad de Fomento Público de Quibdó*, Quibdó, No. 2, October 23, 1919; *A.B.C.*, Quibdó, No. 69, November 18, 1914; No. 96, January 21, 1915.
85. *El Ensayo*, Quibdó, No. 2, October 31, 1898; *A.B.C.*, Quibdó, No. 62, November 1, 1914; *El Citará*, Quibdó, No. 11, November 26, 1919; *El Litoral Pacífico*, Tumaco,

No. 148; Tumaco, March 28, 1914; *El Micrófago*, Tumaco, No. 1, July 12, 1913; *El Fiscal*, No. 46, Tumaco, February 10, 1915.

86. *El Micrófago* No. 14, Tumaco, November 22, 1913; *El Fiscal* No. 2, Tumaco, March 18, 1914; No. 17, June 17, 1914; No. 89, February 10, 1916.
87. *El Litoral Pacífico*, Tumaco, No. 37, October 15, 1910; No. 133, September 6, 1913; No. 184, December 5, 1914; No. 191, January 23, 1915; *El Micrófago* Tumaco, No. 49, November 21, 1914, *El Fiscal*, Tumaco, No. 96, December 14, 1919.
88. *La Palabra*, Tumaco, No. 1, November 5, 1910; *El Litoral Pacífico*, Tumaco, No. 179, October 31, 1914; *El Micrófago*, Tumaco, No. 5, August 9, 1913; *El Fiscal*, Tumaco, No. 7, April 18, 1914; No. 53, March 31, 1915; No. 90, February 16, 1916; *El Micrófago*, Tumaco, No. 38, August 7, 1914; *Unión Obrera*, Tumaco, No. 3, April 19, 1919; No. 9, May 31, 1919; Triana, *Por el Sur de Colombia*.
89. *El Litoral Pacífico*, Tumaco, No. 187, December 26, 1914; Mosquera Rivas, *Recuerdos de un hijo de mineros*, 56–57.
90. *A.B.C.*, Quibdó, No. 96, January 21, 1915.
91. *El Eco del Pacífico*, Tumaco, No. 98, December 31, 1919.
92. *El Fiscal*, Tumaco, No. 3, March 25, 1914; *Virutas*, Tumaco, No. 2, June 17, 1913; *El Litoral Pacífico*, Tumaco, No. 123, June 21, 1913; No. 144, February 28, 1914.
93. Triana, *Por el Sur de Colombia*, 39.
94. González, *Quibdó, Contexto histórico*, 338–40.
95. *La Juventud*, Tumaco, No. 4, October 16, 1920.
96. Interview with Judith Ferrer; *El Litoral Pacífico*, Tumaco, No. 8, January 8, 1910; No. 20, April 23, 1910.
97. González, *Quibdó, Contexto histórico*, 174, 191.
98. For a more detailed treatment of this issue see Claudia Leal, "Música, Raza y región. El currulao del Pacífico sur colombiano," in *Chile-Colombia: Diálogos sobre sus trayectorias históricas*, ed. Fernando Purcell and Ricardo Arias (Bogotá and Santiago: Ediciones Uniandes, Editorial Universidad Católica de Chile, 2014).
99. Triana, *Por el Sur de Colombia*, 71; Merizalde, *Estudio de la costa colombiana*, 153.
100. Norman Whitten, *Class, Kinship and Power in an Ecuadorian Town: The Negroes of San Lorenzo* (Stanford: Stanford University Press, 1965), 78–79; Norman Whitten and Aurelio C. Fuentes, "Baile marimba! Negro Folkmusic in Northwest Ecuador," *Journal of the Folklore Institute* 2, no. 3 (1966); Norman Whitten, *Black Frontiersmen: A South American Case* (New York: Schenkman Publishing Company, 1974), 108–19.
101. Whitten, *Black Frontiersmen*, 114.
102. *El Correo de la Costa*, Buenaventura, No. 7, March 16, 1879; *El Litoral Pacífico*, Tumaco, No. 33, September 18, 1910.
103. *El Correo de la Costa*, Buenaventura, No. 7, March 16, 1879.
104. Merizalde, *Estudio de la costa colombiana*, 153.
105. *El Micrófago*, Tumaco, No. 9, September 27, 1913.
106. *El Litoral Pacífico*, Tumaco, No. 211, September 4, 1915.

107. Claudia Leal, "Usos del concepto raza en Colombia," in *Debates sobre ciudadanía y políticas raciales en las Américas negras*, ed. Claudia Mosquera Rosero-Labbé and Agustín Laó-Montes y César Rodríguez (Bogotá: Universidad Nacional de Colombia, sede Bogotá, CES, IDCARAN, sede Medellín, Universidad de los Andes, 2010).
108. *El Micrófago*, Tumaco, No. 1, July 12, 1913.
109. *El Montaraz*, Barbacoas, No. 27, May 22, 1880; *El Micrófago*, Tumaco, No. 19, December 24, 1913; *El Fiscal*, Tumaco, No. 39, December 9, 1914; *El Correo de la Costa*, Buenaventura, No. 7, March 16, 1879.
110. *El Correo de la Costa*, Buenaventura, No. 7, March 16, 1879.
111. *El Micrófago*, Tumaco, No. 9, September 27, 1913.
112. *El Fiscal*, Tumaco, No. 39, December 9, 1914.
113. Quote from Triana, *Por el Sur de Colombia*, 41. See also *El Litoral Pacífico*, Tumaco, No. 135, September 20, 1913; No. 33, September 18, 1910; Triana, *Por el Sur de Colombia*, 41.
114. Peter Wade, "Music, Blackness and National Identity: Three Moments in Colombian History," *Popular Music* 17, no. 1 (1998): 7–9; Peter Wade, *Music, Race, and Nation: Música Tropical in Colombia* (Chicago: University of Chicago Press, 2000).
115. *El Micrófago*, Tumaco, No. 19, December 24, 1913.
116. George Reid Andrews, *Afro-Latin America, 1800–2000* (New York: Oxford University Press, 2004), chapter 4.
117. *El Montaraz*, Barbacoas, No. 27, May 22, 1880.
118. *El Correo de la Costa*, Buenaventura, No. 7, March 16, 1879.
119. *El Litoral Pacífico*, Tumaco, No. 135, September 20, 1913.
120. *El Micrófago*, Tumaco, No. 9, September 27, 1913.
121. *El Ariete*, Tumaco, No. 2, January 9, 1915.
122. Merizalde, *Estudio de la costa colombiana*, 204.
123. *El Baluarte*, Barbacoas, No. 2, August 8, 1910; *El Litoral Pacífico*, Tumaco, No. 6, November 26, 1909.
124. *El Litoral Pacífico*, Tumaco, No. 119, February 15, 1913.
125. *El Litoral Pacífico*, Tumaco, No. 213, September 18, 1915.
126. Sonderéguer, *Quibdó*.
127. Wade, "Music, Blackness and National Identity"; Adolfo González Henriquez, "La música costeña colombiana en la tercera década del siglo XIX," *Latin American Music Review* 9, no. 2 (1988): 189, 191–93, 198.
128. *El Montaraz*, Barbacoas, No. 10, January 14, 1879; No. 15, May 24, 1879; No. 20, December 18, 1879; *Registro Municipal*, Barbacoas, No. 7, January 10, 1893; *El Telégrafo*, Barbacoas, No. 6, October 4, 1897.
129. This department only lasted until 1909. *El Sur de Colombia*, Barbacoas, No. 2, November 20, 1908.
130. *El Revisor*, Tumaco, No. 2, February 10, 1909; *Gaceta Departamental*, Tumaco, No. 15, February 26, 1909; *El Concejal*, Tumaco, Nos. 86 and 87, October 31, 1910; *El Micrófago*, Tumaco, No. 2, July 19, 1913; No. 49, November 21, 1914; *El Fiscal*,

Tumaco, No. 52, March 24, 1915; *El Anzuelo*, Tumaco, No. 4, May 11, 1919; *La Juventud*, Tumaco, No. 1, September 4, 1920.

131. *El Camarada*, Tumaco, No. 14, May 23, 1915; No. 15, June 13, 1915; *La Juventud*, Tumaco, No. 1, September 4, 1920.
132. *El Litoral Pacífico*, Tumaco, No. 110, December 14, 1912; No. 115, January 18, 1913; No. 135, September 20, 1913; No. 162, July 4, 1914.
133. Luz Mena, "The Spaces and Faces of Music and Dance in Early Modern Havana," Departmental Colloquium, Department of Geography, University of California, Berkeley, February 4, 2004.
134. Interview with Judith Ferrer.
135. Merizalde, *Estudio de la costa colombiana*, 155.
136. Delia Zapata Olivella, "An Introduction to the Folk Dances of Colombia," *Ethnomusicology* 11, no. 1, (1967): 94–95.
137. *El Correo de la Costa*, Buenaventura, No. 7, March 16, 1879.
138. Triana, *Por el Sur de Colombia*, 41.
139. Leal, "Música, Raza y región."
140. Oscar Hernández Salgar, "De currulaos modernos y ollas podridas," in *Músicas y prácticas sonoras en el Pacífico afrocolombiano*, ed. Juan Sebastián Ochoa Escobar, Carolina Santamaría Delgado, and Manuel Sevilla Peñuela (Bogotá: Editorial Pontificia Universidad Javeriana, 2010).
141. AGN, Ministerio de Gobierno Sección 1ª, Tomo 592, f. 313–19; *Revista Oficial*, Quibdó, No. 6, May 24, 1907; Rogerio Velásquez, *Las memorias del odio* (Bogotá: Colcultura, 1992 [1953]), 81.
142. Interviews with Ligia Cabezas Lemos and Aura Helena Sevillano.
143. *El Montañés*, Barbacoas, No. 28, June 10, 1880.
144. See for example *El Litoral Pacífico*, Tumaco, No. 104, September 14, 1912; No. 122, December 28, 1912; *Gil Blas,* Tumaco, No. 18, September 5, 1912; *La Idea*, Tumaco, No. 1, October 15, 1916; *El Citará*, Quibdó, No. 6, October 22, 1919.
145. Pérez, *Selección de escritos y discursos*, 82; *Albores*, Barbacoas, No. 3, February 1, 1906; *El Eco del Pacífico*, Tumaco, No. 10, October 14, 1916; *El Montaraz*, Barbacoas, No. 42, April 30, 1881, *Los Avisos*, Quibdó, No. 11, June 1891.
146. *El Fiscal*, Tumaco, No. 106, September 5, 1918.
147. *El Heraldo*, Quibdó, No. 6, January 1, 1868.
148. *Los Avisos*, Quibdó, No. 20, August 28, 1891; No. 21, September 14, 1891.
149. Velásquez, *Las memorias del odio*, 80–81.
150. *Revista Oficial*, Quibdó, No. 5, May 7, 1907.
151. *Revista Oficial*, Quibdó, No. 6, May 24, 1907. On ideas of blacks as violent and dangerous see Nancy Appelbaum, "Whitening the Region: Caucano Mediation and 'Antioqueño Colonization' in Nineteenth-Century Colombia," *Hispanic American Historical Review* 79, no. 4 (1999): 631–68.
152. Velásquez, *Las memorias del odio*, 77–82.
153. AGN, Ministerio de Gobierno Sección 1ª, Tomo 592, f. 313–19.
154. *Ecos del Chocó*, Quibdó, No. 6, May 10, 1907.

155. Martínez de Varela, *Mi Cristo negro*; Caicedo (1992), 80; Velásquez, *Las memorias del odio*, 45–48, 61–63.
156. *Revista Oficial*, Quibdó, No. 5, May 7, 1907; *Ecos del Chocó*, Quibdó, No. 6, May 10, 1907.
157. Notaría de Quibdó, 1905, f. 347; *Ecos del Chocó*, Quibdó, No. 6, May 10, 1907; *Revista Oficial*, Quibdó, No. 6, May 24, 1907.
158. Teresa Martínez de Varela, *Mi Cristo negro* (Bogotá: Imprenta del Fondo Rotatorio de la Policía Nacional, 1983).
159. James E. Sanders, *Contentious Republicans: Popular Politics, Race, and Class in Nineteenth-Century Colombia* (Durham: Duke University Press, 2004); James E. Sanders, "'Citizens of a Free People': Popular Liberalism and Race in Nineteenth-Century Southwestern Colombia," *Hispanic American Historical Review* 84, no. 2 (2004); Jason McGraw, *The Work of Recognition: Caribbean Colombia and the Postemancipation Struggle for Citizenship* (Chapel Hill: University of North Carolina Press, 2014).
160. My emphasis. Trautwine, *Rough Notes on the Exploration*, 58.
161. *El Micrófago*, Tumaco, No. 35, July 18, 1914.
162. AGN, *Baldíos*, t. 55, f. 457.
163. Of Castillo we know that he was judge in Istmina in 1908 and that he was active in politics, since in 1911, Juan J. Carrasco, a local influential man, recommended him for intendant. AGN, *Ministerio de Gobierno*, Sección 1ª, t. 603, ff. 1–78; *Ministerio de Gobierno*, Sección 1ª, t. 64, ff. 333–35.
164. Interview with Judith Ferrer.
165. Mario Aguilera Peña, "Los últimos fusilamientos legales," in *Pensamiento Jurídico* 6 (1996): 51–67.
166. Claudia Leal, "Recordando a Saturio. Memorias del racismo en Chocó, Colombia," in *Revista de Estudios Sociales* 27 (2007): 76–93.
167. Mirza Mena de Perea, Beatriz Gil Ibargüen, and Beatriz López de Ortega, *Anotaciones socioculturales sobre el departamento del Chocó* (Medellín: Editorial Lealón, 1994), 105–6. The last execution in Colombia happened in 1909.
168. José E. Mosquera, *Diego Luis Córdoba: mito y realidad. Historia de las luchas de los chocoanos por la creación del departamento del Chocó, 1830–1947* (Medellín: Editorial L. Vieco, 2015).
169. AGN, *Ministerio de Gobierno*, Sección 1ª, t. 998, ff. 541–42.
170. González, *Quibdó, Contexto histórico*, 184.

CONCLUSION

1. For this estimate of Latin America's forest cover see John Soluri, Claudia Leal, and José Augusto Pádua, "Finding the 'Latin American' in (Latin American) Environmental History," in *A Living Past: Environmental Histories of Modern Latin America*, ed. John Soluri, Claudia Leal, and José Augusto Pádua (New York: Berghahn Books, forthcoming).

2. Rogério Ribeiro de Oliveira and Joana Stingel Fraga, "Metabolismo social de uma floresta e de uma cidade: paisagem, carvoeiros e invisibilidade social no Rio de Janeiro dos séculos XIX e XX," *GeoPuc* 4, no. 7 (2012).
3. Two recent volumes that use this concept are Anthony Bebbington, ed., *Social Conflict, Economic Development and Extractive Industry: Evidence from South America* (London: Routledge, 2012) and Barbara Göbel y Astrid Ulloa, ed., *Extractivismo minero en Colombia y América Latina* (Bogotá and Berlin: Universidad Nacional de Colombia and Ibero-Amerikanisches Institut, 2014).
4. James Sanders's and Jason McGraw's work best exemplify efforts to understand the historical relevance of blackness for nation building in Colombia. Sanders skillfully reconstructs black mobilization in the southwest and explains how equality stood out as the guiding political aspiration, while McGraw examines war, labor, and even literature as arenas in which Afro-Colombians in the Caribbean struggled for recognition and full citizenship. James Sanders, *Contentious Republicans: Popular Politics, Race, and Class in Nineteenth-Century Colombia* (Durham: Duke University Press, 2004); Jason McGraw, *The Work of Recognition: Caribbean Colombia and the Postemancipation Struggle for Citizenship* (Chapel Hill: University of North Carolina Press, 2014).
5. The two other general histories are David Bushnell, *The Making of Modern Colombia: A Nation in Spite of Itself* (Berkeley: University of California Press, 1993) and Michael J. LaRosa and Germán Mejía, *Colombia: A Concise Contemporary History* (Rowman & Littlefield, 2012). Nina S. de Friedmann denounced the "invisibility" of black people, but in the context of anthropological studies rather than history, Nina S. de Friedemann, "Estudios de negros en la antropología colombiana: presencia e invisibilidad," in *Un siglo de investigación social: antropología en Colombia*, ed. Jaime Arocha and Nina S. de Friedemann (Bogotá: Etno, 1984).
6. Marco Palacios and Frank Safford, *Colombia: Fragmented Land, Divided Society* (Oxford: Oxford University Press, 2002), 102, see also 50–51, 100, 103, 149, 180–82.
7. Safford and Palacios, *Colombia*, 262. Earlier on they assert, "Former slaves from the mines of the Chocó [. . .] tended to migrate to the Pacific coast, where, remote from Spanish authority, they lived by fishing, hunting, and subsistence agriculture," 51. However, migration in the eighteenth century was minimal and later on, when it picked up, black people never severed their ties to the market economy. LaRosa and Mejía, *Colombia: A Concise*, 28, also misrepresent migration in the coast—"Many of the freed slaves settled in the mining areas of the Pacific"—for they were already there.
8. Martha Cárdenas and Manuel Rodríguez Becerra, eds., *Guerra, sociedad y medio ambiente* (Bogotá: Foro Nacional Ambiental, 2004) do address this issue, but this is not mainly a historical study. For the many possibilities that the topic of war and the environment offers see Richard Tucker, "War and the Environment," in *Blackwell Companion to Global Environmental History*, ed. John R. McNeill and Erin Stewart (Oxford: Blackwell, 2012).

9. An exception is Germán Palacio, *Fiebre de Tierra caliente. Una historia ambiental de Colombia 1850–1930* (Bogotá: Universidad Nacional de Colombia, 2006).
10. Jaime Bonet, "¿Por qué es pobre el Chocó?," *Documentos de Trabajo sobre Economía Regional 90*, April 2007, 48–53; see also *Proyecto Biopacífico, Informe Final General, Tomo I: Territorio Biocultural* (Bogotá: Ministerio del Medio Ambiente, 1998); see also César Rodríguez Garavito, Tatiana Alfonso Sierra, and Isabel Cavelier Adarve, *Raza y derechos humanos en Colombia. Informe sobre discriminación racial y derechos de la población afrocolombiana* (Bogotá, Observatorio de Discriminación Racial, 2009).
11. Marco Palacios, *Colombia, Between Legitimacy and Violence: A History of Colombia, 1875–2002* (Durham: Duke University Press, 2006).
12. Perhaps we can find a balanced view that integrates some of the insights of two scholars that have written about this place, Arturo Escobar, *Territories of Difference: Place, Movements, Life, Redes* (Durham: Duke University Press, 2008) and Michael Taussig, *My Cocaine Museum* (Chicago: University of Chicago Press, 2004).

BIBLIOGRAPHY

PRIMARY SOURCES

Álvarez Lleras, Jorge. *El Chocó, Apuntamientos de viaje referentes a esta interesante región del país*. Bogotá: Minerva, 1923.

Arboleda, Sergio. *La República en la América Española*. Bogotá: Biblioteca Banco Popular, 1973 [1867].

Archer, Andrew. "Exploration in the Choco Intendancy of Colombia," *Scientific Monthly* 44, no. 5 (1937): 418–34.

Arteaga, José Benjamín. "Del Urabá. Diario de un misionero," *Revista de Misiones Year 3* 27 (1927): 75–88.

Bell, P. L. *Colombia: A Commercial Handbook*, Department of Commerce, Special Series No. 206. Washington, D.C.: Government Printing Office, 1921.

Brisson, Jorge. *Exploración del alto Chocó*. Bogotá: Imprenta Nacional, 1895.

———. *Viajes por Colombia en los años de 1891 a 1897*. Bogotá: Imprenta Nacional, 1899.

Cochrane, Charles Stuart. *Viajes por Colombia, 1823 y 1824: diario de mi residencia en Colombia*. Bogotá: Banco de la República, 1994.

Codazzi, Agustín. *Memorias de Agustín Codazzi*. Bogotá: Banco de la República, 1973.

Comisión Corográfica bajo la dirección de Agustín Codazzi. *Geografía física i política de las provincias de la Nueva Granada, Segunda parte: informes*. Bogotá: Banco de la República, 1959.

Cordovez Moure, José María. *Reminiscencias de Santafé y Bogotá*. Madrid: Aguilar, 1957.

Cruz, Juan Evangelista. *Visita al Chocó en noviembre de 1920*. Cali: Tipografía Moderna, 1920.

Farhar, F. P. "From Tagua to Buttons," *Bulletin of the Pan American Union* 62 (1928): 801–9.

Friend, Charles. "Notes of an Excursion from the Banks of the Atrato to the Bay of Cupica, on the Coast of the Pacific, in the Year 1827," *Journal of the Royal Geographical Society* 23 (1853).

García, Francisco. "Relación de una excursión al alto Atrato y al río Andágueda, por el reverendo padre Francisco García." In *Relación de algunas excursiones apostólicas en la misión del Chocó*, ed. Francisco Gutiérrez. Bogotá: Imprenta Nacional, 1924.

Granger, Henry. "Gold-Dredging on the Choco Rivers, Republic of Colombia, South America," *Transactions of the American Institute of Mining Engineers* 39 (1908).

Granger, Henry, and Edward B. Trewille. "Mining Districts of Colombia," *Transactions of the American Institute of Mining Engineers* 39 (1899).

Gutiérrez, Francisco. *Informe que el Prefecto Apostólico del Chocó rinde al Ilustrísimo y Reverendísimo Arzobispo de Colombia, como presidente de la Junta Arquidiocesana de Misiones, 1916–1918*. Bogotá: Imprenta Nacional, 1919.

———. *Informe que el Prefecto Apostólico del Chocó rinde al Ilustrísimo y Reverendísimo Arzobispo de Colombia, como presidente de la Junta Arquidiocesana de Misiones, 1919–1923*. Bogotá: Imprenta Nacional, 1924.

———, ed. *Relación de algunas excursiones apostólicas en la misión del Chocó*. Bogotá: Imprenta Nacional, 1924.

Gutiérrez, Rufino. *Datos sobre la historia del ferrocarril del Pacífico*. Bogotá: Arboleda y Valencia, 1919.

———. "Noticias sobre Pasto y las demás provincias del sur." In *Monografías*, Tomo 1. Bogotá: Imprenta Nacional, 1921.

Hamilton, John Porter. *Viajes por el interior de las provincias de Colombia*. Bogotá: Colcultura, 1993 [1827].

Jaramillo, Justiniano. *En el Darién. Informe de una expedición ordenada por el Ministerio de Guerra*. Bogotá: Imprenta Eléctrica, 1910.

Juaristi, Juan Antonio. "Manuscript with information taken in 1963 and 1964 on the formation of several towns located close to Tumaco, transcribed by Father José Miguel Garrido" (unpublished manuscript, n.d.). Archivo Vicariato de Tumaco.

Maetzu, Teodoro. "Prefectura Apostólica de Tumaco. Bellezas de la costa del Pacífico," *Revista de Misiones* 4, no. 34 (March 1928): 67–77.

Martínez de Varela, Teresa. *Mi Cristo negro*. Bogotá: Imprenta del Fondo Rotatorio de la Policía Nacional, 1983.

Merizalde del Carmen, Bernardo. *Estudio de la costa colombiana del Pacífico*. Bogotá: Imprenta del Estado Mayor General, 1921.

Michler, Nathaniel. "Lieutenant Michler's Report of His Survey for an Interoceanic Ship Canal Near the Isthmus of Darien," Senate Executive Documents, No. 9, Vol. 7, 36th Congress, 2nd Session, 1861.

Miller, Leo E. *In the Wilds of South America*. New York: Charles Scribner's Sons, 1919.

Mollien, Gaspard-Théodore. *Viaje por la República de Colombia en 1823*. Bogotá: Colcultura, 1992.

Mosquera, Lisandro, "Monografía general del Chocó," *Dyna* 9 (1934).

Mosquera Rivas, Ramón. *Recuerdos de un hijo de mineros*. Medellín: Editorial Difusión, 1985.

Muñoz, Carlos R. *Problemas de Urabá: informe rendido al señor gobernador del departamento por el visitador fiscal Carlos Muñoz*. Medellín: Imprenta Oficial, 1931.

Ospina, Santiago. *Mina de 'El Salto,' Resolución ministerial y documentos relacionados con este asunto*. Bogotá: Imprenta Nacional, 1925.

Pearson, Henry C. *What I Saw in the Tropics*. New York: India Rubber Publishing Co., 1906.

Prefectura Apostólica del Chocó. *Informe de la Prefectura Apostólica del Chocó durante la administración de los misioneros hijos del inmaculado Corazón de María, 1909–1929*. Quibdó: Imprenta Claret, 1929.

Ragonnet, E. L. "Journal of Voyage." Paris: n.p., 1895.

Restrepo, Vicente. *Estudio sobre las minas de oro y plata de Colombia*. Bogotá: Silvestre y Compañía, 1888 [1882].

Saffray, Charles. *Viaje a Nueva Granada*. Bogotá: Biblioteca Popular de Cultura Colombiana, 1948.

Samper, José María. *Ensayo sobre las revoluciones políticas y la condición social de las repúblicas colombianas (hispanoamericanas)*. Bogotá: Universidad Nacional de Colombia, 1969 [1861].

Santa Gertrudis, Fray Juan de. *Maravillas de la naturaleza*, Tomo III. Bogotá: Biblioteca Banco Popular, 1970.

Seemann, Berthold. *Narrative of the Voyage of the H.M.S. Herald During the Years 1845–51, Under the Command of Captain Henry Kellett, R.N., C.B.; Being a Circumnavigation of the Globe, and Three Cruizes to the Arctic Regions in Search of Sir John Franklin*, Vol. 1. London: Reeve and Co., 1853.

Selfridge, Oliver. *Reports of Explorations and Surveys to Ascertain the Practicability of a Ship-Canal between the Atlantic and the Pacific Oceans by the Way of the Isthmus of Darien by Thos. Oliver Selfridge, Commander US Navy*. Washington, D.C.: Government Printing Office, 1874.

Sonderéguer, Pedro. *Quibdó*. Buenos Aires: Hermanos Maucci, 1927.

Trautwine, John Cresson. *Rough Notes on the Exploration of an Interoceanic Canal by Way of the Rivers Atrato and San Juan in New Grenada, South America*. Philadelphia: Barnard & Jones, 1854.

Triana, Miguel. *Por el Sur de Colombia*. Bogotá: Biblioteca Popular de Cultura Colombiana, 1950.

United States Department of Labor. "The Button and Buckle Manufacturing Industry," 1942.

Vallejo, José. *Por el Atrato*. Jericó: Imprenta de La Merced, 1910.

Velásquez, Rogerio. *Las memorias del odio*. Bogotá: Colcultura, 1992 [1953].

Zawadsky, Alfonso. *Las ciudades confederadas del Valle del Cauca en 1811*. Cali: Imprenta Bolivariana, 1943.

SECONDARY SOURCES

Abad Vélez, Jorge, et al. "Una economía familiar de reproducción simple: el caso de la pequeña minería chocoana." BA thesis, Universidad de Antioquia, 1982.

Acevedo Marin, Rosa, and Edna Ramos de Castro. *No caminho de pedras de Abacatal: experiência social de grupos negros no Pará*. Belém: Universidade Federal do Pará, 2004.

Acosta Solís, Misael. *Tagua*. Quito: Editorial Ecuador, 1944.

———. "Tagua or Vegetable Ivory—A Forest Product of Ecuador." *Economic Botany* 2, no. 1 (1948): 46–57.

Agier, Michel. "El carnaval, el diablo y la marimba: identidad y ritual en Tumaco." In *Tumaco: haciendo ciudad*, ed. Michel Agier, Manuela Alvarez, Odile Hoffman, and Eduardo Restrepo. Cali: Instituto Colombiano de Antropología, IRD, Universidad del Valle, 1999.

Aguilera Peña, Mario. "Los últimos fusilamientos legales." *Pensamiento Jurídico* 6 (1996): 51–67.

Almario, Óscar. *Los renacientes y su territorio. Ensayos sobre la etnicidad negra en el Pacífico sur colombiano*. Medellín: Universidad Pontificia Bolivariana, 2003.

———. "Territorio, etnicidad y poder en el Pacífico sur colombiano, 1780–1930." PhD diss., Universidad de Sevilla, 2007.

Álvarez Arboleda, Juana Francisca. *Vida y obra de un compositor, El maquinista trovador, Petronio Álvarez, "El Cuco."* Cali: Imprenta Departamental del Valle del Cauca, 2011.

Anderson, Warwick. "The Natures of Culture: Environment and Race in the Colonial Tropics." In *Nature in the Global South: Environmental Projects in South and Southeast Asia*, ed. Paul Greenough and Anna Lowenhaupt Tsing. Durham: Duke University Press, 2003.

Andrews, George Reid. *Afro-Latin America, 1800–2000*. New York: Oxford University Press, 2004.

Appelbaum, Nancy. *Mapping the Country of Regions: The Corographic Commission of Nineteenth-Century Colombia*. Chapel Hill: University of North Carolina Press, 2016.

———. *Muddied Waters: Race, Region, and Local History in Colombia, 1846–1948*. Durham: Duke University Press, 2003.

———. "Whitening the Region: Caucano Mediation and 'Antioqueño Colonization' in Nineteenth-Century Colombia." *Hispanic American Historical Review* 79, no. 4 (November 1999): 631–68.

Appelbaum, Nancy, Anne S. Macpherson, and Karin Alejandra Rosemblat, eds. *Race and Nation in Modern Latin America*. Chapel Hill: University of North Carolina Press, 2003.

Aprile-Gniset, Jacques. *Habitats y sociedades del Pacífico Vol. 2: Génesis de Buenaventura*. Buenaventura: Universidad del Pacífico, 2002.

———. *Poblamiento y hábitats del Pacífico*. Cali: Universidad del Valle, 1993.

Aprile-Gniset, Jacques, and Gilma Mosquera. *Habitats y sociedades del Pacífico Vol. 1: La Bahía de Solano*. Cali: Universidad del Valle, 2001.

Arbeláez, Gustavo. *Monografías mineras, Aluviones en zonas auríferas del Telembí y el San Juan*. Bogotá: Editorial de la Litografía Colombia, 1940.

Arboleda, Juan Ignacio. "Entre la libertad y la sumisión. Estrategias de liberación de los esclavos en la gobernación de Popayán durante la Independencia, 1808–1830." Documento CESO No. 10, Facultad de Ciencias Sociales, Universidad de Los Andes, 2006.

Aristizábal, Margarita. "El festival del currulao." In *Modernidad, identidad y desarrollo, Construcción de sociedad y re-creación cultural en contextos de modernización*, ed. María Lucía Sotomayor. Bogotá: Instituto Colombiano de Antropología, Ministerio de Cultura, Colciencias, 1998.

Arnold, David. "'Illusory Riches': Representations of the Tropical World, 1840–1950." *Singapore Journal of Tropical Geography* 21, no. 1 (March 2000): 6–18.

———. *The Problem of Nature: Environment, Culture, and European Expansion*. Cambridge: Blackwell, 1996.

Asher, Kiran. *Black and Green: Afro-Colombians, Development, and Nature in the Pacific Lowlands*. Durham: Duke University Press, 2009.

Aubert de la Rue, Edgard, and Edmond Bruet. "La hoya del río Naya." *Revista de la Universidad del Cauca*, no. 1 (1943): 137—60.

Banton, Michael. *Racial Theories*. Cambridge: Cambridge University Press, 1988.

Barfod, Anders S. "A Monographic Study of the Subfamily Phytelephantoideae (Araceae)." *Opera Botanica* 105 (1991).

Barfod, Anders S. "Usos pasados, presentes y futuros de las palmas Phytelephantoidées (Araceae)." In *Las plantas y el hombre, Memorias del Primer Simposio Ecuatoriano de Etnobotánica y Botánica Económica*, ed. Monserrat Ríos and Henrik Borgtoft. Quito: Ediciones ABYA-YALA, 1991.

Barfod, Anders S., B. Bergmann, and H. Pedersen. "The Vegetable Ivory Industry: Surviving and Doing Well in Ecuador." *Economic Botany* 44, no. 3 (July–September 1990): 293–300.

Barham, Bradford L., and Oliver Coomes. *Prosperity's Promise: The Amazon Rubber Boom and Distorted Economic Development*. Boulder: Westview Press, 1996.

Barona, Guido. *La maldición de Midas en una región del mundo colonial, Popayán 1730–1830*. Cali: Universidad del Valle, 1995.

Barona, Guido, Camilo Domínguez, Augusto Gómez, and Apolinar Figueroa, eds. *Geografía Física y Política de la Confederación Granadina. Vol.1: Estado del Cauca. Tomo II: Provincias de Chocó, Buenaventura, Cauca y Popayán. Obra dirigida por el General Agustín Codazzi*. Popayán: Universidad del Cauca, 2002.

Bauer, Arnold J. "Rural Workers in Spanish America: Problems of Peonage and Oppression." *Hispanic American Historical Review* 59, no. 1 (February 1979): 34–63.

Baulkwill, W. J. "A History of Natural Rubber Production." In *Rubber*, ed. C. C. Webster and W. J. Baulkwill, 1–56. Essex: Longman Scientific & Technical, 1989.

Bebbington, Anthony, ed. *Social Conflict, Economic Development and Extractive Industry: Evidence from South America*. London: Routledge, 2012.

Berg, C. C. "Olmedieae, Brosimeae (Moraceae)." *Flora Neotropica* 7 (July 1972): 1–228.

Bernal, Rodrigo. "The Growth of *Phytelephas seemannii*—a Potentially Immortal Solitary Palm." *Principes* 42, no. 1 (1998): 15–23.

Besson, Jean. "Freedom and Community: The British West Indies." In *The Meaning of Freedom: Economics, Politics, and Culture after Slavery*, ed. Frank McGlynn and Seymour Drescher. Pittsburgh: University of Pittsburgh Press, 1992.

Blanchard, Peter. "The Slave Soldiers of Spanish South America: From Independence to Abolition." In *Arming Slaves: From Classical Times to the Modern Age*, ed. Christopher Leslie Brown and Philip D. Morgan, 255–73. New Haven: Yale University Press, 2006.

Bloch, Hans. "La colonización del Chocó desde el Valle del Cauca." *Boletín de la Sociedad Geográfica de Colombia* 8, no. 1 (1948): 40–42.

Bolland, O. Nigel. *Colonialism and Resistance in Belize: Essays in Historical Sociology*. Benque Viejo del Carmen: Cubola Productions, 2003 [1988].

Bonet, Jaime. "¿Por qué es pobre el Chocó?," *Documentos de Trabajo sobre Economía Regional* 90, April 2007.

Borgtoft Pedersen, Henrik. "Ivory Nuts, Fruits and Thatch: Use and Management of *Phytelephas aequatorialis* (palmae) in Ecuador." Unpublished: n.d., 25 p.

Botero, María Mercedes. *La ruta del oro. Una economía primaria exportadora, Antioquia, 1850–1890*. Medellín: Fondo Editorial Universidad Eafit, 2007.

Botero Villa, Juan José. *Adjudicación, explotación y comercialización de baldíos y bosques nacionales. Evolución histórico-legislativa, 1830–1930*. Bogotá: Banco de la República, 1994.

Bourgeois, Philippe I. *Ethnicity at Work: Divided Labor on a Central American Banana Plantation*. Baltimore: The Johns Hopkins University Press, 1989.

Boyer, Christopher. *Political Landscapes: Forests, Communities, and Conservation in Mexico*. Durham: Duke University Press, 2015.

Brannstrom, Christian, and Stefania Gallini. "An Introduction to Latin American Environmental History." In *Territories, Commodities, and Knowledges: Latin American Environmental History in the Nineteenth and Twentieth Century*, ed. Christian Brannstrom, 1–20. London: Institute of Latin American Studies, 2004.

Bravo Pazmiño, Hernando. "Mineros negros de La Aurora: la creatividad y la supervivencia. Caserío La Aurora, municipio Payán, Nariño." BA thesis, Universidad Nacional de Colombia, 1991.

Brew, Roger. *El desarrollo económico de Antioquia desde la Independencia hasta 1920*. Medellín: Universidad de Antioquia, 2000 [1977].

Bryant, Sherwin. *Rivers of Gold, Lives of Bondage: Governing through Slavery in Colonial Quito*. Chapel Hill: University of North Carolina Press, 2014.

Bucheli, Marcelo. *Bananas and Business: The United Fruit Company in Colombia, 1899–2000*. New York: New York University Press, 2005.

Bunker, Stephen G. "Modes of Extraction, Unequal Exchange, and Progressive Underdevelopment on an Extreme Periphery: The Brazilian Amazon, 1600–1980." *American Journal of Sociology* 89, no. 5 (March 1984): 1017–64.

———. *Underdeveloping the Amazon: Extraction, Unequal Exchange, and the Failure of the Modern State*. Champaign: University of Illinois Press, 1985.

Bushnell, David. *The Making of Modern Colombia: A Nation in Spite of Itself*. Berkeley: University of California Press, 1993.

Butler, Kim D. *Freedoms Given, Freedoms Won: Afro-Brazilians in Post-Abolition Sao Paulo and Salvador*. New Brunswick: Rutgers University Press, 2000.

Cantarino O'Dwyer, Eliane. "Os quilombos do Trombetas e do Erepecuru-Cuminá." In *Quilombos, identidade étnica e territorialidade*, organized by Eliane Cantarino O'Dwyer. Rio de Janeiro: Editora FGV, 2001.

Cantarino O'Dwyer, Eliane, and José Paulo Freire de Carvalho. "Jamary dos Pretos, municipio de Turiaçu (MA)." In *Quilombos, identidade étnica e territorialidade*, organized by Eliane Cantarino O'Dwyer. Rio de Janeiro: Editora FGV, 2001.

Cantor, Eric Werner. *Ni aniquilados ni vencidos. Los Emberá y la gente negra del Atrato bajo el dominio español. Siglo XVIII*. Bogotá: Instituto Colombiano de Antropología e Historia, 2000.

Cárdenas, Martha, and Manuel Rodríguez Becerra, eds. *Guerra, sociedad y medio ambiente*. Bogotá: Foro Nacional Ambiental, 2004.

Carey, Mark. "Latin American Environmental History: Current Trends, Interdisciplinary Insights, and Future Directions." *Environmental History* 14, no. 2 (April 2009): 221–52.

Chayanov, Alexander V. *The Theory of Peasant Economy*, ed. Daniel Thorner, Basile Kerblay, and R. E. F. Smith. Homewood, Ill: Irwin, Inc., 1966 [1925].

Chiriboga, Manuel. *Jornaleros y gran propietarios en 135 años de exportación cacaotera (1790–1925)*. Quito: edición auspiciada por el Consejo Provincial de Pichincha, 1980.

Christie, Keith. "Antioqueño Colonization in Western Colombia: A Reappraisal." *Hispanic American Historical Review* 58, no. 2 (May 1978): 260–83.

Claès, F. "Quelques données utiles sur le Phytelephas macrocarpa Ruiz et Pav." *L'Agronomie Coloniale* 13 (1925): 291–94.

Clare, Patricia. "Un balance de la historia ambiental latinoamericana." *Revista de Historia* 59–60 (January–December 2009): 185–201.

Cleary, David. "Towards an Environmental History of the Amazon: From Prehistory to the Nineteenth Century." *Latin American Research Review* 36, no. 2 (2001): 64–96.

Colmenares, Germán. *Cali: Terratenientes, mineros y comerciantes, siglo XVIII*. Cali: Universidad del Valle, 1975.

———. "La economía y la sociedad coloniales, 1550–1800." In *Nueva Historia de Colombia*, Tomo 1. Bogotá: Planeta, 1989.

———. "La formación de la economía colonial, 1500–1740." In *Historia económica de Colombia*, ed. José Antonio Ocampo, 13–47. Bogotá: Siglo XXI, 1987.

———. *Historia económica y social de Colombia, Tomo II: Popayán, una sociedad esclavista, 1680–1800*. Medellín: La Carreta, 1979.

———. "¿Si será verdad tanta igualdad?" *Boletín Cultural y Bibliográfico* 22, no. 4 (1985): 89–91.

Contraloría General de la República. *Geografía Económica de Colombia, Tomo VI: Chocó*. Bogotá: Litografía Colombia, 1943.

Cook, O. F. *The Culture of the Central American Rubber Tree*. Bureau of Plant Industry, Bulletin No. 49. Washington, D.C.: Government Printing Office, 1903.

———. "Ivory Palms in Panamá." *Journal of the Washington Academy of Sciences* 3, no. 5 (1913): 138–43.

———. "New Genera-Species of Ivory Palms from Colombia, Ecuador and Peru." *Journal of the Washington Academy of Sciences* 17 (1927): 218–30.

———. "The Relationships of Ivory Palms." *Contributions from the US National Herbarium* 13, no. 5 (1910): 133–41.

Coquery-Vidrovitch, Catherine. *Le Congo au temps des grandes compagnies concessionnaires, 1898–1930*. Paris: Mouton & Co., 1972.

Corporación Araracuara. *Colonización del bosque húmedo tropical.* Bogotá: Corporación Araracuara, 1991.

Correa González, Claudia María. "Integración socio-económica del manumiso caucano, 1850–1900." BA thesis, Universidad de los Andes, 1987.

Cosgrove, Denis. "New Directions in Cultural Geography." *Area* 19, no. 2 (June 1987): 95–101.

Cronon, William. *Nature's Metropolis: Chicago and the Great West.* New York: W. W. Norton, 1991.

Dalling, J. W., K. E. Harms, J. R. Eberhard, and I. Candanedo. "Natural History and Uses of Tagua (Phytelephas seemannii) in Panama." *Principes* 40, no. 1 (1996): 16–23.

Dantas, Mariana. *Black Townsmen: Urban Slavery and Freedom in the Eighteenth-Century Americas.* New York: Palgrave Macmillan, 2008.

Dávila, Jerry. *Diploma of Whiteness: Race and Social Policy in Brazil, 1917–1945.* Durham: Duke University Press, 2003.

Day, David T. "Platinum." *Mining Resources of the U. S.* (1906): 551–59.

De Granda, Germán. *Estudios sobre un área dialectal hispanoamericana de población negra, las tierras bajas occidentales de Colombia.* Bogotá: Instituto Caro y Cuervo, 1977.

———. "Onomástica y procedencia africana de esclavos negros en las minas del sur de la gobernación de Popayán, siglo XVIII." *Revista Española de Antropología Americana* 6 (1971): 393–421.

De Groot, Silvia W. *From Isolation towards Integration: The Surinam Maroons and Their Colonial Rulers, 1845–1863.* La Haya: Nijhoff, 1977 [1963].

De Souza, Sônia Maria. *Terra Família e Solidariedade: estratégias de convivência camponesa no período de transição—Juiz de Fora (1870–1920).* Bauru: Edusc, 2007.

Dean, Warren. *Brazil and the Struggle for Rubber.* Cambridge: Cambridge University Press, 1987.

———. *With Broadax and Firebrand: The Destruction of the Brazilian Atlantic Forest.* Berkeley: University of California Press, 1997.

Departamento Administrativo Nacional de Estadística (DANE). *Colombia, una nación multicultural: Su diversidad étnica.* Bogotá: DANE, 2007.

Díaz, Rafael Antonio. *Esclavitud, región y ciudad. El sistema esclavista urbano-regional en Santafé de Bogotá, 1700–1750.* Bogotá: CEJA, 2001.

Díaz, Zamira. *Oro, sociedad y economía. El sistema colonial en la gobernación de Popayán: 1533–1733.* Bogotá: Banco de la República, 1994.

Domínguez, Camilo, and Augusto Gómez. *La economía extractiva en la Amazonía colombiana*. Bogotá: Tropenbos-Araracuara, 1990.

Dumett, Raymond. "The Rubber Trade of the Gold Coast and Asante in the Nineteenth Century: African Innovation and Market Responsiveness." *Journal of African History* 12, no. 1 (January 1971): 79–101.

Duncan, James, and Nancy Duncan. "(Re)reading the Landscape." *Environment and Planning D: Society and Space* 6, no. 2 (June 1988): 117–26.

Echeverri, Marcela. "'Enraged to the Limit of Despair': Infanticide and Slave Judicial Strategies in Barbacoas, 1789–1798." *Slavery & Abolition* 30, no. 3 (2009): 403–26.

———. *Indian and Slave Royalists in the Age of Revolution: Reform, Revolution, and Royalism in the Northern Andes, 1780–1820*. Cambridge: Cambridge University Press, 2016.

———. "Popular Royalists, Empire, and Politics in Southwestern New Granada, 1809–1819." *Hispanic American Historical Review* 91, no. 2 (May 2011): 237–69.

Echeverry Lozano, José María. "Consideraciones raciales acerca del Chocó." *Estudios de derecho* 2 (1942): 297–305.

Escalante, Aquiles. *La minería del hambre, Condoto y la Chocó Pacífico*. Barranquilla: Tipografía Dovel, 1971.

Escobar, Arturo. *Territories of Difference: Place, Movements, Life, Redes*. Durham: Duke University Press, 2008.

Escobar, Paulo Emilio. *Bahías de Málaga y Buenaventura, la costa colombiana del Pacífico, 1918–1920*. Bogotá: Imprenta Nacional, 1921.

Eslava, Jesús. "Climatología." In *Colombia Pacífico*, Tomo I. Bogotá: Proyecto Biopacífico, Fondo FEN, 1993.

Evans, Sterling. *Bound in Twine: The History and Ecology of the Henequen-Wheat Complex for Mexico and the American and Canadian Plains, 1880–1950*. College Station: Texas A&M University Press, 2007.

Ewans, Martin. *European Atrocity, African Catastrophe: Leopold II, the Congo Free State and Its Aftermath*. London: Routledge Curzon, 2002.

Fals Borda, Orlando. *Historia doble de la Costa, Tomo 3: Resistencia en el San Jorge*. Bogotá: Carlos Valencia Editores, 1986.

———. *Historia doble de la Costa, Tomo 4: Retorno a la tierra*. Bogotá: Carlos Valencia Editores, 1986.

Farnhamn, Timothy. *Saving Nature's Legacy: Origins of the Idea of Biological Diversity*. New Haven: Yale University Press, 2007.

Fawcett de Posada, Louise. *Libaneses, palestinos y sirios en Colombia*, Documentos CERES No. 9. Barranquilla: Centro de Estudios Regionales, Universidad del Norte, 1991.

Fawcett de Posada, Louise, and Eduardo Posada Carbó. "En tierra de oportunidades: los sirio-libaneses en Colombia." *Boletín Cultural y Bibliográfico* 29, no. 29 (1992): 3–21.

Fernández, Alcides. *Carabelas y alcatraces*. Medellín: Especial Editores, 1991.

Figueroa, Luis A. *Sugar, Slavery and Freedom in Nineteenth-Century Puerto Rico*. Chapel Hill: The University of North Carolina Press, 2005.

Flórez López, Jesús Alfonso. *Autonomía indígena en Chocó*. Quibdó: Centro de Estudios Etnicos, 2007.

Forero, Enrique, and Alwyn Gentry. *Lista anotada de las plantas del departamento del Chocó*. Bogotá: Universidad Nacional, 1989.

Frenkel, Stephen. "Jungle Stories: North American Representations of Tropical Panama." *The Geographical Review* 86, no. 3 (July 1996): 317–33.

Friedemann, Nina S. de. "Estudios de negros en la antropología colombiana: presencia e invisibilidad." In *Un siglo de investigación social: antropología en Colombia*, ed. Jaime Arocha and Nina S. de Friedemann. Bogotá: Etno, 1984.

———. "Güelmambí: Formas económicas y organización social." *Revista Colombiana de Antropología* 14 (1969): 55–70.

———. "Minería de Oro y Descendencia: Güelmambí, Nariño." *Revista Colombiana de Antropología* 16 (1974): 10–52.

Fundación Inguedé. "Memorias del taller sobre planes de desarrollo de la cuenca del Pacífico y el proyecto Productos del Bosque, El Valle, octubre de 1991." Unpublished (1991).

Funes, Eurípides A. "'Nasci nas matas, nunca tive senhor'—História e memoria dos mocambos do baixo Amazonas." PhD diss., Universidade de São Paulo, 1995.

Funes Monzote, Reinaldo. *From Rainforest to Cane Field in Cuba: An Environmental History since 1492*. Chapel Hill: University of North Carolina Press, 2008 [2004].

Gallini, Stefania. "Historia, ambiente y política: el camino de la historia ambiental en América Latina." *Nómadas* 30 (April 2009): 92–102.

Gamboa, Jorge. "La política de baldíos en el Chocó durante la segunda mitad del siglo XIX." In *Construcción territorial en el Chocó, Vol.1: Historias regionales*, ed. Patricia Vargas, 127–58. Bogotá: ICAN-PNR-Obapo, 1999.

García Estrada, Rodrigo. "El Consorcio Albingia en los inicios de la explotación bananera en Urabá 1909–1915." *Revista Augura* 18, no. 1 (1995): 74–97.

García Márquez, Gabriel, "La riqueza inútil del platino colombiano." *El Espectador*, October, 1954.

García Vega, Eduardo, and Jaime Echavarría. *Mutis y Bahía Solano, 50 años*. Quibdó: Universidad Tecnológica del Chocó, 1984.

Garrido, Margarita. "'Free men of all colors' in New Granada: Identity and Obedience before Independence." In *Political Cultures in the Andes (1750–1950)*, ed. Nils Jacobsen and Cristóbal Aljovín de Losada, 165–83. Durham: Duke University Press, 2005.

Gentry, Alwyn. "Sabemos más de la luna que del Chocó." *Eco-Lógica* 15–16 (1993): 56–59.

———. "Species Richness and Floristic Composition of the Choco Region Plant Communities." *Caldasia* 15 (1986): 71–91.

Giltner, Scott E. *Hunting and Fishing in the New South: Black Labor and White Leisure after the Civil War*. Baltimore: John Hopkins University Press, 2008.

Göbel, Barbara, and Astrid Ulloa, eds. *Extractivismo minero en Colombia y América Latina*. Bogotá and Berlin: Universidad Nacional de Colombia and Ibero-Amerikanisches Institut, 2014.

Gomes dos Santos, Flávio. "Fronteiras e mocambos: o protesto negro na Guiana brasileira." In *Nas terras do Cabo Norte. Fronteiras, colonização e escravidão na Guiana brasileira, séculos XVIII/XIX*, organized by Flávio Gomes dos Santos. Belém: Editora Universitária UFPA, 1999.

———. "A 'safe haven': Runaways, Slaves, Mocambos, and Borders in Colonial Amazônia, Brazil." *The Hispanic American Historical Review* 82, no. 3 (August 2002): 469–98.

Gomes dos Santos, Flávio, and Olívia Gomes da Cunha, eds. *Quase-Cidadão: histórias e antropologias da pós-emancipação no Brasil*. Rio de Janeiro: Fundação Getulio Vargas, 2007.

González, Father Jairo. *Juradó*. (n.d.).

González, Luis Fernando. "Cartografía histórica del Chocó." *Boletín Cultural y Bibliográfico* 33, no. 43 (1996): 112–42.

———. "Ocupación, poblamiento y transformación ambiental del Darién, una revisión histórica." In *Evaluación integral del Darién colombiano*. CD-ROM, Fundación Natura, Universidad Nacional de Colombia, Universidad de Antioquia, 2000.

———. *Quibdó, Contexto histórico, desarrollo urbano y patrimonio arquitectónico*. Medellín: Instituto de Investigaciones Ambientales del Pacífico, 2003.

———. "Sirio-libaneses en el Chocó, cien años de presencia económica y cultural." *Boletín Cultural y Bibliográfico* 34, no. 44 (1997): 72–101.

González Henriquez, Adolfo. "La música costeña colombiana en la tercera década del siglo XIX." *Latin American Music Review* 9, no. 2 (Fall-Winter 1988): 187–206.

Groth, Paul. "Frameworks of Cultural Landscape Study." In *Understanding Ordinary Landscapes*, ed. Paul Groth and Todd W. Bressi. New Haven: Yale University Press, 1997.

Guerrero, L. M. "Un gran establecimiento industrial en el Chocó." *Mundo al Día* (n.d., 1924?).

Guha, Ramachandra. *The Unquiet Woods: Ecological Change and Peasant Resistance in the Himalaya*, rev. ed. Berkeley: University of California Press, 2000 [1989].

Guimarães, Elione. *Terra de preto, usos e ocupação da terra por escravos e libertos (Vale do Paraíba meneiro, 1850–1920)*. Niterói: Editora da UFF, 2009.

Hall, Douglas. *Free Jamaica, 1838–1865*. New Haven: Yale University Press, 1959.

Harms, Robert. "The End of Red Rubber: A Reassessment." *Journal of African History* 16, no. 1 (January 1975): 73–88.

Hassen, Caroline. "La rebelión de los citaráes en el Chocó, 1684–1685." In *Colombia Pacífico, Tomo I*. Bogotá: Proyecto Biopacífico-Fondo FEN, 1993.

Haynor, Genevieve M. "The History of Gold Dredging in California, 1848–1940." MA thesis, University of California, Berkeley, 1941.

Hecht, Susanna, and Alexander Cockburn. *The Fate of the Forest: Developers, Destroyers and Defenders of the Amazon*. New York: Verso, 1989.

Hernández Salgar, Oscar. "De currulaos modernos y ollas podridas." In *Músicas y prácticas sonoras en el Pacífico afrocolombiano*, ed. Juan Sebastián Ochoa Escobar, Carolina Santamaría Delgado, and Manuel Sevilla Peñuela. Bogotá: Editorial Pontificia Universidad Javeriana, 2010.

Herrera, Marta. *El conquistador conquistado. Awás, Quayquer y Sindaguas en el Pacífico colombiano, siglos XVI–XVIII*. Bogotá: Ediciones Uniandes, 2016.

———. "En un rincón de ese imperio en que no se ocultaba el sol: Colonialismo, oro y terror en Barbacoas, siglo XVIII." *Anuario Colombiano de Historia Social y de la Cultura* 32 (2005): 31–49.

Higgins, Kathleen J. *'Licentious Liberty' in a Brazilian Gold-Mining Region: Slavery, Gender, and Social Control in Eighteenth-Century Sabará, Minas Gerais.* University Park: Penn State University Press, 1999.

Hoffmann, Odile. *Comunidades negras en el Pacífico colombiano: Innovaciones y dinámicas étnicas.* Quito: Instituto Francés de Estudios Andinos, Institut de Recherche pour le Dévelopment, Ediciones Abya-Yala, Centro de Investigaciones y Estudios Superiores en Antropología Social, Centro de Estudios Mexicanos y Centroamericanos, 2007. Published in French as *Communautés noires du Pacifique colombien, innovations et dynamiques ethniques.* Paris: Karthala-IRD, 2004.

Isacsson, Sven-Erik. "The Egalitarian Society in Retrospect: Emberá Leadership and Conflict Management under the Spanish, 1660–1810." In *Natives and Neighbors in South America: Anthropological Essays,* ed. H. O. Skar and F. Salomon, 97–129. Gothenburg: Götenborgs Etnografiska Museum, 1987.

———. "Emberá: Territorio y régimen agrario de una tribu selvática bajo la dominación española." In *Tierra, tradición y poder en Colombia. Enfoques antropológicos,* ed. Nina S. de Friedemann, 13–38. Bogotá: Colcultura, 1976.

———. "Indios cimarrones del Chocó (Colombia): Tradiciones y documentación histórica de los emberá desde la Colonia." In *Ethnographical Museum, Gothemburg, Sweden, Annual Report fot 1973,* ed. Kjell Zetterström. Kungsbacka: Elanders Boktryckeri Aktiebolag, 1974.

Jackson, John P., Jr., and Nadine Weidman. *Race, Racism, and Science: Social Impact and Interaction.* New Brunswick: Rutgers University Press, 2006.

Jaramillo Uribe, Jaime. "La controversia jurídica y filosófica librada en la Nueva Granada en torno a la liberación de los esclavos y la importancia económica y social de la esclavitud en el siglo XIX." In *Ensayos de historia social, Tomo I: La sociedad neogranadina.* Bogotá: Tercer Mundo-Uniandes, 1989.

———. "Mestizaje y diferenciación social en el Nuevo Reino de Granada en la segunda mitad del siglo XVIII." *Anuario Colombiano de Historia Social y de la Cultura* 3 (1965): 21–48.

Jiménez, Orián. "El Chocó: Libertad y poblamiento, 1750–1850." In *Afrodescendientes de las Américas, trayectorias sociales e identitarias,* ed. Claudia Mosquera, Mauricio Pardo, and Odile Hoffman. Bogotá: Universidad Nacional de Colombia, Instituto Colombiano de Antropología e Historia, Institut de la Recherche pour le Dévelopment, Instituto Latinoamericano de Servicios Legales Alternativos, 2002.

———. "El Chocó: Un paraíso del demonio." Paper presented at the 2003 meeting of the Latin American Studies Association, Dallas, Texas, March 27–29 (2003).

———. *El Chocó: Un paraíso del demonio. Nóvita, Citará y el Baudó, siglo XVIII.* Medellín: Universidad Nacional de Colombia, 2004.

Jiménez, Víctor. "Guaitadó: Una comunidad minera del río Atrato." BA thesis, Universidad de Los Andes, 1982.

Johns, Michael. *The City of Mexico in the Age of Díaz*. Austin: University of Texas Press, 1998.

Klein, Herbert, and Ben Vinson III. *African Slavery in Latin America and the Caribbean*. New York: Oxford University Press, 2007.

Klein, Herbert, and Francisco Vidal Luna. *Slavery in Brazil*. New York: Cambridge University Press, 2010.

Klubock, Thomas Miller. *La Frontera: Forests and Ecological Conflict in Chile's Frontier Territory*. Durham: Duke University Press, 2014.

Knight, Alan. *Interpreting the Mexican Revolution*. Austin: University of Texas Press, 1988.

———. "Mexican Peonage: What Was It and Why Was It?" *Journal of Latin American Studies* 18, no. 1 (May 1986): 41–74.

Konrad, Herman W. "Capitalism in the Tropical Forest Frontier, Quintana Roo, 1880–1930." In *Land, Labor, and Capital in Modern Yucatán*, ed. Jeffery T. Brannon and Gilbert M. Joseph, 143–71. Tuscaloosa: University of Alabama Press, 1991.

Kopytoff, Barbara. "Early Political Development of Jamaican Maroon Societies." *William & Mary Quarterly* 35, no. 2 (April 1978): 287–307.

Kricher, John. *A Neotropical Companion: An Introduction to the Animals, Plants, and Ecosystems of the New World Tropics*. Princeton: Princeton University Press, 1999.

LaCerte, Robert K. "The Evolution of Land and Labour in the Haitian Revolution, 1791–1820." In *Caribbean Freedom: Economy and Society from Emancipation to the Present*, ed. Hilary Beckles and Verene Shepher, 42–47. Princeton: Markus Wiener Publishers, 1996.

Lane, Kris. "Gone Platinum: Contraband and Chemistry in Eighteenth-Century Colombia." *Colonial Latin American Review* 20, no. 1 (2011): 61–79.

———. "Mining the Margins: Precious Metals Extraction and Forced Labor Regimes in the Audiencia of Quito, 1534–1821." PhD diss., University of Minnesota, 1996.

———. "Taming the Master: Brujeria, Slavery, and the Encomienda in Barbacoas at the Turn of the Eighteenth Century." *Ethnohistory*, 45, no. 3 (1998): 477–507.

———. "The Transition from Encomienda to Slavery in Seventeenth-Century Barbacoas (Colombia)." *Slavery & Abolition* 21, no. 1 (2000): 73–95.

LaRosa, Michael J., and Germán Mejía. *Colombia: A Concise Contemporary History*. Rowman & Littlefield, 2012.

Leal, Bernardo. "'Matar a los blancos bueno es, luego el Chocó acabará.' Cimarronaje de esclavos jamaiquinos en el Chocó." *Fronteras de la Historia* 2 (1998): 143–61.

———. "Paulina Montaño demanda su libertad. Aproximación a una etnografía performativa de un pleito judicial, Chocó, 1838." *Revista Colombiana de Antropología* 46, no. 2 (2010): 409–33.

———. "Pido se me ampare en mi libertad: Esclavizados, manumisos y rebeldes en el Chocó (1710–1810) bajo la lente colonial contemporánea." MA diss., Universidad Nacional de Colombia, 2006.

Leal, Claudia. *A la Buena de Dios, Colonización en La Macarena, ríos Duda y Guayabero*. Bogotá: CEREC-FESCOL, 1995.

———. "La Compañía Minera Chocó Pacífico y el auge del platino en Colombia, 1897–1930." Special issue, *Historia Crítica* (November 2009): 150–64.

———. "Conservation Memories: Vicissitudes of a Biodiversity Conservation Project in the Rainforests of Colombia, 1992–1998." *Environmental History* 20, no. 3 (July 2015): 368–95.

———, ed. *Economía de las comunidades rurales del Pacífico colombiano*. Bogotá: Proyecto Biopacífico, 1995.

———. "From Threatening to Threatened Jungles." In *A Living Past: Environmental Histories of Modern Latin America*, ed. John Soluri, Claudia Leal, and José Augusto Pádua. New York: Berghahn Books, forthcoming.

———. "Manglares y economía extractiva." In *Geografía humana de Colombia, Tomo VI: Los Afrocolombianos*, ed. Adriana Maya, 397–429. Bogotá: Instituto Colombiano de Cultura Hispánica, 1998.

———. "Música, Raza y región. El currulao del Pacífico sur colombiano." In *Chile-Colombia: Diálogos sobre sus trayectorias históricas*, ed. Fernando Purcell and Ricardo Arias. Bogotá and Santiago: Ediciones Uniandes, Editorial Universidad Católica de Chile, 2014.

———. "Recordando a Saturio. Memorias del racismo en Chocó, Colombia." In *Revista de Estudios Sociales* 27 (August 2007): 76–93.

———. "Usos del concepto raza en Colombia." In *Debates sobre ciudadanía y políticas raciales en las Américas negras*, ed. Claudia Mosquera Rosero-Labbé, Agustín Laó-Montes, and César Rodríguez, 393–442. Bogotá: Universidad Nacional de Colombia, sede Bogotá, CES, IDCARAN, sede Medellín, Universidad de los Andes, 2010.

Leal, Claudia, and Eduardo Restrepo. *Unos bosques sembrados de aserríos*. Medellín: Universidad de Antioquia, 2003.

LeGrand, Catherine. *Frontier Expansion and Peasant Protest in Colombia, 1850–1936*. Albuquerque: University of New Mexico Press, 1986.

Losonczy, Anne-Marie. "'Sentirse negro' Empreintes du passé et mémoire collective au Chocó." *Annales. Histoire, Sciences Sociales* 3 (2004): 589–611.

———. *La Trama interétnica. Ritual, sociedad y figuras de intercambio entre los grupos negros y Emberá del Chocó*. Bogotá: Enstituto Colombiano de Antropología e Historia, Instituto Francés de Estudios Andinos, 2006.

Machado, Absalón. "La agricultura del litoral Pacífico." In *Colombia Pacífico*. Bogotá: Proyecto Biopacífico, Fondo FEN, 1993.

Marshall, Woodville K. "Peasant Development in the West Indies since 1838." In *Caribbean Freedom: Economy and Society from Emancipation to the Present*, ed. Hilary Beckles and Verene Shepher, 99–106. Princeton: Markus Wiener Publishers, 1996.

Martínez, Sandra Patricia. "La construcción cotidiana del estado: el proceso de titulación colectiva a las comunidades negras del pacífico colombiano." PhD diss., Universidad Iberoamericana de México, 2010.

Mattos de Castro, Hebe Maria. "Beyond Masters and Slaves: Subsistence Agriculture as a Survival Strategy in Brazil during the Second Half of the Nineteenth Century." *Hispanic American Historical Review* 68, no. 3 (August 1988): 461–89.

———. "Para além das senzalas campesinato, política e trabalho rural no Rio de Janeiro pós-Abolição." In *Quase-Cidadão: histórias e antropologias da pós-emancipação no Brasil*, ed. Flávio dos Santos Gomes and Olívia Gomes da Cunha. Rio de Janeiro: FGV, 2007.

———. *Ao Sul da História: Lavradores pobres na crise do trabalho escravos*. Rio de Janeiro: Universidade Federal Fluminense, 2009 [1987].

Mattos de Castro, Hebe Maria, and Ana Lugão Rios. "O pós-aboliçao como problema histórico: balanços e perspectivas." *Topoi* 5, no. 8 (2004): 170–98.

McCook, Stuart. "Las epidemias liberales: Agricultura, ambiente y glocalización en Ecuador (1790–1930)." In *Estudios sobre historia y ambiente en América Latina II: Norteamérica, Sudamérica y el Pacífico*, ed. Bernardo García Martínez and María del Rosario Prieto. México: El Colegio de México, Instituto Panamericano de Geografía e Historia, 2002.

McFarlane, Anthony. *Colombia before Independence: Economy, Society, and Politics under Bourbon Rule*. New York: Cambridge University Press, 1993.

McGeorge, J. H. W. *Dredging for Gold: The History of Two Successful but Contrasting Enterprises*. Melbourne: N.R., 1964.

McGraw, Jason. *The Work of Recognition: Caribbean Colombia and the Postemancipation Struggle for Citizenship*. Chapel Hill: University of North Carolina Press, 2014.

McNeill, John R. "The State of the Field of Environmental History." *Annual Review of Environment and Resources* 35 (November 2010): 345–74.

Mejía, Eduardo. *Campesinos, poblamiento y conflicto: Valle del Cauca 1800–1848*. Cali: Universidad del Valle, 2002.

———. *Origen del Campesino Vallecaucano, siglos XVIII y XIX*. Cali: Universidad del Valle, 1993.

Mejía, Mario. "La agricultura alternativa." In *Colombia Pacífico*, Tomo II, ed. Pablo Leyva, 656–67. Bogotá: Proyecto Biopacífico-FEN, 1993.

Mejía Pavony, Germán. *Los años del cambio: historia urbana de Bogotá, 1820–1910*. Bogotá: CEJA, 1999.

Melo, Jorge Orlando. "La evolución económica de Colombia, 1830–1900." In *Nueva Historia de Colombia*, Tomo 1. Bogotá: Editorial Planeta, 1989.

———. "Producción minera y crecimiento económico en la Nueva Granada durante el siglo XVIII." *Revista Universidad del Valle* 3–4 (1979): 29–46. Retrieved from http://www.jorgeorlandomelo.com/historia.htm as "Producción de oro y desarrollo económico en el siglo XVIII."

Melosi, Martin. "Mainstreaming Environmental History." *RCC Perspectives*, no. 3 (2011): 31–33.

Mena, Luz. "The Spaces and Faces of Music and Dance in Early Modern Havana." Departmental Colloquium, Department of Geography, University of California, Berkeley, February 4, 2004.

———. "Stretching the Limits of Gendered Spaces: Black and Mulatto Women in 1830s Havana." *Cuban Studies* 36 (December 2005): 87–104.

Mena de Perea, Mirza, Beatriz Gil Ibargüen, and Beatriz López de Ortega. *Anotaciones socioculturales sobre el departamento del Chocó*. Medellín: Editorial Lealón, 1994.

Meyer, Andrew. "In the Choco Colombia." *Engineering and Mining Journal* 142 (1941): 35–39.

Mikesell, Marvin, and Philip Wagner. "The Themes of Cultural Geography." In *Readings in Cultural Geography*, ed. Marvin Mikesell and Philip Wagner. Chicago: University of Chicago Press, 1962.

Millán Echavarría, Constanza, et al. Coordinadora de la investigación. *Buenaventura: un puerto sin comunidad*. Bogotá: Centro de Memoria Histórica, 2015.

Mina, Mateo. *Esclavitud y libertad en el valle del río Cauca*. Bogotá: Fundación Rosca de Investigación y Acción Social, 1975.

Minaudier, Jean-Pierre. "Une région minière de la colonie à l'indépendance: Barbacoas 1750–1830 (Economie, société, vie politique locale)." *Bulletin de l'Institut Français d'Etudes Andines* 17, no. 2 (1988): 81–104.

Mintz, Sydney. *Caribbean Transformations*. Chicago: Aldine Publishing Company, 1974.

———. "The Origins of Reconstituted Peasantries." In *Caribbean Freedom: Economy and Society from Emancipation to the Present*, ed. Hilary Beckles and Verene Shepher, 94–98. Princeton: Markus Wiener Publishers, 1996.

———. "Slavery and the Rise of Peasantries." In *Roots and Branches: Current Directions in Slave Studies*, ed. Michel Craton, 213–42. Toronto: Pergamon Press, 1979.

Mitchell, Don. "Landscape." In *Cultural Geography: A Critical Dictionary of Key Concepts*, ed. David Atkinson, Peter Jackson, David Sibley, and Neil Washbourne, 49–56. New York: Palgrave Macmillan, 2005.

Molano, Alfredo. *Siguiendo el corte: relatos de guerras y tierras*. Bogotá, Alfaguara, 2006 [1989].

Molina Londoño, Luis Fernando. "'El viejo Mainero': Actividad empresarial de Juan Bautista Mainero y Trucco en Bolívar, Chocó, Antioquia y Cundinamarca, 1860–1918." *Boletín Cultural y Bibliográfico* 25, no. 17 (1988): 3–29.

Montoya Guzmán, Juan David. "Las más remotas tierras del mundo: historia de la frontera del Pacífico, 1573–1687." PhD diss., Universidad Pablo de Olavide, 2014.

Morris, Daniel. *Plantes produisant le caoutchouc du commerce*. Conférences publiées par la Sociéte por l'encouragement du commerce, des arts et manufactures de Londres (n.d.).

Mosquera, Gilma. "Los hábitats aldeanos del Chocó: mejoramiento de vivienda y equipamientos comunitarios." *Revista de la Universidad del Valle* 5 (1993).

Mosquera, José E. *Diego Luis Córdoba: mito y realidad. Historia de las luchas de los chocoanos por la creación del departamento del Chocó, 1830–1947*. Medellín: Editorial L. Vieco, 2015.

Mosquera, Sergio. *Diccionario genealógico de la Provincia de Citará, siglos XIX y XX*. Quibdó: Fondo Mixto para la Promoción de la Cultura y las Artes, 1997.

———. *Don Melchor de Barona y Betancourt y la esclavización en el Chocó*. Quibdó: Universidad Tecnológica del Chocó, 2004.

———. *De esclavizadores y esclavizados en Citará*. Quibdó: Promotora Editorial de Autores Chocoanos, 1997.

———. "Los procesos de manumisión en las provincias del Chocó." In *Afrodescendientes en las Américas. Trayectorias sociales e identitarias a 150 años de la abolición de la esclavitud en Colombia*, ed. Claudia Mosquera, Mauricio Pardo, and Odile Hoffmann, 99–119. Bogotá: UN-ICANH-IRD-ILSA, 2002.

Múnera, Alfonso. *Fronteras imaginadas. La construcción de las razas y de la geografía en el siglo XIX colombiano*. Bogotá: Planeta, 2005.

Munro, J. F. "British Rubber Companies in East Africa before the First World War." *Journal of African History* 24, no. 3 (July 1983): 369–79.

———. "Monopolists and Speculators: British Investment in West African Rubber, 1905–1914." *Journal of African History* 22, no. 2 (April 1981): 263–78.

Murphy, Robert Cushman. "Racial Succession in the Colombian Chocó." *Geographical Review* 29, no. 3 (1939): 461–71.

Neumann, Roderick. *Making Political Ecology*. New York: Routledge, 2005.

Nieto Villamizar, María Camila, and María Riaño. *Esclavos, negros libres y bogas en la literatura del siglo XIX*. Bogotá: Ediciones Uniandes, 2011.

Nodari, Eunice, and João Klug, eds. *História Ambiental e Migrações*. São Leopoldo: Oikos Editora, 2012.

Ocampo, Gloria Isabel. "Haciendas y campesinos en el Sinú: Formas de vida y formas de trabajo en 'Marta Magdalena' (1912–1954)." *Boletín Museo del Oro* 20 (1988): 113–29.

Ocampo, José Antonio. *Colombia y la economía mundial*. Bogotá: Siglo XXI-Fedesarrollo, 1984.

Offen, Karl H. "The Geographical Imagination: Resource Economies and Nicaraguan Incorporation of the Mosquitia, 1838–1909." In *Territories, Commodities, and Knowledges: Latin American Environmental History in the Nineteenth and Twentieth Century*, ed. Christian Brannstrom, 50–89. London: Institute of Latin American Studies, 2004.

Olano, Antonio. *La propiedad minera, Su estado legal y modos de adquirirla en la intendencia del Chocó y departamentos que formaron el Antiguo Estado del Cauca*. Bogotá: Talleres Tipográficos de Régulo Domínguez, 1913.

Oliveira, Rogério Ribeiro de, and Joana Stingel Fraga. "Metabolismo social de uma floresta e de uma cidade: paisagem, carvoeiros e invisibilidade social no Rio de Janeiro dos séculos XIX e XX." *GeoPuc* 4, no. 7 (2012): 1–18.

Orlove, Benjamin S. "Putting Race in Its Place: Order in Colonial and Postcolonial Peruvian Geography." *Social Research* 60, no. 2 (Summer 1993): 301–36.

Oslender, Ulrich. *Comunidades negras y espacio en el Pacífico colombiano: hacia un giro geográfico en el estudio de los movimientos sociales*. Bogotá: Instituto Colombiano de Antropología e Historia, 2008.

Pacheco, Margarita. *La fiesta liberal en Cali*. Cali: Universidad del Valle, 1992.

Pádua, José Augusto. *Um sopro de destruição: pensamento político e crítica ambiental no Brasil escravista, 1786–1888*. Rio de Janeiro: Jorge Zahar, 2002.

Palacio, Germán. *Fiebre de Tierra caliente. Una historia ambiental de Colombia 1850–1930*. Bogotá: Universidad Nacional de Colombia, 2006.

Palacios, Marco. *Colombia, Between Legitimacy and Violence: A History of Colombia, 1875–2002*. Durham: Duke University Press, 2006.

Paredes Cruz, Joaquín. *Monografía de Buenaventura*. Cali: Imprenta Márquez, 1949.

Parsons, James. *Antioqueño Colonization in Western Colombia*. Berkeley: University of California Press, 1968 [1949].

Patiño, Víctor Manuel. "El maíz chococito." *América Indígena* 16, no. 4 (1956): 309–46.

———. *Plantas cultivadas y animales domésticos en América equinoccial. Tomo III: Fibras, medicinas, misceláneas*. Cali: Imprenta Departamental, 1967.

Patiño Millán, Beatriz. "La provincia en el siglo XVIII." In *Historia de Antioquia*, ed. Jorge Orlando Melo. Medellín: Editorial Presencia, 1991.

Peard, Julyan G. *Race, Place, and Medicine: The Idea of the Tropics in Nineteenth-Century Brazilian Medicine*. Durham: Duke University Press, 1999.

Peet, Richard, and Michael Watts. *Liberation Ecologies: Environment, Development, Social Movements*. London and New York: Routledge, 1996.

Peluso, Nancy. *Rich Forests, Poor People: Resource Control and Resistance in Java*. Berkeley: University of California Press, 1992.

Peluso, Nancy, and Michael Watts, eds. *Violent Environments*. Ithaca: Cornell University Press, 2001.

Pérez, Louis A. *Lords of the Mountain: Social Banditry and Peasant Protest in Cuba, 1878–1918*. Pittsburgh: University of Pittsburgh Press, 1989.

———. "Politics, Peasants, and People of Color: The 1912 'Race War' in Cuba Reconsidered." *Hispanic American Historical Review* 66, no. 3 (August 1986): 509–39.

Pérez, Santiago. *Selección de escritos y discursos de Santiago Pérez*, directed by Eduardo Rodríguez Piñeres. Bogotá: Academia Colombiana de Historia, 1950.

Pérez Meza, Nimio. *Monografía del municipio de Riosucio*. Medellín: Editorial Lealón, 1988.

Perreault, Tom, Gavin Bridge, and James McCarthy, eds., *The Handbook of Political Ecology*. London: Routledge, 2015.

Pittier, Henry. "A Preliminary Treatment of the Genus Castilla." *Contributions from the US National Herbarium* 13 (1910): 247–79.

Posada Carbó, Eduardo. *El Caribe colombiano, una historia regional (1870–1950)*. Bogotá: Banco de la República-El Áncora Editores, 1998.

Price, Marie, and Martin Lewis. "The Reinvention of Cultural Geography." *Annals of the American Association of American Geographers* 83, no. 1 (March 1993): 1–17.

Price, Richard. *First-Time: The Historical Vision of an Afro-American People*. Baltimore: Johns Hopkins University Press, 1983.

———. *The Guayana Maroons: A Historical and Bibliographical Introduction*. Baltimore: Johns Hopkins University Press, 1976.

Proyecto Biopacífico. *Informe Final General, Tomo I: Territorio Biocultural*. Bogotá: Ministerio del Medio Ambiente, 1998.

———. *Informe Final General, Tomo IV: Los sistemas productivos tradicionales. Una opción propia de desarrollo sostenible*. Bogotá: Ministerio del Medio Ambiente, 1998.

Ramos, Donald. "O quilombo e o sistema escravista en Minas Gerais de século XVIII." In *Liberdade por um fio: Historia dos quilombos no Brasil*, ed. Joao Reis and Flavio dos Santos Gomes. Sao Paulo: Companhia das Letras, 1996.

Ramos, Oscar Gerardo. "La caña de azúcar en la cultura colombiana." Unpublished (1996).

Rausch, Jane M. *The Llanos Frontier in Colombian History, 1830–1930*. Albuquerque: University of New Mexico Press, 1993.

Reclus, Armando. *Exploraciones a los istmos de Panamá y Darién en 1876, 1877 y 1878*. Panamá: Publicaciones de la Revista Lotería, 1958 [1881].

Reid, William A. "A Brief Talk about Tagua . . . ," *Commodities and Commerce Series*, no. 21. Pan American Union: Washington, D.C., 1936, 15 p.

Reis, Joao, and Flávio dos Santos Gomes, eds. *Liberdade por um fio: Historia dos quilombos no Brasil*. Sao Paulo: Companhia das Letras, 1996.

Restrepo, Eduardo. "Economía y simbolismo en el 'Pacífico negro.'" BA thesis, Universidad de Antioquia, 1996.

———. "Ethnicization of Blackness in Colombia: Toward De-racializing Theoretical and Political Imagination." *Cultural Studies* 18, no. 4 (September 2004): 698–715.

———. *Etnización de la negridad: la invención de las 'comunidades negras' como grupo étnico en Colombia*. Popayán: Editorial de la Universiad del Cauca, 2013.

———. "El giro a la biodiversidad en la imaginación del Pacífico colombiano." *Revista de Estudios del Pacífico colombiano* 1 (January–June 2013): 171–99.

———. "Hacia la periodización de la historia de Tumaco." In *Tumaco: haciendo ciudad*, ed. Michel Agier, Manuela Alvarez, Odile Hoffman, and Eduardo Restrepo, 54–86. Cali: Instituto Colombiano de Antropología, IRD, Universidad del Valle, 1999.

———. "Imágenes del 'negro' y nociones de raza en Colombia a principios del siglo XX." In *Historias sobre raza y nación en América Latina*, ed. Claudia Leal and Carl Langebaek. Bogotá: Ediciones Uniandes, 2010.

———. "Los tuqueros negros del Pacífico surcolombiano." In *Renacientes del Guandal: "Grupos negros" de los ríos Satinga y Sanquianga*, ed. Jorge Ignacio del Valle and Eduardo Restrepo, 243–348. Bogotá: Proyecto Biopacífico-Universidad Nacional de Colombia, 1996.

Restrepo, Jorge Alberto, and Manuel Rodríguez. "La actividad comercial y el grupo de comerciantes de Cartagena a finales del siglo XIX." *Estudios Sociales*, no.1 (September 1986): 43–107.

Restrepo Tirado, Ernesto. "Un viaje al Darién (apuntes de cartera)." *Repertorio Colombiano*, nos. 11 and 12 (November–December 1887): 347–401.

Rios, Ana Maria, and Hebe Maria Mattos. "O pós-abolição como problema histórico: balanços e perspectivas," *Topoi–Revista de História UFRJ* 5, no. 8 (2004): 170–98.

Rivas, Nelly Yulissa. "Prácticas espaciales y construcción territorial en el Pacífico nariñense: el río Mejicano, municipio de Tumaco." *Cuadernos de trabajo CIDSE 41*. Cali: Centro de Investigaciones y de Documentación Socioeconómica, 1999.

Robbins, Nicholas A. *Mercury, Mining, and Empire: The Human and Ecological Cost of Colonial Silver Mining in the Andes*. Bloomington: Indiana University Press, 2011.

Robbins, Paul. *Political Ecology: An Introduction*, 2nd ed. Oxford: Wiley-Blackwell, 2011.

Rodríguez, Stella. "Libres y culimochos: ritmo y convivencia en el Pacífico sur colombiano." In *Afrodescendientes de las Américas, trayectorias sociales e identitarias*, ed. Claudia Mosquera, Mauricio Pardo, and Odile Hoffman. Bogotá: Universidad Nacional de Colombia, Instituto Colombiano de Antropología e Historia, Institut de la Recherche pour le Dévelopment, Instituto Latinoamericano de Servicios Legales Alternativos, 2002.

Rodríguez Garavito, César, Tatiana Alfonso Sierra, and Isabel Cavelier Adarve. *Raza y derechos humanos en Colombia. Informe sobre discriminación racial y derechos de la población afrocolombiana*. Bogotá: Observatorio de Discriminación Racial, 2009.

Rogers, Thomas. *The Deepest Wounds: A Labor and Environmental History of Sugar in Northeast Brazil*. Chapel Hill: University of North Carolina Press, 2010.

Romero, Dolcey. "Manumisión, ritualidad y fiesta liberal en la provincia de Cartagena durante el siglo XIX." *Historia Crítica* 29 (January–June 2005): 125–74.

Romero, Mario Diego. *Historia y etnohistoria de las comunidades afrocolombianas del río Naya*. Cali: Gobernación del Valle, 1997.

———. *Poblamiento y sociedad en el Pacífico colombiano siglos XVI al XVIII*. Cali: Universidad del Valle, 1995.

———. *Sociedades Negras en la Costa Pacífica del Valle del Cauca durante los siglos XIX y XX*. Cali: Gobernación del Valle-Colección de Autores Vallecaucanos, 2003.

Romoli, Kathleen. "El alto Chocó en el siglo XVI." *Revista Colombiana de Antropología* 19 (1975): 10–38.

———. "El alto Chocó en el siglo XVI. Parte II: Las Gentes." *Revista Colombiana de Antropología* 20 (1976): 25–78.

Rugeles, Mauricio. "El gobierno realista en la Nueva Granada, 1815–1819." BA thesis, Universidad de los Andes, 2010.

Safford, Frank. "Race, Integration, and Progress: Elite Attitudes and the Indian in Colombia, 1750–1870." *Hispanic American Historical Review* 71, no. 1 (February 1991): 1–33.

Safford, Frank, and Marco Palacios. *Colombia: Fragmented Land, Divided Society*. New York: Oxford University Press, 2002.

Sanders, James E. "'Citizens of a Free People': Popular Liberalism and Race in Nineteenth-Century Southwestern Colombia." *Hispanic American Historical Review* 84, no. 2 (2004): 277–313.

———. *Contentious Republicans: Popular Politics, Race, and Class in Nineteenth-Century Colombia*. Durham: Duke University Press, 2004.

Santiago, Myrna. *The Ecology of Oil: Environment, Labor, and the Mexican Revolution 1900–1938*. Cambridge: Cambridge University Press, 2006.

———. "Extraction Stories: Workers, Nature, and Communities in the Mining and Oil Industries." In *A Living Past: Environmental Histories of Modern Latin America*, ed. John Soluri, Claudia Leal, and José Augusto Pádua. New York: Berghahn Books, forthcoming.

Schwartz, Norman B. *Forest Society: A Social History of Petén, Guatemala*. Philadelphia: University of Pennsylvania Press, 1990.

Schwartz, Stuart B. "The Manumission of Slaves in Colonial Brazil: Bahia, 1684–1745." *Hispanic American Historical Review* 54, no. 4 (November 1974): 603–35.

Scott, Rebecca. "Defining the Boundaries of Freedom in the World of Cane: Cuba, Brazil and Louisiana after Emancipation." *American Historical Review* 99, no. 1 (February 1994): 70–102.

———. *Degrees of Freedom: Louisiana and Cuba after Slavery*. Cambridge: Harvard University Press, 2005.

———. *Slave Emancipation in Cuba: The Transition to Free Labor, 1860–1899*. Pittsburgh: Pittsburgh University Press, 2000.

Scott, Rebecca, and Michael Zeuske. "Property in Writing, Property on the Ground: Pigs, Horses, Land, and Citizenship in the Aftermath of Slavery, Cuba, 1880–1909." *Comparative Studies in Society and History* 44, no. 4 (October 2002): 669–99.

Serrano, José Fernando. "Cuando canta el guaco: La muerte y el morir en poblaciones afrocolombianas del río Baudó, Chocó." BA thesis, Universidad Nacional de Colombia, 1994.

Sharp, William. "The Profitability of Slavery in the Colombian Chocó, 1610–1810." *Hispanic American Historical Review* 55, no. 3 (August 1975): 468–95.

———. *Slavery on the Spanish Frontier: The Colombian Chocó 1680–1810*. Norman: University of Oklahoma Press, 1976.

Skidmore, Thomas. *Black into White: Race and Nationality in Brazilian Thought*. Durham: Duke University Press, 1998 [1974].

Soluri, John. *Banana Cultures: Agriculture, Consumption, and Environmental Change in Honduras and the United States*. Austin: University of Texas Press, 2005.

———. "Labor Rematerialized: Putting Environments to Work in the Americas." *International Labor and Working Class History* 85 (Spring 2013): 1–15.

Soluri, John, Claudia Leal, and José Augusto Pádua. "Finding the 'Latin American' in (Latin American) Environmental History." In *A Living Past: Environmental Histories of Modern Latin America*, ed. John Soluri, Claudia Leal, and José Augusto Pádua. New York: Berghahn Books, forthcoming.

Stanfield, Michael Edward. *Red Rubber, Bleeding Trees*. Albuquerque: University of New Mexico Press, 1998.

Steiner, Claudia. *Imaginación y poder: El encuentro del interior con la costa en Urabá, 1900–1960*. Medellín: Universidad de Antioquia, 2000.

Stepan, Nancy Leys. *"The Hour of Eugenics": Race, Gender, and Nation in Latin America*. Ithaca: Cornell University Press, 1991.

Sutter, Paul. "What Can US Environmental Historians Learn from Non-US Environmental Historiography?" *Environmental History* 8, no. 1 (January 2003): 109–29.

Tapia, Carlos, Rocío Polanco, and Claudia Leal. *Los sistemas productivos de la comunidad negra de la cuenca del río Valle, Bahía Solano, Chocó*. Bogotá: Proyecto Biopacífico, Fundación Natura, 1997.

Taussig, Michael. *My Cocaine Museum*. Chicago: University of Chicago Press, 2004.

———. *Shamanism, Colonialism, and the Wild Man: A Study in Terror and Healing*. Chicago: University of Chicago Press, 1987.

Tirado Mejía, Álvaro. "El caso de las minas de Timbiquí." *Cuadernos Colombianos* 1, no. 1 (1974): 34–63.

Toledo Machado, Maria Helena. *O plãno e o pánico: Os movimentos sócias na década da abolição*. Rio de Janeiro: Editora UFRJ, 1994.

Toro Sánchez, Edgar, ed. *Memorias de Julián Uribe Uribe*. Bogotá: Banco de la República, 1994.

Tortolero, Alejandro. "Water and Revolution in Morelos, 1850–1915." In *A Land Between Waters: Environmental Histories of Modern Mexico*, ed. Christopher R. Boyer. Tucson: University of Arizona Press, 2012.

Tovar, Hermes, Jorge Andrés Tovar Mora, and Camilo Ernesto Tovar Mora. *Convocatoria al poder del número. Censos y estadísticas de la Nueva Granada (1750–1830)*. Bogotá: Archivo General de la Nación, 1994.

Tovar, Jorge Andrés, and Hermes Tovar. *El oscuro camino de la libertad. Los esclavos en Colombia, 1821–1851*. Bogotá: Universidad de Los Andes, 2009.

Trouillot, Ralph-Michel. *Haiti: State against Nation. The Origins and Legacy of Duvalierism*. New York: Monthly Review Press, 1990.

Tucker, Richard. "War and the Environment." In *Blackwell Companion to Global Environmental History*, ed. John R. McNeill and Erin Stewart. Oxford: Blackwell, 2012.

Twinam, Ann. *Miners, Merchants, and Farmers in Colonial Colombia*. Austin: University of Texas Press, 1982.

Ulloa, Astrid. *The Ecological Native. Indigenous Peoples Movements and Eco-Governmentality in Colombia*. New York: Routledge, 2005.

Urrea, Fernando. "La conformación paulatina de clases medias negras en Cali y Bogotá a lo largo del siglo XX y la primera década del XXI." *Revista de Estudios Sociales* 39 (April 2011): 24–41.

Valencia, Adiela. "Poblamiento negro en la hoya del río San Juan, Chocó, 1851–1974." MA thesis, Universidad del Valle, 1997.

Valencia Llano, Albeiro. *Vida cotidiana y desarrollo regional en la colonización antioqueña*. Manizalez: Universidad de Caldas, 1990.

Vallejo, Martha Isabel, Natalia Valderrama, Rodrigo Bernal, Gloria Galeano, Gerardo Arteaga, and Claudia Leal. "Producción de palmito de *Euterpe oleracea* Mart. (Araceae) en la costa pacífica colombiana: estado actual y perspectivas." *Colombia Forestal* 14, no. 2 (2011): 191–212.

Valois Arce, Daniel. *Departamento del Chocó*. Medellín: Tipografía Industria, 1945.

Van Ausdal, Shawn. "Pasture, Profit, and Power: An Environmental History of Cattle Ranching in Colombia, 1850–1950." *Geoforum* 40, no. 5 (September 2009): 707–19.

Van Cott, Donna Lee. *The Friendly Liquidation of the Past: The Politics of Diversity in Latin America*. Pittsburgh: University of Pittsburgh Press, 2000.

Vargas, Patricia. *Los Emberá y los Cuna: impacto y reacción ante la ocupación española Siglo XVI y XVII*. Bogotá: Instituto Colombiano de Antropología, 1993.

Vélez Ramírez, Humberto. "Rafael Reyes: Quinquenio, régimen político y capitalismo (1904–1909)." In *Nueva Historia de Colombia*, Tomo 1. Bogotá: Planeta, 1989.

Vélez Rendón, Juan Carlos. *Los pueblos allende el río Cauca: La formación del Suroeste y la cohesión del espacio en Antioquia, 1830–1877*. Medellín: Universidad Nacional de Colombia, sede Medellín, Universidad de Antioquia, 2002.

Villegas, Jorge A. *Petróleo, oligarquía e imperio*. Bogotá: Ediciones E.S.E., 1969.

Wade, Peter. *Blackness and Racial Mixture: The Dynamics of Racial Identity in Colombia*. Baltimore: John Hopkins University Press, 1993.

———. "Music, Blackness and National Identity: Three Moments in Colombian History." *Popular Music* 17, no. 1 (1998): 1–19.

———. *Music, Race, and Nation: Música Tropical in Colombia*. Chicago: University of Chicago Press, 2000.

Washbrook, Sarah. *Producing Modernity in Mexico: Labour, Race, and the State in Chiapas, 1876–1914*. Oxford: Oxford University Press, 2012.

Weinstein, Barbara. *The Amazon Rubber Boom, 1850–1920*. Stanford: Stanford University Press, 1983.

West, Robert. *Colonial Placer Mining in Colombia*. Baton Rouge: Louisiana State University Press, 1952.

———. *The Pacific Lowlands of Colombia*. Baton Rouge: Louisiana State University Press, 1957.

White Uribe, Henrique. "Apuntamientos sobre la Intendencia Nacional del Chocó y sobre el municipio de Urrao, Antioquia." *Boletín de Minas y Petróleos* 21–22 (1930): 211–304.

Whitten, Norman. *Black Frontiersmen: A South American Case*. New York: Schenkman Publishing Company, 1974.

———. *Class, Kinship and Power in and Ecuadorian Town: The Negroes of San Lorenzo*. Stanford: Stanford University Press, 1965.

Whitten, Norman, and Aurelio C. Fuentes. "Baile marimba! Negro Folkmusic in Northwest Ecuador." *Journal of the Folklore Institute* 2, no. 3 (August 1966): 168–91.

Williams, Caroline A. "Adaptation and Appropriation on the Colonial Frontier: Indigenous Leadership in the Colombian Chocó, 1670–1808." *Bulletin of Latin American Research* 26, no. 2 (2007): 181–99.

———. *Between Resistance and Adaptation: Indigenous Peoples and the Colonisation of the Chocó, 1510–1753*. Liverpool: Liverpool University Press, 2005.

———. "Resistance and Rebellion on the Spanish Frontier: Native Responses to Colonization in the Colombian Chocó." *Hispanic American Historical Review* 79, no. 3 (1999): 397–424.

Wilshusen, Peter R. "Territory, Nature, and Culture: Negotiating the Boundaries of Biodiversity Conservation in Colombia's Pacific Costal Region." In *Contested Nature: Promoting International Biodiversity Conservation with Social justice in the Twenty-first Century*, ed. Steven R. Brechin, Crystal L. Fortwangler, Peter R. Wilshusen, and Patrick C. West. Albany: State University of New York Press, 2003.

Wilson, Edward O., and Frances M. Peter, eds. *Biodiversity*. Washington, D.C.: National Academy Press, 1988.

Wokittel, Roberto. "Apuntes sobre el platino." *Minería* 28 (1934): 1876–78.

Wolf, Eric. *Peasants*. New York: Prentice Hall, 1966.

Wright, Angus. *The Death of Ramon González: The Modern Agricultural Dilemma*. Austin: University of Texas Press, 2005 [1990].

Yacup, Sofonías. *Litoral Recóndito*. Buenaventura: Asociación para la Defensa de los Recursos Naturales y Patrimonio Cultural del Pacífico Colombiano, 1976 [1934].

Zapata Olivella, Delia. "An Introduction to the Folk Dances of Colombia." *Ethnomusicology* 11, no. 1 (1967): 91–96.

Zimmerer, Karl. *Changing Fortunes: Biodiversity and Peasant Livelihood in the Peruvian Andes*. Berkeley: University of California Press, 1996.

Zuluaga, Francisco U. "Cimarronismo en el suroccidente del antiguo virreinato de Santafé de Bogotá." In *Colombia Pacífico*, Tomo II, ed. Pablo Leyva, 406–19. Bogotá: Proyecto Biopacífico, 1993.

———. *Guerrilla y sociedad en el Patía*. Cali: Universidad del Valle, 1993.

INDEX

ABOUT THE AUTHOR

Claudia Leal is an associate professor in the Department of History at the University of the Andes in Bogotá, Colombia. Her first book was *A La Buena de Dios: Colonización en La Macarena, ríos Duda y Guayabero* (*In God's Hands: Colonization in the Macarena, Duda and Guayabero Rivers*) (FESCOL, 1995). She has served as co-president of the Society for Latin American and Caribbean Environmental History. She earned her PhD in geography from the University of California, Berkeley, in 2004.